The Ghost in the Constitution

Contemporary Hispanic and Lusophone Cultures

This series aims to provide a forum for new research on modern and contemporary hispanic and lusophone cultures and writing. The volumes published in Contemporary Hispanic and Lusophone Cultures reflect a wide variety of critical practices and theoretical approaches, in harmony with the intellectual, cultural and social developments that have taken place over the past few decades. All manifestations of contemporary hispanic and lusophone culture and expression are considered, including literature, cinema, popular culture, theory. The volumes in the series will participate in the wider debate on key aspects of contemporary culture.

1 Jonathan Mayhew, *The Twilight of the Avant-Garde:*
Contemporary Spanish Poetry 1980–2000

2 Mary S. Gossy, *Empire on the Verge of a Nervous Breakdown*

3 Paul Julian Smith, *Spanish Screen Fiction: Between Cinema and Television*

4 David Vilaseca, *Queer Events: Post-Deconstructive Subjectivities*
in Spanish Writing and Film, 1960s to 1990s

5 Kirsty Hooper, *Writing Galicia into the World: New Cartographies, New Poetics*

6 Ann Davies, *Spanish Spaces: Landscape, Space and Place in*
Contemporary Spanish Culture

7 Edgar Illas, *Thinking Barcelona: Ideologies of a Global City*

8 Joan Ramon Resina, *Iberian Modalities: A Relational Approach to the*
Study of Culture in the Iberian Peninsula

9 Bruno Carvalho, *Porous City: A Cultural History of Rio de Janeiro*
(from the 1810s Onward)

10 Javier Krauel, *Imperial Emotions: Cultural Responses to Myths of Empire*
in Fin-de-Siècle Spain

11 Luis Moreno-Caballud, translated by Linda Grabner, *Cultures of Anyone:*
Studies on Cultural Democratization in the Spanish Neoliberal Crisis

12 H. Rosi Song, *Lost in Transition: Constructing Memory in Contemporary Spain*

13 Andrés Zamora, *Featuring Post-National Spain: Film Essays*

14 Paul Julian Smith, *Dramatized Societies: Quality Television in Spain and Mexico*

The Ghost in the Constitution

Historical Memory and Denial in Spanish Society

JOAN RAMON RESINA

LIVERPOOL UNIVERSITY PRESS

First published 2017 by
Liverpool University Press
4 Cambridge Street
Liverpool
L69 7ZU

British Library Cataloguing-in-Publication data
A British Library CIP record is available

ISBN 978-1-78694-022-3 cased

Typeset in Borges by
Carnegie Book Production, Lancaster
Printed and bound by CPI Group (UK) Ltd, Croydon, CR0 4YY

To Angela Bertran, Tordera 1927–Sant Cugat
del Vallès 2015, bedrock of my memory

Contents

Acknowledgments

This book has grown at different moments and places, over many discussions in seminars and conferences. I cannot, without undue prolixity, mention all the people and institutions to which I am indebted for their cordial attention and generous invitations. I would like, nevertheless, to register my special gratitude to the center for advanced studies Morphomata, a Käte Hamburger Kolleg housed at the University of Cologne, for a residential fellowship that allowed me to make significant progress on this book in Spring 2014. I am particularly indebted to Morphomata's director Günter Blamberger for his wonderful welcome, exciting discussions, and unstinted display of friendship.

Chapter 7 was originally published in *Plan Rosebud: On Images, Sites and Politics of Memory*, ed. Maria Rudio (Xunta de Galicia and Centro Galego de Arte Contemporánea, 2009). Chapter 8 was included in *War, Exile, Justice and Everyday Life, 1936–1946*, ed. Sandra Ott (Center for Basque Studies Publications, University of Nevada, 2011); Chapter 9 appeared in *Rassegna Iberistica* 90 (October 2009). An earlier version of Chapter 11 was part of the collection, *Unearthing Franco's Legacy: Mass Graves and the Recovery of Historical Memory in Spain*, ed. Carlos Jerez-Farran and Samuel Amago (Notre Dame University Press, 2010). A Catalan version, now updated, of Chapter 13, appeared in *Transformacions: Literatura i canvi sociocultural dels anys setanta ençà*, ed. Margalida Pons (Publicacions de la Universitat de València, 2010). Chapter 14 appeared originally in the volume *Teaching Representations of the Spanish Civil War* that Noël Valis edited for the MLA's Options for Teaching series in 2007. A German translation of Chapter 15 was published in *Latenz: blinde Passagiere in den Geisteswissenschaften*, eds. Hans Ulrich Gumbrecht and Florian Klinger (Vandenhoeck & Ruprecht, 2011). Chapter 16 was published digitally in the volume *Human Rights and Latin American and Iberian Cultures*, eds. Ana Forcinito, Manuel Marrero, and Kelly McDonough, *Hispanic Issues On Line* 5.1 (2009).

To all these editors and publishers, I am grateful for their permission to reprint, in part or entirely, the essays for which they provided a first home.

Introduction

This book has been a long time in the making. Since the publication of *Disremembering the Dictatorship* in 2000, I have worked intermittently on the question of social memory in the Iberian Peninsula. I have done so from the dual subject position of someone who remembers daily life under Francoism in the ordinary, non-metaphorical sense of the term, and of the historian of culture who reconstructs the experience of others, of a generality of others, through acts of secondary witnessing. This combination of points of view is nothing extraordinary; I share it with hundreds, possibly thousands of others. But being aware of the duality helps me (and hopefully my readers as well) to situate my perspective and justify to myself the stresses and omissions, perhaps even to understand my transferential relation to that slice of the past that I study in not always explicit forms of remembrance.

Memory is a synonym for culture and also for life. I do not mean having good or bad memory, which is a matter of neurological endowment, but having long or short memory, which is a matter of experience. Older people live ever more in their long memories, which accounts for the poverty of their short ones. And so it is with societies. Young, barbarian ones remember little but vividly; they are prey to simple, intense representations and prone to mythography. Older, declining societies have civilized their past; they are the peoples with history. The past never goes away, never truly passes. Ernst Nolte's famous dictum about a past that does not want to pass is a truism not just for the Nazi era. At best, the past can be laid to rest, like a corpse, or an exhausted body. Forgotten does not mean "gone." It merely means "out of mind." This book is about a large and decisive part of the twentieth century in the history of Spain, a history that, for those of us born and raised under the dictatorship, began with the Civil War. In our childhood, everything referred back to it, the war was the big bang of our universe. Its genesis was presided by a powerful and remote figure with a mezzo-soprano voice who one fine summer day in A.D. 1936 had cried into the warm, well-lighted republican abyss the command "let there be darkness." For dark, or at least depressingly gray, was the Spain of Franco. Except, perhaps, for its beneficiaries. In time I came to know some of these and many who believed themselves to be such. It is important not to let out of sight the fact that Francoism enjoyed broad support, if one wishes to understand the country's evolution to the present.

As often happens with books on which one has worked at different times that are far in between, my grasp of the historical memory has evolved and this probably shows in the varying and possibly contradictory emphases. Some of the chapters were originally written and published as self-standing articles and I have not attempted to disguise this fact by cobbling them together into an unbroken argument. Hence, the various chapters focus on different aspects of the historical memory that may seem discontinuous and perhaps erratic. All I can say to this potential critique is that, in my mind, the entire book is held together by the intellectual and ethical problem of the Civil War and its consequences as it relates to the burden of memory and its effects in the present, on the social forms of "acting out" repressed knowledge about national identity.

Considering the virtually inexhaustible nature of the materials and the profusion of public debate about the historical memory in the last two decades, this book could have been much longer. A selection inevitably comes at the expense of themes or viewpoints that readers may judge unjustly neglected. There is no counterargument to such objection, other than pointing out that scholarship corrects itself and others will be more alert where I have been remiss or oblivious. Total recall would simply be a repetition of history, and the history of over half a century, with all its derivations, simply does not fit inside the covers of any book, regardless of its volume. No matter how prolific or thorough, the writer must finally give up the notion of an open-ended reflection and bring the study to a close. Nevertheless, in spite of these shortcomings, I feel confident that one thread unifies all the sections of this book, and that is the strong sense that the past is still with us and that memory and its antonym, forgetting, express our relationship to it. Thus, the notion of latency, borrowed from Freud, is key, even if at times implicitly, to my approach.

In his classic study *The Place of Value in a World of Facts*, a book dating back to the time of the Spanish Civil War, exiled German psychologist Wolfgang Köhler confirmed on a neurological basis what Freud had already discerned in the psychic life of individuals and extrapolated to his analyses of the cultural *longue durée* of human groups. Köhler recognized that between an experience and the moment when its effect becomes apparent a great amount of time may intervene (235). His observation makes the study of historical memory (more poignantly than that of history proper) urgent and socially relevant. Because, in historical memory, not only is the original experience of paramount importance, but also the time through which it has traveled before its effect could break the surface of consciousness and become an experience in itself.

It is in the delay not just between the event and its cognition but also between the event and its lived consequences that the distinction between history and memory obtains particular validity. One thing is the original experience and another its long-term effect. This effect can be a phenomenon of consciousness (a memory) or of scholarship (a history), or it can be a political epiphenomenon, and I will be arguing in this book that the significance of Spain's mid-twentieth-century history, for us in the twenty-first century, lies in the persistence of its epiphenomena. To bridge the gap between the experience of the Civil War and the delayed consciousness of its effects I will invoke the concept of latency. By "latency" I do not understand anything metaphysical like a historical waiting room. Here again Köhler is useful, and it will help to quote him at some length:

> If there are any remnants which mediate between my previous mental life and a present recall (or any "memory" in the wider sense), such remnants belong to a world outside the phenomenal realm. Outside this realm I have already assumed nature, more particularly a nervous system in which the correlates of previous experience have occurred. It seems therefore proper to follow the rule that worlds ought not to be multiplied beyond strict necessity, and to construct the remnants of past experience as entities of the physical world, namely of the nervous system. So long as this attempt has not yet been shown to be futile it would not be a sound procedure to assume that these remnants are parts of a third, a never experienced mental world. (236)

The remnants of the past that link past experience with present memory cannot be phenomenal (that is, cannot consist of mental representations), otherwise it would make no sense to say that we remember. And the same applies to a historical occurrence and its late effect. In an anti-Platonic move, Köhler refuses to posit a phantasmagoric realm where the remnants of the past lead a virtual existence before they emerge as memories. Likewise, we do not assume the latency period as a state of suspension outside history. Only, where Köhler assumes a physical persistence of experience in the form of impressions in the nervous system, we conceive of historical latency as the permanent modification of the social and political behavior through the polarizing pattern resulting from the impulse imprinted on the social body by the critical historical experience. For such patterns to lose their efficacy over time, a subsequent event must erase or counter the registered functionality arising from the original experience. This is, for instance, what happened in Germany as a result of the collapse of the Third Reich, the Nuremberg trials and denazification, followed by a complete makeover of the state. Nothing of the sort happened in Spain. On the contrary, it can be argued that the peaceful but flawed transition from Francoism safeguarded the functionalities imprinted in Spain's social body through nearly half a century of a dictatorship that was itself radical confirmation of behavioral patterns previously embedded in Spanish society. Francoism was itself an effect of previous historical experience and in this sense bridged the gap between past and present manifested by the short existence of the Second Republic. What is more, it preened itself on achieving precisely that.

When I claim that the Civil War's and the dictatorship's effects erupt in contemporary Spanish society, I do not mean that the undeniable modifications of this society's political institutions are mere décor or that history remains suspended in an earlier historical period. Spain has changed, just as the subject who identifies with a bygone period in his life is altered by time and circumstance. As Köhler recognizes, the traces of the past are not inert things (244). Historical memory is, like all memory, not a fixed script. The traces left by the past in the form of social relations feel the influence of the environment, of forces and currents that modify both what is remembered and the range and strength of its aftereffects. Francoism was not the same in 1939 and 1945. It changed even more between this second date and the 1960s. Each modification happened in response to the larger historical trends, and at each of these stages Francoism altered the memory of its origin and modulated its alleged purpose. In time, its story was so distorted, the traces of it so jumbled by subsequent revisions, that it finally could erase the record of its original filiation. Thus, not a few historians have denied the fascist nature of the regime inaugurated in 1939; some have gone so far as to deny its totalitarian character altogether, upgrading it from dictatorial to just authoritarian.

However, as Köhler points out, contexts can extend in time. In such extensions, earlier parts may fade behind the current phase of the context, but the present often follows a pattern whose general traits were established earlier (274). This is also true of historical contexts. The transition was the political formalization of an ongoing adaptation to a new social grade. In this process, certain aspects of the previous phases faded out, causing critics to speak of collective amnesia. Ordinarily, social forgetting occurs inconspicuously, but in Spain disappointed expectations of justice and redress, nurtured over long decades, opened a moral void that sucked political values and came to be identified as programmed amnesia. This specific form of amnesia did not emanate as much from a programmatic "pact of forgetting" as from the social metabolism itself. It was the byproduct of the generational relay and of Spanish society's adaptation to new economic and ideological conditions. In other words, a higher standard of living, bringing Spanish identity in line with the European, was purchased at the price of blurring elements of the recent past.

But, however adapted to new demands, the context endures and its functional continuity is responsible for the emergence of remnants of the past that were forgotten only in the public imagination. As a rule, when those reminiscences turn up, they are not considered constituents of the historical memory, but fixations of nostalgic sections of the population incapable of adapting to the present. There are plenty of examples of this form of return of the past. To name but a few: the reintroduction of Francoist insignia in the Spanish flag among certain political associations; the persistence of monuments and street names honoring the dictatorship in towns all over Spain; the recent religious homage to Franco in a mass celebrated at the cathedral of Valencia on 18 July 2016, where Archbishop Antonio Cañizares dedicated the Eucharist to the dictator on the anniversary of the military insurrection; the concentration of legionnaires in Madrid on 24 September 2016 to protest City Hall's decision to change the name of the street named after José Millán Astray, founder of the Spanish legion and mentor of Francisco Franco. And yet, these phenomena are symptoms of a latent memory that relies not only on symbolic props but also on traces left in the social body by the experiences of the past. Those traces pervade the present in capillary fashion, conditioning behavior at all levels of the political and social context. They are responsible for a skewed sense of normality ranging from denial to renewal, as in the obtrusive attitude of neo-fascists and the subtler variations on the right (and sometimes the left) of the political spectrum, which sacrifice the symbolic paraphernalia the better to pursue more substantial goals.

There can be no question that these "returns" constitute a form of historical memory. Thus, it is hardly surprising that the publicly subsidized Francisco Franco Foundation, an anomaly in a democratic European Union, tweeted on 1 April 2016 (the anniversary of the official end of the Civil War) a photograph of Franco's last war communiqué, in which he declared victory, and accompanied the picture with the threatening comment: "We do not forget." Inability to forget, framed by a solid structure of denial, shows the debates about the historical memory under a different light from that of simple forgetting. At stake are not only memory issues but above all issues of political power and, on a different although related level, matters of public responsibility. Francoists do not forget, because the pattern of social functionalities that emerged from the transition was (and could not but be) the pattern that supported the dictatorship and made possible its endurance. It is this pattern that, with an interval in the 1980s and early 1990s, returned the heirs of Francoism to power and has kept them there despite their proven inefficiency, prevarication, short-circuiting of the democratic separation of powers, and massive corruption. Rather than seek the reasons for such counterintuitive behavior at the polls in false consciousness or ideology, it is simpler and intellectually more economic to explain it by memory's latency. At play is the unconscious or semiconscious awareness of a military victory whose ownership no transitional ploy and no amount of democratic posturing has ever taken away. That communiqué of 1 April 1939, revisited sixty-seven years later, elucidates Spain's political tone in the present. "Today, with the red army captive and unarmed, the national troops have achieved their ultimate military objectives. The war is over."[1] Absolute, conclusive victory, achieved without accepting any proposal for negotiated peace and without regard for cost in human lives, set the tone for the administration of the victory, and later for the political style in post-Franco Spain. Reverence for unconditional victory that may not be compromised by negotiation explains the refusal not so much of memory (without which victory cannot be daily ratified) as of the possibility of altering its context in any significant way. Continuity of context rather than the transmogrification of the state through the adoption of formal democracy explains the refusal to this day of a state institution such as the Armed Forces to allow researchers access to its archives of the Francoist period. On 23 March 2016, forty-one years after Franco's death, journalist José María Calleja and attorney Eduardo Ranz addressed a petition to the Ministry of Defense to lift the holds on military, Civil Guard, and police archives older than a quarter of a century, basing their request on the existence of laws for transparency, historical memory, and legal status of the public administrations. As of this writing, the issue has not been settled and the law regulating classified information goes back to 5 April 1968. A Francoist law regulates access to state documents forty-one years after the official demise of the regime that enacted it.

Critics who object to the historical memory because it is tainted with utilitarian motivations are right to point to the inevitable involvement of consciousness with its environment. Memory is not the otherworldly contemplation of an eternal set of representations labeled "historical truth." It is a survival mechanism that makes learning possible. To humans, it also means the possibility of creating and thus changing the world—or

---

1 Throughout this book, translation of the quotations is mine, unless otherwise indicated.

preserving it in its status quo as long as it is feasible. The objectors are wrong in assuming that alternatives to social memory exist, either in the programmed amnesia of totalitarian states or in the accelerated substitution of practices and interests brought about in the name of innovation under the iron law of the market. Societies remember in many ways, and it is important that they do. Any attempt to regulate their memories curtails their freedom, regardless of whether regulation takes the form of exhortation or suppression. What this means in practice is that social cleavage typically pits memories against memories, and the confrontation must be worked out in social space. Only then, and as a rule only provisionally, does the memory settle in the history books. When this happens, and so long as no new scholarship emerges that contradicts the consensual account of the past, there is an illusion of objective truth, of the past understood as it truly was. Such serene views are easier when historians deal with remote periods that seem detached from present concerns, or in rare periods of contextual stagnation, when the functionalities of the past persist unchallenged, whether through censorship and repression of the opposing views or because those views, having drifted into fairyland, have no purchase on present reality.

CHAPTER ONE

Historical Memory
and the Limits of Retrospection

Where remembrance coheres, there, also, is the blood-dimmed tide.
David Rieff, *Against Remembrance*, 128

Intellectual activity, just as the life process, seems to be governed by the law of the pendulum. When satisfaction quiets the irritation of an organ, it establishes a state of organic apathy until a new irritant intervenes. A classic shibboleth affirms that the history of philosophy oscillates between Plato and Aristotle in a circadian rhythm measured not in hours but in centuries. After a half-century of dire warnings about the consequences of forgetting the past, skeptical and even contrarian discourses have emerged against the historical memory. Increasingly, people clamor against the excesses perpetrated in the name of memory by the identities that misuse it. An example of this reaction can be found in David Rieff's book, *Against Remembrance*. Written in the wake of the war in the Balkans, this essay popularized the more rigorous criticism of so-called memory studies pioneered by Charles Meier in the 1990s. Meier's intervention was opportune, considering the trivialization of the concept of historical memory and the race for victimhood status that accompanied the rise of memory studies. In the words of a guest speaker at Stanford, trauma affects everyone, since all of us have inherited some history or other. But if everyone inherits a history, or at least a story—and who doesn't?—surviving a genocidal experience or living under a murderous dictatorship ceases to be a requirement for admission to the club of the traumatized. If memory is inextricable from narcissism, a faculty in service to self-esteem, then mine is as good as anyone else's. And who can set limits to self-pity? Thus, it makes perfect sense to complain about the excesses of memory, although to do so by generalizing trauma inevitably trivializes it.

Beyond the exigencies of political correctness, it is important to weigh the consequences of the current memory surfeit to decide when the fatigue is motivated by legitimate concern with misuse and when by concealment of crimes and the hankering after impunity. We should not ask only, whom does memory serve? but also, who benefits from forgetting? From a psychological standpoint to question the importance of memory makes no sense; hence the question raised by Isabel Wollaston in the title of her book *A War Against Memory?* must be understood in cultural terms. Neither is the past a figment of people's imagination, nor is memory a magic lantern that projects shapes stored in a timeless limbo. Over a century ago, Henri Bergson claimed that between past and present there is no solution of continuity, and the range of memory, understood as the time-bound consciousness of experience, depends on the subject's vital needs. For Bergson, the present turns into the past when it no longer has practical significance. Then it becomes "academic." Indeed, it is the academic approach to the past that makes it "historical." "An event—says Bergson—belongs to the past and enters into history when it no longer interests directly the politics of the day and may be neglected without the affairs suffering from it. As long as its action is felt, it holds on to the life of the nation and remains present" (192).

If we find memory unsettling, it is because we cannot get rid of it. Now we know that everything that circulates in the Web remains forever in an electronic eternity, where it can be accessed at any moment, anachronistically, so to speak. But isn't this, mutatis mutandis, the way the unconscious works? We could define the unconscious as the totality of experiences provisionally located in the shadow surrounding the beam of the subject's intentionality. With this difference, however: that the unconscious cannot be accessed at will but is the magma out of which fragments of experience, often distorted by their temporal relocation, break loose from the original causal chain as a result of complex associations ranging from linguistic correlations to bodily sensations and symbolic interactions. The unconscious, which, with important qualifications, is another name for oblivion, would thus be the paradoxical source of memory. To remember is to recognize, or to "miscognize," something one was already acquainted with. Plato attributed knowledge to the faculty of recollection, and Socratic maieutics resembled a psychoanalytic immersion, in which deductive dialectic replaced spontaneous association.

The most common objection to the historical memory has to do with its untrustworthiness. A commonplace of memory studies is that memory is partial and unreliable. At the beginning of his book, David Rieff contrasts "the critical history of historians and the psychological authenticity but dubious historicity of the collective memories of peoples and nations" (vii). But Rieff's objection to memory has less to do with epistemology than with pragmatic motivations. He says that in the Balkans war he learned to hate and fear historical memory as a depot of ideological weapons that kindles wars and makes peace precarious (viii). As opposed to memory running amuck, Rieff assumes that a critical, documentary history does not encourage war or chill the peace. As a secularized form of administrating the past, history rejects the mythical contents that degrade knowledge and subordinate it to politics and ideology.

I suspect that Rieff here confuses knowledge with its effects. If realities were as easy to disentangle as concepts are, we could accept the practical application of the split between history and memory that Rieff proposes when he argues in favor of the former and against the latter. Let us ignore the contradiction involved in vilifying memory for being tainted with politics while issuing that verdict from within unequivocally political contexts, namely under the influence of a war and its political aftermath. Even abstracting from the explicit background of his judgment, the argument remains flawed, because, where societies are involved, forgetting rests on political factors no less than the memory of which it is the reverse. Forgetting supervenes when people turn their attention to a different reality zone. And shifts of attention affecting entire groups are motivated by collective behavior that we have a right to call political regardless of whether or not it sets into policy. There is no doubt that the Balkans war was exacerbated, perhaps even triggered, by historical memories. But it is no less true that, if memory was so effectual as to set off ethnic violence, it is because the crisis inaugurated by the demise of communism—a system that posited the goal of a post-historical society—allowed the historical relations between the nationalities to emerge in the temporary rebalancing of power. Suddenly, the central authority supported by the obsolete ideology ceased to be legitimate, and conflict between Belgrade and the emerging political agents in the Yugoslav federation gave new relevance to old passions. In a context of growing hostility, memory stood for the return of the repressed.

Rieff's thesis stumbles on the categorical distinction between critical history and mythic history, which he considers incommensurate, as if myth and history had parted ways in a distant past, becoming fodder for the masses the one, and sober fare for a disciplined minority the other. Certainly, Rieff is not the first to discriminate between memory and history. Pierre Nora, in his oft-quoted introduction to *Les lieux de mémoire*, had posited their dichotomy, but, unlike Rieff, he did not neglect to historicize it. According to Nora, memory had become unfeasible after the passing of the nation and the coming of society: "What we call memory today is therefore not memory but already history" (8). Since the nineteenth century, social memory has been an archived, preserved, and materially transmitted memory, one that, in his own words, "deposits its signs as the snake deposits its shed skin" (8).

The distinction between history and memory had been formulated by Maurice Halbwachs, Nora's teacher. In his seminal *La mémoire collective*, the French sociologist stated: "Next to a written history there is a living history that renews and perpetuates itself in time, in which it is possible to find again a great number of these ancient currents that had vanished only apparently" (113). The social transformation of memory inhered in the definition of the collective memory, as did the unconscious retention of a seemingly erased past, which some later event stirs up, as happens under hypnosis or in Proust's famous instance of involuntary memory.

In turn, Halbwachs could have found the history/memory distinction in the work of Charles Péguy, who in a manuscript of 1909 entitled "Dialogue de l'histoire et de l'âme païenne," published posthumously in 1917, commented apropos the historian Jules Michelet: "When he follows his time, he is only a historian. When he follows his genius he is promoted to the rank of memorialist and chronicler" (271). The difference Péguy observes between these genres is not only formal. The memorialist brings the past back to life by means of a spiritual synchronization. For Péguy, "bringing back to life" does not have the weak sense of postmodern spectrality but the strong sense of revoking time. Evoking the origins from within the nation—Péguy actually uses the term "race" (271)—amounts to moving upstream in time, something that only memory can accomplish. Insofar as history entails an exterior perspective on the events, it cannot do the work of evocation. "History," he says, "consists essentially in *passing along* the event. Essentially, memory consists above all in, while being inside the event, not exiting from it, but remaining inside and moving toward its source" (272). A procedure predicated on never considering the facts from outside and retracing their origin as if looking for the source of the Nile is not a critical method. Criticism relies on analysis, on taking the object apart to examine its nature and composition, as well as its relationship with its environment, and this is incompatible with remaining inside the facts that one hopes to establish.

Péguy applies to history and memory Bergson's distinction between chronology and duration, that is between abstract and lived time. Duration, says Bergson, "is the continuous life of a memory that extends the past into the present, whether the present includes the ever-expanding image of the past or testifies through its continuous modification to the ever-increasing load of experience the subject carries along as it ages. Without this survival of the past into the present there would be no duration, only instantaneity" (227). Inclusion in the present of an ever-larger image of the past would entail either a temporal splitting of consciousness, which would always perceive the magma of the past under the crust of the present, or a lifelong anamnesis advancing ever further into the past, so that to age would be another name for excavating one's memory. Most likely it is the density of the past that, as Bergson claims, is responsible for the continuous modification of the present. If we do not admit a teleological reason for change, such as a divine plan or a Hegelian end of history, we are forced to admit that the present is propelled by the accumulated force of the past. If forgetting were a solution of continuity, there would be no purposive action, only arbitrary instantaneity, as goldfish or zapping addicts experience it. Without memory, there is no temporal consciousness or reflexivity, since the latter presupposes a bridge between the present state of consciousness and previous ones.

Detractors of the historical memory are not really apologists for the unconscious, at least not in the sense of advocating the dissolution of reflection. The forgetting they advocate is not literal; nor is the memory they decry. Memory detractors tend to confine their rejection to what they take to be a metaphorical notion of memory. Insofar as it is assumed to be collective, historical memory cannot be memory proper. Rieff: "One simply cannot conjugate the verb remember in the plural unless one is talking about those who lived through what they remember, for we do so as individuals not as collectivities" (58). According to this extreme individualism, intersubjective communities do not exist. Yet, individuals do not think, reflect, or possess an identity apart from the communities that shape them. If memory did not transcend the individual consciousness, sharing experiences or feelings would be impossible, and historical knowledge would be a chimera. There would be no common past founded upon the exchange, sorting out, and confirmation of personal memories. In fact, without being able to remember together, we would not be able to conjugate any other verb in the plural.

Rieff, it is only fair to point out, allows for a limited social memory, that of the group that experienced the events in question—the witnesses, that is. But what does sharing strictly subjective memories amount to? Is collective memory just the sum of personal experiences? Experiences are not identical for everyone, nor are the ways of remembering. Experience shows that, in different contexts or under different circumstances, a person remembers the same facts in dissimilar, even contradictory ways. Narration takes hold of memory and molds it to its own grammar. Indeed, Nietzsche's skepticism, which Rieff levels against the collective memory, can be extended to the personal memory. "Where remembrance is concerned, it would seem that it is Nietzsche who has the last word: 'there are no facts, only interpretations'" (Rieff 25). But Nietzsche's observation is not limited to memory. For him there are no facts, including historical ones. The human being, as a cultural animal, is condemned to interpret, interpretation being the ectoplasm of its subjective condition. Nietzsche, whose theory of eternal return amounts to the inevitable inscription of the past in the present, also rejected the excesses of history, while admitting its necessity ("On the Use and Abuse of History for Life"). According to him, we are only what we, at any given moment, feel of the currents that reach us from the past (*Menschliches, Allzumenschliches, Werke* 1.823).

Thus, when he asserts that "much strength is needed in order to live and to forget, insofar as living and being unjust are the same thing" (*Werke* 1.229), it is evident that he is not praising forgetting in a bout of moralism but in the name of life. Suppressing the past means capitulating to the instincts and entails readiness to accept their violence: "People or times that serve life in this way, that judge and destroy a past, are always dangerous times and people" (ibid.). What upsets the peace and harmony of the inherited situation is not memory but its opposite. Forgetting injustice sets the stage for its renewal. Nietzsche's critique of the past is the converse of the risk avoidance advocated by Rieff. Anticipating Bergson and Péguy, Nietzsche realized that memory is a hypertrophy of consciousness and denounced that the cult of the past sapped vital energies.

When he denied that historical facts could be known independently of structures of meaning, Nietzsche was extending philological principles to the field of history. Etymology refers us to an infinite regression of metaphors. From this intuition, deconstruction drew dramatic consequences, not just with regard to facts but also to their meaning. But, notwithstanding postmodern agnosticism, nothing compels us to embrace a similar nihilism with regard to memory. To say that the referent is permanently deferred is as good as saying that the past is inaccessible; that we can only approach it through poetic or rhetorical tropes that unfold into yet other tropes. But, after all, humans have learned to live and to think with the help of metaphors. Although Rieff begins his indictment of memory with a display of skepticism, denouncing the constructed character and falseness of the historical memory, ultimately the issue hinges on memory's utility. Even in the hypothesis that remembering the past were good and edifying, he says, this would still not satisfy the question of what should we do with memory (49). To this question there are different answers, even if some of these are not to Rieff's liking.

The question about the historical memory need not be settled in the sphere of the *prágmata* (*na energeísoun*), of things to actualize, but in that of the *tá gnôstà*, the objects of knowledge. A memory is a reality of consciousness. What the will does with memories is a problem for the practical reason. To declare a priori that "no increase in the amount of remembering will do any good" (90) seems rash. And to conclude from this axiom that "To imagine otherwise is to leach both the past and the present of their specific gravity" (90) is simply illogical. Certainly, as imprudent as to claim that memory leads to catastrophe is to hail it as a fount of goodness. But if the relation between goodness and truth that we inherit from Platonism retains any validity, we would have to disagree with the ethical promotion of amnesia. In the sphere of praxis, to which Rieff subordinates that of knowledge, forgiveness (an ethical category) must not be confused with forgetting (a gnoseological accident). There is simply no reason why cultivating memory should dissolve the *gravitas* specific to past and present. As we have seen, Bergson talked about the ever-heavier burden that our consciousness carries as we age. Insofar as the load of the past is reflected in memory, it precipitates in the form of practical action in the present.

Is it surprising that, after writing off historical memory as a fiction, Rieff should then draw apparently unassailable consequences from this move? But if fantasy is memory's true environment, why oppose truth and justice to peace? If memory were a black hole into which truth disappears, arguing against it would be futile. It is impossible to get justice out of fallacy. But Rieff does not seem all that comfortable with his own position. He suspects that condemning memory in the name of the status quo is not altogether reasonable, that its demise would not secure peace. Yet, in doubt, he aggravates the case against memory: "The romance that is historical memory is at best a candle we light in honor of the dead and, at worst, a kind of cognitive equivalent of an astrophysical Black hole—a region from which no historical reason and no political sobriety can escape" (91).

Such aversion to memory takes him full circle to embrace mythography by supporting his case with the legend of Spain's happy transition to democracy: "We have an example of this in the so-called *Pacto del Olvido* (The Pact of Forgetting) that was essential to the political settlement that brought democracy to post-Franco Spain. This pact was never formalized but the advent of democracy in Spain came on the wings both of rewriting and of forgetting" (105). If, as Bergson thought, it is not memory but forgetting that needs explaining, Spain's "Pact of Forgetting" clamors for elucidation. This political arrangement departed from the pattern that is typical of such transitions, and this is doubtless the reason why Rieff pressed it into the service of his thesis. But in most post-dictatorial situations, reconciliation is based on collective catharsis through the explicit elucidation and judgement of the past. A festering past can be laid to rest only by processing its traumas with the help of memory.

Furthermore, the Spanish "Pact of Forgetting" did not presuppose, at least at the beginning, the extinction of memory but rather a denial of its relevance in a situation conditioned by political will. The Francoists reoriented their power monopoly toward the goal of surviving the demise of their old ideological shell. The opposition parties accepted the offer in order to participate in the new political game that everyone agreed to call democracy. In those circumstances, the knowledge of the past that had determined the national life until a few weeks earlier evaporated like dew at midday. Consciousness of the past was placed in abeyance, but what do such suspensions have to do with the critical history that Rieff pits against memory?

Rieff is wrong not so much because he credits forgetting for the consolidation of Spanish democracy as because he rejoices in the fact that official forgetting caused the past to be altered. This revision (he calls it rewriting) did not involve rejecting Francoist historiography but rather neutralizing republican memory through an amnesty law that laid the legal foundations for political amnesia. Rieff believes that the ulterior law of historical memory, which, a quarter of a century after Franco's death, gave local authorities license to remove Francoist monuments and inscriptions, "was a blow against the legacy of Francoism but of course it was also a blow against remembrance" (106). He neglects to mention that, by preventing the disclosure of crimes and the attribution of responsibilities, the transition to democracy facilitated society's retention of the essence of Francoism, ensuring its eventual return to political and social institutions. Ultimately, Rieff welcomes, for reasons he considers superior, the programmatic distortion of the past and accepts the myth of the flawless transition as an expeditious maneuver to guarantee social peace.

Confronted with the demands of the *Asociación para la recuperación de la memoria histórica* and the actions undertaken by judge Baltasar Garzón—sued, says Rieff, by "a number of right-wing groups" (108), as if the success of the charges were the work of a cluster of extreme opinion and not evidence of the bias in the law and the judiciary—Rieff allows that a time finally comes when it is legitimate to reclaim the memories previously suppressed, since forgetting also comes with a use-by date (109). Who, when, and for what reason decides that date are questions that in the real world are settled by opportunity. Initially, it would seem that these are questions of power rather than of justice, since the answers depend on the capacity of the various segments of society to participate in the collective memory. But Rieff thinks that memory can be restored without risk in societies that have practiced forgetting long enough, and that it is a luxury only deserved by developed countries. Fragmented by multiculturalism, these countries need some form of social glue, and collective memory supplies it. The problem here would not be an excess of memory but a shortage of it. Obsessed with relating memory to violence, Rieff asks "the question of whether, in rich, peaceful societies, at any rate, *any* form of remembrance remains viable" (126) (Rieff's emphasis). Apparently, the dangers of historical memory threaten undeveloped nations only, those societies that Eric Wolf, alluding to Marx, called "peoples without history." But if the wealthy may be permitted to indulge in historical memory, could it be that the problem of violence does not lie so much in the manipulation of the past as in the power relations between social groups that relate to each other as classes? Do not the great political systems predicate their status on the same distortion of the past that is at work in the break-up conflicts among smaller nations?

Could it be that history's main peril consists in the temptation to make its object absolute? Does not the danger lie in the historian's inability to grasp the object of historical knowledge as a correlative of his own subjectivity? To the extent that the historian does not take himself into consideration, he forgets the relativity of historical consciousness. When that happens, history—whose defining trait is, according to Rieff, that it "really *is* about the past" (96)—tends to become myth. This "really" enfolds a hypothesis about the ontological condition of the past, as if the historian, holding the past in his hands, could dress it with a discourse accurately tailored to its features. But the claim to write history from outside was already self-conscious by the time Leopold von Ranke expressed his desire "to efface myself entirely and allow only things to talk" (cit. Koselleck 133). After the Cartesian critique of inherited knowledge, historians could no longer believe that it was possible to show the past "as it actually was" ("wie es eigentlich gewesen"), to cite Ranke one more time (*Geschichten der romanischen und germanischen Völker von 1494 bis 1514* (1874), cit. Koselleck 134).

Twenty-some years ago, I wrote that myth presupposes the reality of a volitional situation ("El dilema" 253). The will underpins myth, just as Rieff thinks it does memory, which he considers to be at the ego's service (97). The historian tries to stir clear of myth just as early Christians shunned paganism. In fact, debates among historians are not essentially different from theological debates. Both aspire to reduce the multiplicity of causes and processes to a unique canonical narrative. From the time when history became self-conscious, it strove to distance itself from literature, disparaging the latter as mere fiction. In this way, history sought legitimacy as a univocal discourse, discrediting the multiplicity of stories. But, regardless of historians' programmatic intentions, literature suffuses historiography from the moment the materials and their discursive organization rely on expressive models ("El dilema" 274). Claiming to be "really" concerned with the past, that is, to treat it as an independently verifiable reality "presupposes a homogeneous past that can be subsumed under general laws, so that this past is no longer regarded as a distinct time molded by the human reality it contains" ("El dilema" 275). It is rather an abstract time torn from duration, the latter being the shape consciousness takes when it is organized in and through memory.

Historically, the epistemological differentiation between both kinds of discourse, the factual and the fictional, the historical and the mnemonic, was short-lived. Reinhardt Koselleck has shown that opposition between *res factae* and *res fictae*, the opposition on which historians' claim to aseptic handling of memory depends, became untenable after the enlightened scrutiny of their work. Soon it became clear that the distinction between both forms of reporting the past depended on the modality of representation, whether the historian aimed to articulate the essence of the facts or their appearance. Despite the existence of intermediate positions, this categorical distinction persisted until the seventeenth century. It presented the inconvenience of restricting the sphere of reliable history to the immediate past, with limits set by the presence or absence of first-hand witnesses whose accounts would help the historian to report the facts impartially. This naive realism created an awkward division of history into ancient and contemporary. The former started at the instant when the generation of the witnesses disappeared; the latter was confined to the stretch of time that appears in the perspective of the actors. Koselleck observes that both histories were defined by the wishes and agendas, as well as the questions, that emerge in the present. The enlightened historian Johann Martin Chladenius (1710–59) argued the importance of keeping in mind the point of view, because, although history is one, the conceptions vary. He understood that position affects not only the quality of the testimony but also the historian's perspective.

With the acceptance of the relativity of testimony, historians abandoned the notion of absolute objectivity. Bygone time still had ontological consistency, but it was as inaccessible in its totality as the Kantian *Ding-an-sich*. Chladenius had discovered that representation could never be co-extensive with the past. The historian uses the resources of language to create "rejuvenated images" of the past. To that end, he selects, condenses, displaces and resets, proceeding as memory does when it structures the amorphous mass of the past. The same criterion that historians call upon in order not to misrepresent facts, namely collating them and checking them against alternative evidence, applies to the management of memory. Leaving aside the case of intentional distortion, a practice that presents no epistemological difficulty, only an ethical problem, everyone agrees that the historian must avoid partiality. However, this does not mean eschewing the point of view that corresponds to the object, since in that case every account would be partial. For Friedrich Schlegel, the solution to this difficulty lay in discriminating between facts and the judgment of facts. He believed that the very conflict of interpretations tends to produce factual precision, because every party closely scrutinizes the other party's opinions as well as its own for fear of criticism. Nevertheless, Schlegel reached the conclusion that the conflict of historical interpretations did not guarantee factuality, since in order to tell the correct judgment from the others it was necessary to enjoy a superior point of view based on knowledge of the evolution of human nature and of humanity's destiny (Koselleck 147).

This properly historical point of view required a philosophy of history, which Hegel would eventually contribute. For Hegel, history's spiritual principle was the "sum total of all possible perspectives" (cit. 148), but he also thought that the historian had to adopt a judgment on the past as the narrative's organizing principle. And what was this principle? Hegel was not in doubt: it had to be historical reason. But this principle was not supra historical; it did not stand outside the flow of events. It corresponded to a metaphysical hypothesis that was, like every hypothesis, replaceable. And the nineteenth century's most distinguished anti-Hegelian, Søren Kierkegaard, proposed a radically different idea of history. If history were necessary, in the sense of being subject to logic, it would no longer be historical. The necessity of the past, the feeling that history moves forward according to rigorous laws, is a mirage produced by distance. Contemporaries do not perceive the necessity of what occurs, because necessity excludes possibility, which always precedes actualization and is the aspect under which contemporaries perceive the present. "If necessity could gain a foothold at a single point, there would no longer be any distinguishing between the past and the future" (Kierkegaard 96). As foregone reality, the past is absolutely certain, but the fact that it has passed, says Kierkegaard, is the ground of uncertainty and the reason why the understanding cannot assimilate it as if it had been thus for all eternity. And, he adds, "Only in terms of this conflict between certainty and uncertainty, the distinguishing mark of all that has come into existence, and hence also of the past, can the past be understood" (98). That a past exists is beyond doubt. But then we cannot know with any certainty how and why it came to be, and just these happen to be the properly historical questions. To assume that history is a cognitive object of the same kind as a natural phenomenon is to mistake it for an object of the senses and also to mistake the understanding faculty for unmediated perception. Says Kierkegaard:

> The historical cannot be given immediately to the senses, since the *elusiveness* of coming into existence is involved in it. The immediate impression of a natural phenomenon or of an event is not the impression

of the historical, for the *coming into existence* involved cannot be sensed immediately, but only the immediate presence. (100)

The fact that the coming into existence of an existent eludes us makes even the most indisputable fact uncertain. Such uncertainty voids any distinction between history and memory that is based on the objectivity of the event. It would seem therefore that by collective memory we ought to understand the history of the present in Chladenius' sense, that is to say a history that surveys living witnesses, while classic history relies on documents, ossified records of previous life with a status similar to that of archaeological objects. Methodologically, history is neither more rigorous nor more objective than memory; especially if we accept Nora's contention that memory has been devoured by history, leaving behind a passion to remember that translates into a cult of impossible memory (8). If this memory can suffer hypermetropia (seeing historical depth instead of the real proximity of the events), as in the "invention of tradition" denounced by Eric Hobsbawm and Terence Ranger, the historian, on his side, may suffer from myopia and perceive a square tower as if it were round through an illusion produced by distance, as Kierkegaard noted (98).

Documents and sources, the historian's chief materials, do not contain in themselves the criterion of what is worthy of remembrance. But they are indispensable in order to know, at the very least, what does not constitute a historically recountable memory. As Koselleck points out, the sources have veto power (155). Showing that something is untrustworthy or downright false, they can bar the way to an irresponsible interpretation. The sources are insurance against error, but without the historian's discourse they cannot be established as memory. What needs to be added to the sources in order for history to come into being? Calling attention to the fact that existence is unfathomable, Kierkegaard put forward a theory of freedom to explain the origin of historical existence. Koselleck, more soberly, thinks that in order to make the sources speak one must provide a theory of possible history, that is, a conception of what constitutes a significant, faithful relation to the past. Before interrogating the sources or the witnesses, hypotheses must be formulated. If the sources remain silent or reply in ways that exclude the sense of the question, this could mean that the hypothesis is inadequate. Such contingency has no bearing on the question whether digging in the past is good or harmful, the question around which current resistance to memory revolves. But it seems possible to state that any theory of possible history implicitly includes an affirmative value judgment about knowledge of the past. In the last analysis, memory and history are historical variations of the Delphic imperative. My purpose in this chapter has not been to settle a question as complex as the ethical value of memory. I have simply tried to show the weakness of a distinction hostile to it. And at the beginning of this book on the historical memory, I would like to suggest that, if memory is something more than a history of the present, it can only be the social diffusion of the historian's, the reporter's, or the novelist's work, of anyone who approaches the past with a theory of significant causes and a responsible interpretation of the sources.

CHAPTER TWO

Why Memory?
Reflections on a Politics of Mourning

We are an experienced and chastened people that, for lack of memory,
gets little advantage from its punishments and its experience.
Angel Ganivet, *Ideárium Español*

"G ravestones always also serve as 'monuments' warning the living not to
forget their dead—and yet people often forget all too easily, for 'life
goes on.'" (Weinrich 24). These words from Harald Weinrich's magisterial
book on forgetting are an appropriate point of departure for a reflection on
the historical memory, because they express the essence of the problem.
People forget, often deliberately, against the logic that says that one cannot
forget what one tries to forget. Kant wrote in his notebook a reminder that
he should forget his assistant, Martin Lampe, whom he missed after firing
him. If people usually write what they wish to remember, Kant, in the matter
of his servant, wrote to remind himself to forget (122). But if Kant wished
to forget Lampe, most people feel a moral duty to remember their departed
ones. To that end they institute private acts of remembrance: keeping
mementos, discharging promises and obligations to the deceased, filial or
marital acts of piety, and often carrying on an internal form of "presencing"
that sets limits to the process of mourning and disengagement. Societies are
especially oblivious. Like individuals, they exist in time, and time means
fleetingness and loss. But, unlike people, societies have no emotional
attachment to their "memories" and turn their links to the past into
commemoration.

Societies objectivize "memory" through monuments and diverse
technologies of retrieval. One of the most recent is the ascent of the
discourse on the historical memory in the wake of the human catastrophes
of the twentieth century, in particular the Jewish Holocaust, which a
number of scholars identify as the origin of the late twentieth century's
preoccupation with memory. Whether or not it is the actual source for the

rise of the historical memory, the Holocaust has been at its center. It is largely responsible for the emphasis on victimization and for the moral injunction against forgetting, lest the horrific acts be repeated. Paradoxically, for this discourse it is not memory that keeps the past alive with all its dangers, but forgetting that risks reliving it all over again. Historical memory is, as pointed out in the previous chapter, a practical field of inquiry. It has established itself as a public discourse and affected policy, because it rides on the ethical implications of a century of massive destructions. Under these conditions, the grave is not so much a transitional space to objectivize mourning and heal loss as a rupture that, under certain circumstances, reminds people of a discontinuity in the political order. A breach opens in the foundations of the polis when the state hinders the expression of the rupture that death brings about in the everyday and the familiar—when the state, that is, undermines the grave's function as a place of memory.

Antigone's challenge to Creon is based on a confrontation of duties: the duty to remember ("My crime a deed most holy: for the dead/Longer have I to please than these on earth") (Sophocles 215) against Creon's law, which, by forbidding Polynices' inhumation, imposes on the polis a regression to a pre-cultural stage. Because in ancient Greece burial was not a private affair but was taken over by the state, in abjuring his duty Creon disrupts culture and delegitimizes the state that has just emerged from civil war.

Creon's aim is obvious: by refusing inhumation and handing over his enemy's body to nature, he intends to deprive the polis of an occasion for remembrance. Antigone, on the other hand, proclaims a never-ending duty toward the dead; in short, an obligation to remember them precisely as members of the polis. But if life's relentless march causes forgetting, the central problem of the historical memory is not so much to ensure social cohesion by means of collective rituals as to call up and keep alert the awareness of the fissures in the social edifice. Sophocles posits the problem of social division in terms of piety toward the dead, itself an aspect of religious duty in the ancient world, which did not know the distinction between religion and the state. In ethical terms, the dilemma between tending or neglecting the dead, akin to the problem of remembering or forgetting, is bound up with the (religion-derived) issue of forgiveness and its political version, reconciliation. When the ethical aspect is foregrounded, it is not only the ethics of memory that comes into consideration but the ethics of forgetting as well. Both are inseparable aspects of one and the same process of constituting the subject.

Proponents of forgetting sometimes cast memory in the negative light of resentment. Typically, they aim to excise a period of exceptionality pretending that it never occurred, or, what amounts to the same, that its effects have already spent themselves and no longer mortgage the future. Under those circumstances, to insist on remembering—so the argument goes—is to risk a breakdown of the social order. On the flip side of this disposition, reconciliation is often confused with forgiveness, and the latter with forgetting. On account of this confusion, detractors of memory typically interpret the demand for it as a threat to peace and a reversal of the political mandate of reconciliation.

Of these three concepts—forgiveness, forgetting, and reconciliation—only the last holds a sense of social urgency; it alone stands as a social imperative in strictly secular terms. It is the only one that can reasonably be required of citizens after a convulsed historical period. Reconciliation is required by virtue of the social principle that imposes renunciation of violence on all. After a period of social strife, it is the necessary guarantee against a renewal of the convulsions. But the fact that reconciliation is inescapable if society is not to fall apart, does not presuppose the existence of a unilateral principle that forces victims to forgive the harm suffered, much less to accept forgetting as the necessary condition for reconciliation. Nor does reconciliation entail renouncing to prosecute human rights abuses when conditions for bringing them to trial are present. Just as crimes against humanity do not expire, there are good reasons to extend the condition of imprescriptibility to the gravest abuses against the freedom of individuals and of peoples. There are cases in which reconciliation may hinge on the ability of the affected society to prosecute those who were responsible for the abuses. The conditions needed to bring them to trial may not be present, so that those responsible elude justice indefinitely. But this circumstance does not exempt society from preserving the memory of the facts so that, if penal justice is impracticable, acts of restitutive justice may eventually be undertaken for the victims.

It is important to understand that reconciliation, a transaction to facilitate the normalization of coexistence, is not equivalent to a settlement, nor does it erase guilt, since it is powerless to undo the abuses. Reconciliation is a binding declaration of the will to deconstruct the schism between butchers and victims, a rift inaugurated by the former's actions, which only the latter have the power to close. Reconciliation implies the will to coexist with the agents of evil by virtue of a social pact that ensures the victims an end to their victimization and the oppressors' immunity from any form of revenge. Oppressors will often characterize as revenge any intimation of legal action against their privilege or even the mere intention of leveling the playing field. This is a give-away sign of their disingenuity, a clue to the fact that they may be using reconciliation as a ruse. Reconciliation is credible only when the oppressor effectively renounces real and symbolic violence. It fails when it is a maneuver to retain power and status obtained through violence. In such cases, the failure stems from unrelinquished power relying on latent violence to guarantee its status. The risk of violence resurfacing is the reason reconciliation alone is insufficient to heal societies. Even when the call for reconciliation incorporates a religious tone, as in the confessional model adopted by South Africa's Truth and Reconciliation Commission, its effect is limited to generating a climate of respect for human rights. In practice, the South African model did not guarantee that the confessions implied remorse (Gallagher 303), nor could the Commission exact full confessions. And from the moment that it did not push for economic restitution to end the lasting consequences of apartheid, it remained largely rhetorical. Perhaps because it was barred from pursuing more practical goals, the Commission promoted reconciliation based on forgiveness in exchange for knowledge of the facts. Some of the spectacular scenes of forgiveness produced in that context could be attributed to the emotion attendant on the face-off between butchers and victims. But they seem mainly attributable to the religious engagement of the victims. A religious background was responsible for their renouncing to bring their cases to the criminal courts.

From the standpoint of justice, a question remains whether trading forgiveness for narrative did not condemn the victims to censoring their pain, humiliation, and resentment. That question can be rephrased: is it true that hearing the avowal of the perpetrators and telling the story of one's suffering suffices to neutralize the memory of the experience and sublimate the injustice that lives on in the victim's impotence? In Jonathan Teplitzky's *The Railway Man*, Eric Lomax, a former British prisoner of war in a Second World War Japanese camp in Burma cannot find peace until he confronts his torturer fifty years after the events. In the meantime, the Japanese soldier has been suffering remorse and undergone expiation, but this does not help Lomax, who has been tormented by memories and repressed his anger for half a century. Only when Lomax comes face to face with his torturer, and the Japanese accepts to let him break his arm in retaliation, does Lomax find release from his trauma. The reversal of roles proves cathartic, allowing the Briton to forgive and be free of the past, while the Japanese also finds release in that forgiveness. But there is no question of forgetting. On the contrary, remembrance is key to the renewal of both lives. Teplitzky's film was based on a book of the same title written by the real Eric Lomax. Interviewed after the release of the film, Lomax's widow explained that until the night before his reunion with Takashi Nagase, the interpreter who had been present at all the torture sessions, Lomax had been planning to kill him. After meeting Nagase and realizing the genuineness of his remorse, his plan melted away (Lee 37).

Empowering the victim is essential to forgiveness. Only from a position of moral authority can forgiveness take place. Forgiveness cannot proceed from the wrongdoer, as Nagase's case shows. Even after a half-century of self-imposed expiation, he still had to submit to the victim's justice and accept a commensurate amount of suffering before he could regain his peace. Willingly submitting to his punishment, he proved the sincerity of his contrition and nullified the need to carry out the sentence. As a result, the victim not only obtained satisfaction in the recognition of his right to punish, but found freedom and peace in refusing to carry out the sentence, recognizing it as a senseless act. At that point his spiritual wound began to heal.

Mahmood Mamdani points up the inconsistency between South Africa's Truth and Reconciliation Commission's assertion (in the first paragraph of the appendix to the mandate chapter in the Commission's report) that apartheid was a crime against humanity and its failure to identify any victims of this crime. Failing to identify the victims, it could not identify the perpetrators either (Mamdani 54). Furthermore, the TRC did not consider attacks on communities for the purpose of ethnic and racial cleansing or for community policing as part of its mandate (34). Being central to the definition of "crimes against humanity," these violations could not be excluded without compromising the purpose of the TRC. The fact that the Commission found that of all the violations only 15 percent were said to be committed at the height of apartheid, while half of them were said to be committed in the transitional period, and about 35 percent during the popular struggle against apartheid, further called into question the definition of "crime against humanity." If these figures were correct, the TRC's findings would support the conclusion that it was not so much apartheid that was criminal as the situation arising from the effort to eliminate it (35).

One of the problems with the TRC's implementation of its mandate was that it did not recognize cases of victimization except in general terms by referring to "victim organizations" and "perpetrator organizations." Furthermore, in the second paragraph of its report, the Commission states that the fact that it shares the international community's standpoint regarding crimes against humanity should not be taken as a petition for an international court to prosecute those responsible for designing and running apartheid. "Indeed, such a course would militate against the very principles on which this Commission was established" (cit. Mamdani 54). Those principles were not meant to provide gratuitous amnesty but to facilitate an exchange. Perpetrators were promised amnesty; the victims, reparations, and both were supposed to meet on the non-man's land of truth. But, as Mamdani remarks, the core victims of a system of enforced discrimination could not have been individuals but entire communities marked on grounds of race and ethnicity. Doing justice to their grievances required reparations for communities, not individuals (Mamdani 54).

In addition, the TRC foregrounded political activists as victims of apartheid, thus fostering political rather than social reconciliation and avoiding the responsibilities of the state with regard to the entire population. As happened in Spain's transition from dictatorship, by reducing apartheid to a relationship between the state and individuals (33-4), the TRC acknowledged only individual victims, neglecting the fact that entire communities were victims of targeted violations of rights, something that, in the Spanish case, developed into massive insensibility toward the vulneration of collective rights, aggravating the territorial problems. In another parallelism with the Spanish transition, in South Africa mandated generosity toward those responsible for the design and implementation of a criminal regime raised the suspicion that overlooking their responsibility may have masked the conditions of the agreement to dismantle the regime. Once again, the general condemnation of the previous system protected its promoters' physical, social, and economic integrity, showing how political weakness often results in moral duplicity. Mamdani observes that, if the Commission never posed the question whether apartheid was a check on violence or rather the cause of it, this is "because it was in no position to answer it" (36).

In both transitions shortcomings of justice were excused in the name of possibilism. Spanish society, it was said, could not have pressed for more than the legalization of political parties and a system of political representation. And after a visit to Rwanda, the Commission's president, Archbishop Desmond Tutu, declared that "confession, forgiveness and reconciliation in the lives of nations are not just airy-fairy religious and spiritual things, nebulous and unrealistic. They are the stuff of practical politics" (*Truth and Reconciliation Commission of South Africa Report* 5: 351; cit. Grunebaum 308). From the moment it enters into public life, this intersubjective triad of moral action—confession, forgiveness and reconciliation—obtains political status, but politicization does not mean that these actions take place in the order foreseen or in neutral moral ground. As Heidi Grunebaum, a Holocaust survivor, remarked: "Forgiveness relates to memory and recognition, then, not as a right, a claim, or a demand but as the deferred outcome of a long process that includes mourning, the loss, honoring the dead, restituting the land, and reclaiming the language of resistance and survival over the silence of abjection, trauma, and despair" (308). She adds, paraphrasing Thomas Szasz: "For all conditions, terms, modes, and vocabularies of possible endings, healings, and closures have to be made by the historically victimized. There can be no neutral grounds for forgiveness. If there were, the oppressor would have succeeded in imprisoning the survivor's experience of oppression in the language of the oppressor" (309).

Whereas reconciliation, in the terms of the TRC and, a fortiori, of the Spanish politicians of the transition, was a matter of *Realpolitik*, forgiveness is the last stage of a difficult and paradoxical process, if we accept Derrida's view that only the unforgivable can be forgiven:

> If one is only prepared to forgive what appears forgivable, what the church calls "venial sin," then the very idea of forgiveness would disappear. If there is something to forgive, it would be what in religious language is called mortal sin, the worst, the unforgivable crime or harm. From whence comes the aporia...: forgiveness forgives only the unforgivable. One cannot, one should not, forgive; there is only forgiveness, if there is any, where there is the unforgivable. (32–3)

Julia Kristeva accepts the radicalism of Derrida's position but confines it to the private sphere; more precisely, to the privacy of the psychoanalytic relation. She believes that within this relation aporetic forgiveness occurs not as erasure of guilt but as an opportunity for the inner transformation of the subject. But although such conversion is possible in the private sphere, where the analyst becomes, to a point, transferential co-participant in the subject's guilt, this solution is not admissible in the public sphere. Kristeva considers that forgiveness is out of place in the life of the state, because society is based on the conventions of jurisdiction and punishment for transgressions. Without insurmountable limits and social reaction to their transgression, society could not endure. "There is a public discourse, and it must be continued as a discourse of condemnation, of settling accounts" (283).

Between Kristeva's separation of private (psychoanalytical) and public spheres, and the separation of religion and state in modern political praxis, there is an obvious parallel. Contrition and transformation—in old-fashioned language, spiritual rebirth—emerge from intimate exchange with an Other who—paradigmatically, in the case of the psychoanalyst— wields interpretive authority and the power to originate narratives, a divine prerogative. Conversely, the public sphere is agnostic with regard to the inner self. Defined by the impartiality of the law and the objectivity of punishment, it never escapes historical immanence. Even when the state undergoes revolution, it remains ignorant of forgiveness. This means that it cannot truly break with the past. Whereas forgiveness is atemporal, in that it operates outside the sphere of action and has the effect of nipping its potentially endless expansion in the bud, history is an unbroken series of causes and effects, which in the public sphere translate into the sequence of crime and punishment.

Kristeva invokes Hannah Arendt's definition of forgiveness as the allowance of renewal, of rebirth (281). In *The Human Condition* (1958), Arendt considers forgiveness the faculty of changing the impact of the past on the present and opening the possibility of a future, that is, a time free from the determination of the past and made possible by engagement in the present. She relates forgiveness to the human capacity to promise, that is, to make an ethical stand in a temporal dimension that is, by definition, unknowable and uncontrollable. "Without being forgiven, released from the consequences of what we have done, our capacity to act would, as it were, be confined to one single deed from which we could never recover; we would remain the victims of its consequences forever" (237). The capacity to forgive and to promise, on which the renewal of social life depends, refers to everyday transgressions resulting from the unpredictability of action with respect to its consequences; in other words, it relates to the unconscious magnitude of every human action (Friedland 32). Although Arendt recognizes that forgiveness is absent from the Greek world and emerges within the theocratic society of Israel, she claims that it pertains to the secular sphere and was situated on the level of interpersonal relations by the founder of Christianity. "The discoverer of the role of forgiveness in the realm of human affairs was Jesus of Nazareth. The fact that he made this discovery in a religious context and articulated it in religious language is no reason to take it any less seriously in a strictly secular sense" (238). According to her interpretation of Luke 5: 21-4, where Jesus performs a miracle to prove that "the Son of man hath power upon earth to forgive sins," it is his claim of the power to forgive, rather than the miracle, that shocked people (239 n. 76). An orthodox Christian reading would take the passage as proof of Christ's divinity, but Arendt sees in it evidence of Jesus' claim that forgiveness does not derive from God but "must be mobilized by men toward each other before they can hope to be forgiven by God also" (239). The duty to forgive is based on the sinners' unconsciousness, on their not knowing what they do. It refers to "an everyday occurrence which is in the very nature of action's constant establishment of new relationships within a web of relations, and it needs forgiving, dismissing, in order to make it possible for life to go on by constantly releasing men from what they have done unknowingly" (240). Forgiveness does not apply to the extremity of crime and willed evil (239). Such crimes, according to Jesus, "will be taken care of by God in the Last Judgement, which plays no role whatsoever in life on earth, and the Last Judgement is not characterized by forgiveness but by just retribution" (240).

According to Arendt, dealing justly with the offenses that Derrida calls unforgivable and Kant "radical evil" is not a human faculty. Offenses of that scope are unpardonable, precisely because they cannot be punished, since no punitive equivalence exists for them. "All we know is that we can neither punish nor forgive such offenses and that they therefore transcend the realm of human affairs and the potentialities of human power, both of which they radically destroy wherever they make their appearance" (241). Destroying the potentialities of human power—of power that remains recognizably human—and the realm of ordinary human affairs is a good gauge for what constitutes a crime against humanity. Such crimes shatter the capacity of acting humanely, both for the victims, who are demoted to infra-human status, and for others, who are deprived of the capacity to feel and to respond to the plight of the victims. As for the perpetrators, being in the grip of radical evil sinks their conscience below the level of interpersonal comprehension where humanity abides and forgiveness takes place.

If Derrida identifies a need for forgiveness although, or rather because, forgiveness is impossible, and Kristeva circumscribes forgiveness to the endless negotiation of the psychoanalytic relation, Arendt for her part removes judgment and forgiveness of serious crime from the human sphere. As for minor, half-conscious or unconscious offenses, these belong to the network of interpersonal relations in people's groping living forward. On the contrary, crimes against humanity, that is, serious offenses against human groups, are not private, everyday trespasses but events in the public sphere. To deal with the victims and perpetrators of these crimes as individuals only is a contradiction of principle. The very concept of crime against humanity renders the offense universal: the perpetrator attempts against that which is human in the victimized. But if the public sphere is not legitimated to grant forgiveness in the name of the victims, who is entitled to do so? Only God, says Arendt. But, since the unforgivable cannot be punished, her reply necessarily places it beyond the scope of human judgment. In such circumstances, how can the political need of reconciliation be advanced in those cases where radical evil emanated from the state or was perpetrated in its name and under cover of its legality?

In reference to the Holocaust, Richard J. Bernstein remarks: "we need to recognize that there are ruptures and evils that cannot be overcome, that cannot be reconciled (and to which we cannot reconcile ourselves). We must resist what Adorno so incisively characterized as extorted reconciliation. There are wounds that leave *permanent* scars. There are evils that cannot be sublated" (75). Forgiveness cannot be exacted from the public sphere; it must emanate from the victims and proceed within the limits and conditions they stipulate. Reconciliation is necessary to social life, yet cannot be mandated. After crimes are committed against a community or category of citizens, scars remain in their souls and memory crisscrosses the social space creating a topography of trauma, despite efforts to obliterate it under masses of revamped architecture of re-functionalized purpose. How can the social body overcome its fractures in post-traumatic periods? How can it evolve where fixation exists? Or, in Arendt's terms, how can a society afflicted by historical evil free itself from the past and turn that liberation into the promise of its future?

Avishai Margalit provides a possible answer. He perceives a middle way between Arendt's complete exclusion of forgiveness for radical crime from the circle of human potentiality and Derrida's aporetic call for an unfulfillable duty (or necessity) to forgive. Margalit believes that while only God can forgive those crimes that Kant called "radical evil," men can nonetheless undertake the labor of forgiveness. They can initiate a long, interminable process of reconciliation that will not eliminate the scars or dissipate the memory of the deeds, but might allow them to live with the pain and the humiliation. Such forgiveness cannot be implemented politically but only voluntarily, as a difficult process of growth and learning—somewhat like Kristeva's psychoanalytical relation.

> Forgiveness of this sort is not a policy but rather a case of overcoming resentment and vengefulness, of mastering anger and humiliation. Such overcoming is the result of a long effort rather than a decision to do something on the spot ... Only the decision to begin the process is voluntary; the end-result of complete forgiveness is not voluntary any more than forgetting is, and so it cannot be guaranteed ... Forgiveness in the perhaps unattainable ideal sense is overcoming all traces and scars of the act to be forgiven. (cit. Friedland 37)

This is also Karen Hoffman's view on the nature of forgiveness, which she considers mainly from the viewpoint of the victim's release. In an article on the unforgivable, she claims that forgiveness is the inner transformation not of the perpetrator but of the victim. "When a person has been wronged, she naturally experiences negative, often vindictive, reactive attitudes towards her wrongdoer. It is these attitudes and emotions that the victim overcomes through the process of forgiving" (15). Overcoming of resentment through forgiveness does not, however, remove guilt, which persists objectively, regardless of the presence of subjective guilt feelings. Removal of guilt, says Hoffman, echoing Arendt, may be possible for the divinity, but since it is not in the victim's power, questions about its morality do not arise (15). Because "persons rather than deeds are the true objects of forgiveness," speaking of unforgivable deeds is inconsequential (18). Forgiveness is not for the sake of the deed but of the victim's overcoming resentment, and also of the perpetrator's potential transformation. To ignore the possibilities for moral transformation of the wrongdoers is to treat them as no longer human beings, a profoundly unethical attitude (19). Nevertheless, forgiveness is not to be taken lightly. "The wrong must be understood to be such for forgiveness to be at issue. If a victim fails to acknowledge the serious moral wrong he forgives, then he has not so much forgiven as he has justified, excused, or condoned the offense he suffered" (22).

In the case of serious offenses, such as inflicting psychic trauma, forgiveness cannot be stipulated, nor can the memory be erased without deepening the offense. What can be done, without indulging the passion for vengeance, is to engage in collective mourning that includes acts of restitution, in full awareness that such acts do not dilute guilt or settle the account. It could be objected, however, that if collective mourning and restitution do not erase the past, they are rendered futile by that failure. Are they then worth the conflict and the social strain? The answer to this question is not in doubt. Mourning's effectiveness lies in the fact that it acknowledges the gravity of the deeds and opens the possibility of coexistence on the basis of that acknowledgement. But if there are crimes that cannot be forgiven, once the process of mourning begins, does not its intrinsic incompletion risk transferring the guilt to the generations that came onto the scene after the commission of the crime? The question has practical urgency, not only with regard to the paradigmatic case of Germany, whose policy of collective restitution faces permanent claims based on the idea of the Holocaust's incommensurability, but also with regard to countries such as Turkey, or certain Latin American republics that perpetuated the colonial marginalization and, in some cases, the genocidal liquidation of their native populations, but have yet to admit their responsibilities. Spain would be among these countries, not only with respect to the enslaved and decimated native populations of America, and to the damage inflicted on their languages and cultures, but also with respect to human rights abuses during its last Civil War and, especially, after the nationalist victory and the establishment of Francoist legality.

The answer to the question raised above is incontrovertible: guilt is not inherited. Those who were born after the events, just as contemporaries who resisted them, are neither moral nor juridical subjects of actions that took place prior to their coming into the world. A different matter is that people incur obligations through participating in a tradition from which they derive not only their identity but, more importantly, advantages and benefits. As Ruth Kluger observes: "You do have a stake in your nation's past if you want to be embedded in a tradition, and if you are serious about claiming your heritage, you have to take the good with the bad and own up to the crimes that were committed by your parents and grandparents. But that isn't the same as guilt and doesn't require forgiveness" (311). The last sentence is crucial. One does not need to be or feel guilty to recognize that, by inheriting a history one has become its present vehicle and extender. So long as one does not reject the legacy and renounces the identity and benefits it bestows, one remains immersed in it and acts as the unwitting propagator of its effects. To the extent that someone assimilates their nation's history and epistemology, that person participates in the national past, whether they celebrate it or repudiate it, whether they defend, criticize, deny or consign it to an unconscious state of latency.

Taken as a whole, post-Franco Spanish society chose to live in such a state of false consciousness. It behaved as if the future, redefined as the double conquest of democracy and modernity, could be hitched to the unprocessed legacy of the previous half-century merely by plugging new generations into it. And it did so without warning them of the moral dangers lurking in the acceptance of that legacy. The democratic transition was taunted as a skillful case of social surgery, as the painless removal of a not-so-malign tumor, nonchalantly setting the country on a course of endless progress and exemplary democracy without concern for the possibility of metastasis. Even when events revealed the delusional nature of this belief, as in the *coup d'état* of February 1981, the response of those with political responsibilities was to limit the fallout to the narrowest circle of the conspiracy, to interpret the uncertain victory of the new system as proof of the democratic convictions of the country's principal institutions, and to mollify the powerful conservative forces by slamming the brake on the reform and reversing key aspects of it. For years, though, the legends of an exemplary transition and of the political maturity of the electorate were fed to new generations of Spaniards and to a European Union eager to dispose of the embarrassing Spanish exception. In the view of distinguished witness and direct participant, Jorge Semprún, "the Spanish transition from dictatorship to democracy is the sole example I know [that proceeded] according to the Hegelian model, that is to say, was produced according to the concept of *Aufhebung*: of dialectical preserving-surpassing of the past in the bringing about (in presence and in the present—or in precedence?—) of the future" (115). The irony and the risks of the *Aufhebung* were lost on Semprún, who, writing at the height of Spain's triumphalism in the *annus mirabilis* of 1992, could still write: "This maturity of the Spanish people, its extraordinary political intelligence, will have been the main historical factor of this crucial period" (115).

The truth of the matter is that the bearers of historical guilt engineered Spain's transition with the compromise of a weak opposition whose corruption would emerge in a string of scandals soon after it came to power. Reconciliation, the key rhetorical feature in the change of political scene, rested upon the impotence of the victims, on whose hopes for redress the blithe triumphalism of the moment poured contempt. Semprún hinted at this historical insouciance in the phrase I have quoted in the epigraph to chapter 12 , but he failed to delve into the consequences of his observation. Unlike transitions in South Africa and Peru, Spain's political realignment proceeded on the assumption that silence rather than truth, and censorship rather than confrontation, was the best formula for transcending the historical situation. The result was indeed an *Aufhebung*, a "preserving" of the essence of the dictatorship in the synthetic democracy that represented the new stage of the dialectic. As a result of this simple maneuver around an uncomfortable past, amnesty could be declared a terminal law of the dictatorship. Amnesty, the form forgiveness takes in the public sphere, did not follow in this case from acknowledging the crimes and from contrition but was conceived and implemented as a final act of political arrogance, whereby the victims were cheated of justice and history of truth. By means of the Amnesty Law of 15 October 1977, the Francoist forces still in control of the state after the pre-constitutional elections of 15 June, used the popular clamor demanding the freedom of the dictatorship's political prisoners to grant themselves and all those implicated in the Francoist repressive apparatus immunity from prosecution for the crimes of the regime. Codified and put into effect before the new regime drafted its supreme law, this self-given amnesty became an impassable bulwark against any attempt to vindicate the rights of the victims and redress the wrongs inflicted on them. It made mockery of reconciliation, nullifying the victims' moral authority and depriving them of their capacity to provide sense beyond nonsense ("donner du sens par-delà le non-sens"), to use the formula that Kristeva employs to define forgiveness ("Diversité dans la tempête").

This is not the place to discuss the political logic of the reforms. But it should be pointed out that, beyond the necessity of consolidating democracy in a context of abiding authoritarianism and militarism, playing up the myth of the transition's exemplarity turned political analysts into accomplices in the cover up of the crimes. They share responsibility in the organized refusal of moral satisfaction and the duty of restitution to the victims. In 2002, the affair of the "Salamanca papers" was a spectacular symptom of the moral confusion produced by false closure on the past. "Salamanca papers" refers to the archives seized by the Franco police through a newly created "State Delegation for the Recovery of Documents" after the fall of Catalonia. Trainloads of documents, both public and private, were impounded and sent to Franco's headquarters in Salamanca, to be filed away in a general archive newly created for repressive purposes. For years, the archive was used by a "Special Court for the Repression of Freemasonry and Communism." Created in 1940 to persecute those implicated in the defense of the Republic, this court passed death sentences based on information culled from the confiscated materials. In the 1980s, the reconstituted Catalan government requested the return of its archives on several occasions, and on 17 March 1995 the government of Felipe González, needing the support of the Catalan minority in Congress, issued an order of restitution. Such "caving in" to Catalan demand triggered the largest demonstration in Salamanca's history. From a balcony in City Hall, Falangist writer and local celebrity Gonzalo Torrente Ballester shouted to a cheering crowd that the Catalan documents belonged to them by right of conquest. Cowed by this reaction, the government did not dare to implement its own order. When the conservatives won the general elections the following year, they refused to return the documents to Catalonia. In fact, the government of José María Aznar tried permanently to block the restitution by renaming the old archive "General Archive of the Spanish Civil War." Creating a centralized repository for historians and researchers on the Civil War became the excuse to avoid restoring the documents on the argument that doing so would disrupt the "unity of the archive." Francoist unitarianism had now transferred to a haphazard collection of documents ransacked from all kinds of offices and private homes. In 2002, a civic platform calling itself the "Dignity Commission" undertook the challenge of educating liberal groups and individuals in Salamanca about the injustice of retaining stolen documents, carrying out a long-term campaign for restitution.

When the socialists returned to power in 2004, the way was open for partial return of the documents. The resolution elicited grotesque behavior from Salamanca municipal authorities and the archive's management. When the trucks arrived to load the first consignment, the drivers found the building fenced with barbed wire. After the first truckloads had arrived in Barcelona, Salamanca city hall renamed the lane where the archive is situated. Since then it is called "Calle del Expolio" (Plunder Street), not in memory of the Francoist lootings, as it might seem, but of Catalan impudence in "taking away" what the city had obtained through military victory. The authorities' behavior prompted the grandchildren of Miguel de Unamuno, former rector of the university and the city's foremost personality in modern times, to complain to Mayor Julián Lanzarote. In a letter dated 9 December 2005, the illustrious family objected to the use of their grandfather's dictum "you shall win, but will not persuade" in the campaign against the devolution of the documents. Their letter clarified the interpretation of the famous phrase pronounced in the auditorium of Salamanca University to a gathering of fascists on 12 October 1936. "The manipulation of historical truth that this represents is obvious. You know that this phrase was addressed to rebellious officers in 1936, to the Franco army that stole those papers in Barcelona and took them to Salamanca" (Unamuno Adarraga, et al.).

Although by now a large part, though not all, of the documents have been returned, and Salamanca has been compensated for the "loss," the story is far from over. Encouraged by the absolute majority obtained by the conservatives in the Spanish elections of 2011, and taking advantage of rising anti-Catalan sentiment throughout Spain, Salamanca officials have recently demanded the return of the documents to Plunder Street. This is not the only case of arrogant refusal to take the necessary steps to produce genuine reconciliation rather than the definitive—because legitimized by a rule of law state—humiliation of the victims and the defeated. In the crossfire of accusations and counter-claims, it is important to distinguish between war crimes in a context of mutually inflicted violence, and the crimes committed by a hegemonic dictatorship against a defenseless population. Because the distinction is often blurred, the task of reconciliation was made more difficult than it was already by confusing the categories of militant and victim. This allows Francoists to parade their own victims of "red terror" in cynical disregard of the fact that they implemented their own "justice," unhampered by considerations of fairness and due process, during four long decades.

Although responsibility for the war is usually laid at the doorstep of the Francoists, there will never be universal agreement on this point, much less on the notion that, the war being the consequence of unilateral aggression against the constituted legality, all dead in defense of the Republic may be counted as victims *in extenso*. Victims of Francoism proper are those individuals and groups who, unencumbered by the violence of the war, suffered because of their loyalty to the legitimate institutions, their accidental geographic location, their religious, class, ethnic, linguistic or even familial ascription. It would be inappropriate to consider as victims persons who lost their wager in favor of dictatorships of a different sign. The resentful loser does not have a moral claim to reparation *except* insofar as their punishment was unreasonable and violated human rights. The possibility of losers camouflaging as victims is eagerly exploited by the victors, who denounce all demands for justice as desire for revenge.

Ignoring this categorical distinction, the so-called "pact of forgetting" favored institutional irresponsibility and the confusion between the divisive memory of the war and that of specific crimes. In Germany, a post-bellum government effectively disassociated from the Third Reich took responsibility for the crimes of National Socialism. In the United States, the federal government has apologized to the Native American nations for genocidal actions going back to the previous century and maintains reparation agreements with them. Even in Euzkadi, where government violence stemmed unilaterally from the Madrid government, Lehendakari Juan José Ibarretxe in 2007 asked forgiveness in the name of the Basque people from all victims of ETA, a clandestine organization without representativity or ties with the Basque government. Unlike these and other countries, Spain vehemently rejects every suggestion that the government should take similar steps in relation to the individuals and groups injured by the Franco repression. The conservative right hides behind its new post-transition identity and contends that any demand for apologies, let alone reparations, seeks to reopen old wounds. When in power, the left argues that it would be inappropriate for its government to ask for forgiveness, since this would be tantamount to the victims apologizing for the crimes of their butchers. There is in all this an extraordinary amount of confusion and no less exceptional irresponsibility. Confusing the status of victim with membership in a political party, the socialists transferred the onus to their rivals, showing themselves incapable of grasping the state's responsibility regardless of who governed when fundamental rights were violated. And historical responsibility is greater in the absence of rupture between the state that perpetrated the crimes and the state that declines the obligation to repair them.

Those who refuse the state's obligation to the victims of Francoism, endorsing the moral failure of the successive governments of post-Franco democracy, would have done well to heed Paul Ricœur's position vis-à-vis François Mitterrand's assertion that the French state did not have to ask forgiveness for the crimes committed by the Vichy government. According to Ricœur, the fact of an institutional break in 1945 did not hamper the nation's continuity as a historical community embodied in the institutions of civil society, which exist within the frame of the state (122). For this reason, the state has a duty to respond for the totality of the national history instead of selecting only what it finds advantageous in a massive act of bad faith. But, beyond philosophical reasons, there is also empirical evidence about that continuity in the payroll of the state employees. If one opens the register of high-level functionaries in 1948, says Ricœur, it is possible to verify that two-thirds of them were already in their posts in 1942 (123). It is hardly necessary to add that if one opens the Spanish registry in 1980, it will be possible to confirm a nearly absolute continuity with 1975. In fact, the continuity in the nomenclator would still be high by century's end, given the consolidation during this period of the political, economic, and bureaucratic powers whose foundations were laid under Franco.

The quality and strength of democracy can be gauged by the social penetration of the ethics of recognition, and, as in the case of Germany, by acceptance, not of guilt, which is not inherited, but of the price of an identity and of partaking in a tradition which, in addition to assets, also contains liabilities. Such liabilities are actual debts stated in collective episodes that dignity and decency do not suffer societies to deny. Given history's irreversibility, its torts can only be redressed in the present in symbolic and material deference to the victims. Such deference is what the term "politics of mourning" ought to convey. Without this meaning, all the rhetoric about the historical memory is little more than a mere emission of sound amidst gesticulating fury.

CHAPTER THREE

Memory and Imputation

The most useful memorial for past injustice is keeping the debate
about it alive, rather than freezing it in a monument.
Heribert Adam, "How Emerging Democracies Deal
with the Crimes of Previous Regimes"

At some point in the recent past, the term "historical memory" was pried
loose from its originating theory and set adrift on the sea of prevalent
discourses. There it floats, tugging previously unrelated issues in its tow.
Since nothing happens without a reason, a measure of historical necessity
must account for the broad diffusion of the concept. In Spain, the emergence
of a public debate about the historical memory toward the turn of the
twenty-first century was a belated adaptation of debates already prevalent
elsewhere. To be sure, Spain had a fertile past to cultivate, and soon after
the end of the dictatorship the theme of remembrance emerged as a natural
continuation of the critique of the regime, which had seeped into the arts
and the popular culture for over a decade. As a consequence of the duration
and pervasiveness of the dictatorship, in Spain the historical memory has
centered almost exclusively on the Civil War and the Franco era. Only
recently, the extension of historical memory to earlier periods (for instance,
the eighteenth-century War of Succession to the Hispanic Monarchy) has
produced comparable levels of acrimony.

Spanish history has altered or suppressed enough aspects of the past
to fuel intense debates. It is not scarcity of materials but rather the lack of
ethical initiative that explains the country's intellectual lag. This can be seen
in the mechanical extrapolation of concepts developed in other contexts.
Proof of this dependence can be seen in the often implicit, and occasionally
explicit, placing of Spanish experience under the interpretive auspices of
extraneous models once they are globally established. For instance, the
term "Spanish Holocaust" brazenly profits from the academic prestige of

the most influential studies of memory.[1] It is hard to avoid the impression that, in Spanish discourses on memory, the rhetorical cart often precedes the historical horse—that the universal expansion of the memory discourse after the 1960s, rather than a social demand for "recovering the past," was responsible for the rise of the memory debates in Spain. Had the Civil War not been at hand as a horizon of regret, scholars would still have found opportunities to work on Spain's "historical memory." This is because discourse constitutes "reality," and intensely broadcast discourses impose themselves with the force of self-evidence.

Under these conditions, "historical memory" is a placeholder for issues that have little to do with memory proper. Justice or truth governed oppositional discourses during the Franco years. If discourse on memory was able to displace earlier discourses of social vindication, it is because memory was ascendant in other contexts of denunciation of abuses and demand for recognition. In other words, memory became hegemonic because it not only updated the classic discourses of vindication but also held out the promise of effective redressing, provided the victims could accredit their status. Typically, the demand for historical memory foregoes strict demands for justice. Time and again, the victims insist that they are not seeking retribution but merely setting straight the record of the past. Nor does this "setting straight" hinge on an essentialist notion of truth, which objectivist historians often wield against the alleged pitfalls of memory. Rather, memory has to do with experienced truth, or, better yet, with the truth of experience. And, despite claims to a "merely" narrative satisfaction, whereby the victims obtain a voice and therewith the opportunity to tell their untold stories, there is evidence that memory discourses can interrupt the social consensus. They go beyond the pursuit of epistemological effect in that they assess responsibility, no matter how diffusely, and seek symbolic gratification for the victims.

Nothing else was possible in post-Franco Spain, since the individuals directly involved in the drama of the war and the post-bellum repression had for the most part disappeared from the historical scene. Insofar as the goal was not merely cognitive but included compensatory aspirations, the historical memory became a tool to foist responsibility on social groups, political parties, and institutions that inherited the privileges or otherwise benefited from the ideologies and practices of the perpetrators. On this level of political struggle, vindicating the memory of three-quarters-of-a-century-old war crimes and of abuses committed under a legal system that

---

1 Paul Preston, *The Spanish Holocaust. Inquisition and Extermination in Twentieth-Century Spain.*

was never formally repudiated was bound to fail. In her study of revenge and punishment, "An Eye for an Eye," published in *Les Temps Modernes* in February 1946, in a context of account setting with Nazi collaborators, Simone de Beauvoir explained that the goal of retaliation is to reestablish reciprocity between human consciousnesses. Precisely the reciprocity denied by the butcher when he turns his victim into an object and arrogates to himself alone the privilege of subjectivity. To be recognized as a subject, says Beauvoir, is every person's aspiration and its denial by others the supreme injustice (136). Seeking vengeance, the victim wants to turn the tables on the butcher, and, by making him share the victim's abjection, hopes to force on him the realization that they also shared the privilege of subjectivity. In this desire, Beauvoir discerns "nothing less than the coercion of freedom" (137) and thus a contradiction. Only a free admission of guilt will satisfy the victim's moral injury; anything else risks lowering the victim to the level of the butcher's inhumanity. What we really want, says Beauvoir:

> is to cast a spell on the enemy's freedom, to seduce it like a woman: the alien consciousness must remain free with regard to the content of its acts; it must freely acknowledge its past faults, repent and despair; but an external necessity has to force it to this spontaneous movement. It must be led from without to extract from itself feelings nobody could impose upon it without its own consent. This contradiction is the reason that revenge's aims can never be satisfied. (137)

Beauvoir's acute observation shows the vanity of legislating memory. The political appropriation (or expropriation) of the psychological and philosophical concepts of memory is one of those facts whose obviousness leads people to misunderstand its nature and to misrecognize its effects. Regulating memory can appear as a triumph of applied reason, a public initiative relying on the notion of the general good and thus incumbent on progressive thought. If the marketing of drugs, the labeling of foods, and air traffic are commonly regulated, why not the public memory of historically significant matters? Should citizens not be protected from the toxicity of disinformation circulated by irresponsible ideologues and unscrupulous revisionists? Well-intentioned citizens and militant organizations demand the government's participation in not only setting up protocols but even legislating on the contents of historical memory, on what will and will not be remembered, without grasping the self-destructiveness of this aim. Government sponsorship of public memory can only be pursued in oblivion of the fact that it betrays a previous politicization of memory. To demand a state policy on historical memory is to ignore that the memory thus invoked is tautological. This becomes clear if we substitute truth for memory.

Although states routinely claim the right to impose a verdict of truth in penal proceedings, courts of justice handle truth only in the restricted sense of circumstantial demonstrability and procedural correctness. In their terms, truth has nothing to do with the word's semantic import in a philosophical or a religious sense. The former requires an irrevocable intuition subtended by rigorous logic; for the latter, truth is more often than not affirmation of a dogma, that is, of something unintelligible that must be asserted on faith. In the religious sphere truth is normally designated as belief.

Subjectively, the certainty arising from the two variants of truth might be indistinguishable. Wittgenstein remarks: "It would thus be possible to speak of a mental state of conviction, and that may be the same whether it is knowledge or false belief. To think that different states must correspond to the words 'belief' and 'know' would be as if one believed that different people had to correspond to the word 'I' and the name 'Ludwig,' because the concepts are different" (*On Certainty*, Proposition 42, p. 8e). But even if both correspond to "states of conviction," truth in a philosophical sense is not just any kind of conviction but one emanating from unimpeachable logic. Which is to say that, although one may use the word "I" or the name "Ludwig" for different people, the common denominator does not assimilate all the individuals named Ludwig or everyone who self-designates with the pronoun "I" to the same person. More significantly, unlike philosophy and religion, law courts do not deal with absolute truth, but with the probabilistic truth deemed sufficient to arrive at a usable correlation between the universal code of law and the particular case at hand. Hence, for the law, the term "conviction" also has a different meaning from that envisaged by Wittgenstein. It does not refer to a subjective state but to the completion of a formalized procedure.

That truth cannot be legislated should be self-evident to a secular society. Kant asserted as much when he defended the autonomy of the philosophical disciplines, as opposed to theology, in *The Conflict of the Faculties*. But the essence of politics is not to establish absolute truth—i.e. a truth undiminished by the observer's position—but to achieve partial objectives. That is why politics is par excellence the realm of the multiple, and political truth the will-o'-the-wisp of the pragmatist's epistemology. The ethical charge of the term "historical memory" easily slips into unthinking rejection of skepticism with regard to state-regulated historical memory. Thus, what is in principle the ethical component of memory transmutes into a coercive injunction to remember, and, in practice, to do so in specified ways. Furthermore, the unwarranted association of progressive politics with the implementation of a law of historical memory conflates the critique of the political arrogation of what must be remembered with conservatism's alleged refusal to countenance the past. To the hasty association between memory and political color can be objected that such association is circumstantial and may be easily turned around as the object of memory changes. Historically, it has been the conservative classes that have worked hardest to keep the past alive in the form of tradition and in institutions that strive to minimize the impact of chance and project to the future decisions that have been made in the past. It can also be argued that legislating memory is the positivized expression of censorship. Something must be remembered so that something else can fall away from memory.

This is the aporia: either the memory law is purely formal and neutral with respect to contents, in which case it has no teeth, or it is bound up with the determination of content and thus with its exclusion too. In this case the law will reflect the dominant ideology and discharge its mandate in factional, partisan ways. If the law is intended to impose on a part of society the evidence of its past crimes through an act of external necessity—the only possible reason for legislating on memory—failure to elicit the free recognition and repentance for crimes committed reveals its futility. Forced admission of guilt no longer has anything to do with memory.

If guilt is exacted or enacted on the basis of "memory" rather than evidence (as in the Moscow trials of the 1930s or in confessions extorted through torture), compulsion may impose a narrative but it will hardly elicit subjective consent. In non-totalitarian situations, forcing history through the legislative apparatus will either cripple the law or split society into irreconcilable camps, each with its own historical memory and conflicting demands on the law. This was in effect the outcome of the promulgation of a law of historical memory on 26 December 2007 in Spain. Not only has the law failed to resolve the issues it was conceived to settle, but the conservatives' readiness to reorganize their discourse along the lines of their own victimization (for instance, in the egregious vindication of torturer Melitón Manzanas as a victim of Basque terrorism, extending benefits to his family) is a strategic response to the emergence of memory discourses.

"Collective memory" is a metaphorical extrapolation of the notion of personal memory, whereby society is treated as a conscious individual that defines its identity through sustained acts of recollection. Extending the metaphor, one could reasonably say that, with regard to its past, Spain suffers from multiple personality disorder. It is not just that Spain, like other societies, is divided by class, ethnicity, and material interests, but rather that, unlike other societies, it lacks a common past. Spain relates to its past as a subject suffering from split personality. I do not mean only that there are multiple narratives organizing the same set of events framed as a historical period. The situation is more radical than that: there is no agreement about the events themselves. People disagree not merely on how things happened but on what happened. Events that are preeminent in one version of the past are peripheral to another version or do not feature in it at all. Often the problem cannot be resolved by combining the various narratives, as if by adding their elements a complete and objective account of the past could emerge. It is not a case of truth being in the middle but rather one of mutually exclusive pasts. The narratives being incompatible, they are also irreducible to a minimum common denominator. At this point, the suspicion of "false memory syndrome" becomes plausible.

False memory is part of what Ian Hacking calls "false consciousness," the state of having false beliefs about the subject's identity and about its past. The so-called "oblivion pact" of the Spanish transition to democracy was not merely the suppression of conflictive memories in order to forge ahead and keep post-Franco Spanish society on a balanced path, but a deliberate attempt to stabilize that society in its prominent features by giving a new lease of life to fabricated beliefs about national identity. To achieve this goal, any questioning of the past on which that identity was predicated had to be discouraged or curbed. Not all the past was ejected in a futuristic project of self-rebirthing; only that past whose recollection and public awareness might have produced discontinuity and brought about an actual re-foundation of the state.

The agreed-upon obligation to forget was not total but selective. Following Hacking, we might call it wrong-forgetting (259), by which a political strategy of suppression is to be understood. This process should not be confused with repression in the psychoanalytical sense. It does not refer to the kind of loss of the past implied in the often-abused notion of trauma. In repression, experiences undergone by the subject are inaccessible to consciousness and cannot be retrieved, except—theoretically—through symbolic and associational analysis; in other words, mediated through the analytical narrative of complexes. Such repression is never the result of a deliberate decision by the subject, but a defense mechanism whereby the self blinds itself to an experience or desire that it is unable to countenance and eliminates any trace of the mechanism of ejection from consciousness. This handling of an unwelcome knowledge does not describe the nature of the Spanish pact of forgetting. Here the operative term is not repression but suppression, that is, the deliberate elimination of the uncomfortable memory, which becomes unavowable without, for all that, lapsing from consciousness.

The pact of forgetting was no mere erasure. It involved production of false memories, that is, events or behavior that never happened or happened in a different way (for instance, the late and post-dictatorship memoirs of conspicuous Falangists and Francoists who "recalled" their "early" opposition to the regime and their "deep" democratic convictions.[2] Far from being an isolated phenomenon, in the late 1970s and early 1980s, such "confessions" of strategically articulated memories were profuse. Modification of the past was not the exclusive province of Francoists. On the other side of the political divide, many people "remembered" their heroic struggle against the dictatorship, publicizing their alleged contributions to bringing about the collapse of a regime that, in point of fact, survived itself. Journalist Francesc-Marc Alvaro denounced this imposture of the left in *Els assassins de Franco*. In transitional periods, illusive memories tend to replace actual memories, with the consequence that this kind of remembrance amounts effectively to a blockage of memory, albeit not one defined by amnesia, because one continues to "remember." Nor is false memory a particular case of the indeterminacy of memory as such. Just as mandated remembrance is impotent to conjure up the past, a "pact of forgetting" does not make it go away. Although preemptively unnamable, it remains active in the motivational structure of people's behavior.

In a broad sense, it is true that, for later generations that have grown unacquainted with the facts, the past starts looking legendary. But faulty transmission does not amount to forgetting. One can forget only what one knows, and this is not the case of children who are denied information about the world before their birth. Those children will nonetheless continue the history of their society by living out the consequences of a misrecognized past. Unawareness of the causes of action weighs heavily on a society's potential for change. Societies reproduce through inertia, and it was certainly in the name of stability rather than change that the political agents of the Spanish transition evicted the recent past from public awareness. For their part, proponents of the Law of Historical Memory wished to revisit the past in order to unblock the political stalemate and move beyond the circle of cynicism and resentment. While this is all true, the fact is that lack of an objective grasp of the history leading up to the present has been the norm rather than the exception in every society. And the argument can be

2 For instance, Pedro Laín Entralgo, *Descargo de conciencia (1930–1960)*. In the 1980s, Joaquín Ruiz Jiménez, interviewed by a journalist of the TASS news agency, declared: "By 1970 I no longer had any doubts that Francoism was the greatest calamity for Spain" (Krasikov 61). Ruiz Jiménez had held significant posts in the Franco state: Director of the Instituto de Cultura Hispánica in the 1940s, ambassador to the Vatican from 1948 to 1951, and Minister of Education in the 1950s. In this position of great responsibility, he chose Falangist intellectuals—Laín Entralgo among them—as his closest collaborators.

made that recurrent slippage of the past has been the key to regenerating the social weft over centuries and possibly millennia. Thus, one should ask what is specific to the Spanish "memory struggles."

One answer could be that earlier societies, being more continuous with their past, did not think themselves determined by it as much as we do. Doubtless, people always appealed to the past to legitimize the current state of affairs, shielding the present behind the armor of tradition and received knowledge. But pre-modern social orders did not depend so much on an irreversible sequence of events as on a permanent structure of things: a divine plan, a cosmogony, a revealed or arcane mystery, and on rituals to renew the relation between the human and cosmic orders. In pre-Christian societies time was circular. As Mircea Eliade argued, before the invention of history humans could abolish the past by annihilating time and ritually recreating the world (80). The advent of Christianity inaugurated a teleological history whose eschatological completion was illuminated by the Golgotha drama. The proclaimed uniqueness of that event gave the past an irreplaceable significance and inaugurated a temporal structure that secular history would inherit. But, in the Christian analysis, the past, while interpretable, has transcendental significance: it defines the soul's ulterior destiny. And, in the Hegelian reinterpretation of that story, the past is a dialectical stage in the manifestation of the totality according to laws of historical necessity. In this account, memory was not yet enshrined as the duty of self-knowledge, inasmuch as the ruse of reason was supposed to advance historical rationality behind the backs of great individuals—the "concrete universals"—who are the dupes of the world spirit. But, if we have come to think of ourselves as decisively molded by the past and of society as either "redeemed" or "condemned" by memory, it is because of the triumph of what Hacking calls "memoro-politics" (260), an accepted doctrine involving the belief that, since a person is constituted by memories and a society by its past, any lacuna or gray area of amnesia robs the person or society of an important part of its identity.

On the other hand, in the now old-fashioned and largely forgotten existentialist language, the past is the fall-out from the subject's self-transcendence in the unavoidable exercise of its freedom. That existence precedes essence amounts to a negation of identity in Locke's sense of consciousness merging with each and every one of its memories. Jean-Paul Sartre's notion of a temporalized consciousness means that the latter is never equal to itself, but a "nihilating" movement whereby nothingness "is *made-to-be* at the heart of man and which forces human-reality to *make itself* instead of to be" (*Being and Nothingness* 440). Yet the past is not nothing. It is the accumulated irreversibility of choices that freedom has made in pursuit of itself as an in-itself. And, to the extent that, once made, choices cannot be retrieved, they become part of the situation to be transcended.

From the moment that it repudiates the existence of objective values, Sartre's philosophy makes it difficult to ground judgment. What counts for him is whether the choice implied in every action affirms or denies freedom. Accorded freely through an existential decision, value is the meaning retrospectively given to choices that in and of themselves are arbitrary. Value arises from the concrete situation, which the choice illuminates. For Sartre, claiming that the past, memory, or the unconscious determines choice is dishonest. But if the existentialist chooses without reference to pre-established values, the choice is made nonetheless in view of the anticipated consequences. And since freedom is a distant, possibly inaccessible, absolute, the relative freedoms constitutive of the concrete horizons defining each effort at self-making must be measured by the consequences of the choices involved.

Existentialism's commitment to justify the possibility of judgment in the absence of a priori values bears on the problem of certainty and imputation for historical wrongs. Being interrelated, these two notions are easily swapped. Thus, claims about just wishing to establish the facts are suspect, while appealing to the wrongs inflicted as the conclusive argument for regulating the historical memory is disingenuous. In both cases, two categories are conflated that should be kept analytically apart. In the first case, establishing the facts serves to introduce the juridical notion of imputation under the mantle of epistemology. In the second case, with the appeal to "do something" in the face of historical outrage, a pre-juridical demand for justice invades the epistemological sphere, replacing truth with the moral admonition to "remember." It is evident that the epistemic certainty that comes from establishing facts about human rights abuses triggers a demand for justice that is morally compelling and must be satisfied before society can be placed on a footing of reciprocal trust. But an epistemological travesty takes place when, from the indisputable requirement of justice, people infer the need to legislate on the shape and significance of the past. It is knowledge of the past that, under certain circumstances, grounds legal recourse for justice. The justified desire for justice should not determine the way the past is remembered.

In the twentieth century, "historical memory" arose as an alternative to history with a view to transcending the merely epistemological representation of the past, a representation whose legitimacy lies in the historian's cognitive neutrality, or at least in disciplined refraining from apologetic or prosecutorial bias. Unlike history, which attempts to establish the motifs and implications of actions, "memory" often aims to assign responsibility, placing the past on a moral scale. The scale is itself subject to history and therefore varies with the slant taken by the historical memory. But history is a messy discipline. For instance, people agree on the abstract definition of genocide, not always on what counts as one. Disagreement does not necessarily stem from the facts being denied (as in negationism) but rather from the weight laid on them, that is, disagreement oscillates depending on the perspective from which facts are interpreted. Moral outlook and intention reduces or enhances their consequence, as does their assignation to a theory or semantic field.

"Responsibility" is a juridical concept, denoting obligation to make good or compensate for an infringement of right or to be punished for it as established by law. If the term were understood strictly within the confines of the law, there would be no need for legislating the obligation to take into account the torts committed by social groups or institutions in the past. The International Court of Justice at The Hague deals with precisely such historical torts in the manner of a criminal court. It does not require international legislation on historical memory, which, in addition to being uncontrollable, would be superfluous. Most legal systems include civil liability and penal procedures for wrongs committed in the past, and some of these infringements are imprescriptible. But the term "responsibility" has spread beyond the confine of its juridical definition and as a result has become blurry and affected by considerable vagueness. Semantic overflow takes away not only the term's conceptual rigor but its efficacy as well. In the case at hand, how is one to assess responsibility for the damages of a civil war? If people, including historians, cannot even agree on who was responsible for starting the war, how is a consensus on the distribution of responsibility to be reached? And if an unlikely agreement were to unite all participants into settling the issue of efficient responsibility, what specific agent could then be called on to account for the rhizomatic proliferation of injustice in a totalitarian dictatorship like the Franco regime? The very generality of the charges impedes the assessment of concrete obligations and the exaction of penalties. How does one place a "regime" in the dock of that regime's self-surviving juridical apparatus? Making Franco the ultimate embodiment of the system he represented was that system's expedient to dispose of the open-ended demand for "responsibilities" during the transition. Personification is a common rhetorical device, but its power seems inexhaustible. If, under exceptional circumstances, an individual personifies a weft of social and political interests, the demise of that individual places that same weft beyond the possibility of moral or judicial recourse.

Ricœur observes that the founding concept for the juridical meaning of "responsibility" must be looked for outside the semantic field of "respond"

(13). He finds it in "imputation." This term was already in use when "responsibility" had not yet moved beyond the narrow political sense in which people spoke about the sovereign having "responsibility" toward the British parliament, i.e. being obliged to respond to it. To impute is to ascribe to someone a culpable action, one that infringes a prohibition or an obligation. Imputation, from Latin *putare*, to reckon, to estimate, includes the idea of calculation, from which we derive "compute." It introduces the metaphor of the moral account that must be settled. And it is on the question of settling old accounts that the demand for historical memory hinges. Into this demand for "memory" slips a claim for compensation, be it purely moral, such as an abstract satisfaction, or material, as in the paying of damages. It represents an impotent softening of the demand for penal justice, such as came into effect in the Nuremberg trials or in the cases tried at the International Court of Justice. As Ricœur points out, a certain depenalization of responsibility is implied in the demand for simple compensation (24). In this respect, the Francoists who survived Franco benefited from the shift from the desire for legal prosecution (a hope of the anti-Francoists and an anxiety for members of the Franco regime) to demands for restitution, which, given the passivity of Spanish society, were soon whittled down to appeals for moral compensation, unheeded for the most part.

Prosecution was in fact taken off the table when the Franco regime, democratically reelected under a new name, granted itself immunity through the amnesty law of 1977. Since that law was pre-constitutional, there was no legal impediment to striking it down after the new Constitution was approved in 1978. But, in the absence of political pressure to challenge the law, it remained in force. In time, it seemed as if the granting of immunity implied absence of culpability. Individuals involved in human rights abuses during the Franco era remained in public office, continued to play political roles and to enjoy social privileges in post-Franco times, as did their children and grandchildren. Ten years after its promulgation, the law of historical memory of 2007 not only remains ineffectual at indemnifying the victims of repression; it cannot even be invoked to illegalize the historical fascist party, Falange, or to shut down the Fundación Francisco Franco, whose declared program is "to spread the memory and the work of Francisco Franco," a euphemism for encouraging a political regression to the values and methods of the military dictatorship. Connivance between an institution devoted to the spread of antidemocratic ideals and Spain's ruling class transpires in the continued support the Fundación Francisco Franco receives from the Partido Popular, Spain's majority political party.

In some sense, the emergence of "historical memory" correlates with the restriction of access to legal redress, showing that the memory enterprise is not primarily epistemological but is part of a general pattern, by no means restricted to Spain, of countering the shrinkage of the juridical field, and in particular the field of penal determination, with an unprecedented extension of the field of moral responsibility (Ricœur 27). How far does responsibility go? Since a society is a web of inextricable relations, where does responsibility stop? At the government? The institutions? The police? The Church? The educational establishments? The Press? How about the financial institutions? Private business, too? Recently, denunciation of the Franco government's negligence in the outbreak of an epidemic of poliomyelitis in the mid-1950s, causing 1,600 deaths and close to 11,000 children impaired for life, raised the specter of systemic malpractice and culpable deception, leading to unnecessary suffering of the affected children and their families (Armengou and Belis). Since the negligence was imputed to the government's decision not to spend limited foreign currency on the importation of vaccines from the United States, denunciation of medical malpractice would appear to be predicated on a diffuse ideological contamination rather than on limited knowledge and incompetence. The regime's cruelty would somehow reflect on doctors and medical personnel, themselves tainted by the corruption associated with the Franco era. However one decides on this matter, it seems indisputable that the emergence of this and similar scandals half a century later was motivated by the authority acquired by the memory discourse and the diffuse notion of responsibility. There is a tradeoff between the inability to bring political criminals to justice and the proliferation and ramification of cases of ever more tenuous responsibility, to the point that the entire period and a good part of the society is held morally accountable.

The problem becomes a question of the scope of responsibility, of how far into the past (and into the future) moral accountability reaches and how broadly it extends in the present. In other words, where does one situate the efficient cause of the evils denounced, so that the subsequent chains of effects can be plausibly imputed to that origin? If Francoism was not *causa sui*, who or what caused it? Where should one stop in tracing the precedents of its violence, in cataloging its conditions, and identifying its distant effects? If the Holocaust is taken as paradigm-setting for historical memory, as has often been the case, it is possible to observe that historians do not limit its horizon to the rise of Hitler, but trace its origins long before the Nuremberg laws of 1935, and even the publication of *Mein Kampf* ten years earlier, to turn-of-the-century Viennese anti-Semitism, to Arthur de Gobineau's *Essay on the Inequality of the Human Races*, to Richard Wagner, all the way to Martin Luther. In short, it becomes an indictment of German culture as a whole, and even of Christianity, in the extreme militancy of Daniel Goldhagen, who traces the origins of modern anti-Semitism to the central texts of the New Testament and demands the suppression or at the very least the annotation of some of Christianity's canonical texts as anti-Semitic (274–6) and asks for the Catholic Church to pay reparations to the state of Israel in material and political form (212). In response to the criticism that his book provoked, Goldhagen defended himself by saying that the very title and the beginning of the book state that his purpose was in moral, not historical analysis; that he was interested in the Catholic Church's emulating Germany in soul-searching, breast-beating, and "the duties of repair" for "debts incurred" (Rothenberg). And this is precisely the hitch: that a historian should arrogate to himself the authority of "moral analysis" while failing to observe his professional deontology.

The Goldhagen case has the virtue of highlighting an issue: is the memory practitioner interested in scrupulously reconstructing the past or rather in indicting a present institution, such as a state or a church, with practical outcomes in mind? To achieve this goal, the "moral interpreter" must show that the arraigned institution is continuous with one that in the past was guilty, by commission or omission, of crimes against individuals or a human group. But continuity cannot be taken for granted. The post-civil rights United States is not the pre-Civil War land where slavery was legal. Regardless of current racism, the historian is not entitled to judge as if abolition had not occurred and legal guarantees against discrimination did not exist; as if, in other words, history could be dissolved into moral judgment whose premises and conditions of possibility are, in fact, the product of that very history. One premise of fair law is that it will not apply retroactively. But, granted that crimes that were legal in former times must be judged criminal even then, how fair is it to impeach present society for the crimes of a previous one? The unfairness is so glaring that Goldhagen defended himself against accusations of being anti-German by claiming that the notion of collective guilt is indefensible and that his books aimed at the restoration of individual responsibility. Individuals, he now says, may be judged for their individual deeds and moral choices and not those of others or of some group. But, in the same breath, he adds that institutions bear ongoing responsibility (Rothenberg), regardless of whether their current stance coincides or departs from that of the past.

He had already stated this position in *A Moral Reckoning*, where he wrote: "Guilt and blame is never collective, never incurred for a person's identity but only for his individual choices to act (and not to act) and for the consequences of those choices. Only individuals are guilty or blameworthy, and they are so only for their individual offenses" (212). However, he immediately added: "a person, by choosing to be a member of an institution that owes restitution, obliges himself to accept the institution's duty as his own, and then must discharge that obligation as best he can" (212). All Catholics, therefore, owe restitution to Jews on the basis of the Church's historic anti-Semitism. And how does a present-day institution bear the guilt of previous ages if guilt and blame is not collective or incurred for reasons of identity? Simple, says Goldhagen. "A religious institution such as the Catholic Church has ongoing duties and obligations, incurred by its and its officials' own past deeds" (212). And, in case anyone were to object that this would make guilt inheritable, Goldhagen advances the notion that, in the case of the Church and similar institutions, they legally "have the status of persons" (212).

He does not, in other words, admit the possibility of reform or transformation. So long as an institution is the historical heir of a previous one, it inherits all of its past, regardless of whether it was monolithically unified or crisscrossed by ideological and behavioral fault lines. In the case of the Catholic Church, Goldhagen claims exactly this, ignoring its troubled history of schisms, reformation attempts, and ideal universality, holding Catholic teaching responsible for the emergence of anti-Semitism and ultimately for the Holocaust. The Church, of course, abets this ahistorical view of responsibility by claiming to hover above history, preserving the essence of a 2,000-year-old religion through the ups and downs of secular history.

But, in the case of slavery, it is possible to object that neither does the Constitution of the United States provide any foundation for it (on the contrary, it states the creed of natural equality among all humans) nor is the country continuous, except in name, with the pre-Civil War federation of the former British colonies. To claim otherwise would be to ignore the irreversible moral break consummated by a bloody civil war pitting an abolitionist North against a pro-slavery South. To prove otherwise, Goldhagen refers to the hundred years of segregation and ongoing economic inequality as evidence of the resilience of the slavery factor. But it could be argued that segregation was *another* legalized crime against African Americans, one that again divided Americans (and not only blacks against whites) until its abrogation. If torts are, as Goldhagen ultimately conceded, committed by individual agents against individual victims, those torts are themselves situated in time and space. They do not extend infinitely. Except in a world of inexpiable guilt, crimes do not project their repercussions to all future generations in runaway traumatic transference. Guilt is not inherited; each generation builds up its own. It is closer to the historical truth and to sound juridical practice to consider each crime a transgression in itself rather than a toxic cloud of evil drifting from one historical moment to the next.

Goldhagen's polemical books against collective institutions beg the question of forgiveness in transitional times. Amos Friedland has studied this issue in three Jewish post-Holocaust thinkers: Hannah Arendt, Avishai Margalit, and Jacques Derrida. I will dwell on Arendt only, because of the three she is the one that most clearly opposes Goldhagen's irreconcilable spirit of endless responsibility and infinite reparation by declaring humans inherently incapable of dealing justly with the nature of evil. Arendt, famously vilified by the Jewish community for considering Adolf Eichmann a pitiful, mediocre human being rather than an outsized impersonation of the atrocious, is of particular interest because she responded to Hegel's idea of the complete elimination of evil through the advent of absolute Spirit (Friedland 25) by carefully considering the words of the founder of Christianity. In Luke 17, Arendt finds that Jesus "preached forgiveness for all those sins which in one way or another can be explained by human weakness, that is, dogmatically speaking, by the corruption of human nature through the original fall" (28). Nevertheless, Jesus "once mentions in the same context that there are others who caused *skandala*, disgraceful offenses, for which 'it were better a millstone were hanged about his neck and he cast into the sea.' It were better he had never been born" (28).

Arendt considers forgiveness in relation to the action of promising, to which it is inextricably related, in that both are oriented toward the future. This, comments Friedland, may seem counter-intuitive: forgiveness concerns the past, which cannot be undone, while promising concerns the future, which cannot be secured. However, the act of forgiving can help break the fixity of the past, allowing the sinner and the aggrieved to move on. Forgiveness makes it possible for a future to take place. It opens for action a time that is not entrapped in the pitfalls of the past. By bringing forgiveness into the realm of human interaction (rather than of the divine), Jesus achieved status as a political thinker and not only as a religious one (Friedland 30). To be forgiven, according to Arendt, are the trivial, everyday offenses that people commit without knowing. It is the unknowingness that makes the action forgivable. However, forgiveness "does not apply to the extremity of crime and willed evil" (32). These will be judged by God in the Last Judgment, "which plays no role whatsoever in life on earth" and "is not characterized by forgiveness but by just retribution" (32).

Here Arendt sounds as implacable as Goldhagen, but in an unexpected turn she says that what men cannot forgive they may not punish. The logic cuts two ways: what men cannot punish, they are not in a position to forgive; and that which is unforgivable they are unable to punish (33). Punishment is only legitimate if it balances the debt, and this assumes that punishable debts can be forgiven, so that whether the punishment is carried out or not does not affect the releasing of the individuals involved from the hold of the past. It is therefore of the utmost importance to decide whether the unpunished crimes of the Franco dictatorship, presumably forgiven through the amnesty law of 1977 and the political reconciliation formalized with the Moncloa stability pacts of the same year, belong to the category of unknown trespassing or to that of willed evil.

In Arendt's reading of the passage on forgiveness in Luke's Gospel, the possibility of reconciliation between sinner and sinned against rests on the absence of evil, which permits demotion of the wrongful actions to unconscious trespassing. Jesus makes forgiveness a moral obligation but by no means an automatic one. The possibility of forgiveness (and the obligation to forgive) hinges on "repentance," a change of mind in the trespasser, starting with acknowledgement of the punishable action. It is precisely this condition that was lacking in the Franco establishment's extortion, rather than entreaty, of reconciliation on their own terms and for their convenience. "Reconciliation" was indeed the guiding thread or master narrative of the political resolution of the dictatorship. But if one believes that Francoism willingly incurred extreme crime and its deeds were of a nature that could not be forgiven or reconciled, then one must conclude that they cannot be punished, in the sense that any punishment would be incommensurable with the fault and thus arbitrary. But if justice cannot be served in such cases, because evil transcends the scope of human lawfulness, can historical memory do anything more than preserve the awareness of an opprobrium that cannot be undone or excised? To remember, in such cases, is also to realize that, insofar as the evil deed is not expunged, it retains its force and thwarts the transformation of would-be forgivers and would-be forgiven into free agents.

Goldhagen's insistence on endless institutional responsibility is reasonable when the institution enshrines and perpetuates the principles that caused the damage in the past, making it repeatable in the present. This is the morally, if not always judicially, relevant meaning of continuity. Thus, when the Spanish governments of the 1980s refused to apologize for crimes perpetrated in the name of Spain's unity on the pretext that the post-Franco state was discontinuous with the Franco regime, those governments were guilty of bad faith. Elected officials of the post-Franco era knew that the regime that issued from the so-called transition to democracy was based on continuity, not rupture, with the previous one. The reestablishment of the monarchy not only linked up with the conservative Spanish tradition but solemnized the legacy of the previous regime. At the height of his power, Franco had arranged the transmission of authority in the 1947 Law of Succession. This law established that Franco would choose his own successor, who would then be ratified by the Spanish Cortes. In 1969, after years of grooming the young boy under his supervision, Franco appointed

Juan Carlos as his political heir, and the prince famously swore allegiance to the Fundamental Laws of the Regime before the Francoist Cortes in 1975. In this way, *de jure* succession became *de facto* continuity.

Francoism was not defeated; to bring itself into line with the European Economic Community and to receive international sanction, it decked itself out in democratic trappings. But the social and economic, and to a great extent the ideological, balance of power remained in place. There was no formal recantation or abjuration of the past. Conspicuous offenders against justice were not disqualified from public office, nor were the institutions purged of fascist elements. The self-dissolution of the Franco establishment was a crafty piece of political engineering. The fiction succeeded by inducing a memory vacuum and a legal loophole, correlating the social amnesia with an amnesty law. To this day, that loophole prevents the revision of political trials under the Francoist "justice" and makes it impossible to prosecute crimes committed under the mantel of that legality. When examining magistrate Baltasar Garzón, of the Central Court of Criminal Proceedings, initiated an investigation in 2010, he was diligently denounced by a fascist group for abusing his powers and preventively suspended from office. In 2012, Spain's Supreme Court cleared him of that charge but barred him from continuing the investigation by expelling him from the judiciary for a period of eleven years. The pretext was an unrelated charge of wire-tapping in a money-laundering scandal involving the conservative party. The Gürtel case exposed bribes paid to the Partido Popular, which governed Spain and several autonomous communities when the Supreme Court ruled on Garzón's case.

Spain's flawed transition to democracy, its failure to disengage fully from a criminal past and to give symbolic satisfaction to the victims, helps to answer the question how far the consequences of injurious actions extend to the future. By making allowance for the old legality in the new, Spain's politicians and their supporters de facto ratified the political system they claimed to leave behind, implicating the country's future in its criminal past. The post-Franco evolution of the Spanish state bears out Ricœur's answer given to the question of how far responsibility extends in time: "Stated in terms of scope, responsibility extends as far as our powers do in space and time" (29). The ability of Franco's political heirs to continue to exercise power over the groups that were aggrieved by his regime is the strongest possible indicator of their ongoing responsibility. By adding new grievances in the post-Franco era, such as the state terrorism of the Socialist party, cultural eradication of minorities, discriminatory redistribution of taxation, and other entrenched forms of symbolic and effective violence, the post-Franco regime has dilated the state's responsibilities, projecting them deeper into the future.

We are responsible only for harm that we are capable of inflicting. If historical memory is conceived as a means of casting the net of responsibility in the present, as it clearly is, its apologists must confront the question whether the groups and institutions of whom responsibility is demanded were capable of inflicting pain and willing to do so. And, in the case of legacy institutions, whether they still are. To this caveat should be added that denial of wrongs committed in the past, or denying the wrongfulness of injurious actions otherwise admitted to, is itself a form of injury typified as moral harm. The problem with the uncontrolled expansion of responsibility is that it dilutes the assignment of penalty to the point where it disappears in any legally meaningful sense. A totalitarian system like Francoism was the result of countless interventions at every level of society. It cannot honestly be concentrated in the personality of its figurehead, but expanding responsibility to every bureaucrat or compliant participant under the vague, all-embracing notion of collaboration leads to the paradox that a large part of Spanish society, if not all, could be held accountable on some capillary level of complicity. But when everyone is responsible, no one is. And perhaps this was the shrewdest of Francoist strategies: to recast political participation as social adaptation.

The transition achieved the miracle of political transubstantiation. By lifting the state by its bootstraps and transferring the whole apparatus from legality to legality, Francoists and a submissive opposition avoided breaking with a disreputable history. The new political dispensation transfigured the past rather than repudiating it. But to justify human rights abuses by appealing to constituted legality, i.e. the legality of an unjust, murderous system, is unacceptable. Individuals and institutions directly involved in criminal behavior should not be exonerated by appealing to an illegitimate system's ratification of their acts. Nor should they be allowed the benefit of legal cover by alleging historical necessity. Doing so amounts to ignoring the consequences of their actions and removing them from the sphere of responsibility. Those who plead immunity on such terms incur bad faith as much as those who admit their arguments.

But in a totalitarian system founded on explicit injustice any action can yield deleterious consequences without consciously envisaging them. A teacher can be guilty of spreading the dominant ideology, a priest of legitimating an execution with his presence, a functionary of lending a concrete face to the regime. Their actions and omissions are inextricable from the functioning of the political machine. And yet, if the unintended consequences of their behavior are considered the sole criterion of their actions, the possibility of imputation vanishes into diffuse liability. This is the ultimate survival strategy for the agents of an iniquitous past: to camouflage in the state of opinion that they contributed to create by shaping the worldview, assumptions, and political reflexes of succeeding generations. This is what analysts mean when they denounce that institutional Francoism perpetuated itself in social Francoism. To the success of this strategy contributes the scattershot tactics of the champions of historical memory, who, by casting a very wide net, arraign a historical era instead of the individuals on whose authority specific crimes were committed.

But dilution of responsibility through a vague demand for memory runs the risk of rendering the guilt ethereal by generalizing and thus diffusing the causes of wrongful behavior. At times, memory is invoked to bridge the temporal gap between the actions denounced and the effects held to endure in the present. Then it gives the impression of being a last-ditch attempt to put a face or a name on injustices that have been either forgotten or pushed into anonymity. On those occasions memory becomes indistinguishable from imputation. But when the temporal gap is so wide that reparation is no longer practicable, the possibility of meaningfully ascribing the crime to an agent disappears, and memory becomes historical, that is, removed from the practical possibility of imputation.

CHAPTER FOUR

Denial and the Ethics of Memory

Truth has not single victories; all things are its organs,
not only dust and stones, but errors and lies.
Emerson.

The greatest paradox in the popular debate about the historical memory
could well be the concern with its frailty, the almost conspiratorial
alarm at its suppression, and widespread demand for its protection by
means of specific legislation, foundations, archives, monuments, museums,
ceremonies, and other public initiatives intended to anchor the past in
society's awareness. In the face of massive preoccupation with the dominant
tendency to forget—a byproduct of society's evolution—and, in the case of
Spain, with an alleged machination to accelerate this tendency with regard
to the Civil War and the ensuing military regime, it is important to look
at the facts. And the facts show that, on the intellectual plane in general
and that of history in particular, there was no forgetting during the years
following the Franco dictatorship. There was selection of the narratives,
strategic emphasis on certain elements at the expense of others, depending
on who told the story, whose viewpoint became the cornerstone for the
edifice of the past in historical recollection, whose interest and for what
goals dictated the syntax of the narrative, determined its agents, interpreted
their motivations. To admit memory's subjective organization (how could
memory, an affair of consciousness, not be subjective?) is not to declare
it threatened or abolished. It is merely to place it where it belongs: in
the relative space and temporality of reflective consciousness, from where
positivist historians of the nineteenth century and their belated epigones,
who claim to represent a "scientific" history based on the aseptic handling
of the facts, had taken it. Claiming collegiate ownership of memory, and
unaware of the historical origins of their own disciplinary language game,
such historians mistake archival documents for facts.

Although it is often said that the victors write history, denouncing its distortion is not the exclusive task of the vanquished. Francoists were not the only ones who covered up their crimes and obscured their atrocities. Often, when someone calls on society to remember, it is not to center the scale but to legitimate a partial version of the past as if it were the complete account. Long after its official conclusion, the Civil War continued to be fought on the ideological front. At stake was the desire to secure legitimacy in the present by imposing a narrative about the past. In time, the difference between the contenders has grown ever more diffuse. But, thirty years ago, the blocks were sharply distinguished, each claiming the moral high ground with a story lacking in nuances.

David Herzberger proposed the thesis that fiction writers were the unofficial alternative to Francoist historiography. But novelists, in this scheme of things, were not exactly conveyers of historical truth, or even of genuine memory. Rather, they challenged the mendacious official historiography by subverting its mythic ordering of history. And the bolder and more experimental of these writers chucked narrativity altogether, sublimating this collapse into a triumph of "pure fiction" (13). In a troubling move, though, Herzberger notes that "the salient issue at hand, therefore, is not what empirically real objects are represented by the fiction and history of postwar Spain (I am not concerned, for example, with what may or may not have happened in the bombing of Guernica during the war), but rather from which textualizations do the works of history and fiction most fully reveal their capacity to mean" (13–14). Meaning here is freed from representation— a bad word in academic criticism of the 1990s—with the consequence that the writer's "challenge" to official history did not come from a more honest and precise account of the facts but from a higher virtuosity in the manipulation of form, "meaning" being in this context something like the displacement of syntactic (rather than semantic) air produced by more voluminous and involved "contextualizations."

According to Herzberger, the protagonists of this anti-history would have been not so much the "testimonial" writers who self-ascribed to the social realism of the 1950s, a style inspired by the contemporary theories of Georg Lukács, as those who in the 1960s and 1970s adapted the formal innovations of the *nouveau roman*, stream-of-consciousness, and the theories that Philippe Sollers, Jean Ricardou, and others began publishing in *Tel Quel* in 1960. The social realists of the 1950s, while constructing "a homology of the real" in the present, were—says Herzberger—echoing an implied past that defied the history of the state. However, they did this by creating counter-myths "rather than through the sublation of the process within which the past is controlled and made known by Franco historiography" (12). In other words, social realists were the dupes of a naive theory of narrative that placed them at the opposite end but on the same level as Franco historians. Their novels implied a personal memory that refuted the sense of official historiography, but behind the antagonism and, I should add, the formal differences, the two genres shared a common element in subjectivity and essential fictiveness. Later writers like the Camilo José Cela of *San Camilo, 1936*, certain works of Gonzalo Torrente Ballester, and Juan Goytisolo, on the other hand, "assert the end of historiography. They do so by privileging the power of words as the primary foundation of power within an aleatory narrative of deferral" (13). In this sentence it is easy to recognize prevalent notions of the 1990s: the Foucauldian focus on epistemic power and the Derridean idea of permanent deferral of meaning. Ironically, logocentrism is simultaneously affirmed and rejected (or "sublated," in another temporal giveaway), in that words, or rather texts, are seen as the foundation of power (even Francoist power), while power is "subverted" through a form that denies narrative necessity and refuses stable significations. More than presenting alternative accounts of the past, narratives inspired by the New Novel called attention to the unreliability, if not downright untruth, of nationalist mythography.

A work like Juan Goytisolo's *Count Julian* (1970) did not propose an alternative history to the nationalist construction of the Generation of 1898 and the orthodox fundamentalism of Menéndez y Pelayo. Rather, Goytisolo re-appropriated Jean Genet's idea of betrayal as challenge to the ossification—contemporary criticism spoke of "reification"—of life in cultural dogmas. Like many a New Novel, Goytisolo's text lacked a plot—unless one considers a plot the meandering of an individual through the streets of Tangier. The novel's combination of observation and subjective subversion not only alters history's lineal progress but raises skepticism about the possibility of establishing a causal chain originating in a privileged event, such as the Arab invasion of the Iberian Peninsula and the consequent origin of Spain's national identity in the Reconquista. The New Novelist, wrote Vivian Mercier, "often finds himself unwilling or unable to make this distinction between subject and object" (5). Some of the Spanish novels of the 1970s called into question this very distinction, thereby contesting the truth status of the nationalist historiography before and after the Civil War.

With the phrase "the age of suspicion," the title of an essay published in 1956, Nathalie Sarraute described the modern reader's skepticism toward fiction, signaling the crisis of the idea that readers willingly suspend their disbelief. Coleridge, the coiner of this expression, had remarked that writers often resort to cognitive estrangement in order to profit from readers' ignorance or lack of information to encourage them to suspend their tendency to disbelieve. 1970s narrators employed formal estrangement to obtain the opposite effect. By breaking the realist spell, they called attention to the constructed nature of all narratives, and the observation spilled over onto the episodes of national history, which thereby could be understood from the viewpoint of myth. Even the Civil War of thirty years earlier— still alive in people's memory—could be projected as legend, the way Juan Benet did in *Volverás a Región* (1967), where the war is fought in the vaporous geography of enchanted history bordering on myth.

In the closing essay of *Pour un nouveau roman*, "From Realism to Reality" (1963), Alain Robbe-Grillet wrote that all writers think they are realists. However, whereas previous writers claimed to produce a record of reality, the realism of the New Novel consisted not in transcribing reality but in constructing it. "Novelistic writing does not aim to inform, as does the chronicle, the testimonial, or a scientific report; it constitutes reality (175). Now that the poststructuralist tide of formalist theory has subsided (and a broader Iberian Studies paradigm has made progress in academic work on Spain), a different canon of contestation of Francoist history has emerged in testimonial novels from the 1960s, such as Joaquim Amat-Piniella's *K.L. Reich* (1963), Joan Sales' *Incerta Glòria* (1956), Aurora Bertrana's *Entre dos silencis* (1958), Jorge Semprún's autobiographical narratives beginning with *Le grand voyage* (1963), Agustí Bartra's *Crist de 200.000 braços* (1958 and 1968), and Mercè Rodoreda's *La plaça del Diamant* (1962), all of them written in the kind of realism that correlates language to experience and memory.

Many of these works differ from more recent accounts in the honesty with which their representation of the past balances the distribution of blame. Sales' novel, one of the first to treat the Spanish Civil War from a republican viewpoint, denounces the persecution of Catholics in the rearguard; Bertrana presents the case of a German officer stationed in a French village where the German army has committed a massacre he does not approve of, has taken no part in, but understands that he must expiate for. An educated, principled, and compassionate "aggressor" caught in the turmoil of a history he regrets. And Rodoreda pits the fanaticized Quimet against the levelheaded Mateu, both victims of the war. She describes the persecution of Catholics by the anarchists, while denouncing the reactionary attitude of the "law and order" upper class, all without taking the action of her novel outside a narrowly circumscribed district of republican Barcelona. That a balanced memory was possible in the 1950s is further borne out by an entry in Joan Fuster's diary. Writing about Arthur Koestler's *Spanish Testament* on 12 July 1954, Fuster objected:

> Koestler does not go so far—as some Spanish Marxists—as to assert that "nothing happened" in the republican zone. But he does suppress

what happened. This is the great mistake, or the great fraud, of foreign testimonies in the war of 36. In their writings there is deliberate confusion. It was possible to place oneself on the level of principle and defend one or the other antagonist. It was possible to place oneself on the level of fact and attempt to produce a statistical account of the crimes perpetrated by both sides. But no: almost no one has done this. Everyone has taken the easiest path: to exalt the principles to which one was partisan and to blame the enemy for the crimes committed. This is what the philo-fascists and the philo-Marxists have done. (128)

Fuster was not arguing for the moral equivalence of the two sides in the war, or for a self-cancelling historical guilt. Provoked by Koestler's book, he does not go into the reasons of the rebels or of the republicans but into the resolution, now just as hard as then, between objectivity and political commitment. He does not conceive of objectivity merely in quantitative terms—the pending statistical balance—although this would furnish important data, but in terms of equanimity, applying the juridical concept of crime to the violence perpetrated in excess of the accepted rules of engagement. Crime presupposes a victim, and the tendency to think in opposites translates the pair victim/perpetrator into the conceptual polarity of guilt (or accountability) and innocence. François Maspero points out the fallacy of this equation by distinguishing between innocent victims and combatants among the inmates of Nazi death camps. For him the category of "resisting deported" excludes the notion of victim. One fought against Nazism with full knowledge of the facts, knowing that deportation and death could mark the end of the combat. For that reason, he says that he never considered his father, the sinologist Henri Maspero—who was deported as a member of the resistance and died in Buchenwald in 1945—as a victim (27). But such trenchant discrimination is not the rule. A posteriori many crave the status of victim, made attractive by its correlation with innocence. Since, by definition, crime entails guilt, people jump to the conclusion that victimhood involves innocence. From here to identifying defeat with victimhood there is a small conceptual step, and it is this step that interested parties took, portraying the Civil War as a Manichean story of good and evil, with the opposites neatly divided by the political line.

Narrating the past, especially one as drenched in primitive violence as the Spanish Civil War, should never be a formulaic exercise. Instead of filling in ready-made functions in a conventional story, the narrator ought to open spaces for ambiguity, overlap, and contradiction. The account should take stock of the complexity of human crises. According to Fuster, it was the failure of foreign observers to do just this that caused their reports to mislead through their presumed testimonial value. "The advocates of the contenders have used every opportunity to assure the world that the victims—whether these or those—were always innocent. What no one will admit is that among the victims on both sides there were innocent and guilty" (128). And he specifies, out of a desire for semantic precision: "Perhaps guilty is not the right word: let us say, instead of guilty, people who justly provoked the enemy's hatred" (128). The last phrase begs the question. The question, first of all, of when is mortal hatred justified, but also whether just hatred alters the substance of the facts and neutralizes their criminal nature. An anarchist patrol that kills a class enemy does so with an ideological sense of justice. Equally justified, in their own minds, are the members of a court martial that summarily passes a death sentence on men arraigned for rebellion against self-proclaimed "forces of order." These were recurrent situations during and after the war. And it is such misguided belief in the justice of the violence deployed that still troubles the historical memory and narrows the chances for an objective settlement of the accounts.

With the term "justly" Fuster avoids simplifying the historical facts to fit the requirements of the law, which depends on unambiguous notions of guilt and innocence. In Fuster's use, the term "justly" does not have acquitting value but, on the contrary, it limits the scope of "innocence" in a context of social violence escalated to the level of all-out civil war. It is to illustrate the limiting function of the category of justice and to prevent its appropriation by one of the parties, that Fuster recalls the blood spilled by both sides. This blood, he says, "disqualifies and will continue to disqualify until all confess their crimes and accept their responsibilities" (130). And it is not, or not primarily, the bloodshed in the battlefield but the murders perpetrated in the rearguard that qualify as crimes for which the guilty and their ideological heirs have yet to accept responsibility. At the time the crimes were committed, they were justified by appealing to revolutionary or reactionary necessity—so much ideological foam on the surface of unrestrained passions. In his memoirs, Claudi Ametlla, chronicler of the destruction of political culture in Catalonia, described how, regardless of political filiation and prewar behavior, business people and management, technicians and middle-class professionals, not to speak of religious individuals, were systematically persecuted and murdered on the republican side. "After a few weeks, all people with leadership functions in production have disappeared. They are abroad or in hiding and lying low far from their homes, depressed by fear and incomprehension of what is happening" (142).

Relatively early and in a context not so much of suppression as of manipulation of memory, Fuster put his finger on the true dimension of the problem. A half century later, this problem remains unsolved and no politically motivated law will resolve it, because the solution does not depend on the coercive power of the state, but on society's overcoming the psychological barrier of denial. This barrier is neither gratuitous nor casual. As Stanley Cohen asserts: "Denial is hard work, because our actions nearly always conflict with our self-image" (62). Refusal to lower the self-image to the level of the actions goes a long way toward explaining the distance between the lurid rhetoric of patriotism (on the right), of social justice (on the left), and the petty passions and disgraceful motivations that fed the violence on both sides. Although some half-hearted precautions were taken to dissimulate murders (death certificates for postwar executions by Falange or the army typically indicated "heart failure" or "internal bleeding" as the cause of death, while anarchists took their victims "for a walk"), the insulation of the two sides in the war did not require them to mask or cover up their atrocities. Guernica was an exception, and that only because it made world news unexpectedly.

In the wake of theoretical interest in trauma and its effects on survivors of human catastrophes, some cultural analysts have applied this notion to the social effects of the Spanish Civil War. It is a questionable application. An objection to deploying the notion of trauma to explain the unsatisfactory presence of the memory of the war in the public sphere is that absence from public discourse does not correlate with psychological repression. Another objection is that the notion of trauma refers to a psychic defense mechanism that expels unwelcome impressions from the ego's sphere of reflective action and sends them into the unconscious. To assume the possibility of a similar expulsion of uncomfortable knowledge from the public sphere, as the expression "pact of forgetting" suggests, would seriously compromise the idea of moral agency and question the existence of freedom. Neither morality nor freedom is possible where reflexive action is impaired, as would be the case if awareness of a social crisis of the magnitude of a civil war had been truly repressed. But in the public sphere the notion of absolute repression and irretrievable memory is untenable. As Cohen points out, "Perpetrators and observers only pretend to forget. This hardly ever happens to victims. They may have phases of forgetting or denial, but most of them, most of the time—contrary to the repressed trauma model—are quite unable to shut out their memories" (131).

For all the talk about the repression of history, the facts of the Civil War are generally known, at least in the rough, and their very nature corrodes the tranquil image of a reconciliation unchallenged by the wrenching need laboriously to negotiate an accommodation between butchers and victims. The appeal to reconciliation seduces with the voice of reason: to live together, people must heal the wounds of the past; resentment has to morph into understanding; the past must give way to the future. As Cohen warns, this voice, especially under the catchword of "national reconciliation," can be a strategy to avoid accountability and a form of historical denial (238). Genuine reconciliation presupposes full knowledge of what happened. It cannot take place if one side rejects responsibility for any wrong and the other side never meets with admission of the gravity of what was done to it. Post-dictatorship Francoists were reconciled (and then, not all of them) in the sense that they understood that their supremacy could not endure in the form of an authoritarian regime and took the necessary steps to adapt to the new circumstances. They were not reconciled, or wished to be, in the sense of accepting responsibility for the wrongs inflicted by the regime that had used history to their advantage.

In its essence, the war had been about nothing else. From the beginning, the conspirators understood that it was necessary to spread terror among the civilian population. In the guidelines sent to his fellow conspirators, General Emilio Mola, the coup's ringleader, said that action had to be extremely violent, that exemplary punishment had to be meted out to the leaders of parties, unions, and associations that did not join the military coup ("Instrucción Reservada No.1, Base 5ª," in Sánchez Pérez 346). Full-blown massacres with a high number of victims were not collateral damage, a byproduct of the rebellion, but its intended goal. The official story of the victors traces the military rebellion to the assassination of José Calvo Sotelo, a philo-fascist member of Parliament; but the fact is that the coup had been planned for months and scheduled for an earlier date, then postponed for tactical reasons. Calvo Sotelo's assassination caused general consternation and may have precipitated the events, but the fact is that Mola's difficulties in securing the support of Navarre's *requetés*, a snag that had been delaying the coup, cleared on 12 July, the day before Calvo Sotelo's murder. And with this support Mola now saw the way expedited for the overthrow of the republic. Calvo Sotelo's martyrdom as the motif of the rebellion is one of those *post hoc ergo propter hoc* inversions typical of ideology. Calvo Sotelo's murder was used to deck out high treason as honorable discharge of patriotic duty. As a pretext, it throws light on the significance of victimhood for purposes of social control through manipulation of the public discourse long after the events.

Recognition of the close relation between facts that are substantially known and the categories of victim and perpetrator is lacking in contemporary Spain. Missing is the public understanding that the war sought to construct a social reality based on those categories, that these were not meant to be the temporary reflection of the state of affairs emerging from the vicissitudes of battle. Understanding this crude but effective structure of Francoist society was actively discouraged during the transition, because recognizing the identity between the aims of the war and the social objectives that it facilitated would have resulted in a widespread call for responsibilities. Since remission of the crimes could be entertained only after the discharge of responsibilities, those implicated in building a society structured around winners and losers went out of their way to prevent anyone identifying them with the facts. This is why the facts themselves, although essentially known, have not been surmounted and float like unassimilated lumps in the collective memory.

With respect to memory, the protagonists of historical violence have equivocated, behaving in an opaque manner. After Franco's death, many Falangists, army officers, judges, police, and collaborators cleaned up their CVs, creating a trompe l'œil effect. These people were the same that had signed death penalties, tortured people, stolen property, kidnapped children, imprisoned union leaders, and passed iniquitous laws. When individuals like Falange co-founder Ernesto Giménez Caballero, or the pro-Nazi minister of the Interior and Falange president Ramón Serrano Suñer, were interviewed on national television, they did not look like ferocious ideologues responsible for the deaths of hundreds of thousands. They sounded calm, unremorseful, almost reasonable; they knew themselves protected by the circumstances of a remote era that, to the new generations, seemed an entirely different place.

The era, not they, was responsible for the terrible things they recalled with shocking detachment: the bloodletting on a grand scale, the irrational hatred, the mass trials without guarantees, the torture. Committed by alter egos they no longer related to, the unspeakable crimes had been blown away by history. How could they ever be pinned on these aging, frail, even-spoken, old-fashioned men, who seemed to explore their memories without bumping into anything troubling? One might disagree with their conservative views, just as one disagrees about the color in a canvas or the interpretation of a poem. But who could be so callous as to accuse them of barbarity? Of exterminating political opponents? Of crafting policies of cultural genocide? All those things had been done by strangers who might have worn the same uniform and even the same name as they, but were most certainly other people. And then, war excuses everything. One simply has no idea how bad things were back then.

On the other hand, while asking society to sanction the discontinuity on which their continued wellbeing depended, the victors and their heirs clung to privilege and influence obtained through the very actions they asked others to forget. Hence the paradox: it is necessary to remember that events happened in a particular way and to forget anything that contradicts that memory. People have to know that a war was won by those who were reasonable, realistic, and levelheaded; that it was lost by the irrational, the fanatics, the scum. To achieve this state of political schizophrenia, it is necessary to alter the record, shredding the compromising evidence or preventing access to it. Furthermore, it is necessary to erase even the memory of having tampered with history, not just for the sake of one's conscience but so that the resulting social order may appear as the effect of natural continuity. Then the great rupture of the war can be scaled back to the level of a self-inflicted wound that has already healed and whose scar is a hieroglyph that is best ignored and forgotten.

The notion of trauma does not explain the reluctance to associate the facts with the ethical categories of victim and perpetrator. Trauma is a slippery category, and to wield it in the context of protracted, generalized repression drains it of exegetical efficiency. In a context like that of a civil war followed by a long dictatorship, the psychic wound refers inexorably to the blood that was spilled and is a permanent reminder that someone did the spilling. If trauma there is, its causes are far from unconscious. They are simply unacknowledged. The enthusiasm with which most Francoists embraced the opportunity to switch to a constitutional regime would make one think that they never had anything to do with the dictatorship. In fact, this is what they would have us believe. It was the easiest way to reject responsibility for the injustices perpetrated with their consent. And so, in the 1970s, many Francoists assured fellow Spaniards that they were personally unhappy with the regime; that they had been instrumental in softening it and making it more humane; that it was impossible for them not to act the way they had; that the laws were different then. The transition was a massive exercise in denial.

Denial was and remains the first line of defense for those who committed crimes in the past and those who justify them in the present. Freud recognized in denial (*Verneinung*) a psychic form of defense far more destructive than repression, in that deniers do not ignore the truth but actively work to destroy it. The denier refuses to admit what he knows to be the case. The denying mind splits into a part that knows and one that acts as if that which it knows were not real. Whether it slides into delusion or remains in the balance of a double conscience, the schizophrenic attitude corrupts the denier. It is not unreasonable to speculate that denial is at the root of the profound immorality of Spanish life since the transition to democracy, of the extensive corruption that corrodes the institutions and the political parties, the dependence of economic life on political favor and vice versa, the media's collusion with political power, the purchase of votes through policies that amount to bribery, the decades of living "as if": as if Spain were the epitome of an exemplary transition; as if, from one day to the next, it had become a paradigm of democracy; as if the separation of powers were anything more than a formality; as if, by a miracle of mutation, the country had skipped two centuries and become a beacon of modernity; as if its privileged reception of massive European funds had, like a magic wand, transformed the Francoist frog into a socialist prince; as if Spain's per capita income, one year before the country was engulfed in a crippling crisis, was about to overtake Germany's— in the memorable phrase of President José Luis Rodríguez Zapatero (Moreno). But the clock struck twelve and the princess was back in her rags. After 2008, the unemployment rate climbed to 27 percent, 50 percent among the young, the highest in Europe, fueling a new wave of emigration among the better educated and offering the spectacle of a crumbling system to a stunned population. Broken beyond fix is now the very system that had been glorified in the transition: a king that abdicated amidst scandals in exchange for immunity from prosecution; a government party that has inexplicably weathered a storm of corruption revealed as systemic; an electoral deadlock that saw repeated elections in June 2016 and the inability to form a new government for nine months as of this writing; a constitution converted into a roadblock to democratic freedoms; and a constitutional court cynically used by sectional interests. Much of this can be traced back to the original sin of the transition: collective denial as false overcoming of the past.

Nothing draws attention to the persistence of the archaic morality that Umberto Galimberti calls "neighborhood morality" (*morale della vicinanza*) as the tendency of historical memory to reproduce the conflict it claims to overcome. Neighborhood morality, which Galimberti defines as that which tends to defend the familiar clan or small community and to ignore the rest (113), is Manichaean. Being in effect a double morality, neighborhood morality relies on an endogenous and an exogenous code at once. According to this distinction, the stranger, the foreigner, the outsider, even the outlier, are in principle guilty, while the insider is innocent, not because his crimes are unknown—small communities are transparent to themselves—but because they are overlooked. Fuster rightly associated denial with refusal of responsibility. With the expressions "philo-fascist" and "philo-communist," he alluded to the neighborhood morality that made these political ideologies something like self-enclosed communities of belief. Their reciprocal accusations and self-portrayals as victims of the other's brutality serve as warning against blanket demands for recognition of victim status among certain groups.

Although groups typically apply for victimhood status with the hope of obtaining some tangible reward, the historical memory discourse introduced a cognitive component in the struggle for acknowledgement. Now, it was said, victims did not aspire to retribution or even to compensation, only to disclosure of the facts. This aspiration seems reasonable; only, knowledge of the essential fact, the spilling of blood, is the a priori condition of historical memory discourses. Without it, they would not have emerged. Are these discourses circular, then? Obviously, the answer to this question must be negative. But, if they are not circular, they may be disingenuous in their disinterestedness. The stakes are not more revelations of historical detail, but the adjudication of responsibility for what we already know.

Since historical memory cannot add significantly to the social knowledge of the crimes committed in the war and the dictatorship, pleading victimhood can only serve two purposes. Obtaining recognition for undervalued classes of people, such as the losers of the war, and reorienting society to make it capable of rebalancing the status quo through compensatory measures. The Enlightenment added recognition (*Anerkennung*) to Christian morality, making appreciation of the individual in this world one of the essential human needs, and consequently a human right. In this context, recognition amounts to respect. It refers to the elemental respect due to relatives of the people buried anonymously in mass graves throughout Spain. To the tortured ones. To those sentenced in trials without guarantees, whose relatives now seek—so far in vain—the posthumous reversal of their sentences. The refusal with which they have met in Spanish courts of law and the indifference their endeavors arouse in the political institutions prove the failure of Spanish society to confront its ghosts.

Both aspirations—obtaining recognition and overhauling social morality—aim for justice, but whereas the first can be achieved on the symbolic level—through memorials, documentaries, interviews, and other means of honoring victims—the second requires the state to accept responsibility for crimes committed in its name. For this reason, it runs against the inherited social order, whose highest aspiration is to preserve itself. A state rarely accepts its responsibilities willingly. As a rule, it is coerced into doing so, as Germany was in 1945 and Japan in 2015 on the issue of the comfort women (Korean sexual slaves for the Japanese army during the Second World War). More frequently, though, the lifting of the denial follows a negotiated reassessment of the past, with truth seeping gradually into the interpretation of the facts, the way light filters through the crack of a door or the blind of a window and gently dissolves the dimness of a room.

I have pointed out that Freud conceived of denial as a dike against the return of the not-so-repressed. But when the unconscious disgorges a fact that consciousness has previously expelled, the subject engages in a dialectical relation of expulsion-return. Denial is the public form this dialectic takes. Against the subject's will, the past pervades his present experience because it has never been truly repressed. This is a past that will not go away, in Ernst Noltes's suggestive phrase. In an article published in the cultural section of the *Frankfurter Allgemeine Zeitung* on 6 June 1986, Nolte, a conservative historian, alleged a refusal by the German Federal Republic to deal with National Socialism in such a way as to lay it to rest and keep it from haunting the present. His opinion that Nazism should be understood in historical context and that the genocide against Jews had been inspired by the Soviet Gulag provoked hefty criticism. This article sparked the notorious *Historikerstreit* of the mid-1980s, during which Nolte was accused of relativizing the Holocaust. He had been asked to participate in the Römerberg talks, but shortly before the event the organizer informed him that the topic of "the past that will not go away" had been given to Wolfgang Mommsen, a historian of leftist persuasion. Nolte interpreted this decision as a form of censorship, withdrew from the conference, and published his paper in the *Frankfurter Allgemeine Zeitung*.

Interestingly, Nolte faulted the German establishment with not confronting the Nazi period historically, whereas the Spanish debate about Francoism has been characterized on the left by accusations of unwillingness to confront the past, and on the right by refusal to do so with the argument that it would reopen old wounds. For the right the past is already past; it is the left that will not let it go away. But, as we have seen, denial is also a way of keeping the past from passing. And, willingly or not, retaining the past as a defining factor of the present turns memory into fixation. Since memory is the co-presence of the subject and the emotional echo of something lived, denial imprisons the subject in the object of his obsession. Paradoxically, to deny the past is emotionally to block the future.

A half century ago, Fuster realized that Spanish society was going to remain trapped in the past, incapable of transforming memory into history and moving resolutely into the future. Transforming memory into history is not as simple as some historians believe and some politicians wish. It does not happen by virtue of claiming the exclusive right to handle the past for a professional guild. Progressing from memory to history is not a matter of artificially delimiting an area called "the past," much less of delegating the right to demarcate its legitimate from the non-legitimate frames of relevance. It is, rather, a matter of settling the present's debt with the past, so that the past can finally settle into history, at which point it can be innocuously turned over to the historians. The facts must be given pride of place, says Fuster, even on the spiritless level of statistics, but they will continue to elude us until responsibility for the crimes is assumed. Only then can a line be drawn between the past that returns and the past that passes forever.

In a context of generalized denial, however, the past cannot be merely a phenomenon of consciousness. In that situation, importing memory discourses from other contexts in the hope of stirring the public consciousness is useless. It may be possible to add interpretative details by reference to better studied historical processes, to confirm hypotheses, or to reformulate narratives in view of new theoretical tools or political typologies, without for all that getting one inch closer to the moral resolution that the votaries of historical memory aim for. When I say that memory is not exclusively an affair of consciousness, I mean that its ethical dimension eludes the frame of strict representation of the facts. If we accept the analytic distinction between memory and history, whether identifying memory and tradition with Pierre Nora, or memory and collective identity with Maurice Halbwachs, we will conclude that the non-rational component of memory is precisely the ethical dimension that Fuster missed in the sectarian testimonies of the Civil War. Let us note in passing that this ethical dimension precedes the lines of defense identified by Freud. It is by reacting to the demands of this pre-rational dimension that the self brings those defenses into existence. One of the forms taken by this reaction is rationalization; that is, accommodating the facts to the superego's ethical demands.

If the historian's mission is to establish the facts objectively—statistical calculation being, according to Fuster, the most basic factual determination— it behooves literature to describe the causes and effects of denial. Literature's fictive, might-have-been dimension permits the imaginary portrayal of truth growing or dwindling through the acceptance or rejection of responsibility. Literature has always sounded out the ethical depths of humanity. It has gone deeper than any other discourse in the task of exemplifying the dilemmas of conscience, not because it can muster a higher degree of objectivity than other types of discourse, but because its archaism, reflected in its weaker disciplinary specialization, brings it closer to the emotional roots of consciousness. Literature handles facts in the raw, with all their emotional dross. It transmits, with greater accuracy than other kinds of documents, the spirit of a time suspended in memory, without sacrificing the ambiguity and the contradictions inherent in the experience, those aspects of the truth that are the first casualties of rationalization.

CHAPTER FIVE

Warming Up for the War:
The Cultural Transmission of Violence
in Spain since the Early Twentieth Century

It is doubtful that a society's relation to its past can be sufficiently described in terms of memory. And little is gained by qualifying memory as historical. "Historical memory" is not just a redundant concept but also a flawed one. It is flawed, because, if we accept Pierre Nora's methodological distinction between history and memory, those two terms are mutually exclusive. But also, because, as currently used, their conflation confuses epistemic with ethical issues. In 1992, the same year that the last volume of Nora's *Les lieux de mémoire* appeared, Jan Assmann introduced a subtler distinction between cultural and communicative memory in his book *Das kulturelle Gedächtnis*. By "cultural memory," Assmann means memory that orients itself to fixed points of reference in the past: symbolic figures, legends of origins or of conquest, and myths, which can also turn up in historical narrative, the difference being not so much in the nature of the objects as in the method by which they are enlisted for the practice of social remembrance. Cultural memory is not archival, documented history but history as remembered by people, the trace of the past in the popular imagination. By "communicative memory," he means a form of remembrance that relates to a recent past, one whose references are broadly shared by contemporaries. This kind of memory depends on witnesses and disappears with them. It constitutes a history from below, objectified in social rituals, dance, myths, clothing, decoration, painting, landscape, architecture, and so on. When a generation disappears, a society's communicative memory is altered, sometimes in dramatic ways. Thus, as the age factor becomes more pressing and post-traumatic societies take stock of the limits of their communicative memories, there is usually a flurry of activity to record the testimonies of the surviving members of the relevant age group. This has been the case in Spain since the turn of the century, when discourse about the historical memory surfaced and became more urgent.

The fact that a great deal of the memory relating to the Civil War and the military dictatorship falls within the bounds of the communicative memory contributes to the confusion between epistemic and ethical approaches to the past. Such confusion is understandable and perhaps inevitable in the context of Spain's *Historikerstreit*, given the conditions of the country's exit from dictatorship and its inability to steer clear from that legacy in the supervening decades. But the attempt to legislate the preservation of the "historical memory" in a law approved by the Spanish Parliament in October 2007 is self-defeating. The problem is not just that the law, by speaking generically about all the victims of the war and the dictatorship, failed to discriminate between innocents that were preyed upon and culpable fatalities, such as the police torturer Melitón Manzanas, assassinated by ETA in 1968 and awarded the gold medal for civil merit in 2001; or that it excluded practical measures like supporting the exhumation of mass graves and the identification of corpses. The problem was, rather, that legislating memory in a regime that was founded on a blanket amnesty law and has whitewashed the cultural memory of its recent past, could only ensure the new law's epistemic vacuity. To make matters worse, the "law of memory" was de facto derogated after the conservatives won the elections and refused to allocate funds for its implementation in the state's general budget in 2013 and 2014.

When I say that legislating the historical memory is absurd, I am far from saying that providing redress for the victims of a dictatorship is wrong or impracticable. I am saying that this objective should have been politically delimited and diligently pursued at the outset of the current regime or as soon as Spanish society was able to muster some ethical energy. But in the absence of consensus or of a majority supporting some form of redress, the shaky compromise on an ineffectual law failed to solve the ethical problem and fell short of an integral "recuperation" of the past, by which I mean a sustainable description of the causes of contemporary social and political relations. In the form it was approved, law 52/2007 did not envisage retroactive justice. It merely acknowledged that abuses were perpetrated. From an epistemic viewpoint, it would have been far more useful to attack the inertial constraints on research, broadcasting, and education.

Lingering political and judiciary bias is in evidence, for instance, in the refusal of Spanish courts to revise Francoist trials, in which the death sentence was often a foregone conclusion; in the removal of evidence, such as the transportation of 800 tons of soil mixed with human remains from a common grave in the Valencia cemetery to a quarry in Sagunt in May 2006; in the censorship routinely practiced by Spanish media on politically inconvenient topics; in the unlawful use of the state apparatus to persecute political adversaries, as in the notorious GAL affair under the socialist government of Felipe González; in the attacks of the neo-Francoist government of José María Aznar against the Basque press in 1998 and the jailing of journalists. Jabier Salutregi, director of the left-wing daily *Egin*, spent seven years in prison on charges of membership of a terrorist group. Other members of the board also received prison sentences. In 2003, the same government, through a subservient judiciary branch, shut down *Egunkaria*, the single Basque-language-only daily, arresting members of the editorial board, who later denounced their having been tortured while in custody. In 2010, Spain's high court acquitted them. The previous year the Supreme Court had concluded that *Egin*'s activity had not been illegal. It was too late for the journalists who had completed their sentences, or for the 210 workers who had lost their jobs with the journal's closure. In June 2016, during the last days of the government of Aznar's successor, Mariano Rajoy, the so-called "Fernándezgate" affair blew up in the midst of the campaign for the general elections. The digital journal *Público* revealed recordings in which Minister of the Interior Jorge Fernández Díaz, with the approval of Prime Minister Mariano Rajoy, connived with the director of the anti-corruption agency in Catalonia to fabricate scandals against Catalan politicians and anonymously leak them to the media in order to remove them from office. In an unforgettable phrase, the agency's director reassured the Minister by saying: "We have destroyed their [Catalan] health system."

To question the value of a law of memory is not to relativize the murderous character of the Franco regime or to cast doubt on its originally fascist nature, admittedly tempered and modified after 1945.[1] It is to mistrust the institutionalization of an official truth that advertises itself in memory sites and celebrations, as it deflects the social energy that would obtain from a comprehensive understanding of the past. Denouncing the Francoist abuses and decrying their impunity need not be ineffectual. But even without the scandalous impeachment of a judge for contravening the Francoist self-amnesty law of 1977 in his attempt to investigate the crimes of the dictatorship, it is apparent that the heirs of the regime have had ample time to mount an aggressive defense and are now capable of countering the

---

1 Pointing out that by the mid-1940s and 1950s formulas for mobilizing the masses linked to national syndicalism were becoming stale, Carlota Coronado Ruiz and José Carlos Rueda Laffond argue that "this can be interpreted as an apparent de-ideologization of the Franco regime, or perhaps more accurately, as the success of more lax identity values (economic development, social mobilization [*sic*] and economic well-being) deriving from both the patriarchal nature of the dictatorship and the incarnation of a certain spirit of openness" (52).

left's reclamation of historical memory with a memory of their own.[2] And, indeed, their allegations of persecution and assassination of civilians by the "reds" cannot be dismissed or relativized without loss of ethical face. The massacre of prisoners considered fifth columnists in Paracuellos del Jarama, the right's iconic example of Republican brutality, compares with its own massacre of civilians in Badajoz. In Catalonia, the anarchist organizations, legitimized by the incapacity or unwillingness of the elected politicians to disarm them, conducted a ferocious campaign against the "class enemy," instituting a veritable state of terror against anyone suspicious of not seconding their behavior. The anarchists took the military attack against the democratic regime as the cue for their own assault on the "bourgeois republic" with a ferocity they had never displayed against the monarchy.

In the sober view of the facts, it is disingenuous to play down the crimes of the left by presenting them as understandable reactions to fascist brutality. Retaliatory murder is still murder, and the precedent of the Badajoz bloodbath does not lessen the gravity of the execution of political inmates at Madrid's Modelo prison, as some historians of the left have speciously argued (Espinosa Maestre, *Contra el olvido*, 221). If we condemn the fascist use of terror as a deterrent, we can hardly invoke deterrence to underplay the murders committed by the other side. Francisco Espinosa Maestre does an excellent job of showing how the historians of the Franco regime and the new conservatives cooked the figures of Republican violence while sharply underrating the significance of the Francoist crimes or denying them altogether. But merely opposing the number of victims of one side to those of the other is futile, because no unambiguous moral judgment can be extracted from a quarrel about numbers. Trying to wrestle political legitimacy in this way can be counterproductive if it can be argued that the reason for the imbalance was the greater opportunity of the winners to purge their enemies. This was in fact the case where the military coup triumphed immediately or in the areas occupied after republican resistance crumbled. Furthermore, the left's traditional exoneration of republican violence by claiming that uncontrolled groups were responsible for rearguard murders

2 One instance, among a stream of neo-Francoist publications led by Pío Moa, is Nicolás Salas' *La "otra" memoria histórica*. The pseudo-novelty of an alternative memory, which in fact recycles the themes on which the Francoist "legitimacy" was based since the beginning of the Civil War until the death of the dictator, challenges the gradual emergence during the period of controlled democracy of many of the facts that were suppressed and buried under the debris of lies that constitutes Francoist historiography. Thus, by proclaiming the justice of a synthesis between their old themes and the newly excavated facts, the "new historical revisionism" challenges democracy *tout court*.

seems specious to its opponents. Certainly, the legitimate authorities made some effort to uphold the appearance of the rule of law, however distorted by the crumbling institutional guarantees, whereas the rebels declared the law void and replaced it with military and paramilitary expediency to eradicate the disaffected. Even so, where the revolution prevailed, the Republican authorities did not react as the crisis demanded, did little or nothing to quell *that* rebellion, and lost control of the situation. In Madrid, the Communist Party created a parallel authority, which in the course of the war managed to gain control of the army and eventually of the government as well.

The left can reasonably argue that on the Republican side ideological persecution of the political adversary was often beyond governmental control, which is to admit that government was ineffective; but to defer judgment on the red terror because the Republic was compromised by the war effort plays into the hands of its enemies. After all, the Francoists justified the *coup d'état* by the need to rescue the country from lawlessness and disorder, and Spanish conservatives still adhere to this narrative.

In view of the facts, it is fair to say that the "historical memory" has been selective on both sides of the political spectrum, although perhaps not to the same degree. Francoist historiography descended to the level of propaganda, but the left also produced narratives along party lines. Leftist historians tend to gloss over episodes of violence that, in their view, do not qualify as crimes. In his book on the Empordà region, Josep Pla recalled the pointless, ruthless blowing up of the town of Llers by the retreating Republican army in February 1939, a few days before it crossed the border and turned over its weapons to French authorities. About this event, he wrote, all have been silent, on both sides (149). Not exactly hushed up, but tidied up in technical descriptions of military strategy was the willful sacrifice of juvenile recruits at the Ebro River battle. When historians discuss this episode, they rarely mention the 30,000 boys in their teens, mostly from Catalonia, who were deliberately exposed to certain slaughter. Recruited in 1938 and 1939 on orders of Manuel Azaña, these teenagers were pitted against Franco's experienced and materially superior army and forced to hold their positions, with the river behind their backs to prevent retreat. Down the river, says Mercè Rodoreda in her novel *Quanta, quanta guerra...*, flowed the corpses of soldiers, which their comrades had no time to bury (55). Even after the republican offensive stalled, and it became clear that the situation had become untenable, Prime Minister Juan Negrín refused to withdraw the troops. The adolescents, snatched from school to face Franco's artillery in parched terrain without cover, were no different from those whom, in the last footage of Adolf Hitler, a quivering Führer greets before sending them to meet the red army at Berlin's gates. But, unlike Hitler,

Negrín is not considered a monster by most.[3] To be sure, armies have at all times recruited children and adolescents, and Article 77.2 of the Additional Protocol I to the Geneva Conventions of 12 August 1949, relating to the Protection of Victims of International Armed Conflicts, adopted in 1977, admits the recruiting of children above the age of fifteen, a condition met by Azaña's mobilization of adolescents. What makes the episode on the Ebro River revolting is the misuse of young, inexperienced troops on a mission with predictable consequences. Yet, sympathy for the Republican cause bought its leaders indulgence for criminal decisions rationalized on grounds of military emergency.

The left, no less than the right, has been lenient with its political figures. Most interesting, in this regard, is the negotiation of Negrín's reputation in light of Spain's changing political climate. As Pelai Pagès i Blanch writes in "Juan Negrín o la reinvindicación de la derrota," after decades of neglect or vilification, Negrín is being extolled as one of the most modern and daring politicians of the 1930s. It is difficult to understand this revaluation, says Pagès i Blanch, unless we see it in the context of the ongoing revisionism of the left, which has been taking place for some time in parallel to that of the right (15). This newfound admiration for Negrín and his violent repression of the revolution would be inexplicable if it did not serve the ongoing recentralization of political power. To those for whom vindicating Franco is distasteful, Negrín offers a model of authoritarian involution on the left.

Renegotiating the historical facts in light of present interest skirts the problems with interpreting the Civil War as a class conflict in a nationally homogeneous society. When pressed, left-wing Spanish nationalists admit that the national question did play a role in the eruption of violence, but they immediately dwarf its significance, considering its recollection an inconvenient and distorting perspective.[4] This avoidance on the part of the left suits the right's own myth of the coup as a national uprising against the aggression of international communism. Such jaundiced view of twentieth-century Spanish history is not merely a matter of interpretation but incurs

---

3 In the popular mind, Hitler's monstrosity is an explanation of his anti-Semitism and the moral reflection of the Nazi policy of exterminating the European Jewry. The point here is that dispatching the children soldiers to confront the red army when the war was lost and Hitler about to go into his bunker is monstrous in itself. The same moral revulsion is produced by the general that places the school-children at the head of the bridge to stop the U.S. army in Bernhard Wicki's film *Die Brücke* (1959).

4 "To forget that the class nature of the struggle that began in July 1936 overshot by far the nationalist question—as has been done sometimes in Catalonia and the Basque Country—is a serious distortion of history" (Espinosa Maestre 283).

in the denial of the facts that historians of the left typically associate with their right-wing colleagues.

Skewing the causes of the Civil War biased the interpretation of Francoism and over time led to the growing acceptance of the dictatorship among the younger and more conservative generations of Spaniards. Accommodation to the past is now flagrant in certain regions and among certain age groups. According to a poll taken by the Center for Sociological Research in 2000, 46.4 percent of respondents opined that the Franco regime had good, as well as bad, aspects (Centro de Investigaciones Sociológicas 1–2). There is reason to believe that the percentage of people who justified the dictatorship grew during the following decade. A pattern of playing down, disregarding, or bluntly denying what does not fit with the established accounts of the war is inextricable from the continuous edging up of sociological Francoism over the last decades. The low profile of substate nationalism in the left's accounts of the war and the disingenuous confusion of Catalanism with the class enemy in some of these accounts prepared the psychological conditions for the success of neo-conservatism in the 1990s. With its denial of the national question, the left contributed as much to this success as did the right by destroying archives and blocking access to public documents well into the democratic period. Any attempt at a detailed reconstruction of the past was compromised during the transition to democracy when Rodolfo Martín Villa, vice-president of the Union of Democratic Center (UCD) government, dissolved the *Movimiento Nacional* in April 1977, and a massive destruction of documentation related to the repression ensued. In the following years, expressions of Spanish nationalism were subdued due to its association with the Franco regime, but in the 1990s they rose in crescendo, goaded by the reemergence of the peripheral nationalities, attaining a feverish pitch in the new century.

The surging of competing national memories put pressure on the centralist narrative about the war and the dictatorship, and its advocates reacted by dismissing the alternative memories as "nationalist fibs" and "crybaby" complaints. But setting aside the competition for the dubious honor of victimhood, as if the massacres on one end of the Peninsula lessened the repression at the other end, it suffices to peruse the fascist literature before and after the war to realize that the Basque Country and Catalonia were singled out for violent intervention. They were "the two cancers in the body of the nation" that, according to Millán Astray, "Fascism, Spain's remedy, comes to exterminate ... slicing healthy, living flesh like a scalpel" (cit. Preston 29–30).

Such outbursts were by no means exceptional before, during, and even after the war. Why are they ignored or at best subordinated to the story of conservative versus revolutionary politics? The answer lies at hand if one considers how, after Communism's meltdown in the 1980s, a figure like Negrín could be rehabilitated and admired for his inflexible recentralization. Such celebrations of authoritarianism on the left are not unrelated to the rehabilitation of fascism among sectors of Spanish society. Thus, an anthologist of José Antonio Primo de Rivera's writings, Julio Antonio Gonzalo, starts the foreword to his neo-fascist primer by recalling the priorities of Spanish nationalism on the eve of the Civil War: "In 1936 Spain was about to break up through pressure from the Basque and Catalan separatist parties, which began to be imitated by other Spanish regions. Then the socialist left, not all, because in the ranks of Spanish socialism there were always some who were Spaniards out of conviction ... threw its lot with the enemies of historical Spain. Then came what inevitably had to come and afterwards Spain lived the longest peace time of its contemporary history" (vii).

As if the relevance of the Franco dictatorship to contemporary politics were not sufficiently clear, Gonzalo spells it out:

> Today, in 2006, absurdly, it seems that Spain is again about to break up. Today there are no African army, *requetés* or Falangists ...The fact is that being part of a more or less disaggregated Europe, a Europe of consumers and merchants that seems about to renounce its historical patrimony and Christian roots, [this membership] will not help to buttress Spain's unity. Will the Spanish people know how to respond on this occasion as they did on previous occasions? (vii–viii)

Leaving aside the language, redolent of the aggressive harangues of fascist leaders in the 1930s, what stands out in Gonzalo's call for action is the metaphysical certainty about an entity, Spain, whose malfunctioning parts must be purged "as on previous occasions." The author patently expects the reader to fill the suggestive dots in the primer's title, *If Spain wants to commit suicide....* And expects him to fill them in a manner consistent with his sense of historical urgency.

Today the assignment of moral responsibility for the war is a matter of interpretation. The polemic has not abated and it retains much of its passion. The conditions under which the country transitioned to democracy reveal the limits of the alleged national reconciliation. There was as much fear as calculation in Felipe González's officious praise of the army (which was still Franco's army) shortly after he attained power in 1982. The army, he declared, is the backbone of the modern state. Many years later, González came out of political retirement to say: "We decided not to talk about the past." To which Espinosa Maestre shrewdly comments: "this attitude was already a way of confronting the past" (178). Espinosa Maestre adds that in

1985, when the socialists approved a *Law of the Historical Patrimony*, which included a section on the documentary and archival patrimony under Title VII, they felt no urgency to preserve, catalogue, and release the Francoist documentation. Not only did they neglect the "obligation to allow the study [of the documents] by researchers" (VII, art. 52.4), but their negligence was deliberate. Later, with revisionism under way, state television depicted the Franco years in the soft glow of nostalgia programs such as *Cuéntame cómo fue*. Exploiting the popular appeal of the historical memory at this time, *Cuéntame* purported to assist in the intergenerational transmission of the past. In reality, it concealed the harsher aspects of the Franco era, including the role of television as a tool for state propaganda. In other words, it replicated the political control of television in the 1950s and 1960s in unselfconscious *mise en abîme* (Coronado Ruiz and Rueda Laffond 52).

No one seriously disputes the Franco regime's violent nature. But the meaningful and rarely asked question is about the violence itself. Always taken for granted in the voluminous literature about the war, the nature of the violence, its origin and rationalizations, seem more in need of reflection than the statistical disputes and political background of the actors. When the body count is over and the political chips are down, the riddle remains. How was such explosion of violence possible in the guts of a Western, self-declared Christian society?

If we admit that the Civil War still casts a shadow on Spanish culture, then we cannot reduce its significance to the legend of good and bad violence. The sense of being ethically in the right has shifted with the times and fortunes of the competing ideologies. Morality hinges on the interpretation of the facts, and interpretive authority is conditioned by the centrality or marginality of the interpreting community with respect to power. Emanuele Severino asserts: "To be in the right, to be in the good, to be psychologically normal means to be a victor, it means force" (96). And, certainly, the defeated were treated as aberrant during the dictatorship, while the victory of the nationalists soured considerably when Franco's regime met with international rebuke after the Second World War. In a context of alternating moral values, in keeping with the outcome of wars, the question cannot really be, who endorsed the violence, but: why did so many people find themselves in its grip? And whence did it arise?

Violence is inherent to human nature. No civilization is unfamiliar with its ravages. But if we refuse to consider it in universal fashion, that is, if we are unconvinced that something can be learned from an abstract theory of violence, then we need to comprehend violence in the actions and discourses of its devotees. We must see it emerging in a historical situation not as reflex aggression (which would take us from history to zoology) or as the means of last resort to a specific end (which would place it in the ambiguous realm of utilitarian reasoning) but as a considered, self-reflexive attitude amounting to a cultural value (or, arguably, an anti-value). And, although war is its most spectacular manifestation, to the point of constituting the central cultural factor in antiquity through its intersection with the juridical and the theological (Bahrani 213), violence cannot be restricted to or narrowly identified with the "war machine," that is, with state institutions and rituals. As a mode of social behavior, violence can take different forms. Like other modalities of action, it morphs into phenomena of different magnitude, intensity, and signification, depending on circumstance and the available cultural codes.

Since cultural phenomena morph in time, it is important to consider their early stages. In other words, one has to historicize what appears to be their natural expression. But violence can be traced back to a time preceding the constitution of the state, whether we accept Hobbes' description of violence as the natural condition of humans or agree with Pierre Clastres' idea of primitive violence as a mechanism of social preservation. If we emphasize its evolutionary genealogy, we run the risk of regressing on a historical slide, from war to war, into the distant past, or mixing up phenomena as colorful as they are hackneyed: Goya's etchings, bullfights, the Inquisition, honor plays, and so on. But if we resort to such commonplaces, can we hope to understand the explosion of violence that tore Spain asunder in a way unparalleled by any other country in the self-destroying Europe of the 1930s? Clearly, we need to tread into the cultural memory with caution, assisted by the communicative memory of the survivors and by historiography proper. This methodological combination shows that, while Spanish fascism activated a form of cultural memory by resorting to symbolic figures from the past, to mythic origins of the nation and imperial legends, it was nonetheless conditioned by the communicative memory of a generation that in a mere three decades had lived through a series of political upheavals capable of shattering a society's essential bonds and triggering recurrent bouts of killing.

The abolition of social bonds amounts to loss of legitimacy and the consequent disappearance of power in favor of violence, in Hannah Arendt's description of this phenomenon as a compensation mechanism. The Second Spanish Republic's attempt to rebuild the legitimacy whose loss had eroded the monarchy miscarried. As the government failed to restrain the use of violence, a reversal of means to ends resulted, a situation in which, as Arendt explains, the means of destruction determine the end, "with the consequence that the end will be the destruction of all power" (54). And, along with power, of the legitimate order that alone sustains it. In the event, the reversal played itself out as a two-pronged assault on the republic by the revolution and the coup-d'état. Acting beyond the boundary of legitimate power, each of these extremes condemned itself to replace legitimacy with terror, which Arendt defines as "the form of government that comes into being when violence, having destroyed all power, does not abdicate but, on the contrary, remains in full control" (55). While this description is true to the events in Nazi Germany and in postwar Spain, positing unchecked violence as a government-eliciting and government-maintaining tool begs the question of stability. A regime of unchecked violence is unsustainable. For this reason, those who deploy violence to bring about political change rarely admit its self-validating force, but appeal instead to prior motifs. In the case of the Civil War, it is easy to show that violence was wooed long before it replaced political argument.

Looking beyond the immediate causes of the Civil War, which most historians locate in the political and economic upheavals of the third decade of the twentieth century, the first thing that meets the eye is that in Spain ideological violence long preceded the war. One of its witnesses, Claudi Ametlla—civil governor of Girona and Barcelona and member of Parliament during the Second Republic—was reminded of the history of Spain: "the Carlist wars, the alternations between moderation and furious repression, the Inquisition, and finally the entire history of Spain, brimming with such cruel fits of insanity" (217). There is little doubt that violence is learned and its memory travels down the generations. But referring it to the entire course of history does not help to understand its recent episodes. A shorter time span is hermeneutically necessary. Social violence and inordinate military repression were both present in turn-of-the century Spanish society. General Severiano Martínez Anido, notorious for his cruelty as governor of the colonial enclave of Melilla, brought to Barcelona unheard-of brutality during his governorship in the 1920s. His methods exacerbated the social warfare, and assassinations between the thugs of his "Free Union" and those of the anarchist organizations became routine. Later, as Minister of the Interior during the dictatorship of Miguel Primo de Rivera, he contributed decisively to the repression of political parties.

By the time the Civil War broke out, violence had seeped into the social imaginary to the point that it could explode in rural areas isolated from the political turmoil of the large cities. Manuel Ortiz Heras comments that the violent incidents that followed the failure of the *coup d'état* in Albacete in 1936 "cannot be related to any kind of political violence, which hardly existed and then only in a few, concrete localities in 1934" (75). One must treat such statements with caution. The agitation in the Andalusian countryside during the early 1930s was responsible for the Second Republic's most damaging public order scandal, the massacre at Casas Viejas, a village in the province of Cádiz, where on 12 February 1933 the republic's elite guard put down an anarchist rebellion. The guards burned down the cottage in which the ringleaders had barricaded themselves with their families, then proceeded to search the village, arresting any men found with weapons, leading them to the smoldering cottage and shooting them in cold blood in reprisal for the death of one guard during the assault of the cottage.

Even if political ideologies were unequally present throughout the Spanish countryside, politics gave latent conflicts a pretext to emerge during the troubled years of the republic and especially in the aftermath of the military attempt to overthrow it. We cannot avoid the conclusion that, if in rural areas the underlying conflict was pre-political, an effect of the long-standing tension built into the ownership and exploitation of the land, it nonetheless translated into the prevailing language of the times. Politics became a conduit for violence, the formal medium through which it surfaced. But this is to say that violence had long been accepted as a valid alternative to the negotiation of conflict, and the new political language merely assisted with the delivery. Recognized as a socially structuring principle, violence morphed into politics, donning its ideological costumes.

In Albacete, many victims of the popular fury were landowners identified as the class enemy. Others were shopkeepers and small businessmen perceived as "bourgeois" and branded as "fascists" along with members of the liberal professions, teachers and students, regardless of the fact that many had been active in the proclamation of the republic (Ortiz 89–90). Lumping together as "bourgeois" or "fascist" people with such varied backgrounds, including liberals, shows how indiscriminately ideology trickled from the centers of political culture to the countryside. As one would expect, the villages with the highest incidence of violence were those where political sentiment had peaked since the proclamation of the republic (del Rey 92). But we need not conclude from this correlation that politics was the efficient cause of the violence, only that ideology was an efficient vehicle for its discharge. Given the opportunity, political stereotyping facilitated the sudden release of tension between the haves and the have-nots in a milieu that proved impervious to the liberal democracy that the republic had attempted to implement.

Although some historians now contest the totalitarian nature of the Franco regime, they cannot deny its loathing of liberal democracy. In a certain sense, the question is moot, because the defeat of the Axis in 1945 imposed a strategic reversal on Franco, effected through the "de-Nazification" of his cabinet and the curtailment of Falange's political influence. But if Francoism was not intrinsically fascist, as some analysts insist, the only thing that kept it from a full-fledged identification was its extreme conservatism. Franco reinforced the army's role as custodian of an age-old social configuration and utilized the Falange to provide his power-grab with a political subtext. Conflation of radical violence with reactionary rhetoric was responsible for Francoism's ability to transition from a wartime alliance with Nazi Germany, which included military participation alongside the Wehrmacht in the Eastern front, to postwar military agreements with the United States.

Thus, it is possible to see Franco's fascist interlude as incidental to his conventional authoritarianism. According to this view, he would be no different from the rest of the military officers who plotted against the republic: Sanjurjo, Mola, Fanjul, Goded, Rodríguez Barrio, Queipo de Llano, etc. These men were determined to use force in order to overturn the February elections, which had brought a Popular Front government. The extreme conservatism of the social groups supporting their plot could be gauged by the call of the journal *El Pensamiento Alavés*, on the day after the elections, for an insurrection that would be kindled in an "essentially counter-revolutionary region," which would rise up "if necessary as a new Covadonga that would serve as a place of refuge for those who fled from the revolution and undertook the Reconquista of Spain" (in reference to the alleged origin of the crusade to retake the Iberian Peninsula from the Muslims that had overrun it in the eighth century) (Casanova 138). It was a call to recoup a status quo conceived as essential to Spain's identity and threatened not only by revolution but also by modernity broadly understood.

Since the Restoration (1874), the state had increasingly identified its enemies with the social groups proposing democratization and decentralization. After 1898, the monarchy met those demands by suspending the constitutional guaranties, declaring martial law, and deploying the army to suppress social unrest. As Carolyn Boyd points out, "conservatives and traditionalists applauded military violence when it was directed against 'separatists' and revolutionaries" (301). Since then the army had been a nationalist hothouse prone to radicalization and rebelliousness, encouraged in this attitude by the social groups that benefited from its self-identification with the nation.

Confusion between corporate and national interests through the army's self-attributed patriotic representation made its violence hard to criticize. It enjoyed broad support when it targeted the Catalan social movement, and impunity encouraged the army in its vigilante role. As Carolyn Boyd reminds us, the *Cu-Cut!* incident in 1905, when hundreds of officers destroyed the headquarters of this journal and of *La Veu de Catalunya*, proved that violence could be politically advantageous. The army's assault against the Catalan press did not elicit disciplinary measures or the awarding of damages to the victims, but resulted in the suspension of constitutional guarantees in Barcelona. The government approved a special Law for the Repression of Crimes Against the Fatherland and the Army, granting the armed forces jurisdiction over the press. The libidinal factor, which, according to Freud holds an army together (*Group Psychology* 16–17), was thus cemented on brotherly violence condoned by the paternal Commander-in-Chief. And while this violence continued to be trained on the secular object, namely the Catalans, considered internal enemies since the Reaper's War of 1640,[5] eventually it would react upon the republican government, which had offended the army's nationalist sensibilities by promulgating a Statute of Autonomy for Catalonia in 1934.

Violence, of course, inheres in the armed forces, but as a state apparatus the army owes its existence to a government that sets the conditions and limits to the use of violence. However, since the nineteenth century, the state had proved incapable of restraining the army, which staged countless *pronunciamientos*. Government incapacity to prevent insubordination further eroded military discipline. When the Civil War broke out, anarchy, long endemic to civil society, had festered in the army, which had come to conceive itself not as an instrument of the state but as its arbiter, that is, not as a means to political goals but as an end in itself. However, it is not to a loose notion of anarchy as refusal of deference to a higher authority, but to anarchism in the restricted, political sense of the term that we must turn for an explanation of the outbreak of violence in the 1930s. To be precise, anarchism in a context of dissolution of the colonial empire and amidst rising fears of further territorial breakup in the Iberian Peninsula itself.

From Rose of Fire to Civil War

In Barcelona there had been sporadic anarchist terror since the turn of the century. Taking advantage of this climate, Alejandro Lerroux, an accomplished demagogue and founder of the Radical Party, opened a front against the "bourgeois" Catalan movement. Marshaling his "young barbarians," a kind of shock troops, he specialized in breaking up political meetings and attacking rival parties during elections. The "young barbarians" were not above political murder, as shown by their attempt on the life of Francesc Cambó, leader of Solidaritat Catalana, a coalition of Catalan parties, in 1907. Despite his fanatical rhetoric, Lerroux lacked a theoretical corpus to pave the way to popular insurrection (González Calleja, "La razón" 99). Overtaken

5 At this time, Francisco de Quevedo wrote: "Catalans are a monstrous abortion of politics" (*La rebelión de Barcelona* 465).

by the events during the Tragic Week of 1909, he fled the scene. But, as an agent provocateur suspected of being on the government's payroll, Lerroux succeeded in aggravating the tensions in Barcelona, preparing the way for the social warfare that flared up in 1917. After that year, violence became integral to Spanish life in a climate of dwindling legality.

In 1921, anarchist terrorism led to employers' counterterrorism, and society descended into violence, with each side justifying its transgression of the moral limits by the violence of the other side. On a small scale, it was already the logic of civil war. And, indeed, historian Albert Balcells links the uncontrolled anarchist violence during the first months of the Civil War to the memory of the political gang wars of the early 1920s (11). The impunity with which the anarchist patrols operated in the months after the *coup d'état* of July 1936 recalls the breakdown of justice during the 1920s, when the anarchist organizations pressured juries to pass absolutory sentences and intimidated witnesses, preventing trials from going forward for lack of evidence. Such license for social murder encouraged the emergence of so-called "white" terrorism, planting the seeds of the hatred that would explode in 1936.

The anarchist organizations were caught in their own trap. Having endorsed the use of collective violence in preparation for the general strike of 1917, they could hardly chastise the individual acts of violence originating in their own milieu. In his book *Terrorismo*, CNT leader Angel Pestaña acknowledged that "although the Union collectively had no part in the planning and execution of the attempts, it condoned them, helping those who had committed them elude justice" (cit. Balcells 65). Just as cavalier was the contempt for the law on the employers' side. In his memoirs, Amadeu Hurtado, dean of the Barcelona Lawyers' Association, recalled that his upper-class friends jeered at him for complaining about the murder of two CNT defense lawyers. Insensitivity to violence was widespread. "Law and justice," he writes:

> had no chance to hold sway, since they did not dispense the holy violence that was the only norm in those dramatic hours. If the verdicts of penal justice could not provide the lightning satisfaction of legalized wrath, it was considered better to push them aside, clearing the way for the crimes of a justice meted out by sectarians who justified their atrocities in the name of expediency. Blood called for blood instead of complaints and juridical procedures, and people believed that in the end it would become apparent which of the two bloods prevailed. (406)

The radical momentum was not quenched with the demise of the monarchy and the instauration of a republic, and the enemies of the new regime took advantage of bursts of revolutionary violence to advance their reactionary agendas. In his one-sided *Historia de la Segunda República*, published shortly after the end of the Civil War, Josep Pla catalogued the crimes that took place under the republic, wallowing in the impression of anarchy and of government taken hostage by the revolutionary parties, producing an image that narrowly mirrored the victors' official line. As early as 3 August 1932, less than sixteen months into the life of the new regime, Pla notes:

> The number of violent incidents remains very high and the homicide chronicle is terribly monotonous. The sensibility of public opinion gets coarser by the day, becoming ever duller. Facts that in all civilized countries, which in every human society would have been considered serious—precisely because of their political background—become simple gossip columns due to their abundance and persistence. Human life in Spain goes down in value, loses significance. (2.123)

Then, in April 1936, three months before the start of the war, he depicts an uncontrollable situation: "the country is a whirl, the number of violent events taking place is inestimable, personal insecurity, complete. The history of Spain sinks into a simple account of acts of violence and of terror" (4.374).

Pla's history of the Second Republic is certainly one of unrestrained violence, but instead of analyzing its nature and the reasons for its social authority he merely presents it as the consequence of the republican governments' partiality, of its incompetence or inability to uphold the principle of authority against the revolutionary owners of the regime. In doing this he neglects a more essential question, which nonetheless cries out from observations such as this: "The Constituting Parliament, by virtue of its generous ideas, had abolished the death penalty; in fact, however, Spaniards had placed the most blatant violence at the center of their collective life" (2.153). It is as if the derogation of the state's monopoly on death, associated with the monarchy by virtue of the supreme attribute of sovereignty, had only secularized the social determination of the right to live, transferring this principle to the new sovereign, the people, of which the insecure, beleaguered new state could not claim unambiguously to embody the representation. Hurtado had been more perspicuous when, observing that violence had replaced every social norm and become the single principle of social discrimination, he had spoken of "holy violence."

Existing work on the historical memory tends to ignore the hallowing of violence in twentieth-century Spanish culture. This may be due to the difficulty of tracing its phenomena (death sentences, executions, exhumed bodies, etc.) beyond the deceivingly simple dialectic of aggression and revenge. To be sure, violence is often rationalized or justified in terms of expediency. But even when considered instrumental, it retains a numinous quality and irrational appeal. It is, in Severino's distinction, a supplement to faith rather than an adjunct of truth. "Is not faith, as such, the original form of violence?" he asks (83). Severino suggests that essentialism forecloses the attempts to adapt behavioral attitudes to the relativities of social interaction. The point is not that faith does not bow to rational argument—faith in reason can be as dogmatic as any other faith—but rather that it does not countenance the evolution of human dispositions and thus of social truths and interpersonal arrangements.

One is tempted to trace the Spanish cult of death to the mystical tradition. If the gods are, as Émile Durkheim believed, the self representation that a society provides for itself, then the mysticism of cruelty in the agonizing, tortured body of Christ worshiped in every church, at most schools, and in many homes throughout Spain would seem to speak for a socialization of pain and the transfiguration of atrocities through eschatological exaltation. This seems to be the case in Miguel de Unamuno's most famous poem, "El Cristo de Velázquez" (1920), which contains verses such as: "through You death has become our mother, / through You death is the sugary refuge that sweetens life's bitterness," and then again, "You saved death," a heretical reading of St. Paul's doctrine of death's defeat through Christ's resurrection: "O death, where is thy sting? O grave, where is thy victory?" (1 Cor. 15:55). Unamuno would later recoil at General Millán Astray's cheering death during an act at the University of Salamanca in the early days of the Civil War, but he did not make death less of a fetish. On learning that during the course of the Civil War the Legion's fourth battalion had lost 8,000 men (a figure equivalent to the Legion's entire strength at the beginning of the conflict), Millán Astray invited all the officers present to lavish consumption of wine in the local casino (Preston 36). One in religious-lyrical form and the other profanely, both the university rector and the general subscribed to a negative theology that turned death into life's highest expression.

For this coincidence of opposites, the timing is important. Usually remembered in stark contrast at the tension-laden act at Salamanca, the immoderate army officer and the wizened university rector were both expressions of the nihilism that Ernst Jünger saw spreading over the entire first half of the twentieth century, "a time of apostles without a job" (*Über die Linie* 24). "Nihilism" was the term used by German theologian Friedrich Heinrich Jacobi to refer to lack of positive belief; the term's religious connotation was inherent from the beginning. But it was in Russia, in the 1870s, that the word obtained a political meaning with the rise of the *Narodnik* movement and its gospel of the propaganda of the deed, which reached France, probably with Russian exiles, in the 1880s, when a number of "martyrs" for the cause shocked French society with a spate of highly visible terrorist acts, accompanied by the terrorists' attempt to use the courts as a lectern for pedagogical self-immolation.

On 9 December 1893, Auguste Vaillant detonated a bomb in the Chamber of Deputies in Paris while in session. He was himself wounded in the act. While at the hospital, he confessed voluntarily and in writing in a letter addressed to the judge. His purpose was partially attained. Shaken by the action and by the confession, French society engaged in soul-searching, and mainstream writers used the opportunity to attack the government and the politicians for ignoring the suffering of the destitute classes. Some voices, such as the chemist Eugène Turpin, the inventor of Melinite, condoned the desperate actions of those who resorted to violence to protest against an unjust state of things (Guilleminault 72). On the very evening of the bombing of the Chamber of Deputies, Émile Zola declared: "it's the epic of violence that's beginning under our eyes" (Guilleminault 72). Others would follow Vaillant. One week after his execution, on 12 February 1894, a bomb went off in the café Terminus of the Saint-Lazare train station. Responsible was Émile Henry, an educated young man who for the last two years had been publishing articles in the anarchist journal *L'En Dehors*, in which he extolled violent actions that "wake up the masses" (Guilleminault 90). Georges Sorel would later systematize these ideas in his influential *Reflections on Violence* (1906), a book that Unamuno, who was a militant socialist until 1897 and remained a party sympathizer well into the 1920s (Roberts 90-1), probably read. Sorel is, from an intellectual point of view, the real apostle of modern violence. He extracted the irrational kernel of violence from Marx's "scientific" notion of the class struggle, convinced that violence could jolt the middle class into rediscovering its ancient fighting ardor. In turn, this would allow the working class to develop the intensity required for its historical mission, a hope that Unamuno—forever the champion of an agonic way of life—also expressed in 1919, when the social conflict came to a head in Barcelona. In an article published in *El Mercantil Valenciano* on 16 February ("Del engaño politico"), he rejoiced in Sorelian terms over the candor of violence and its potential for unmasking political deceit. "Better violence, that is to say, tyranny, than secrecy, that is to say, despotism. As long as they sweep away the priests of deceit, all those practitioners of fiction and falsehood, let the mobs of naked-hearted men appear" (cit. Roberts 91).

The World's Only Hygiene

Violence is no longer politics by other means but naked-hearted expansion of an "I" emancipated of ulterior motives. Speaking of massacre, Wolfgang Sofsky writes that "it is violence that governs the event. Collective excess cuts itself off from political or social objectives" (cit. Wieviorka 261). Violence, for Sorel, was also a revelation. It served to unmask the reformists and idealists, who dulled the class war and delayed the triumph of the proletariat. It was important, he claimed, "to thrash the orators of democracy," so that no one would entertain any illusions about the character of violence (105). Granted, a sense of instrumentality lingers in these statements. But in these practical and, so to speak, purposeful uses of violence it is not hard to perceive the fascination with the pure energy that consumes and is self-consuming. At the end of chapter 6, on "the ethics of violence," Sorel asks why in certain countries acts of violence produce an ideology capable of inspiring sublimity (240). The ideology-productive nature of violence may be an illusion. Objectively, violence and ideology stand in the opposite relation, the perceived sublimity of violence being the result of inspiring ideologies. In fact, it is not ideology but violence that constitutes the mystery. Ideology is its eliciting or ulterior justification. Violence is too strong a beverage to take undiluted. It needs mixing with sublimity and with rationality. It depends on language for its transmission and remains latent in language during periods of inactivity, before exploding again into action. But, when it does, it is the phenomenon itself that needs to be observed in order to understand it, rather than the aims its perpetrators summon to account for actions whose source they often fail to comprehend.

The Sorelian cult of violence was not the upshot of methodical analysis but of faith in the impending downfall of liberal society. It was the faith itself. And because it was an end in itself, nothing precluded its adoption by fascists and anarchists alike. A Basque like Unamuno, José Félix de Lequerica wrote his doctoral dissertation on Sorel. In 1931, he sponsored the publication of Ramiro Ledesma Ramos' weekly *La conquista del Estado*. In 1932, he was arrested for his involvement in a premature attempt at a coup-d'état led by General José Sanjurjo. Lequerica also financed the publication costs of Falange's journal *Arriba* and formally joined Falange at the start of the Civil War. In August 1944, when Franco appointed him ambassador to the Vichy government, the choice was seen as a setback for Franco's new policy of rapprochement to the allies, because Lequerica was perceived as an enthusiast of the Axis (Bowen 56).

Fascism, as Luciano Pellicani has argued, was a local and milder adaptation of the communist revolution, with which it shared the goal of overthrowing capitalism and setting up a centrally directed economy. Violence was the social lever to reach the intended goal; it was also a fount of lurid metaphors for the harsh, grisly aesthetic of the new era. Praising the "fertile manure provided by thousands of corpses," Bruno Spampanato declared in 1930 that Russian Bolshevism was "the prelude to fascism" (Pellicani 61). In 1939, *Gerarchia* (a title that was imitated in Spain by the Falange) featured a declaration of war on the bourgeoisie by Titta Madia, stating that "The bourgeois must be flushed out, stalked out like a wild rabbit; he has to be torn up like a weed in the grass" (cit. Pellicani 63). However, when confronted with the practical administration of power, dreams of apocalyptic revolution jarred with the reasons of state. Mussolini disappointed many in the fascist leadership by not dissolving private property and destroying capitalism, just as Franco, who, incidentally, contributed to the journal *Jerarquía*, disappointed Falangist "hierarchs" when he failed to liquidate the industrial bourgeoisie and upset their dream of economic autarchy. Nonetheless, he made up for that by granting them the *ius primae noctis* in the repression.

Spanish Falangists took their cue from Italian fascists in spirit and in detail. José Antonio Primo de Rivera's motto, that it was time for "the dialectic of fists and pistols," recalls Giovanni Gentile's encomium of the "billy-clubs of the fascist squads as God given" (Pellicani 73). In March 1933, Falangists launched a journal titled *El Fascio*, which the government hastened to suppress. But the formal similarities should not disguise the fact that Spanish fascists—Falangists and *Jonsistas*—adapted the idea of the totalitarian state to more traditional objectives. National unity loomed prominently in their agenda, but, different in that respect from Italy or Germany, it was not conceived as the resolution of the class conflict in a modern state but as the completion of the politics undertaken by the Catholic monarchs in 1492. The historical reference, bizarre as it may seem, had some logic. But it was not, as it is often said, the logic of political unification, which did not in fact occur at this time, since the crowns brought together through the royal wedding retained their original laws, privileges, and jurisdictions. What did occur under these monarchs was religious unification through forced conversion and the introduction of the Inquisition in the territories of Aragon with the policies of Cardinal Cisneros, supported by Queen Isabella of Castile. The completion of the Reconquista by the Catholic monarchs eliminated the violence directed against an outside enemy and inaugurated the internal violence characteristic of civil wars.

This new form of violence corresponds to the monotheistic violence that knows no limit because it tolerates no divergence and no falling away from the faith, as Jan Assmann has shown in relation to the fierce treatment of the population of Canaan by the Israelites in contrast to their behavior in the conquest of foreign cities (Deut. 12:2-3). The reason for this double standard was that Canaanites were Hebrews who had not adopted the monotheistic religion (*Monotheismus* 40). The old notion of *bellum sacrum*, originating with the crusades, had been wielded by the "servile," "traditionalist," or "fundamentalist" side in every one of the Spanish civil wars of the nineteenth century. An archaic line of transmission passing through Catholic seminaries and religious schools, as well as family traditions in certain rural regions, conveyed the idea that unrestrained violence was permitted and even required against the enemies of the faith, whether they were *afrancesados* (supporters of French enlightenment ideas), liberals, socialists, anarchists, communists, or simple democrats (Ugarte Tellería 159-60). To a great extent, then, the unbounded brutality of the Spanish Civil War stemmed from the division into "good" and "bad" Spaniards, the "sons of light" and the "sons of darkness," as Cardinal Pla y Deniel referred to the two sides in a pastoral letter at the beginning of the Civil War. Similarly, on 16 September 1936, Antonio García, Bishop of Tuy-Pontevedra, wrote in the Official Bulletin of his Bishopric that the war was a religious crusade in which the "good sons of Spain" fought "men who, although born in Spain, had expelled Spain's spirit from their hearts" (López Campillo, et al. 141).

"Goodness," in the politico-theological terms that guided the Spanish "salvation movement," as Franco called the revolt in his *Official Note to All Spaniards* (21 July 1936) (López Campillo, at al. 138), meant compliance with a form of political monotheism that exacted unrestricted violence against the unfaithful, the lukewarm, and the worshipers of political idols. In this light, the military *coup d'état* could be likened to divine intervention, and its leaders to instruments of God. This is how the priests of Seville saw the role of the city's military authority, General Gonzalo Queipo de Llano, "instrument of God for the realization of that great miracle, the National Uprising" (Pons Prades 67). A consequence of Spain's feeble enlightenment was that national identity became inseparable from politico-theological principles and its mark was unconditional devotion to a unity that could only be grasped performatively, hence violently, as a purgative campaign against those who did not nurse the idea in their hearts. The conflation of the Holy Spirit with Spain's spirit was obvious in Franco's reference to the military headquarters as "sanctuaries of the fatherland" in his allocution to the Armed Forces on 25 July 1936 (López Campillo, et al. 142). But the impulse to purify with the sword—or with fire, as anarchists undertook by burning churches and convents soon after the declaration of the republic and again early on in the war (Resina, "From Rose of Fire")—was not so much an expression of religious fanaticism as the rediscovery and recycling of local forms of violence in the "national" history. Appealing to those anachronistic themes in the language of violence endowed the impulse to action with the sublimity that, in Sorel's view, is indispensable to an "ethics of violence."

Even before it turned up in the Spanish bishops' language, the notion of a crusade requiring sacrifice was inscribed in the *Puntos iniciales* (Starting points) of the manifesto of Falange (*Falange Española* no. 1, 7 December 1933). Julio Ruíz de Alda, co-founder of Falange, had called for a "crusade of violence" in the second issue of the journal *No importa* (6 December 1936; cit. López Campillo, et al. 139). The idea that the rebellion was a "holy cause," for which participants must be ready to lay down their lives, was present in General Emilio Mola's secret instructions to the military conspirators ("Instrucción Reservada Número 1, Base 3," in Sánchez Pérez 344). Franco merely repeated a counterrevolutionary commonplace when he appealed to the notion of crusade in his proclamation of Civil War ("Proclama a todos los españoles") on 21 July 1936. Nationalist faith gave meaning to the unleashing of violence in a climate of fanaticism in which, as the *Joint Letter of the Spanish Bishops to the Bishops of the World* declared, war was "an armed plebiscite" between spirit and matter ("Carta" 8), and thus a merciless struggle of metaphysical proportions.

Political monism had been slow in coming, but it reached doctrinal character when Ramiro Ledesma Ramos, founder of the JONS, preached nationalism as the principal duty of Spanish youth. Taking the lead from the older generation of writers, such as Angel Ganivet, Unamuno, Ramiro de Maeztu, Ramón Menéndez Pidal, and José Ortega y Gasset, who famously offered a recipe for national regeneration based on Castilian supremacy, Ledesma merely drew the implications of their thinking when he interpreted Catalonia's and Euzkadi's demands for devolution as carry-over from the Empire's disintegration. "It is not by chance," he said, "that these unsettling phenomena [Catalan and Basque autonomic demands] have emerged after this date [1898], when the overseas disaggregation was completed and concluded, as if the historical cancer was now ready to sink its teeth on the unity of the peninsular territories" (66). He was not in doubt about the remedy: "The trajectory followed by the disaggregating forces is something that cannot be defeated or stopped except through war, that is to say, through revolution" (67). And the new Spanish reality "must, of course, begin with a violent triumph over them [Catalan and Basque separatists]" (67). This was doubtlessly the meaning of his invitation to Spaniards to unite in a "dangerous and delightful enterprise of reconquest" in the manifesto he issued on 14 March 1936 (Ellwood 214).

Falange's conception of the national state was, with added frills and trappings, that of its more traditional precursors. Even the celebration of violence was a frank admission of a conviction already expressed, if in more subdued ways, by their intellectual precursors. Maeztu had written: "Long live Force! To those who weep, punch them in the eyes" (cit. González Cuevas, "Política de lo sublime" 111). Unamuno had been preaching intolerance and imposition, and vindicating Castilian aggression as early as 1905: "No matter what shortcomings the Castilian people might have for living in modern culture, one must admit that it owed its predominance to its generosity, its fine sense for imposition, and its resolve to compel others to accept its beliefs" ("La crisis actual del patriotismo español" 1293). José Ortega y Gasset, who was, after Unamuno, Spain's most influential intellectual, considered societies that are steeped in military values to be of a higher type than those imbued with the gentler habits of commerce (*España invertebrada* 57). These and other writers undermined the liberal line of thinking, which since the seventeenth century had associated commerce with the progress of nations (Hirschman 59–63).

Radicalizing their teachers' soft spot for aggression, a younger generation of Castilian intellectuals geared up to put rhetoric into practice. Ortega had asserted that only Castile could grasp Spain's political essence (*España invertebrada* 61) and had endorsed "a suggestive project of life in common," presumably devised by a Castilian leader and supported by a glorious army (59). José Antonio Primo de Rivera rephrased it by defining Spain as a "unity of destiny in the universal" ("España y Cataluña"). Although the enterprise remained conveniently vague in his formulation, it was inspiring. Onésimo Redondo campaigned for a policy of Castilian exaltation leading to a new imperial era. And Ernesto Giménez Caballero, in his book *La nueva catolicidad* (1933), associated the authors of the Generation of '98 with Hitler, Lenin, Kemal, and Mussolini, flashy leaders who had succeeded in concentrating the national forces in their countries. Inspired by their example, Giménez Caballero wished for Spain's national revival through a crusade undertaken "in the name of a Cesar and in the service of a God" (González Calleja and Limón Nevado 19). Although he was considered a theoretician of the Avant-Garde, Giménez Caballero appealed to the pet themes of the Spanish reaction. There was a whiff of déjà vu in these pretended modernizers. But, then, fascism lacked an original ideological corpus. Its specificity lay in excess, and, as Michel Lacroix points out, it is not an excess of what is left behind but of that which has already been said and is simply reaffirmed with intolerance and violence (352).

Spanish fascists profited from widespread acquiescence to direct action, which anarchists had naturalized among large sections of the population. From Sorel, they borrowed the spite against liberalism in a political environment in which even liberals were forced to admit the deterioration of the Western democracies (Lippmann 13–15). Ledesma preached direct action, but instead of making it a weapon of the working class, as Sorel had, he linked it to Ortega y Gasset's call for the leadership of a select minority (Ledesma 83). Direct action, said Ledesma, did not always amount to armed violence, but violence was for Spanish youth "a profound echo of moral realization, of heroism, of mettle and resolve" (83). Incongruously with his idea of a leading minority, he condemned political action when it stemmed from "small visionary groups" (83), a sign that, notwithstanding his limited following, he envisioned a youth movement on a national scale. By virtue of the elevated aims embodied in the totalitarian state, Ledesma affirmed that "our hand would not tremble before any resolution, no matter how grave and bloody" (88).

He did not merely preach violence; he also followed Sorel in supplementing it with myth as the most efficient means to mobilize the masses. Myth, he asserted, is more powerful than rational explanation (cit. González Cuevas, "Ledesma" 18). The origin of Spanish fascism confirms Severino's opinion that violence stems from faith rather than from the possession of a self-evident truth to be arrived at philosophically (90). Unamuno's insistence on Spain's need for a faith that overcomes the mind, vehemently argued for in his eccentric *Our Lord Don Quixote* (1914), had already removed the safety pins of rationality and opened the floodgates to pugnacious voluntarism.

Two mythic strands can be discerned in Spanish fascism. First, the myth of national destiny, a secular variation on Catholic providentialism. Secondly, the aestheticizing of death, ritualized in the cult of the Fallen and the absent one. From European interwar nationalism, fascism borrowed the ceremonials of memory that George Mosse has called "tangible symbols of death" (34). But fascist memory, monumentalized in the Valley of the Fallen and romanticized in death's mystical comradeship, rests on the forgetting of the corpses. The lofty ideas proclaimed in the manifestos have been purged of empirical content. In fascist texts and spectacles, "death is not bloody or horrible; it presents a graceful face, that of the young soldier who died with a smile on his lips. Fascist aesthetics rest on a highly significant ellipsis, that of agony" (Lacroix 343).

The Groom of Death

Death was revered not only in the Falangist myth of the Fallen, but also in the Spanish Foreign Legion, the elite corps founded by José Millán Astray in 1920, from which Franco emerged wrapped in an aura of heroism to become the Caudillo. Shortly after founding the Legion in 1920, José Millán Astray invited Franco to join him, forging a friendship based on brutality and absolute submission to one's superiors. Paul Preston describes the legionnaires as "automatons who followed orders without thought" (15). The commanders exacted a fierce discipline from the recruits, but in compensation they pulled all the stops on the atrocities committed against the colonial population. In a calculated reversal, Franco would later give his Moorish troops free rein in the Spanish villages taken during the Civil War. A sense of impunity is, Michel Wieviorka observes, "decisive for the passage to barbarity; it is indispensable for cruelty" (272). All the more so, we may add, when impunity is sanctioned by authority. The sense of impunity, which goes a long way to explain the pre-revolutionary social warfare in the 1920s and 1930s, was consciously turned into an instrument of combat by the "Africanist" army officers and eventually into policy by the Franco regime.

Millán Astray's war cry was "¡Viva la muerte!": "Long live death!" and the Legion made in fact an ostentatious cult of the death it inflicted. If nuns called themselves "brides of Christ," in reference to their mystical wedding with the Crucified, the legionnaires called themselves "grooms of death," making this moniker the title of their most famous hymn. At the end of his life, Franco glided like a shadow through El Pardo palace, his residence outside Madrid, somberly humming "El novio de la muerte" (Oliver 76): "I am a bridegroom of death going to join such a loyal companion with strong bonds." At heart he was still the legionnaire. The mystique of death had survived decades of political stewardship of a country he had always governed with the chilling fanaticism that his former senior officer had inspired in him during his years in Africa.

Millán Astray is an instructive case with regard to the figurations of violence in the 1930s. The self-referential violence that he worshipped in the emptiness of death brimmed with pathological manifestations but lacked ideological foundations. To provide them was Falange's contribution. Millán Astray admired its organization and became an official member after Franco incorporated the armed forces to the single party. In a famous speech at the University of Salamanca in 1936, where he notoriously clashed with Miguel de Unamuno, Millán Astray proclaimed that fascism was the only remedy for Spain. His boisterous style contrasted with Franco's puritanical sobriety, but, as Roger Caillois observed, "[c]ertain kinds of sobriety are more fearsome than the lack of restraint" (163). For Franco, Falange was an ideological windfall, providing interim structure to the pure culture of violence and submission he had developed in his African years. Placing Falange under his personal headship was not simply a way to dispose of a political rival. Manuel Hedilla, the Falange leader whom Franco jailed prior to subordinating the party, lacked José Antonio's prestige and was no challenge to the Caudillo. Removing him so uncompromisingly ensured the Falange's submissiveness, but, above all, by taking over the party Franco got hold of a ready-made totalitarian ideology, which he placed at the service of his personal rule. Thus, the programmatic principles of Falange inspired the ideological principles of the new regime formulated in the booklet *Los XXVI Puntos del Estado Español* (1940), which, as Enrique Rodrigues-Moura points out, includes twenty-six of Falange's twenty-seven points (174 n. 21). Clad in that ideological breastplate, Franco could climb the political rostrum and stand next to Mussolini and Hitler (and, closer to home, Salazar) as chief of a New State.

Julio Aróstegui points out that violence succeeds politically through two different actions: ideologization and instrumentalization. Ideology serves to make violence acceptable, passing it off as ethical and creative, while its instrumentalization relies on institutions and organizations (40). The apparent incongruence between Franco's traditionalism and his leadership of Falange, a self-styled revolutionary party, is best understood by the latter's weakness. Before the war, Spain's would-be Führer, José Antonio, did not lord over a paramilitary force like the *Sturmabteilung* of the NSDAP. The JONS had organized its militants into assault commandos in Madrid, but even after its unification with Falange in 1933, their combined forces were not capable of mobilizing enough blue shirts for a march on Madrid. Unable to follow Sorel's path through syndicalist violence, José Antonio had to rely on the *coup d'état*, as propounded by the royalist Charles Maurras in France. And, indeed, Falange's middle-class thugs resembled Action Française's *Camelots du roi* more than the syndicalists at the other end of the political spectrum.

Rather than on a revolutionary mass movement, Falange placed its hopes on the army's inherent conservatism. So embedded was the *coup-d'état* in the army's tradition, that the generals who plotted against the republic did not feel the need to justify their action with any political program, let alone theory. They were merely "saving the fatherland" with a "program" formulated at the beginning of the century by Joaquín Fanjul in *Misión social del Ejército* (1907). In this book, Fanjul, who would later be one of the chief military conspirators against the Second Republic, asserted that the army was the keeper of the "patriotic religion" against separatists and revolutionaries. Here again, the conflation of religion and violence underscores that element of faith that Severino identified in the latter. It was faith's self-referentiality that sanctified the violence and rendered it imperative for good Spaniards. For faith, in the country's history, has always been synonymous with obedience.

"Apolitical" Dictatorship

The reactionary precedents of the so-called "national uprising" explain why Falange failed to displace the conservatives from the institutions and ended up subordinating itself to the army, rather than the other way around, as had been the case in Italy or Germany. Despite routine appeals to youth, the liturgy of leadership, the Roman salute, the boots, the torchlight parades, and the use of emblems, "many elements of the politics of the 'sublime' were subsumed by a radical politico-theological perspective" (González Cuevas, "Política de lo sublime" 109). The detour taken by the fascist cult of violence through Spain's central institutions implied that the modern radicalism of this cult was appropriated for pre- and even anti-modern causes, inserting it in the *longue durée* of Spanish reaction. In the words of Manuel Vázquez Montalbán, "Curiously, in Spain, the Church and the Army rerouted to their logical mill the mass movement of the Crusade and of the ever-deferred national-syndicalist revolution. That is why Spanish fascism always resembled the traditional reaction of Counter-Reformation Spain" (16). This is also the reason why in Spain fascism's avant-garde overtones could be mimicked by reactionary groups intent on preserving the traditional structures of power. José María Albiñana's *Partido Nacionalista Español* adopted the fascist phraseology for the purpose of restoring the monarchy as guarantor of the traditional order. After 1934, unable to compete with Falange, Albiñana reverted to the defense of Castilian agrarian interests, threatened, as he saw it, by the Catalans' and Basques' refusal to buy Castilian wheat at monopoly prices. He then declared fascism, now brokered by José Antonio Primo de Rivera, to be "foreign" and incompatible with Spanish nationalism (González Calleja, *Contrarrevolucionarios* 135).

As a restoration of the state through the reaction of its time-hallowed institutions (the Church, the Army), the "national revolution" could pose as apolitical. During the war, Colonel Antonio Vallejo Nágera asserted that: "The National Movement is above human passions, above political sectarianism and the class struggle" (Vallejo Nágera, *Sinfonía* 8). Franco himself appears to have believed that "politics" was a scourge of parliamentary democracies, a flaw from which he had redeemed the country. In a familiar anecdote, he was said to have counseled an advice-seeker: "do as I do, and do not get involved in politics." Whether genuine or apocryphal, the anecdote expresses the Francoist conviction that the state of exception, made permanent, healed (or cauterized) the wounds inflicted on the national body by political passions. The archaic belief in a Christian monarchy unifying the earthly sovereignties through supra-political faith was reclaimed for new immanent uses through the elevation of the cult of nationality to the status of a transcendent religion. And, as in the times of religious unification, now remembered as Spain's Golden Age,[6] the ruthless purging of heretics and dissenters bonded the community of the "addicted," as those committed to the regime were called.

In a certain sense, fascist "apoliticism" mimicked the syndicalist rejection of "politics." Both ideologies attacked "bourgeois" parliamentarianism, the latter in the name of an allegedly scientific theory of human nature; the former in the name of eternal values grounded in a national mystique. The right's pretended apoliticism was in effect a doctrinal straitjacket intended to crush political disagreement under the weight of symbols that were fanatically imposed. A certain historicism was here at work, but a singularly non-dialectical one. Falange's "unity of destiny in the universal" turned out to be no revolutionary horizon but nostalgia for Castilian hegemony, which imperial reassertion would restore. Hence the constant references to Spain's glorious past, to Charles V, the Catholic Kings, Philip II. Hence, too, the name of Falange's major postwar magazine, *Escorial*. None of this had anything to do with a futuristic Utopia or a politics of the sublime. It recalled principles of legitimation used in the Renaissance to support the transference of the theological-political principle of absolute authority to the Castilian nation identified with its king. José Antonio Maravall explained how, in the sixteenth century, Antonio de Guevara had combined Castilian particularism with the promotion of a quasi-divine idea of the prince and the legitimation of unquestioning obedience. Universal empire was for Guevara the expression of God's will. He shared the contradiction between universalism and particularism with many renaissance humanists, who wavered between acceptance of the traditional idea of empire and a vivid pre-national sentiment (198). In the end, he resolved the contradiction by treating the idea of universal empire as a protensional aspiration that justified the political behavior of his own particular lord, the emperor Charles V (199).

Franco, Spain's *Caudillo* through God's grace—as the motto in Spanish coins declared—turned to this theological foundation of absolute authority in a gesture that found support in Falange's own recourse to a form of the nostalgic sublime anchored in the combined authoritarianism of Church and Army. In the nineteenth century, Juan Donoso Cortés had devised the

6 The term "Golden Age," used since the middle of the eighteenth century in the sense of "great achievement" in Castilian poetry, became a designation for Spain's high imperial era in the work of the German Hispanist Ludwig Pfandl (1881–1942). It was popularized during the twentieth century, becoming established in Spanish literary historiography after the Civil War. For a history of the concept, see Abad Nebot, "Sobre el concepto literario de 'Siglo de Oro.'"

formula for superseding constitutional legality through a metaphysical idea of the nation. His formula read: "When legality suffices to save society, legality; when it does not suffice, then dictatorship" (188). He also furnished the opposition between party strife, understood as un-Spanish, and the supreme unity of command that replaces politics with national vigor. "When the invading forces concentrate in political associations, then necessarily, of their own accord, the forces of resistance collect in one hand without anyone being able to prevent it, without anyone having the right to prevent it. This is the clear, luminous, indestructible theory of dictatorship" (189–90).

Olivier Abel observes: "the appeal of the conscience to a law superior to the law of politics is the very logic of fundamentalism" (77). Donoso Cortés appealed to such a law on the basis of an ontological understanding of society and the state. In view of this fundamentalism, it is impossible to sustain the opinion that Donoso "is opposed to any form of absolutism, any totalitarian theory of the state" (McNamara 343). Given his claim of an absolute foundation of government in a stern adaptation of the Augustinian tradition, his alleged opposition to political absolutism can only be endorsed in the sense that the mature Donoso refused secularism and in fact any modern theory of the state on grounds of innate human depravity. To be acceptable, any theory of the state had to correlate with religion. Only a return to some form of theocratic monarchy was capable of saving post-revolutionary man.

After the Civil War, Francoist jurisprudence elaborated a theory of dictatorship inspired by Carl Schmitt's construal of Cortés' principle of decision as ethical/metaphysical grounds for discarding legitimism and establishing a dictatorship. Schmitt provided legal–theoretical cover for the re-founding of the state on the basis of the worst of political crimes: plunging the country into civil war. This premise meant that not only in the memory but at the root of the new state was the violence called for by the translation of political conflict in terms of the final struggle against radical evil (40). The violence unleashed by the rebel army in the name of the purification of a fallen society was thus made to embrace both its purpose and justification. In *Representación política y régimen español* (1945), Francisco Javier Conde wrote: "The dictator is such precisely on account of the situation that he himself is called to produce with his own action. By reason of the goal to be accomplished, all the legal barriers that could frustrate it must be suppressed" (cit. Tahmassian 64). In juridical treatises of Schmittian inspiration, violence is conceived as the just means to restore a unity allegedly upset by those who, for that very reason, are designated as irreconcilable enemies and slated for destruction. From a theological-political perspective, the cult of violence leads to a form of the sublime imbued with a sacrificial disposition, with the cold, righteous sacrifice of all that is perceived as hindering sacred unity. As González Calleja explains, "fascism looked on violence as an aspect of its nature and as a proud manifestation of the national essence rather than as a secondary political mechanism. Violence was not an exceptional means to conquer power but a permanent symbolic representation of national discipline and unanimity" (González Calleja, *Contrarrevolucionarios* 130).

The Return of the Unrepressed

Violence merged with essentialism in the fascist discourse of the 1930s and remained ensconced in the values of Francoism and beyond. It remains a recognizable index of national discipline in Spain's conservative discourse. Spanish fury, the charge of the bull blinded with rage, the impulsive appeal to masculinity measured by physical courage, these are real or illusory national traits. Their widespread prestige means that individuals are not the autonomous source of these aggressive values, but grow into them through cultural adaptation. But how did Spanish society come to nurture those values? Martín Alonso talks about a drama unfolding through its inertia (120). In the 1930s, Spain rushed down the incline of its own tragic history. Ricocheting from the country's last imperial war, the inertial violence, deprived of an object and a reason, morphed into the figures of radical youth and more seasoned generals who dreamed of resurrecting the old glory in the garb of new conquistadors. Theirs was a poor philosophy of history based on an eternal fatherland populated by epic figures. But it was enough to pass their petty class interests and territorial resentments for an unconditional imperative. On the other side, anarchists and communists partook of a more substantial philosophy of history, one that prescribed an answer to present conflicts in a future *telos*. If the right saw history as a tableau representing an eternal set of truths and values, the left was steeped in apocalyptic determinism. For both, meaning exceeded the lives of individuals. These could be dispensed with as either disrupters of a prelapsarian unity or as obstacles to history's unfolding justice.

In relation to violence and the cultural memory, it should be noted that, in Spain, public discourses on memory have been unwilling to tackle the question of responsibility, that is, of causality. Facing that question required attaching specific acts of violence to the persons who committed them and then searching for clues to their behavior. Instead, the historical memory discourse has, for the most part, been bogged down in disputes involving blanket accusations against whole classes of people, replicating a dialectic that proved murderous in the 1930s. But, as Judith Butler points out, acts of violence are committed by individuals who "are not dupes or mechanisms of an impersonal social force, but agents with responsibility. On the other hand, these individuals are formed, and we would be making a mistake if we reduced their actions to purely self-generated acts of will or symptoms of individual pathology or 'evil'" (15). The point is, of course, not to deflect responsibility from individuals to specific conditions or to dissolve it altogether in the spirit of the times. It is rather to acknowledge the formative power of collective representations, and to suggest that, even if justice can no longer be procured for the victims of the Civil War, it is never too late to rethink the relation between those acts and the historical representations that anointed them with the blessing of the ideal.

CHAPTER SIX

Guernica as a Sign of History

I n his classic study of aerial bombing, *On the Natural History of Destruction*, W. G. Sebald denounced the failure of postwar German literature to address the trauma caused by the bombing of German cities toward the end of the Second World War. The lack of descriptions of the air raids was particularly disturbing to Sebald, who believed that only artistic representation can convey the terror of the firestorms in great cities laid to waste in a matter of hours. To be sure, there is no lack of graphic material showing the ruins of Hamburg, Cologne, or Dresden, and a *Trümmerliteratur* and *Trümmerfilme* appeared from the end of the war to around 1950. But these images were the laconic witnesses of a demoralized society on which the Nazi period still cast a shadow. Sebald missed a resolute engagement with the experience of the destruction itself, which, he claimed, had vanished from public discussion due to the presence of "an almost perfectly functioning mechanism of repression" (12). He was convinced that "there was a tacit agreement, equally binding on everyone, that the true state of material and moral ruin in which the country found itself was not to be described" (10). He regretted the German authors' inability to transform the immediate experience of the bombing into a reflective moral truth capable of being assimilated by the collective memory of Germans.

Various critics have challenged the notion of a fatalistic silence surrounding the bombings. Joachim Güntner, writing for the *Neue Zürcher Zeitung* on 7 December 2002, denied the existence of a literary taboo, although the audience for this subject was never large ("Der Bombenkrieg findet zur Sprache," cit. Vees-Gulani 337). Others uphold the notion of a taboo but criticize Sebald's psychological approach as inadequate and supplement it with a political theory of repression. Where Sebald, apropos the work of Alexander Kluge, detected a paralyzing fatalism that looks onto the technological conditions of the destruction as a falling out from autonomous history "and back into the history of nature" (67), Wilfried

Wilms considered that "a taboo on remembering is not only a private psychological affair, but also a political one" (181). For Sebald, fear of being accused of revisionism weighed on the German writers, who found it very difficult to present Germans as victims. Wilms admits this, but he adds that such fear played into the hands of the Allies, who, being engaged "in the process of cultural reorganization," had every reason "to steer clear of the recent technological mass murder" that they had perpetrated (188). For Wilms, Sebald himself suffered under the taboo that he denounced, as his study "is sustained by a gesture that seeks and finds blame or failure on the side of the now ashamed and speechless German perpetrator who makes a taboo of the massive destruction of his home and life" (188).

This view, invested as it is in shifting blame to the Allies, could be easily interpreted as lending support to those readers who, as Sebald himself declares in the third, additional part of his essay, understood his Zurich lectures as reinforcing the notion of German victimhood or even Jewish conspiracy. Such reactions, although to be expected in light of some of his assertions, incommoded Sebald, who wrote this part of the essay, Susanne Vees-Gulani points out, as "a form of 'damage control' as Sebald here clarifies the role of Germans in the war" (340) and lays out the order of responsibility by reminding his readers of Germany's preeminence in the development of aerial bombing. "The intoxicating vision of destruction coincides with the fact that the real pioneering achievements in bomb warfare—Guernica, Warsaw, Belgrade, Rotterdam—were the work of the Germans" (Sebald 105). Thus, it is never a question of Sebald denying or relativizing his country's responsibility in the induction of a new level of destruction that came home to roost: "The majority of Germans today know, or so at least it is to be hoped, that we actually provoked the annihilation of the cities in which we once lived" (104).

But this sensible reminder is precisely what Wilms faults Sebald with: "At the very end of *On the Natural History of Destruction*, and like a good pupil, he mitigates his own criticism and reminds readers once again that Guernica, Warsaw, Belgrade, and Rotterdam established the Germans as pioneers in area bombing" ("In Search" 204). For Wilms it is morally irrelevant that Germany was the undisputed aggressor; he faults the first postwar reporters, Janet Flanner and Martha Gellhorn, for colluding to hide from British and American readers the destruction of German cities by their air forces, building a case for mixed responsibilities on the words of Swedish reporter Stig Dagerman, who early on sought to discharge Germans of civil accountability for the suffering inflicted on a whole continent: "the German distress is collective whereas the German cruelties were, despite everything, not so" (cit. Wilms, "In Search" 195).

But was it not precisely the question of national responsibility that became the bone of contention in the history of the German Federal Republic? In the light of the *Historikerstreit* of the 1980s, Wilms' effort against Sebald to lift that responsibility by placing Germans squarely on the side of the claimants must be read as part and parcel of reunified Germany's slow but sure bid for power in international politics. That much does, in fact, Wilms concede: "I suggest that today's literary and political events challenge the largely undisputed allotment of roles that were established and consolidated at the end of World War II" ("In Search" 187). But the passage at the end of *On the Natural History of Destruction* where Sebald recalls the series of area bombings originating with Guernica is significant not on account of the author's brainwashed self-deprecation but of the accurate tracing of the origins of the technological rampage in which the Allies reactively indulged, raising it to a new level of criminality not in Dresden or Cologne, which were, so to speak, mirror images of Warsaw, Coventry, or Rotterdam, but in Hiroshima and Nagasaki, which no power of the imagination could ever rationalize as retaliation on the level of Pearl Harbor.

Although Guernica pales in comparison with the number of victims and the material damage in these other cities, and even with the protracted bombing of Madrid and Barcelona, places that do not show up on Sebald's list, it stands for a symbolic landmark in the history of aerial attacks on civilian populations. Guernica's significance does not lie principally in the tonnage of explosives dropped on its inhabitants. In the city of Barcelona alone, over a million kilograms of bombs were dropped in the course of the Civil War and 1,800 civilian buildings were partly or totally ruined. Thanks to historian Edoardo Mastrorilli, there is now documented evidence that the Italian aviation that bombed Barcelona for 72 hours between 16 and 18 March 1938, causing 900 casualties, targeted the civilian population with the objective of spreading terror and weakening the republican's resistance (Riart). If the number of casualties in the Catalan capital was relatively low (several thousand in the course of the war) it was due largely to the effective system of underground shelters designed by Ramon Perera, a civil engineer whose experience was foolishly dismissed to great cost of life by the British at the Hailey conference in the London Institution of Structural Engineers during the Second World War (Armengou and Belis 213–22).

Guernica's enduring importance lies above all in the fact that, unsuspected by the Spanish nationalists and the German air command, it was to become not exactly a victory of propaganda for the republic, as Raymond L. Proctor speciously asserts (131), but one of those uniquely revealing experiences that Kant called "signs of history." Guernica's uniqueness lies, on the one hand, in the disproportion between the alleged purpose of the attack and the violence deployed and, on the other hand, in the blurring of the truth that followed the transgression of a moral boundary. Ultimately, Guernica's historical significance arose from the struggle to define what had happened in light of the indignation called forth by the rubble and ashes of a small provincial town. The disproportion between means and ends made the bombing unsuitable for an ordinary war narrative. As a result, it fell into a moral and intellectual twilight zone, the very zone where Sebald later claimed the bombing of German cities had vanished. The parallels and similarities run deep, even if in the case of the Basques there can be no question of a self-imposed taboo. A dearth of literary representation surrounds the destruction of Guernica as much as that of German cities. Only, unlike Dresden or Hamburg, Guernica did find effective and definitive artistic symbolization in the outraged brush strokes of Pablo Picasso.

Although no one ever accepted the responsibility for its devastation, the escalation of the damage from previous operations and the incongruity between the ostensible target and the given orders did not escape the Luftwaffe's servicemen. In transmitting the orders, Condor Legion chief of staff Wolfram von Richthofen identified the Rentería bridge and the roads leading to it as the target. Seemingly, the idea was to cut off the retreat of the republican troops and to encircle them prior to General Varela's moving into the area. But the bombers were ordered to fly at 6,000 feet, a height from which they could hardly be expected to take off such a small target without a great waste of materiel. Nor was the massive deployment of antipersonnel bombs readily comprehensible, and even less so the use of incendiaries, in a ratio of one to three according to Von Richthofen's journal, for a total of over 2,500 thermite bombs capable of reaching a temperature of 5,000 degrees Fahrenheit (2,760 degrees Celsius) when ignited. What use could firebombs be against a stone bridge? They could, however, be devastating in a town that the map showed to be a mere 300 yards away (Thomas and Morgan Witts 213). To take out a seventy-five-foot-long and thirty-foot-wide bridge, a few Stukas, used elsewhere for precision bombing, would have sufficed. Yet the operation launched forty-three bombers and fighters from the Burgos and Vitoria airfields to drop 100,000 pounds of high explosive, fragmentation, and incendiary bombs in sharp deviation from Von Richthofen's usual economy of ammunition. The ratio was about 400 pounds of explosives for every square yard of bridge. In effect, this was the largest force ever assembled for an air attack in Spain, an extravagance that belies the professed target. Oddly, the bridge remained intact after the massive raid, as did the Astra-Unceta weapons factory, which did not even come under attack, although it was used a posteriori to justify it. Missing the ostensible target after such lavish expenditure of resources makes absurd Colonel Jaenecke's reporting to the Special Staff that "In and for itself Guernica was a total success of the Luftwaffe" (cit. Brieden, Dettinger, and Hirschfeld 71). And it makes Von Richthofen's enthusiastic diary entry for 30 April 1937 not only absurd but nonsensical.

> When the Junkers arrived, smoke was everywhere (from Von Beust, who had attacked with three airplanes), no one could recognize the bridge, the roads or the city outskirts anymore and dropped the bombs right into the middle of it. The 250 kilogram ones threw up a high number of houses and destroyed the water main. Now the incendiaries had time to develop and work their effect. The construction style of the houses: tile roofs, wooden balconies and wood section workshops, led to complete destruction. —The population was outdoors largely on account of a holiday, the majority of the others left the town right at the beginning. A small part died in the impacted shelters. —Bomb craters can still be seen in the streets, simply great. —The town was closed for at least 24 hours; it was the accomplished precondition for a great success of our 250 kilo bombs and EC.B1. (cit. Brieden, Dettinger, and Hirschfeld 72)

The latter referred to the thermite incendiaries produced by I.G. Farben. The elation of the report makes no sense, unless the bridge was never the primary object of the operation but a cover for the testing of a new warfare technique designed to terrorize entire populations. For a man who had given orders to shoot anything that moved near the bridge and on the adjacent roads, Von Richthofen's wishful declaration that the majority of the population was spared because it had been outdoors and left the town at the start of the bombing does not square with the drama of people machine gunned as they attempted to flee, or with fields strewn with dead sheep and slaughtered animals. His men had taken to heart his order to consider hostile anything that moved. And what did he mean by making the destruction of Guernica the precondition for a great success of the high explosive and incendiary materials? It is plain that in his mind Guernica had been the laboratory on whose results the future success of the new weapons hinged. Hence his elation: "Simply great," he summarized.

The "great success" of the Luftwaffe in the annihilation of a civilian target devoid of military importance flipped immediately into high-level political secrecy and rotund denials. And here, I think, is where the tragedy of a small Basque town acquired its epochal significance, which, as Ian Patterson points out, "has tended to overshadow the bombing of Madrid and Barcelona and the systematic bombing, from 19 January to 31 March, of the Catalan coast" (67). The Franco press office, headed by Luis Bolín, immediately set off a propaganda campaign blaming the destruction of Guernica on Asturian miners, allegedly dispatched by the Bilbao government to dynamite the town. Franco's headquarters at Salamanca gave a somewhat different version, blaming retreating Republican units for setting Guernica on fire. Very soon, though, a strikingly dissimilar version of the events surfaced through Father Alberto de Onaindia's interview in the French newspaper *L'aube*. Onaindia was a canon of Valladolid cathedral. He happened to be in Guernica on the day of the bombing. His interviews for the Belgian, French, and British press sparked controversy but could not be as easily dismissed as were Basque government communiqués. Yet, in France, the Havas news agency did not distribute the interview. The *New York Times* dismissed Onaindia as "just an unfrocked young priest," and in London the Catholic weekly *The Universe* and the *Catholic Times* repeated General Queipo de Llano's embroidery that the Pope had excommunicated Onaindia. The Vatican itself ignored a letter of Onaindia's protesting the bombing of innocent Christians (Patterson 44–5). Most interesting was T. S. Eliot's comment in the July 1937 issue of *Criterion*:

> The situation in Spain has provided the perfect opportunity for extremists of both extremes. To turn from the shrill manifestoes of the Extreme Left, and the indiscretions of the Dean of Canterbury, to the affirmations of Mr. Jerrold and Mr. Lunn, is only to intensify the nightmare. On the First of May, *The Tablet* provided its explanation of the destruction of Guernica: the most likely culprits, according to it, were the Basques' own allies, their shady friends in Catalonia. (cit. Patterson 37)

Eliot's reliance on the *Tablet*, whose wild theory of Catalan involvement did not square even with the versions advanced by Franco's chief of press, by Queipo de Llano, or Salamanca headquarters, displays the arrogance of the detached intellectual who feels he can dispense with the facts by manipulating some self-evident axiom, in this case the depravity of Catalan revolutionaries. No matter that Catalonia was cut off from the Basque Country, or that anarchists exerted no influence on the Catholic leaders of the Basque Nationalist government, the wilder the lie, the more it satisfied the class and national prejudices, the easier it was taken for the truth. Who would pass on the opportunity to taint the Basques and the Catalans at one stroke? Neither Bolín nor Queipo de Llano, both certified liars, had been as inventive as the *Tablet*, but then, they knew that neither the map nor the structure of republican command would bear out that big a fib.

Eliot's cavalier settling of the issue reveals the liberal's superstition that truth lies in the balance between the extremes and can be arrived at through innate ability to discern the middle. Such bias, to which intellectuals are especially prone, benefits the extreme that is capable of the most cynicism, or quite simply the position that the intellectual most sympathizes with and inadvertently centers his imagination. In this case, Eliot did not pursue the facts but spun them around pre-existing opinion. His intellectual failure illustrates that of Western civilization to assess its own progress or regress. Guernica became a sign of history because it was one of the rare occasions on which the meaning of words like "progress" or "regress" could be exceptionally established. And it was the failure of people like Eliot properly to react to that meaning that threw light on the Western predicament.

One could say in Eliot's defense that Guernica was submerged in organized deception. Shortly after Colonel Jaenecke informed the Special Staff about the "total success of the Luftwaffe," orders were received to hush the German involvement. The minister of war in Berlin, Field Marshal von Blomberg, cabled the Legion's High Command repeatedly, asking who was responsible for bombing Guernica. The reply was "Not Germans." Clearly, orders had been given to deny the action (Thomas and Morgan Witts 285) and the question is: who had given them? Ribbentrop, the German ambassador in London, asked General Hugo von Sperrle, who commanded the German forces in Spain, if it would be possible to send an international fact-finding commission to Guernica, to convince the world that German planes had not destroyed the town. In 1974, Condor Legion pilot Von Knauer remembered that explosive specialists were sent to Guernica to remove the remainders from the tailfins of the bombs, duds, and other evidence. Only then was Ambassador Ribbentrop notified that he could send a commission (Brieden, Dettinger, and Hirschfeld 73).

The Franco government itself sent a commission, which unsurprisingly established that Guernica had been destroyed by fire after a bombing that the report claimed had been minimal and the number of victims not above one hundred. The same report blamed the republicans for explosions that went on after the air raid and for preventing the putting out of fires, suggesting that they were responsible for starting them. In Great Britain, Sir Arnold Wilson MP used the commission's report to discredit *The Times* correspondent, G. L. Steer, who had broken the news of the bombing. Oddly, Wilson credited a Franco commission with impartiality, finding comfort, like Eliot, in the notion that truth is the compromise that refutes two contradictory statements (*Guernica* vi).

If Guernica had been a "great success," in Colonel Jaenecke's euphoric words, no one was rushing to claim it. The Germans were incommoded and decided to hush the whole affair. Werner Beumelburg does not allude to it in his history of the Condor Legion, *Kampf um Spanien* (1939), nor does Karl

Georg von Stackelberg's *Legion Condor. Deutsche Freiwillige in Spanien*, of the same year. And it is completely overlooked in the booklet devoted by the Reich's propaganda department to the Luftwaffe's Civil War campaign. This is an expedition book with pictures showing the pilots' exploits and their moments of leisure in an exotic southern country. But while no reference to Guernica appears in this profusely illustrated book, the reproduction of Hitler's reception speech to the returning German pilots in Berlin's Lustgarten made it clear that the terror that had revolted the world was not expected or even wished to be forgotten:

> If the international warmongers should ever realize their intentions of attacking the German Reich, their attempt will meet with a repulse from the German people and the German army, of which the propagandists for the encirclement [of Germany] do not yet seem to have an appropriate idea. In this sense, my comrades, your fight in Spain was as much a lesson for our enemies as a fight for Germany.

While the Germans were willing to forego the propaganda value of their bombing exercise, the Spanish Nationalists denied any link between the air attack and Guernica's destruction. Only toward the end of the Franco regime did the Nationalists admit that Guernica was destroyed by bombing but, passing the blame entirely to their former allies, insisted that it did not happen with their previous knowledge or consent. However, Herbert Southworth, author of the best researched book on the bombing of the Basque city, cites a telegram, previously published by pro-Franco historian Vicente Talón, sent on 7 May 1937 from Franco's headquarters to the Condor Legion for the information of Berlin. This telegram restates the thesis of limited tactical bombing and subsequent destruction by arson, but it admits that the attack was requested by front-line units "directly to Aviation," that is, to the Nationalist air command, which would have transmitted the request to the German pilots. The action, states the telegram, consisted in the bombing of crossroads; lack of visibility, however, caused bombs to fall on the town, which the Reds proceeded to set on fire (cit. Southworth 372). For the purpose of informing the Condor Legion, the telegram was useless, its obvious intention being to cover up for the pilots vis-à-vis the Berlin authorities, which were plainly meant to be kept in the dark. Had Berlin known the facts, Salamanca would have had no reason to ask the Condor Legion to furnish its superiors in Germany a story that both the Spanish Nationalists and the German pilots knew to be false (Southworth 372–3). Hence, despite its occultation of the full extent of the bombing, the telegram acknowledges that it was ordered by the Rebel Air Command. This admission strengthens the hypothesis that Guernica was destroyed because of its symbolic status for the Basques, with the intention of cowing Bilbao into surrender.

The Nationalist story benefited from the attitude of the neutral countries. In France not only did the Havas news agency suppress father Onaindia's eyewitness account, but it distributed a false report favoring the Nationalists. Neither of these actions could have taken place without the knowledge of the Quai d'Orsay. For its part, the British government allowed the Nazis to slander *The Times* while keeping secret the information sent by Ralph Stevenson, its consul in Bilbao (Southworth 397).

The dispute about Guernica was no mere propaganda war but an effort to determine the moral level of the times. Once the concept of total air warfare, advocated by Giulio Douhet in his 1921 book *The Command of the Air*, had been put into practice, the responsibility for infringing the hitherto accepted "rules of engagement" in battle proved too heavy to shoulder in face of the indignation it provoked. Admitting responsibility would have crushed the Nationalists' carefully groomed image of Christian knighthood. For breaking the taboo on the massive targeting of civilians, the Germans played the role of midwife. They furnished the technological and military efficiency without regard to humanitarian considerations. But the Nationalists, in their decision to use borrowed air power to terrorize civilians, were like Faust postponing the day of reckoning. To judge by their convoluted denials, it would appear that they did not immediately grasp how far behind they had left the human consensus on what war justifies. By raising the threshold of tolerance for destruction to the status of a new rule of engagement, they were opening an ominous door to the unprecedented murder of civilians in European and Japanese cities. In this way, the Nationalists' "no holds barred" policy became a sign of the history to come.

The term "sign of history" stems from Kant, and I borrow it from Jean-François Lyotard's application of it to the breakdown of the prevalent discourses of modernity. Discussing the philosophy of the beautiful and the sublime in Kant's third Critique, Lyotard points to the de-realization of the object of aesthetic feelings and the absence of an aesthetic faculty of knowing and proposes the relevance of the criteria of aesthetic judgment for the historico-political object, "which as such has no reality, and for any political faculty of knowing, which must remain inexistent" (168). Politics is neither a form of knowledge nor a positive object, because only things are real that can fill their concepts with intuitions. But the series of events that comprise the history of humanity is not a datum but rather "the object of an idea." In other words, the ideational character of history makes of what Kant calls "the common being," i.e. the being of the human collectivity, the referent of a phrase that must be either cognitive or teleological. If it were cognitive, "the common being" would be subject to intuitive perception and to the principle of contradiction. If teleological, it would be ruled by finality in organized beings, and in rational beings this means moral finality. Insofar as the facts of its destruction were disputed, distorted, or denied, Guernica remained on the cognitive or phenomenal level as a datum to be ascertained, for instance by the findings of a commission. But as soon as its status as a historico-political object came into view, it shifted to the teleological sphere, where it became a sign of moral finality, i.e. of human purpose.

The type of common being that regulates the basic human consensus defines a historical period. Any break with that consensus that oversteps the moral limits, such as occurs in revolution or in war, replaces the hitherto existing common being with another. In so doing, the break recreates the object as a new datum for the cognitive faculty, but cannot present this object as a datum for the historico-political imagination. The world grasped the material facts of the destruction of Guernica immediately, and it reacted to them according to the existing human consensus. But it took a considerable amount of time before it could endow those material facts with a generally accepted symbolic meaning; before, that is, the Guernica phenomenon could crystallize into the historical idea of Guernica. Far from being exceptional, this dislocation of meaning was within the logic of things.

Insofar as war pursues an ideal as well as a material goal, superposing some notion of human finality on what is and must always be the resolution of existing form into formless matter, the understanding of war is based on the confusion between the schemata of intuition and the analogies with which the mind works when it deals with ideas. The mind treats the objects of symbolic knowledge *as if* they were concepts for the understanding. Only this confusion explains why Guernica, a mere footnote in the three-year-long Spanish Civil War, could become an *ideomachia* where two competing historical speculations clashed. But symbolic objects are not phenomena, and their teleological significance cannot be derived from the laws governing intuitions. Hence, says Lyotard, "the progress of a common being for the better is not to be judged on the basis of empirical intuition, but on the basis of signs" (168). This distinction explains why many years after the bombing of Guernica some Condor Legion pilots, judging strictly from the viewpoint of their senses, still failed to grasp the upheaval around an action that they considered similar to others they had undertaken at the time. Thus Baron von Beust stated that "Guernica was not different from any of the other missions" (cit. Brieden, Dettinger, and Hirschfeld 77).

But if the historico-political is not an object of the intuition but an *as if* object subject to the play of analogies, for Kant nevertheless a datum (*Begebenheit*) does in fact exist that allows it to be presented to the understanding. This datum is

> the way of thinking of the spectators as it reveals itself on the occasion of this drama of great transmutations in which is expressed a taking of sides for one set of antagonists against their adversaries, a taking of sides so universal and yet so disinterested ... that it provides the proof ... that there is a character of mankind as a whole and (because of its disinterestedness) that this character is a moral one at least as a disposition, and this character not only allows us to hope for human progress, it is already this progress, insofar as its scope is within reach of what is possible at present. (cit. Lyotard 170)

In other words, the historico-political event is not an empirical datum, but the moral response that it arouses is. And since this response rises above the particular interests of individuals and attains universal validity as an expression of the moral disposition of humanity, it can be taken as a gauge of the progress achieved by the latter. Guernica was thus a privileged sign of history in that, by revealing the removal of the last holds on unlimited destruction, it also affirmed the moral disposition in humanity, not only through the outcry it provoked in the conscience of the common being but perhaps even more so in the failure of cynical nerve among those who were unable to rise to the teleological significance of their own actions.

CHAPTER SEVEN

Delenda est Catalonia:
The Unwelcome Memory

> In the year 1940 even the trees seemed mussed up.
>
> Josep Pla

T he worldwide surge of an ethics of memory in the last quarter of the twentieth century was kindled by that century's crimes against sizable human groups. Raphael Lemkin named this sort of crime "genocide" in his 1944 treatise *Axis Rule in Occupied Europe*. Shortly after, on 11 December 1946, the General Assembly of the United Nations condemned genocide in its resolution 96. Although the Spanish Civil War has often been considered the preamble to the Second World War, Spain has escaped the moral blemish associated with ethnic persecution in a way that other European countries have not. On the contrary, Franco profited from the legend of his protection of Jews (Avni 179–99; Rother) to ease his acceptance by the Western powers. Certainly, the atrocities of the Spanish Civil War pale next to the magnitude of the destruction in the Second World War and the enormity of the violence against Jews and other groups. There was a difference of scale, but also something else. For the first time in modern European history, a state organized the physical annihilation of an ethnic group. In Spain no such outright extermination took place, and despite the commission of human rights abuses, by 1946, Franco had begun to de-Nazify his regime and initiated a rapprochement to the West, resuming full diplomatic relations with the United States in 1951 and gaining admission to the United Nations in December 1955.

With Spain's membership in the European Union and in NATO in the 1980s, the Civil War seemed remote and the dictatorship anecdotal to the point that some historians disputed its fascist nature.[1] In part, this milder view of the Franco dictatorship is the result of his timely maneuver to

---

1 Stanley Payne, for instance, asserts that "scarcely any of the serious historians and analysts of Franco consider the generalissimo to be a core fascist" (476).

disengage from the Axis before the end of the Second World War while shedding the fascist rhetoric and ceremonial; but it is also influenced by the general assimilation of the regime's self-representation as a stern but on the whole lawful and orderly government. Dressing up its crimes in the semblance of legality was the regime's principal strategy to falsify the historical truth. The authorities of the New Spain went to the trouble of staging court martials with predetermined outcomes, often after collective trials lasting a few minutes. The so-called *causa general*[2] was a blanket process, largely on the basis of denunciations, for the purpose of prosecuting "those that had served or directly or indirectly aided the red-separatist cause" (Cenarro 291). Aiding indirectly often meant failing to join the military uprising. For this crime, people were convicted of military rebellion by the very rebels who had toppled the constituted government.

Francoism aimed to justify its illegitimacy by fabricating an epic of liberation from a foreign conspiracy, with the USSR playing the role of instigator rather late in the day. At the close of the Franco era, misrepresentation and distortion gave way to the strategy that I have called "disremembering." This refers to a deliberate eradication of memory as the perceived condition for freeing up the imaginative energies necessary for change ("Short of Memory" 90–1). Disremembering also takes place when the work of memory condenses long-term historical processes into disproportionately symbolic figures like Franco or schematic representations of the past, such as the various ideological reductions of the Civil War. The result is the flattening of historical complexity and the corresponding shedding not just of the diverse responsibilities but also of the consciousness of events, and thus of the possibility of understanding what happened then and may happen again within a different constellation of factors.

When public concern with the historical memory arose in the 1990s, it focused almost exclusively on the Civil War and its aftermath. The war's drama and the span of the regime that came of it eclipsed other events that had been no less traumatic or decisive in shaping the national consciousness of Spaniards. Today few people fathom how brutal the assimilation of the territories of the Crown of Aragon by Castile was 300 years ago, how radically the social and political structures that had defined the self-understanding of its populations for centuries were altered in the space of a few years. Perhaps it is inevitable that recent catastrophes eclipse

2 The *Causa general Informativa de los hechos delictivos y otros aspectos de la vida en la zona roja desde el 18 de julio de 1936 hasta la liberación* was launched by decree on 26 April 1940. The Supreme Court Prosecutor (Fiscal del Tribunal Supremo) was in charge of the investigation.

earlier ones. Because experience cannot be inherited, it is easily replaced with ideologies. Focusing intensely on a narrow strip of memory does not guarantee reliable knowledge of the past. On the contrary, often that intensity has the effect of shading other areas. I will develop this proposition in three stages, each introduced by its respective thesis. The first thesis is that the relatively recent popularization of the historical memory, focused exclusively in the middle decades of the twentieth century, serves as a screen memory for other events that are more efficiently repressed. My second thesis is that the evacuation of these unwanted memories dispenses with the historical logic that turns them into episodes of a historical constant. My third and last thesis is that the historical memory, as promoted by Spanish politicians and intellectuals, rearticulates the basic plot of nation building, fulfilling one of Renan's conditions for its success: in order to live as a nation, a people must not only have achieved much together; it must also have forgotten a great deal together.

Naturalization of the Unacceptable

I proceed now to develop my first thesis. Unless toppled by force, a regime of terror that becomes entrenched will remain influential well beyond its disappearance. It is not just that such regimes become rhizomatic and penetrate the inner recesses of the institutions, public and private; more importantly, they have time and means to shed their more violent features when terror no longer pays off. Continuity of purpose under a different legality explains why those who profit from the inherited narrative are loathe to revisit the past and keen to destroy its material traces. The case mentioned earlier of the disposal of bodily remains from a mass grave in Valencia will serve as an example.[3] In May 2006, the City Hall, long in the hands of the Partido Popular, started building in the municipal cemetery on the spot where a large part of the 26,000 people who were executed in the city after the war had been buried. Not coincidentally, this happened during the fluster of activity surrounding the exhumations of republican victims throughout Spain. On 18 May, as opposition to the construction grew, City Hall transferred 800 tons of soil containing human remains to a quarry in nearby Sagunt. Such breaches of basic humanity bring to light the difficulty of establishing a common discourse about the past in a society in which the impunity of some meant the humiliation of many and the complicity of all.

After the year 2000, the excavation of unmarked graves put in circulation gripping images of aging people gathered by the sites for the chance of

3 See page 73, this volume.

recognizing a shred of cloth, a shoe, a medallion, that gave away the identity of a skull filled with earth or a heap of bones. Nothing in these images suggests the visual reconstruction of trauma, but rather a narrative of abject silence on the one hand and arrogant triumph on the other. Yet, here too, as in the most shocking reconstructions of trauma, silence gives way to eloquent emotion. For instance, when an elderly woman tells of her desire to kiss bones that have been underground for sixty years.

Unlike the world-shaking images of the Nazi genocide, exposing the distress that underlies Spanish conviviality has not unsettled the political order. The pain was privatized for too long for there to be any political fallout now. At first, silence was ensured through terror, then by the rising standard of living. It all happened according to plan. If the victims nonetheless speak up, their voice is neutralized by the memory of the victors, who trot out their own dead to balance the emotional score. In any case, justice was precluded by the general amnesty that became the cornerstone of the transition to democracy, and then by the enduring convergence of interests that were the basis of Franco's political longevity. Discussions about historical memory are the last ripples of the conflict that broke out in the 1930s. What was once an all-out war now returns as an epistemic tension to define what will be known. Failure to achieve historical inclusiveness, to produce a history that accommodates the experiences of all concerned inside a general horizon of understanding suggests the persistence of a fault line at the core of Spanish society. In this context, to confront the material evidence of democracy's troubled foundations is not, as it was for Benjamin, to "seize hold of a memory as it flashes up at a moment of danger" (255). Rather, because of the fragility of Spanish democracy, discourse on historical memory often contributes to leveling the past. Not the poignancy of memory but its diffusion is what promises to heal the social fracture.

What the Tale Does Not Tell

Second thesis. Foregrounding certain ideologies as screen memories re-signifies the Civil War in line with a narrative that developed when the war was already underway. According to this story, the Civil War was the rehearsal for the imminent clash between communism and fascism on a world scale. But, as Dan Diner points out, the romantic iconography of the Spanish Civil War as a global struggle between classes and ideologies bypasses the complexities of the international power arrangement. "Spain was not the arena for a decisive round in a civil war over values spreading over the globe ... For decades, the opulent revolutionary portrait of the Spanish Civil War would help mask one of Nazism's most characteristic features: the biologism of its weltanschauung, located outside the horizon of all usual social interpretations of reality" (57). The same is true with respect to one of the Spanish right's deepest and to this day most unacknowledged motivations: its violent hatred of cultural difference, epitomized, above all, in their loathing of Catalans. The virulence of this odium cannot be accommodated within a romantic story of revolution and reaction, and so it is typically muffled or altogether hushed by reference to the general violence.

But the romantic plot that presents Spain as the advanced arena of the struggle between the two emerging ideologies overlooks the fact that in Spain both of these ideologies were irrelevant before the war. The ranks of Falange swelled quickly when the war began and, especially, after it ended, underscoring this party's opportunistic nature rather than its organic development. Communism grew as a consequence of the republic's isolation by the Western democracies, maneuvering rather circumstantially and not without difficulty into its postwar position as undisputed ideological winner of the conflict. Even Franco's hostility to the Soviet Union during the Second World War was more tactical than retaliatory, an offshoot of his stalling policy with regard to Germany's demand that Spain enter the war on its side (Beaulac 2). It was only later that he would portray himself as a timely anti-communist, rather than the anti-democrat he was all along. Never mind these uncomfortable truths, the tale of a Spain torn between fascists and communists prevailed because it met the requirements of both the Communist Party's strategic interests and the Generalissimo's survival under Cold War conditions. Thirty years later, the same legend, with democracy replacing communism, helped the regime evolve in the prescribed direction. By the 1970s, the Civil War had taken the back seat in the collective memory and the tale could be rewritten as the story of a clash between extremists with a very large mass of democrats caught in between. To the latter belonged many erstwhile Falangists and communists whose former militancy now it was in bad taste to recall.[4]

If in the last analysis all dead are equal, the political implications of each death differ, and history is precisely the articulation of those differences. In 1936, a part of Spanish society chose the path of violence. This part deserves eternal blame. But once the Civil War started, neither side remained

---

4 Conversely, in a more reason-defiant move, communism is presented as part of the struggle for democracy, which of course begs the question of the new split of the world into mutually opposing blocks immediately after 1945. Santiago Carrillo, former Secretary General of the PCE, the Spanish Communist Party, writes: "The time has come to assert more loudly and firmly than ever before that, more than a civil war, the Spanish war was the first round of World War II, which was fought between fascism and democracy" (16).

innocent. I am not interested in arguing that the violence unleashed by one of the sides was quantitatively and qualitatively different from the other's, or that the republican excesses resulted from a revolutionary situation which the legitimate government could not control. I am concerned, rather, with showing an aspect of the violence completely blurred by the ideological tale, a violence that was group-specific and fed by deep-seated prejudice rather than by the hostilities arising from the war. In the rearguard thousands of people were killed for their religion or lack thereof, for their wealth or their poverty; in other words, for their association, however superficial, with groups that the circumstances had made it possible to blacklist. We lack a specific term for these targeted assassinations of people based on their essential or circumstantial identities. But if, under certain conditions, to kill people for what they are rather than the choices they make in the context of belligerence falls under the general description of genocide, then such crimes, though committed under the mantle of war, come close to the notion of crimes against humanity. At the very least, they should not be confused with political or military casualties, or callously explained away as "war excesses." I argue that, in the Spanish Civil War and postwar, the violence that targeted an ethnic group as such was genocidal in intent if not in scope, and that this kind of violence was directed against the Catalans with a passion and resolve that transcended class antagonisms. Furthermore, such violence, rather than a footnote to the general conflict, was integral to the military strike against the Republic. And it was programmatic in the Falange ideology that provided the conceptual underpinnings for the New Spain. To subsume that specific violence under the sum total of brutalities unleashed by the war not only obscures its nature but the nature of the conflict as well. It is nothing short of deceptive. Ramón Serrano Suñer, nationalist minister of the interior, made it clear that the annihilation of the Catalans as a people was an objective of the military rebels from the beginning of the war. It was not analytically that, in the midst of the offensive against Catalonia, he reminded those fighting for the fascist victory: "There are many reasons for this war, but the principal one is unity" (*El diario vasco*, 1 January 1939, cit. Raguer 72).

Serrano was only one of many nationalist leaders who declared without restraint what today can hardly be said in public, namely that one of the principal objectives of the rebels was to solve the so-called Catalan problem once for all. He is echoed by Santiago Carrillo, former Secretary General of the Spanish Communist Party and a member of the Junta for the Defense of Madrid during the Civil War, who, shortly before his death, admitted the centrality of the Catalan issue to the attacks against the Republic (*La crispación en España* 35). Furthermore, he recalled that opposition to any devolution of power to Catalonia came not only from the traditionalists but also fiercely from the left (42). Many years after the facts, Carrillo voiced what legions of historians on the Civil War have muted, namely that the derogation of Catalonia's statute of autonomy was an overt goal of the fascist block united under the CEDA of José María Gil-Robles (80). For it was this region's stubborn persistence in its historical personality that Spanish nationalists considered a threat to the state; therefore, they were determined to eradicate not only its representative institutions but the Catalan personality itself.

Although Franco's draconian policies against Catalans cannot be called genocide, because he did not pursue their physical extermination, many were killed, tortured, and imprisoned for their identity, to the point that renouncing it became a condition of survival.[5] It was this compulsory renunciation, the constrained stepping into another social ontology, typical of forced conversion, that best describes what happened in the early forties in Catalonia. The unscientific character of the Spanish elites, responsible for the low predicament of biological doctrines in Spain, prevented anti-Catalanism from developing genocidal solutions. Nevertheless, ideological racism, that is, the belief that Catalans were innately deprived of superior values and destined for subordination to the values of Spaniards, was widespread in the 1920s and 1930s. This belief took the semblance of a philosophical axiom in Ortega y Gasset,[6] and turned up in scientific get-up in the pseudo-psychological investigations of Dr. Antonio Vallejo-Nágera,[7] but the

5 To this strategy should be added the bouts of self-hatred stimulated by opportunism. For an instance of this classic attitude among subject peoples, see José María Fontana, *Los catalanes en la guerra de España*, 195–200 and *passim*.

6 Ortega, asserting that "the industrial ethic ... is morally and vitally inferior to the warrior's ethic" (57), measured "the historical quality" of a people by its army's performance in war (58). While the implications of this stance for democracy are transparent, its ethnic implications are lost unless the book is historically contextualized. Published in 1921, this book was Ortega's reaction to the democratic challenge posed by the Catalan Lliga Regionalista to the Castilian monopoly on Spanish politics. The Lliga merged the interests of Catalan industry with the general interests of Catalans, much as Castilian interests were conflated with those of its traditional elites. From the military defeats of Catalonia by Castile, Ortega concluded something like a natural right of Castile to dominate the "weaker" ethnic group. Furthermore, his glorification of the warrior spirit was a somber reminder to Catalan politicians that their challenge to Castilian authority would ultimately be settled by force, the real test of ethnic quality for Ortega.

7 Vallejo, who was influential with Franco, suggested the exclusion of the children of the trading classes from the professions: "For the State and for Society it is dangerous that the son of a businessman or an industrialist practices the liberal professions, because he usually commercializes them" (*Política racial* 28–30). Given

disposition can be traced at least as far back as the turn of the century, to the medical poetics of Nobel laureate Santiago Ramón y Cajal (Sosa-Velasco 25) and the diffuse anti-Catalanism pervading the press and the work of many writers.

This unremitting state of opinion should have alerted scholars to the inadequacy of deriving the repression of Catalonia solely from the political conditions that emerged during the war. As I will show, abhorrence of Catalans transcended transient political dispositions and was a paramount incentive to destroy the Republic that, in the view of many Spaniards, had disgraced itself by granting limited autonomy to Catalans. The Spanish National Movement was not, as would later be portrayed, a reaction to foreign intervention, but the ricocheting of the return of Catalan institutions to the arena of national politics. If the Nazis pursued a politics of Germanization through de-Semiticization of German society, the Spanish National Movement aimed at the de-Catalanization of Spanish politics and culture. It would be wrong to push the parallelism to the point of equating the extermination of European Jews with the annihilation of Catalan society in the 1940s, but it is also wrong thoroughly to dissociate events that took place inside the same time frame, when the ideological commitments of the German and Spanish national movements overlapped. Hence, whereas the term "genocide" is not applicable to Franco's policy toward Catalonia, the qualified term "cultural genocide" is a fitting descriptor for what went on for a considerable number of years.

What happened in Catalonia between 1939 and 1945 was comprised in the first and second drafts of the Genocide Convention of the United Nations, which defined cultural genocide as the destruction of the specific character of a group by forced transfer of population, forced exile, prohibition of the use of the national language, destruction of books, documents, monuments, and objects of historical, artistic or religious value (Kuper 30). The disappearance of cultural genocide from the final text blurred the seriousness of the crime and assured impunity to offending countries. Yet, precisely this exclusion was a sign that cultural genocide had to be reckoned with. At the United Nations, it was the representatives of the colonial powers that opposed defining as a crime what was still common practice in non-self-governing territories (Kuper 31). In the end, the Convention accepted a proposal by the Swedish representative to add the word "ethnic" to describe the collectivities protected under the UN charter. Although meant to protect groups with

the identification of commerce and industry with Catalans in the 1930s, the import of Vallejo's advice to the Franco government in the name of the Hispanic race required no exegesis. Vallejo was aware of the Nazi Nuremberg laws.

a distinctive culture or language, in practice the word "ethnic" proved ambiguous. Its semantic spread was anthropological rather than political, and in the end it did not cover the national minorities in the West. Thus it came about that, despite an appeal by Catalan president in exile Josep Irla,[8] the UN did not stand up to Franco's policy of cultural eradication.

Recounting the Civil War as uniquely a class struggle obfuscates what went on in concrete historical space. Such simplification obviates the long-standing conflict between the industrial interests of Catalonia and the landed oligarchies of central and southern Spain, a conflict without which it is impossible to understand the history of Spain from the middle of the nineteenth century to the Civil War. It further obviates that this economic conflict was riddled with political tensions between a Castilo-centric Spain and a Catalan-driven federalism. For a century and a half, economic and cultural power had been shifting toward the eastern seaboard, making a political reform of the state inevitable. The collapse of the empire in 1898 was the waking call to radical change, but Spanish intellectuals could only think of restoring the Castilian ascendancy. The Generation of '98, José Ortega y Gasset, and scores of lesser intellectuals devoted their energies to salvaging the trappings of imperial supremacy within national confines. Catalans believed it was time to rebalance political power. The republican Constitution of 1931 met their demands halfway by providing a Statute of Autonomy for Catalonia amounting to modest devolution. But even this limited charter was unacceptable to a majority of Spaniards. The debates that took place prior to approval of the Statute in the Spanish Cortes reveal a conviction among the deputies that Catalan culture is intrinsically inferior and at the same time a threat to Spain. In the previous decade, Ortega y Gasset had summarized this sentiment in his assertion that "Only Castilian heads contain the special organs required to comprehend the great problem of an integral Spain" (61). And, in an ominous anticipation of what was to come, he had declared: "in the fact of being capable of prevailing on others can be found the indisputable sign of being worth more than the others, and thus of being entitled to rule" (*España invertebrada* 115).

Here was Hegelian logic at its least dialectical. And this logic had a following in Spain. During his time as lecturer at Mannheim University, Onésimo Redondo became acquainted with national socialist ideas, and

8 Irla informed the United Nations subcommittee of inquiry on the Spanish question: "As one can see from the features of Francoist domination in Catalonia (leaving deliberately aside the well-known mistreatment of political detainees, the murders and tortures, as well as the lists of cases of plundering and abuses of all sorts), the dictator took to heart the famous phrase of a degenerate king: 'Delenda est Catalonia'" (526).

on his return to Spain he founded the Juntas Castellanas de Actuación Hispánica in August 1931. This was the seed of the Spanish National Movement. Redondo was so taken by the Nazis' racial doctrine that he reproached the sister organization La Conquista del Estado for its lack of anti-Semitic activity (speech in Valladolid 1931). Redondo would provide this missing element after the two fascist cells fused into the Juntas de Ofensiva Nacional Sindicalista (JONS), which would later merge with Falange Española. "Spain," he wrote, must assert its racial spirituality and save the world, rather than succumb in a few years to the surreptitious force of an inferior people" (*Libertad* 8, 3 August 1931). In a speech pronounced at the headquarters of the JONS in Valladolid on 12 March 1932, he blamed Spain's decadence on Judaism, which aimed to dominate the world through capital, the press, and universal suffrage. In hallucinated rhetoric, he denounced liberal democracy as the instrument of an international conspiracy of Spain's eternal enemies.

Redondo may owe his virulent anti-Semitism to his origins in rural Castile, where the peasantry retained archaic memories of ancient religious struggles, or it may be the sign of his subsequent identification with Nazism. But, in Spain, anti-Semitism risked operating in a vacuum, unless someone could take the role of the Jews. At bottom, Redondo, like Spanish fascists generally, was more interested in ideological than in racial purification. He aspired to the sacred unity of Spain, meaning absolute Castilian hegemony, and thus he exhorted his fellow countrymen: "Let Castile utter the words of racial wisdom that prevail over the vast confusion of the moment: let it use its unifying force to establish justice and order in the new Spain" (*Libertad*, 10 August 1931). This ideal justified a holy war: "it is both legitimate and righteous to use the necessary violence against the barbarian international Marxism, against the anti-Spanish separatism, and against the freemasonry that has destroyed and defiled the Fatherland a thousand times" (*Libertad*, 30 July 1934). Less than four months after the constitution of the republic, he warned: "Catalonia is on its way to becoming independent. And this goal can definitely not be consummated without Spain perishing. Thus, we believe that Castile, the only region that asks nothing of Spain because it feels responsible for Hispanic life, will feel constrained to take up arms" (*Libertad*, 3 August 1931). One month earlier, Ramiro Ledesma Ramos' journal, *La Conquista del Estado*, had also announced a violent response to Catalonia's demand for autonomy: "Catalonia is not a nation that may claim this kind of rights. Even if Catalonia's separatist clamor were absolute, that is, unanimous, without one single exception, Spain should reply to its petition of independence with the language of artillery." Ledesma ended the article with a dire prediction: "If a majority of Catalans insist in blocking the Hispanic path, we will have to consider the possibility of transforming this land into a colony and transferring the armies from North Africa there" (*La Conquista del Estado*, 4 July 1931, cit. Benet, *Cataluña* 76).

The destruction of Catalonia's personality was announced from fascist publications and in the speeches of the movement's leaders prior to the insurrection of July 1936. When the war began, Catalonia was already the enemy. Its identity, above all its political resurfacing and the stirring of its civil society, challenged Castile's supremacy. The Spanish National Movement was revanchist in the strict sense of the word, a way of regaining territory that Castile considered lost to its authority. Redondo was explicit:

> Finally, we can say that our hour has come. And to make our warning more clamorous and Castile's excuse impossible, behold that the toppling of the anti-Spanish civilization [abroad] coincides with the sway in Spain of the anti-national state. Under these circumstances, Castile anticipates the pleasure of its impending revanche. (*JONS*, No. 2, June 1933; cit. Aparicio 172–3)

Spanish fascism was the promise of a Castilian renaissance. It flattered the Castilian peasantry with appeals to its racial superiority, stirring ancient anti-Semitic memories to bolster its resentment of the new bearers of the cultural difference. When the Valladolid deputy to the republican Cortes, Antonio Royo Villanova, a member of the agrarian group who distinguished himself in the anti-Catalan campaign, voted in favor of granting Catalan co-official status in Catalonia, he fretted that his decision was contrary to the Castilian spirit, observing: "I am certain that, at this moment, people in Castile do not approve what I am doing" (cit. Ferrer i Gironès 157). A cursory reading of the parliamentary debates apropos the co-official status of Catalan in June 1932 shows that the majority of the representatives of the young republic, including intellectuals like José Ortega y Gasset, Miguel de Unamuno, and Francisco Giner de los Ríos, passionately opposed the restitution of the linguistic rights of which Catalans had been deprived by the Bourbon monarchy.

For the fascists, the war was a struggle between Spain and anti-Spain. Like all negative concepts, the idea of anti-Spain could be filled with just about anything: Jews, liberals, communists, Catalans, and in the end the masonic-red-separatist hydra. But in order to mobilize people efficiently the idea required an implicit referent. Just as anti-Semitism smoothed the progress of Nazism because it was pervasive in European society, fascism could not have become the dominant ideology in the Franco camp if anti-Catalanism had not run deep in all Spanish classes regardless of ideology. Julián Zugazagoitia, the republican minister of Interior in the first Negrín government, and secretary of Defense in the second, admitted: "Franco's decree abolishing Catalonia's autonomy had passionate supporters among the republicans" (cit. Balcells 183). Juan Negrín, the last prime minister of the Republic, was one of them. When his government withdrew from Valencia to Barcelona in 1938, he lost no time voiding the Generalitat's competences and impounding its financial resources, prompting Antoni Rovira i Virgili to write: "Politically, the situation of Catalonia is worse today than in 1640 and 1714. Now people from other lands attack us from outside, and people from other lands boss us around inside. In this war, we Catalans are caught in cross-fire" (18). Manuel Azaña, the president of the republic and its former prime minister, wrote in his journal on 29 July 1937:

> Someone I know asserts that it is a law of Spanish history that Barcelona must be bombed every fifty years. The system of Philip V was unjust and harsh, but solid and convenient. It has worked for two centuries. (cit. Balcells 179)

Spanish republicans, monarchists, and fascists fought over the nature of government. On the national question, they were all in agreement. For Catalans, the war had an existential urgency; winning or losing made the difference not between this or that government but between having or not having a future, and thus having or not having a past. In his memoirs, Xavier Benguerel points out that, for Catalans, losing the war amounted to losing their self-consciousness.

> Often "to lose the war" meant for us "losing the country altogether" ... We were distressed by the idea of losing the small fatherland that we had recovered at the beginning of the century ... It was evident that this great undertaking was about to turn into pure loss; that everything whose anxious palpitations and tired, wounded panting we could already hear, but which was still historically alive; all this was the only history we had materially at hand to recognize ourselves in some tradition, some demeanor, some personality, and it was going to be destroyed, perhaps forever. (Benguerel 272–3)

A sense of impending doom affected other writers. In Mercè Rodoreda's great novel, *The Time of the Doves*, one of the characters says that the war has been thrust on Catalans; if they lose it, they will be wiped off the map. That prediction was born out by the events. Soon after the war, Francisco de Cossío, editor of *El Norte de Castilla*, wrote: "No more 'Esquerra' and no more 'Lliga,' no right-wing or left-wing, moderate Catalans or radical Catalans; all that is over forever. ... We made the war for this purpose and win it for this purpose" (cit. Benet, *Desfeta* 16–17). Even Catalans who joined the Franco forces were regarded with suspicion by their comrades in arms. Speaking their mother tongue was out of the question for those who risked their lives for the National Movement. As the *Diario Vasco* proclaimed on 16 April 1937, "Dialects or regional tongues have been a terrible weapon wielded by separatists and plunged into the heart of Spain" (cit. Solé i Sabaté and Villarroya, *Cronología* 35). In Franco's rearguard, people were fined for speaking in Catalan over the telephone and warned by the military censor against writing letters in this language (36). In 1939, the newspaper *El Correo Catalán* was suspended for three weeks for mentioning a conservative youth association, the Traditionalist Youth of Barcelona, by its Catalan name in the laudatory article published the day after Franco's army took Barcelona. In the event, the newspaper was punished for the difference between a "u" and an "o" and between a "d" and a "t" (47).

Since arbitrary violence requires justification, the fascists marshaled a rhetoric of national purity conceived in linguistic terms. There was one superior language, and inferior, bastard tongues. When Franco's army took the Catalan town of Balaguer, its press warned: "We do not want to hear the cretinous patois of the dialectal pseudo-purism artificially concocted by intellectuals on the payroll of the Lliga and the industrialists" (Solé i Sabaté and Villarroya, *Cronología* 41).

Spite against the industrialists, shared by the extreme right and the extreme left, was sheer anti-Catalanism. If Castile had been industrialized, the Falangists would have been pro-business and modernizing, like the Nazis. Territorial envy was explicit in some of the rebel generals' plans for post-bellum Catalonia. General Alfredo Kindelán, head of Franco's air force during the war, spoke in the 25th issue of the journal *Occidente* (January 1938) of plans to destroy Barcelona and Valencia. Toward the end of the same year, General Queipo de Llano declared: "We will make Madrid Spain's largest industrial center; Valencia will continue to be Spain's garden; of Barcelona we only want the building lot" (Pons Prades 67). The rebels' hostility toward the industrialists of the Lliga Catalana is worth noting, in view of the notion, still sustained by many scholars, that this party supported Franco's coup. But the Lliga neither took part in the conspiracy nor came out in support of the insurrection on 18 July. In fact, it declared its loyalty to the republic in the party's newspaper la *Veu de Catalunya* before the anarchists shut it down and began hunting party members. For all the idealism that some historians lavish on the revolution, the climate in the rearguard can be gauged by the arithmetic of the executions. In the course of the war, 383 members of the Lliga were murdered by anarchists, as against 108 Falangists. The FAI threatened to eliminate the most conspicuous reporters of the liberal press.

Francesc Madrid, Eugeni Xammar, Joaquim Ventalló, Agustí Calvet (Gaziel), Just Cabot, Claudi Ametlla, Josep Maria de Sagarra, Josep Pla, and many others fled from the anarchist committees, in some cases hours before the death squads came looking for them (Torra 152–3).

Expropriated, tortured, and often assassinated by revolutionary committees, some members of the Catalan middle class set their hopes on the army as the swiftest remedy to the breakdown of government. Does this mean that the Spanish Civil War was also a Catalan civil war? It means that, in the face of unleashed violence, Catalans were compelled to take sides, and often the side was decided by one's position in relation to the barrel of a gun. Those members of the Lliga who threw their lot with Franco for the sake of a return to legitimacy saw their hopes dashed. Catalan conservatives did not partake of Franco's victory except in subordinate positions, and then mostly at the local level. There were very few Catalans in key offices of the National Council of Falange or in the Cortes, not to say in the ministries, and no provincial governor was Catalan. As Carles Santacana remarks, Catalans were shut out from these functions, on the one hand because there were hardly any Catalan ultra-right leaders before 1936, and on the other hand because it was difficult to incorporate former members of the Lliga (Santacana 2000). Its founder, Francesc Cambó, died in exile in 1947, after working for Franco's victory as the lesser evil. How did Franco manifest his gratitude? Upon taking Barcelona on 26 January 1939, rebel army officers occupied the Fundació Bernat Metge, Cambó's cultural society, and destroyed his private archive because it was in Catalan (Solé i Sabaté, *Cronologia* 49–50).

Spanish nationalists did not draw fine distinctions between conservative and radical Catalanism. Or between Catalanists and Catalans for that matter. Even the Archbishop of Toledo, Primate Cardinal Isidro Gomá y Tomás, author of the collective letter of the Spanish bishops to promote Franco's cause among world Catholics, came under suspicion because he was accompanied by two Catalan priests on a visit to the Archbishop of Burgos (Berzal, cit. Raguer 73). The intensity of ethnic hatred during the postwar cannot be concealed with statements about the general violence against republicans. Josep Maria Solé i Sabaté, a specialist on this period, asserts: "The first idea one gathers about the Francoist repression in Catalonia after consulting all documents, data, names, and circumstances, is that it had a general character, affecting all sectors and spheres of the population" (*La repressió* 263). In this climate, the indiscriminate oppression of the working class was part of a policy of curtailment of the Catalan economy. In 1942, the Consejo Superior de Cámaras de Comercio e Industria sent a report to the government complaining about the low productivity of workers, about

50 percent lower than before the war. The reason, the employers argued, was "the worker's physical wasting through malnutrition" (Associació Catalana d'Expresos Polítics, 93).

Defeat had severe consequences for all republicans, but nowhere was the eradication of civil society as ruthless as in Catalonia, where repression went well beyond the political opposition, in effect redefining the everyday as political. "Separatist" was the word. There was a separatist language, separatist music, separatist sports and entertainment, even separatist names. In every Catalan lurked a potential separatist, who betrayed himself by his accent or the simplest reflex act. The less Castilianized a person was, the more likely his or her punishment. That is probably the reason why the repression was harshest in rural areas, where the population was uniformly Catalan and immigration from outside Catalonia negligible or non-existent (Solé i Sabaté, *La repressió* 268). What Catalans could expect from the new regime could be inferred from the demeanor of the occupiers. Upon taking Lleida, the nationalist troops shot the commemorative plaque on the cathedral's belfry, because it was inscribed in Catalan. If there remained any doubts about the intentions of the victors, the prebendary of Salamanca cathedral, José Artero, quickly dispelled them during the reconciliation Mass at the Cathedral of Tarragona on 23 January 1939 by proclaiming: "Catalan dogs! You're not worthy of the sun that shines on you!" (cit. Raguer 375).

The entire population was suspect. In order to work, people had to procure certificates from trusty individuals—a military officer, a Falangist, most often the local priest. Six weeks after the fall of Barcelona, the Head of the National Service of Primary Education estimated that over 1,000 Catalan teachers had been removed from their posts. The screening of intellectuals was far reaching. In Girona, 80 percent of all people in the areas of culture and the press were barred from any work with a public dimension (Costa, cit. Solé i Sabaté, *Cronologia* 108). At the University of Barcelona, about half of the faculty were dismissed (Casassas 330). Representatives of the principal Catalan institutions had been hunted down all along. In the early days of the war, Franco troops ambushed and shot Josep Sunyol, the president of the Football Club Barcelona. In August 1937, the Christian Democrat Manuel Carrasco i Formiguera, a councilor of the Generalitat, was captured en route to Biscay, taken to the Burgos prison, and sentenced to death. Franco refused to trade him for prisoners and himself ordered the execution in defiance of a plea from the Vatican. In 1940, the president of Catalonia's government, Lluís Companys i Jover, was arrested by the Gestapo at Le Baule-les-Pins (France) and handed over to Franco. He was found guilty of "military rebellion," which in the rebels' language meant that Companys represented republican legitimacy. On 15 October, he was executed in the moat of the Montjuïc castle in Barcelona.[9]

Thousands were put to death in those years of mock legality. Under the command of General Yagüe, "the butcher of Badajoz," and of Lieutenant General Orgaz, dozens of people were executed nightly at the Camp de la Bota, a stretch of beach at Barcelona's city limits. Overall, 3,385 people were sentenced to death by court martial, about 1.2 percent of the population (Balcells 248). Although this number is comparatively low and is matched by executions in other regions, it must be reckoned against the disproportionately high casualty count for Catalonia during the war, and against the size of the Catalan exodus. One-sixth of Catalonia's population fled before Franco's army. Those who stayed behind believed that they had no reason to fear the new authorities. The contrast between their confidence and the number of incarcerations and executions gives us the repression's true dimension. So many were detained that the adult population decreased more than it had during the war. Barcelona was full of prisoners. In the city's penitentiary, with capacity for 5,000 inmates, 12,000 were crowded. Other buildings were converted into prisons: a hemp factory in Poble Nou, the convent of Sant Elies, the Communications Palace. The fortress of Montjuïc, which had been used as a military prison throughout the war, now held republican officers.

One by one, the vital institutions were eliminated and civil servants replaced with personnel from Falange and veterans of the Franco army. On 28 January, two days after the fall of Barcelona, the Ministry of National Education shut down the Autonomous University of Barcelona and banned the teaching of Catalan culture in all disciplines. The Institut d'Estudis Catalans, Catalonia's elite research institution, was closed. The "Foot-Ball" Club Barcelona was nearly dissolved, but the regime decided to Hispanicize its name, changing it to Club de Fútbol Barcelona, to eliminate the Catalan flag from the club's escutcheon, and to nominate its presidents and the members of the Executive Board. Even then, the club, unlike its rivals, was hindered from recruiting foreign players, and whenever it was convenient, its team could be reminded of its obligation to lose.[10] The general director of

---

9 One of the first decrees of the rebels declared: "All those opposed to the triumph of the Movement to save Spain will be executed after extremely summary trial, no matter what means they use to attain their perverse objective" (cit. Josep Fontana 19).

10 In 1943, during the first leg of the semifinal of the Copa del Generalísimo, F.C. Barcelona had beaten Real Madrid 3–0. Before the start of the second leg, the Director General for State Security visited the dressing room and reminded the Barcelona players that they played only thanks to the regime's generosity. Real Madrid won that game 11–1.

the principal Savings and Loan Association, La Caixa, Josep M. Boix i Raspall, was court-martialed and condemned for "assisting the rebellion," meaning quite simply that he had not resigned his position during the war (Solé i Sabaté, *Cronologia* 120). Choral societies and the hiker's association Centre Excursionista de Catalunya were outlawed, and libraries and publishers' warehouses purged of Catalan books. The house of Pompeu Fabra, the eminent philologist who standardized the Catalan language, was ransacked and his superb library burned in the street. He had fled to France a few days earlier. Prewar marriages were invalidated because they had been logged in Catalan in the civil registry, and even death certificates were rejected unless they were in Spanish.

Over time, the repression changed according to the regime's assessment of the international situation. From 1939 to 1943, that is, until the end of the battle of Stalingrad, there was generalized violence and a blatant substitution of Spanish for Catalan culture. From 1944 to the early 1950s, the aim was assimilation through the promotion of cultural production in Spanish while keeping Catalan culture away from the public. The strategy now was to interrupt the cultural transmission, and everything was done to degrade Catalan to the level of a patois. Now it was no longer strictly forbidden, but it was not authorized. After Franco signed the treaty of cooperation with the United States and the Concordat with the Vatican in the mid-1950s, the repression became subtler: limited manifestations of Catalan culture were tolerated, but nothing in the sphere of mass culture. Consigned to intimate circles, the language was expected to suffocate. Publication data shows how this worked. In 1933, publications in Catalan were 23.1 percent of all publications in Spain. In 1975, the year Franco died, publications in Catalan were 4.5 percent of the Spanish total (Solé i Sabaté, *Cronologia* 15). In four decades, a thriving market for Catalan literature had been destroyed and several generations brought up illiterate in their mother tongue. The use of Catalan, nearly universal among the popular classes before the war, receded during the Franco years and it has continued to shrink under the democratic governments, which have not been neutral on this issue.

The desire to stamp out the Catalan identity was unconditional. Even the name "Catalonia" was avoided in official discourse and often replaced with a vague nomenclature (the North East, or even the East, *el Levante*), just as the names of towns and of streets were changed to erase the topographic memory of an entire society. As late as 1961, Joan Ballester i Canals, who had experienced the Francoist concentration camps at the end of the Civil War, was sentenced to nine months and one day in prison for displaying a map of the Catalan-speaking lands in the window of his bookstore in Barcelona.

There is no point in tracing the persecution of Catalan culture down to the petty, cruel details. The data is hard and staggering. But it is worth recalling that the attack against this culture has been the most persistent attempt on a European culture in modern times. The fact that it was able to survive Francoism has often been used as an argument to play down its persecution. But if it had perished, who would remember it today? Another hindrance to the historical memory is a specific form of denial that questions the very notion of cultural genocide. To such skeptics one can only reply that, even if Catalans were not massively confined to concentration camps (although many were in such camps at the end of the war, and nearly 2,000 of them were transported to Nazi death camps in Central Europe),[11] their treatment between 1939 and 1943 was inspired by the Nazi ideology.[12]

In those years, Spain's relations with the Reich were strong. This is only logical, given the evidence that the coup against the Republic had been planned with the support of the German government (Carrillo 119–30). The Gestapo supervised the impounding of Catalan archives and their transportation to Salamanca to create a database for the repression. The Civil Governor of Barcelona, Wenceslao González Oliveros, welcomed Heinrich Himmler to the city on 20 October 1940, only five days after the execution of president Companys, and the Reichsführer-SS declared himself horrified by the crimes of the anarchists. On 10 October of the following year, seventy-five members of the Hitlerjugend visited the city. In the early 1940s, Barcelona was a support base for German submarines. German business opened offices there, and pro-Nazi publications were printed. In 1941, the Assembly Hall of the University of Barcelona, decked out with a huge Nazi flag and a bust of Adolf Hitler, was used for an exhibit of Nazi books and periodicals. At the officers' residence, a German room was decked out with Swastikas and presided by Goering's portrait and a sculpture of Hitler (Fabre, et al. 33–4). Nearby, on Diagonal Avenue, a monument to the Condor Legion was erected in memory of the German air force that bombed the city in terror strikes of unprecedented intensity. Azaña's musing about the

11 On this subject, Montserrat Roig's work *Els catalans als camps nazis* remains fundamental, and, in the order of testimonial fiction, Amat-Piniella's novel, *K.L Reich*.

12 Josep C. Vergés affirms that on different occasions he heard his father, the publisher Josep Vergés Matas, say that Franco, in his conference with Hitler in the closed railway car in Hendaye, asked the Führer to transport Catalans to extermination camps. Since there is no record of the talk between the two dictators or a known source for the information, it is impossible to validate Vergés' account. The relations of Vergés Sr. with people who stood high in the Franco hierarchy may have given him access to privileged knowledge, but arguments from silence lack weight. I owe this information to a personal communication from Josep Vergés.

need to bomb this city regularly was thoroughly and methodically fulfilled, although unfortunately for him it happened when Barcelona had become his government's last refuge.

None of this is part of Spanish collective memory, but it is precisely the blurring of its significance in the context of the 1940s that sheds light on our present. With this I come to my last thesis. The nationalist fixation on cultural uniformity spared most Catalans their lives but condemned them to die as a people. That purpose was not fulfilled during Franco's lifetime, but the foundations were laid for a goal that remains programmatic. But if Catalans are to disappear some day as a culturally distinct people, then it is crucial that the process should seem inevitable. It matters greatly that the memory of the new Spaniards be free of knowledge of the violence perpetrated against this culture. Only in the twilight zone where legitimacy overlaps with officialdom can attempts to alter the preordained course of events be denounced as unnatural: indeed, as the very cause that justifies renewed attacks on this stubborn relic of freedom. Renan's observation that a nation rests on collective forgetting is now being put to the test.

The need to forget is historically modulated. In the mid- and late 1970s, a blanket forgetting was advanced as the condition for Spain's democratization. More recently, revisionism has taken the form of denial. Despite the availability of documentary proof and a rich testimonial literature, a reversal theory came into circulation, according to which, Spanish is now persecuted in Catalonia. It would take another chapter to show that whatever linguistic, cultural, and collective economic discrimination exists today still displays the classic coercion of a minority by the majority through the apparatus of the state. The urgent question in this regard is: how did cultural discrimination obtain a good conscience? The short answer is: it never had a bad one. Franco became a convenient catalyst of responsibility for policies that condensed centuries of domination, an ideological scapegoat for a nation eager to abject its ethnic hatred, which at a certain point evolved toward a final solution of the Catalan problem. The solution did not prove quite final, but its failure does not justify the *post hoc, propter hoc* argument, whereby the insufficiency of the effect proves the inexistence of the cause.

The argument goes like this: if Catalan society survived the dictatorship with comparatively high economic development, then Franco could not have been really anti-Catalan. And if there was no cultural genocide, then the bemoaned contrast between Catalan culture before and after the Civil War must be a nationalist fabrication. If nonetheless the data bears out the claim that Catalan culture was devastated in the 1940s and has been tottering on the brink of extinction ever since, then, its enemies argue, the replacement of Catalan by Castilian culture evinces the natural decay of an inferior culture in contact with a superior one. In this way, post-Franco society comes full circle to the Darwinian notions about cultures once embraced by the European fascisms.

The state of denial in which many Spaniards find themselves with regard to Catalonia's claim on historical memory begs the question: what role does denial play in the formation of a democratic society? If any form of genocide, including the cultural, calls for a reform of the polity that malfunctioned in the past, reform must begin with the discourses that define the identities of the groups involved. I have contended that to assign all responsibility to Franco, or even to Francoism, is a severe misrepresentation of the facts. Minorities are not oppressed without the complicity of a great part of society. Unfortunately, this truth has made little progress in Spain, where the facts have not been assimilated. Still, a society can be healed only through self-analysis and a reorientation of its attitude toward the erstwhile victims.

We would come nearer to understanding the Spaniards' infatuation with the historical memory if we could relate it to the roles discerned by trauma theory in relation to severe abuses of human rights. Extrapolating from trauma theory is not abusive, because its basic plot does not hinge on the extreme of genocide but is apt to describe other forms of collective assault. Typically, those who work on historical memory tend to focus on the roles of victims and perpetrators. But, even when disputed, these are fairly straightforward categories. The intellectually challenging role is the bystander's. In presence of the bystander, questions inevitably arise: what was his or her share in the fate of the victim? How much exegetical latitude is the bystander allowed? At what point is inaction guilty? Is the bystander morally obliged to bear testimony? What is his or her responsibility as a member of the culture that exerted violence against a minority? Was the bystander critical, complicit, or neutral? And what does neutrality mean in a context of mounting prejudice and looming violence?

I do not presume to have answers to all these questions. My undertaking was more modest. It was to show that, as the era of perpetrators gave way to that of bystanders, the emergence of concern for the historical memory makes it possible to deepen the shadows around the zones of intense illumination. Does the renewed discourse on behalf of the victims of the Franco repression pursue another factitious consensus, which, like the pact of silence during the transition, liquidates the issue of the victimized minorities and allows the Francoist idea of unity to set? If so, the staging of the historical memory signals a general failure of the responsibility to remember those aspects of the past that cast an unfavorable light on our culture. As with trauma, what is done to and through the historical memory raises questions about the attendant roles. But, unlike what happens in actual violence, in the work of symbolic violence perpetrators can do little without a receptive audience. The bystander has become the arbiter of the historical memory. This figure may soon be called upon to decide whether the perpetrators will again ride the crest of the tide.

CHAPTER EIGHT

Allez, Allez!
The 1939 Exodus from Catalonia and Internment in French Concentration Camps

> All at once, Martí Carulla left the group behind and found
> enough courage in himself to start running. He stopped, raised
> his arms emphatically and after looking intently at the sky,
> kneeled down and placed his lips on the boundary stone.
> "I am already in France!" he shouted naively as he overstepped the limit.
> "You can't see anything but everything's there," he said affected, "Martí, since
> you're already in France, can you tell me when are we going to return?"
> "Don't think about returning; it's a loser's idea."
> "Are we anything else?"
> No one replied. We crossed the border, drenched in moonlight, silent.
> Xavier Benguerel, *El vençuts*

Xavier Benguerel's novel, *Els vençuts* ("The Vanquished") (1969), begins with the evacuation of Barcelona in the last days of January 1939 and ends when Joan Pineda, the novel's fictional author, leaves the camp of Sant Cebrià (Saint Cyprien) in Roussillon. In the foreword to this work Benguerel comments on the paradox besetting the writer who hovers between objectivity and verisimilitude. Later, he would write in his memoirs: "In 1955, when I published *Els fugitius*, what was rigorously historical was objected to on grounds that it was 'exceedingly literary.' The way I have recently 'imagined' it in *Els vençuts* has been deemed absolutely verisimilar and logical" (*Memòries 1905-1940*, 301). The inversion of the reception between historical and fictional discourses calls for analysis of the status of historical truth in collective memory and of the role of testimonial fiction in revising epistemological routines in the present. In the case of Benguerel, the difference between the two texts mentioned is not in their adscription to this or that discursive modality (literary versus historical narrative) but in the method of composition and, above all, in the history of its reception. Benguerel wrote *Els fugitius* upon returning from exile in 1955, a time when the story of the losers in the Civil War could not gain a foothold in public life, and the experience of exile was lost on the generations that had grown up or lived in Spain after 1939 (*Els vençuts* 15).[1] This experience was incommunicable, in part because it had no semantic equivalent in 1950s Spanish life, then again in part because the biographical interruption experienced by the exiles entailed a rift in national and cultural continuity that had not yet been resolved and was potentially irresolvable: "Exile is a permanent situation; so much so that in certain moods I feel that all of us who returned after some years used to exchange looks, silences, strange and scarce words, which confirm the fact that exile does not end, that it cannot end" (*Els vençuts* 15).

By 1969, when Benguerel published *Els vençuts*, censorship was somewhat less stringent, and he found it possible to complete the subject "as far as my capacity and the current circumstances permit" (*Els vençuts* 15). Circumstances were different indeed, not only in terms of opportunity for the vision of the defeated, as this sequel to the earlier novel was boldly titled, but also because, if in 1955 sympathetic understanding was hindered by silence, thirteen years later it could be thwarted by surfeit: "it may be risky to try to arouse again retrospective interest for certain episodes about which much has been said" (*Els vençuts* 16).

If for years insufficient context precluded reception of the testimonies of the Holocaust, as revealed by Primo Levi's initial difficulties with the publishing industry, is it farfetched to speculate that negative context, in this case the stigma that adhered to the Civil War exile, might have prevented Benguerel from broaching the subject of the concentration camps in the mid-1950s? If in the 1940s Levi found it difficult to talk about Auschwitz, because of the shame that attached to the victim's degradation and because of the listener's inability to fathom the reality of the extermination camps, Benguerel, as a returned exile leading the drab life of the defeated, did not find it easy to surmount the psychological (in fact, social) hindrance to exposing one of the most humiliating experiences undergone by the Spanish republicans. Nor could he expect sympathy from a hypothetical readership in the Western democracies, if France itself, sitting at the victors' table, hushed the reality of its concentration camps.

In 1969, when he revisited the theme of the republican exodus, Benguerel admitted to the "serious error" of not "'going into' the hideous French

1 The censorship objected to the title of the book. It was published under the personal responsibility of historian Jaume Vicens Vives.

concentration camps" (*Els vençuts* 15). But he also confessed his decision to write "the new work that a certain change of climate would allow me to move forward according to my intimate project" (*Els vençuts* 16). This new project included "going into" the camps as part of a testimonial account that, as he pointed out, was "imagined," even if prompted by "great responsibility" (*Els vençuts* 16). The extent to which it was "imagined" becomes apparent in the episodes in his memoirs that depart significantly from the novel, in that Benguerel himself was never confined to a concentration camp. He crossed the border through a mountain pass, the Coll de Manrella, and was sent by gendarmes on to the border town of El Voló (French Le Boulou), where thousands of republicans were massed prior to their internment. Benguerel was fortuitously rescued from this fate, taken to Perpignan, and then to a writer's hostel in Roissy-en-Brie before his passage to South America was paid by the Catalan Center in Santiago de Chile.

Thus, he avoided the cold, hunger, lack of hygiene, disease, neglect and shame, humiliation and abuse, sadness, and death that thousands of men, women, and children suffered in so-called shelters for months and even years. It may have been from a sense of unmerited privilege that he felt compelled to write about the camps *as if* he had not been separated from the mass of refugees. After avowing the "grave error" of not "going into" the camps, he made this theme the focus of his new novel, where his "imagined" account achieves the effect, as he put it, of seeming "verisimilar and logical" (*Memòries* 301). This verisimilitude owes a great deal to Jaume Pla's report of his experience in the camp of Sant Cebrià, but also, I suggest, to Benguerel's remorse for dodging the fate of his equals, a feeling that underlies his effort to empathize with them and account for their misfortune. In the foreword to *Els vençuts*, he writes: "If the reader of this new book does not realize that many of its pages were written anxiously, with a feverish hand and with immense, incalculable regret, I will consider that I have failed in my purpose" (*Els vençuts* 16). The keyword here is *recança*, regret for having done or neglected to do something.

Regret powers memory and disciplines writing, providing the "as if" or "imaginary" dimension that turns fiction into testimony. If Benguerel's partly fictional, partly autobiographical narrative lacks the authority of the personally and somatically experienced, it nevertheless wields the authority of the literarily effective. In fact, not a few accounts of concentration camps by actual internees adopt conspicuous novelistic traits, and some even the luxury of the lyrical. Agustí Bartra's "Crist de 200.000 braços," for instance, rejects the idea that camp life can be adequately represented through mimesis and resorts instead to an extraordinary image verging on the surreal. "At the camp, the usual images of life belonged to a past in which everyone dived in search of his own lost time, in an irascible copula between imagination and phantoms arising from dreams" (*Crist de 200.000 braços* 127). One hundred thousand men exposed to the cold, the rain, and the wind on the Argelès beach must come to terms with a reality that can no longer be deciphered through the repertoire of accustomed images. Lack of a visual vocabulary capable of articulating the unbelievable sends the captives on a Proustian search for familiar images through the fury of the imagination and the oneiric vapors of the unconscious. From this quest for a visual semantics arises the surreal image of the Shiva-like Christ that gives the title to the novel. This structuring image makes sense of the atypical experiences of the internees where everyday images fail to do so.

> It was an enormous city of defeat that imposed its vast unreal quality with its terse, concrete and fragile elements, a barren lazaretto for a huge lying torso with two hundred thousand arms. And its isolation from the world, the rigid siege that clustered them in one thousand naked lives, revealed above anything else the fear that pervaded an era of contempt for man. (*Crist de 200.000 braços* 127)

Although Bartra spent half a year in the concentration camp at Argelès, he also delegated the narrative voice to another writer. *Crist de 200.000 braços* professes to be the notebook of Pere Vives i Clavé, a camp mate of Bartra's who was later interned at Mauthausen and murdered with a gasoline injection into his heart. His internment and death inspired Joaquim Amat-Piniella's Mauthausen novel *K.L. Reich*. Thus, three years after becoming the chief character of Bartra's novel, Vives again received literary homage from a fellow prisoner. Through the fictional voice of Vives, Bartra proclaims the status of his work as a testimonial legacy stemming from ethical commitment to memory. "I seriously doubt that I will be granted the power to use what I have written here for a work that, if it were realized, would be the throbbing and moving testimony of someone for whom not to forget is the central duty of his soul" (*Crist de 200.000 braços* 163).

Bartra's book is fundamentally about the formation of a community of exiles, a mystical body collected from the *disjecta membra* of defeat and held together by the memory of common suffering and the triumph of moral survival. In my opinion, the humanistic values of this book belie the central thesis of Francie Cate-Arries' *Spanish Culture behind Barbed Wire*, which purports to show "how Spanish Republicans in exile begin to construe a shared sense of nationhood through the unlikely discursive vehicle of the French concentration camp" (33). Even if we accept that national identity was reaffirmed among internees who found themselves rejected, isolated, and mishandled as foreigners, it is hard to see how a "shared sense of nationhood" could have emerged from the camps, unless that sense had gone into them in the form of a lost cause and broadly shared feelings of social estrangement—in other words, through purely negative psychological dispositions. More importantly, what evidence is there of a shared national community spontaneously achieved in captivity, when that goal had just cost Spain a civil war and was at that very moment being relentlessly pursued by the winners through repressive measures?

Cate-Arries inadvertently furnishes examples of the dislocation between state and nation on the republican side. Citing an eyewitness of the last days of republican Barcelona, she glosses: "Mistral, amid her fellow Republican supporters frantically preparing to leave Barcelona, sees in the pieces of papers, these scraps of identity, the physical proof of a nation state in ruins" (27). If we turn to the actual words of her witness, however, we find that she does not mention a ruined nation state but merely "an organization that is falling apart" (27). What were those scraps of identity? What did they identify? How did they refer to a nation state that, according to this interpretation, was being destroyed, ironically, by its national army? As a matter of fact, the scraps of paper that greeted the rebels like tumbleweed in a ghost town came from the archives and centers of widely different political organizations, including the anarchist and communist, as well as various Catalanist parties. They came from newspaper offices and stockrooms, from militants of all colors, and from the Generalitat's commissariat of propaganda. Did these sectors amount to anything like a nation state? Throughout the war, they collaborated uneasily while pursuing widely divergent political agendas. With goodwill, such a precarious coalition of interests could be described as an organization, though perhaps more precisely as disorganization, but hardly as a nation state.

Another signpost of interpretive trouble is the witness who, shortly after leaving Barcelona, saw peasants prudently burning the republican and Catalonian flags (27). Where is the nation state in this cautious disposal of two different national emblems? Plainly, for these peasants, the *senyera* symbolized the nation and the tricolor the "organization," that is, the political form of the state. And this dichotomy, far from disappearing, was reaffirmed rather emotionally in exile. Benguerel, who is not mentioned in *Spanish Culture behind Barbed Wire*, relates his subjective moral pressure to write "about one of the probably most impressive chapters in our contemporary history" to "the single fact of having been a Catalan writer that perhaps helped me to fulfill ... my duty" (*Els vençuts* 16). On 20 April 1939, Agustí Centelles—the outstanding photojournalist of the Spanish Civil War—began a description of the concentration camp at Bram in the form of a letter to his son, explaining at the outset: "I write in Catalan so that whatever our fortunes and wherever we are—you, your mother, me and other members of the family who may be with us—you may have the pride and satisfaction of calling yourself a Catalan" (65). To add one more example: in 1969, exactly thirty years after his internment, Lluís Ferran de Pol recalled that during his stay in the camp of Sant Cebrià, he read poems of Joan Salvat-Papasseit to his fellow veterans. Thus, it was the poet of *Les conspiracions* and *La gesta dels estels*, not Machado, whom Cate-Arries presents as representing the inaugural moment of Spanish national identity remade in exile (37), that sustained the sense of national community for a group of Catalan soldiers:

> I have not forgotten that in the concentration camp of Sant Cebrià, in the Roussillon, under a torn canvas on a rainy day, my artillery men did not tire of hearing me read aloud the poetry of Salvat-Papasseit. Later they often asked me for it, and there, by the sea, with the snow-covered Canigó as our farthest horizon and defeat as our sole possession, we all huddled together to listen to "the fixed price of anguish." (Ferran de Pol 58 n. 38)

It would be easy to collect other examples showing the retention of the diverse national identities of the losers, who therefore could not constitute an "exiled nation" marked by a deterritorialized identity (Cate-Arries 31). This distinction does not, on the other hand, exclude their solidarity as human beings fallen on hard times. If we ask what elements were essential to the emergence of something like an exile identity, we should not appeal to formulaic concepts and must turn instead to the experience of the exiles. The beginning of an answer is provided by the citation with which I started this reflection. In the fictive reconstruction of the conversation between Benguerel and his fellow fugitives at the moment of crossing the boundary, we discover the border's arbitrariness and a sense of its magical, taboo-like efficacy. This border exists only by virtue of its indexicality: a boundary stone, a physical object that one can easily overstep, set in the middle of nowhere marks the transition from a spiritual domain to another. "You can't see anything but everything's there" (*Els vençuts* 89). "Everything's there" speaks of a vision of hope in the depths of dejection, of plenitude in the absence of concrete certainties, of illusion when in fact "you can see nothing." This is of course an expression of Benguerel's irony setting up the psychological terrain for the shock of disappointment awaiting republicans who flocked to safety in a country they believed to be germane to their values. To be sure, Iberian republicans who entered France through official crossing points like El Portús or La Jonquera did not find the border so easy to overstep, but the significance of the moment, overpowering the arbitrariness of the political division, took hold of their minds with no less consequence. Antoni Rovira i Virgili went into France through El Portús on 31 January, riding on the bus used by the Generalitat to evacuate Catalan writers. He reflects upon the moment of crossing:

> We know quite well that this part of France into which we have come is still Catalonia. But now the official line has a true meaning. We leave one state and enter into another one; we go away from the enemy's persecution and come into the protection of a different sovereignty. For this reason, I renounce all reflection on the Catalan identity of the Roussillon and on the fact that the state line is, in some ways, fictitious. For our group, the psychological moment of the change of country is this moment of entry into the territory of the French state.
>
> Regret mixes with joy. We are protected and are personally saved, but we are in exile. (Rovira i Virgili 157–8)

Rovira's wife looks back to the country they are leaving. On her mind is probably the question that Benguerel puts in the mouth of one of his characters: "When are we going to return?" Thinking of returning is a loser's idea, says another character, prompting the riposte: "Are we anything else?" (*Els vençuts* 89). This time the question meets with silence. The "everything's there" of exultant border crossing elicits the "we are nothing" as a self-definition of the exiles. Apparently, the concept of loser does not imply an ontological class but is merely the expression of bereavement, the sign of an absolute divestment of positive ties. Deprived of the credentials that go with having a home and civil status, the exiles receive a new, negative identity at the moment when their past is wiped out and no future can yet be discerned. Ferran de Pol expresses the losers' dispossession by means of the phrase "with defeat as our sole asset" (58 n. 38).

Defeat was in fact the first thing the fugitives experienced upon crossing the border. A few hours earlier and few miles behind the border, the dignity of the republican fighters still held up under the illusion of reassembling and taking up the combat elsewhere. "Now," says Avel·lí Artís-Gener in his memoirs, "the disaster appeared to us in its true dimension and this happened paradoxically when we were no longer facing the adversary, were not fired upon, and did not repel the attacks. What could have been a pleasant stroll through a peaceful land became the four-dimensional representation of defeat" (*Viure i veure* 3.8–9).

Congruent with their status as losers, the protection offered by French sovereignty was negatively qualified, amounting to the bare distancing from a murderous regime. Such purely jurisdictional safety was granted grudgingly and at the price of dehumanization. "Full of irrational authority, [the mobile guard deployed to meet us] meted out a harsh treatment without the remotest sign of compassion, which we sufficiently deserved" (*Viure i veure* 3.8). Of the half-million people who crossed the French–Spanish border in 1939, about half were interned in improvised concentration camps. For reasons of national security, and because the Spanish republicans were perceived as politically dangerous by the conservative French government, they were not placed in military camps, which were equipped to receive them; instead, they were massed in stretches of beach at Argelès, Sant Cebrià, and El Barcarès without a roof over their heads but prudently fenced off with barbed wire and watched by gendarmes and mounted Senegalese guards. Artís-Gener describes the arrangements at the camp in Prats de Molló:

> The "concentration camp" was an old vineyard on the side of the Tec river, with the badly shaved beard of the vines trying to breathe through the layer of snow. They had marked out its perimeter with loops of barbwire and Senegalese soldiers, who, passionate for a vengeance that was full of common sense, did not waste the opportunity to assert their presence to *whites* that represented oppression, and handled that limp mass with an irrational authority that was deeply rooted.
>
> That was all: the small hut [for the commander of the mobile guard], the barbwire fence and, inside, the vineyard, the snow and us. (*Viure i veure* 3.11–12)

Artís-Gener surrounded the words "concentration camp" with quotation marks to stress the inadequacy of the makeshift arrangements into which republican exiles were imprisoned. From his standpoint as a victim of French hospitality, the word "concentration camp" overstated the physical reality. But today French analysts refuse to call "concentration camps" the detention centers erected in French territory in the 1930s, preferring the euphemisms that began to circulate shortly after their creation. Marc Bernardot considers the term inappropriate inasmuch as French "foreigners' camps" (*les camps d'étrangers*) did not aim to destroy but to expel or, when this was not immediately possible, to segregate the unwanted inmates while waiting for expulsion (xx). He recognizes nonetheless that these camps became a repressive tool under pretext of an exceptional political situation. Under these conditions, the rule of law and individual guarantees were suspended, while discretionary powers were granted to the police within the space of the camp (Bernardot 121). But, as Giorgio Agamben states without circumlocutions, the camps do not owe their existence to the deterioration of ordinary law, but were from the beginning the intended consequence of suspending the rule of law within perfectly delimited confines: "The camps were not born out of ordinary law, and even less were they the product—as one might have believed—of a transformation and a development of prison law; rather, they were born out of the state of exception and martial law" (*Means Without End* 37).

The problem with appealing to the exceptionality of the political situation to explain, if not justify, the duress to which large contingents of asylum seekers were officially and deliberately subjected is that it tends to rationalize the exceptionality of the measures. In 1939, the exceptional political situation was not France's but Spain's and, in particular, that of the defeated republicans who crossed the Pyrenees fearing for their lives, some of them dying of exhaustion, hunger, or maladies contracted in the camps without benefit of medical care or hospitalization. Not to speak of the propaganda and the pressures applied to the refugees to accept repatriation that in many cases led directly to imprisonment or execution upon reentering Spain. In any case, the consequences of an exceptionality that mobilized national anxieties and xenophobia were grave and, as Anne Boitel points out, predicated from the beginning on a hypocritical terminology employed to refer to these sites of human "parking" (23).

Although the denomination "concentration camps" was used by Interior Minister Albert Sarraut for the centers created to intern the Spanish exiles, the Vichy government soon introduced a distinction between concentration camps (*camps de concentration*), such as Vernet and Rieucros and shelters (*centres d'hébergement*), such as Gurs, Argelès, and future installations (Burgess 207). But, as Boitel comments, "ultimately, terminology is a mirage, since life conditions in either case are dramatically the same" (23). Furthermore, the categorical decoupling between "foreigners' camps" and "concentration camps" does not appear essential after some of these camps became intermediate stations for the Nazi camps. This was true, in particular, of Rivesaltes, which in the summer of 1942 became a Centre National de Rassemblement des Israélites, an antechamber to Auschwitz, in the words of Michel Cadé, while still retaining a majority of Spanish republicans among the inmates (15–17).

On the other side of the border, republican exiles experienced an unexpected reversal of their hopes. Their expectation of finding again the civil rights of which they had been deprived was soon dashed. At the points of crossing, greedy gendarmes confiscated personal items, aggravating the refugees' state of dispossession. Profiteers swarmed into the border villages to exchange currency at abusive rates and to pick the spoils of defeat from people whom hunger forced to sell any valuables they had managed to cling to. In view of this reception and of the ensuing treatment, it is impossible to accept the notion that France observed the republican tradition of asylum

(Weil 206). On the contrary, what strikes the reader of the testimonies is the severity of the conditions and the persistent deprivation of basic human needs. As Greg Burgess puts it: "One seeks in vain a humanitarian impulse in the manner in which they were received and accorded asylum while under French protection. Instead, the gesture displayed in the admission of the Spanish republicans pales next to the overwhelming economic and security preoccupations of French officials" (Burgess 206). Such hypocrisy is captured by Benguerel's description of the first encounter with French authority shortly after crossing the border.

> Leaving Maurellàs we were stopped by two gendarmes on bicycle.
> "Refugees?" asked one of them, and without waiting for a reply: "You must go on to Le Boulou ... *Allez! Allez! ... Et maintenant vous êtes libres!*" exclaimed the younger one, smiling. (*Els vençuts* 103)

The refugees would hear the words "*allez, allez!*" many times while being rounded up and herded into concentration camps. This word would remain in their memory associated with mechanical repetition and dehumanizing intent. Thrown upon the sand of Sant Cebrià's beach in the company of 95,000 other internees, exposed to the rain and the cold with no shelter besides the sand in which they dug themselves to keep bodily heat from dissipating, the narrator takes the full measure of their situation: "Even more impressive was, on turning the other way, to see the swarm of black spots scattered on the sand, like small heaps of slag, of useless scraps, of waste ... Who had said to them the slightest word of comfort, of hope? Only that glacial, inhuman command: "*Allez, allez ... !*" (*Els vençuts* 185).

This command, remembered obsessively by many witnesses of the Spanish and Catalan exodus, is fraught with the quality of testimony. Through the years, it retains its peremptory concreteness. Its alienating timbre rings in our ear, distinguishing the lived from the imaginary, fiction from history. That word, reiterated many times along the roads of Roussillon during late January and early February 1939, was the single official communication, instruction, or advice offered to the hundreds of thousands who crossed the Pyrenees at the peak of winter to place themselves under the protection of asylum laws presumably in force. The order to press on to an appointed destination, made comminatory through doubling and iteration, appears external to the subject of enunciation; it is not this or that particular gendarme that speaks but the Third Republic and France itself. The word's paradoxical status between constative referentiality (its suggestion of a destination) and performativity (as a command, it brings about the motion it purports to connote) displays the grain of truth (in this case, the rejection and repulsion) that is the hallmark of testimonial literature.

Such vague, though by no means open-ended, directionality appears in retrospect as a clue, sign, or rule governing the fate of the exiles—a clue they were at first incapable of fully decoding without, however, being insensitive to its ominous sound. In time, the redoubled command became the symbolic referent for a narrative that took shape in the camps and precipitated in a plethora of stories voicing the experiences of thousands of people of all ages and walks of life. What these stories articulate was not, or not primarily, a new national identity, but more modestly a shared meaning that could then be reincorporated into the tellers' personal lives while being recognized or understood by other agents engaged in the social construction of the past.

It is in this becoming public of the personal that the distinction between fiction and testimony founders, a distinction that proved difficult to make by early readers of Benguerel's novels. And it is tempting to conjecture that the seeming fictional quality of *Els fugitius*, a novel based on fact, stemmed from its silence on the subject of the camps, and thus from an incomplete configuration of the actions and suffering endowing a particular historical episode with narrative meaning. In the time between conception and reception, the missing theme had been shaping the shared meaning of the protagonists and had already emerged—as Benguerel later admitted—as a full-fledged referent and potential organizer of the social memory of the vanquished. Ultimately, if the words *"Allez, allez!"* achieved the status of a symbol, if those four syllables encapsulated the refugees' experience on the yonder side of the border, it is because they were perceived as the expression of their newly found status.

If Paul Ricœur is right to say that, "in the final analysis, narratives have acting and suffering as their theme," then accounts of exile in France are quintessentially narrative (*Time and Narrative* 56). The actions involved aim at the most basic of epic functions, anticipating the survival of the internees without ever predicting a happy outcome, so that beyond representing sheer endurance in the face of hardship the narratives foreground the continuity of something like essential humanity. It is in and through these actions that the agents recognize themselves as the source of their deeds and thus, within limits, as masters of their own will.

The accounts of life in the camps are typically concerned with small actions: collecting scraps of materials to put a roof over people's heads, fetching the daily rations of soup, tending a companion who has fallen ill, taking leave of someone who is departing, cutting out a flute from a reed, or carving pieces of wood. These are all actions with a double import: a pragmatic one geared to survival and a symbolic one engaging the ethical quality of the action. It is this symbolic quality of work with no social transcendence outside the camps but with huge, immanent importance that draws out the ethical meaning of every action and every gesture. Whether undertaken in abnegation or insensitive to the fate of those around, whether purposeful or absurd, the trivia of survival acquires momentous meaning within the narrative. Telling the quotidian life of the camps from the point of view of their residents raises these minimal acts (rudimentary actions of a collective subject constrained to play both the role of Robinson and that of Friday) to the level of cultural re-founding. Above all, actualizing the potential stories inherent in the scattered experiences that made up life in captivity is continuous with those experiences. Such continuity between austere experiences that were entangled in a complex political and historical past, and the stories that bring that entanglement to the fore, transforms the "primitive life" in the camps into complex accounts of the breakdown of liberal ethics under the shadow of rising totalitarianism.

Benguerel's attempt to "stir retrospective interest for certain episodes that have been much talked about" was plainly an effort to maintain continuity and not let the suffering or the conditions that engendered it disappear into a dreamy and disputable past (*Els vençuts* 16). His novels, as much as the personal memoir or the intimate diary, were a deliberate effort to redeem the suffering of the vanquished. His attempt to stir retrospective interest joins similar efforts in projecting the horizon of the defeated beyond the limits of the barbed wire and to merge it with the reader's horizon in productive intersection. Fiction, in this broad sense, is not absolutely distinguishable from history. In the last analysis, both aim to make relevant for the present the actions and suffering of the bygone and the lost.

A hermeneutic approach to so compelling a discursive modeling of the past would shuttle back and forth between semiological anchoring points like the, in principle, semantically diffuse "*allez, allez!*" and the horizon of experience in which those words became ominously oppressive. Fiction, however, in the sense of a specific form of literary discourse, short circuits the interpretive movement between the anchoring points and the horizon of interpretation, collapsing the two into a form of presence that formally, if not existentially, is equivalent to the experience itself. Reading these works, we hear the ominous words through the ears of exiles who, after a difficult, wearing trek over the Pyrenees, reach the other side of fear hoping for a place to rest and recover. Semantically, those words are the opposite of a greeting, and this reversal of expectations stands for the sign of an absent welcome, unequivocal proof that desire meets its Other, and the latter becomes the negative condition of testimony.

CHAPTER NINE

The Corpse in One's Bed:
Mercè Rodoreda
and the Concentrationary Universe

I n the prologue to her novel, *Quanta, quanta guerra...*, published in 1980, Mercè Rodoreda observed bleakly: "Around the people of my time there is an intense circulation of blood and corpses. Because of this intense circulation of tragedy, in my novels, at times perhaps inadvertently, war, to a greater or lesser extent, is a theme" (14). This remark is often assumed to refer to the Spanish Civil War, which provides the novel with its obvious background, although this matter-of-fact statement speaks about a time, not a specific event—in Catalan, "my time" ("la meva època") is colloquial for "my generation," or, more precisely, the time of one's youth. This means, in effect, that Rodoreda saw her lifetime marked by an overabundance of corpses. But nothing in that phrase implies that she circumscribed her observation to her own country. It was not, or not only, in Catalonia that tragedy made the rounds. Rodoreda saw herself in the maelstrom as unintentional witness to the vast mid-century tragedy. That tragedy certainly included the Spanish Civil War, but also the massive exodus and inhumane internment in French concentration camps, which she was spared by being lodged with a small contingent of writers in the château of Roissy-en-Brie, an Auberge de Jeunesse some nineteen miles from Paris, courtesy of the French government. From there she moved to Paris, from where she fled on foot with the crowds that took to the French roads when the Germans marched in on 14 June 1940. Next, she lived in Limoges and Bordeaux, returning to Paris after liberation in 1944. It was there that she wrote one of the earliest literary pieces on the Nazi death camps, the short story "Nit i boira" ("Night and Fog"), published in 1947 in *La nostra revista*, a journal issued in Mexico by Catalan exiles. It was later reissued in the collection *Semblava de seda i altres contes* (1978).

"Nit i boira" is remarkable not only for its anticipation of the title of Alain Resnais' famous film with the script by Jean Cayrol, but also for the economy with which the author, who did not herself experience the camps, recreates the physical impressions and the moral deconstruction of an inmate, perspicuously placing his spiritual dismantling at the center of the concentrationary universe (to use David Rousset's coinage). The story begins with this striking sentence: "If all who are here could go back into a belly, half of us would die trampled by those who tried to go first. A belly is warm and dark and secluded ..." (294). More than *in medias res*, the story begins *in medias desperationis*. Its first sentence evokes the frantic scramble of people fighting to escape from the gas chamber while knowing there is no exit. Rodoreda does not mention the gas chambers, but her evocation of the desire to be unborn as a way of escaping an inhumane death recalls the desperate spasms of those whose nudity in a cold, dark, and closed room placed them on the tragic side of their impossible rebirth. The concentration camp as anti-uterus is a powerful metaphor for the extremity of an experience that a whole range of literature assures us is unrepresentable, a coercive truism that received its core of truth from the certainty of camp survivors that their knowledge could be fathomed only by those who shared the experience. In the last chapter of *L'univers concentrationnaire*, David Rousset wrote that "normal men do not know that everything is possible," echoing Goebbels' definition of politics as "the art of making what seems impossible possible" (cit. Agamben, *Remnants of Auschwitz* 148). Both Nazis and survivors were outside the realm of normality and normativity; to them the camps became a revelation of the limits of the rational apprehension of reality as foundation of knowledge. For Rousset, "They—survivors—are set apart by an experience that cannot be transmitted" (117). The electric barbwire had created a categorical distinction within the human species.

Rodoreda's story defies the implicit injunction against furnishing literary representations of the death camps *unless* one is a survivor. Only for the survivor, the argument goes, is the taboo on representation revoked by the duty to bear witness. "Nit i boira," however, makes no claim to being a report on the camps. Rather, in the tradition of the short story, it seeks to gain and communicate insight into that experience. That it does so with great economy proves, incidentally, that depicting credible states of mind does not presuppose identity between subject and object. One could say that in her articulation of the subjective core of the experience comes forth the essence of the mid-century tragedy, that its truth could be fathomed by anyone who listened intently to the murmur caused by the intense circulation of corpses and blood.

Starting with the irrepressible desire for a dark, enclosed space where one can hide, Rodoreda communicates the experience of total exposure in the camps, where life—*das Leben*—has become naked *bios*. The desire to veil existence in the dark recesses of being becomes the fate of the anonymous inmate whose monologue declares and also effects his withdrawal into the self. The narration opens a space of reflection in the instant just before death, much as Ambrose Bierce had done in "An Occurrence at Owl Creek Bridge" and Borges in "El milagro secreto." Rodoreda lets us eavesdrop on the musings of a man at the end of his tether, a Muslim. But if the Muslim, whom Agamben calls the "complete witness," is the one who cannot speak, and the speaker is the pseudo witness, then the questions arises, "Who is the subject of testimony?" (*Remnants of Auschwitz* 120). These are, of course, the terms in which Agamben posits the relation of witnessing to speech. Rodoreda's answer is implied by her choice of narrator. In her story, the Muslim speaks, but his voice is not an utterance. Inaudible, we hear it only insofar as it is ventriloquized by writing. Writing becomes the human agent of the inhuman, but in arrogating this function it mimics testimony, burying the original voice in the anonymity of narration. The narrative speaks for the dead because it is the story of a dead man speaking. Removed from life, the story is, quite literally, the dark and enclosed space of subjectivity.

"Nit i boira" thus refers us not only to the *Nacht und Nebel* code for extermination but also to the twilight zone where the Muslim meanders on the threshold of death. "Earlier, I used to say: pretend you're dead. That was when I had not yet realized that I am a shadow" (294). But to feign death one must be alive, and the Muslim no longer *is* in a meaningful sense of the term. Wolfgang Sofsky describes these beings, a creation of the death camps, as "nameless hulks" that are "still nominally alive" (294). Nominally alive but already gone. As the empty shell of a departed humanity, the narrator knows himself to be the projection of a receding life. "I am silent now. Nothing justifies their turning me into a shadow" (294). The survivor is supposed to write in shame, feeling that his survival was purchased with the sacrifice of those who were not spared. Primo Levi put it succinctly when he described the law of the Lager as "eat your own bread, and if you can, that of your neighbor" (*Survival* 160). Others have pointed out that exacerbated egotism was a condition of survival, or that the best were those who did not come back. Again Levi: "The 'saved' of the Lager were not the best, those predestined to do good, the bearers of a message: what I had seen and lived through proved the exact contrary" (*The Drowned and the Saved* 82).

Rodoreda proposes something different: to show or rather imagine the shame of the Muslim's voyage into silence, of that "I am silent now" of which only fiction can provide an insight. Is this witnessing? Certainly not by the accepted account. Rather, it amounts to paradoxical and not just fictional self-witnessing. For who really knows, except those who will not live to tell? Levi entertained no doubts about the limits of testimony:

We, the survivors, are not the true witnesses. This is an uncomfortable notion of which I have become conscious little by little, reading the memoirs of others and reading mine at a distance of years. We survivors are not only an exiguous but also an anomalous minority: we are those who by their prevarications or abilities or good luck did not touch bottom. Those who did so, those who saw the Gorgon, have not returned to tell about it or have returned mute, but they are the "Muslims," the submerged, the complete witnesses, the ones whose deposition would have a general significance. (*The Drowned and the Saved*, 83–4)

Hence, the survivor can speak of his shame when recuperating the moral yardstick of ordinary civil life. But this is a different shame from the shame that accompanies silence. Robert Antelme captured a sign of this ultimate shame in the student from Bologna who flushed the moment the S.S. selected him for sacrifice just hours before liberation (231–2). Agamben attributes the blushing of this victim to intimacy with his murderer (*Remnants of Auschwitz* 104). Going red in the face gives away the presence of shame, or so people believe; but nothing proves that it is the emotional price of survival, as Levi suggests in *The Drowned and the Saved*, where he relates survivors' shame to feelings of having been diminished. "Not by our will, cowardice, or fault, yet nevertheless we had lived for months and years at an animal level" (75). The student's sudden, morally inexplicable shame is brought on by the abrupt exposure to fate. It is the shame of individuation, of being randomly selected, an emotion akin to the panic of the lamb taken away from the flock.

It is not of this shame that Rodoreda speaks. She describes an affection that grows like a tumor in the body, pushing it toward death. Such shame is not called on by random murder but itself calls on the murderer. In her story, the Muslim embodies the law of the camp, according to which delaying death comes at the price of self-degradation. Primo Levi's "eat thy neighbor's bread, if you can" is the concrete articulation of this commandment, which took many forms, from abusing the elderly and weak to betrayal and denunciation. Infinitely worse than the liquidation of deportees on arrival was their programmed degradation, the escalated extortions and impositions that forced many to extinguish moral feelings and turn into accomplices of those who destroyed them. Rousset wrote: "Those who must die go to death with a calculated slowness in order that their physical and moral decline, achieved by degrees, ends up making them realize that they are damned, expressions of evil and not human beings" (72).

"Nit i boira" is a cameo study of calculated damnation. The Muslim in the story is made aware of the transference of the sadistic pleasure derived from extermination. "The more who die here, the more I like it. It is a joy so deep, so complex that it is indescribable" (294). Because internment in the camp establishes an ontological distinction between the human and the subhuman, he yearns for nothing as much as for people. "People sleep, get up, wash their hands, know that streets are for walking and chairs for seating. People are neat. They do their needs in a corner and close the door to keep others from seeing them. They have handkerchiefs. They turn off the light to make love" (294). It is the yearning for a world that has not been deprived of taboos and stripped to its primary egoism, a world with habits and memory.

On the other side of the barbed wire, such a world still exists. On this side there is only the stink. And Meier. "Meier died some time ago" (294). Meier was not "neat." He urinated in bed, and he was the narrator's bedmate. The first night the narrator felt his upper leg wet, he flew into a rage and poked a spoon into Meier's neck. His bedfellow responded by sinking his knee into the attacker's belly. Later Meier became valuable to him. When he died, the narrator pretended that Meier was ill and kept him in his bed for two days in order to eat his ration of soup. The corpse was not as repulsive as the living man, because it did not urinate. "And corpses ... one was used to them. For many nights now I had been sleeping with my head separated from a mound of one hundred or two hundred corpses only by the boards of the barrack" (297). Then someone noticed and tried to take the extra ration of soup. This led to a fight and the usual punishment. And then Meier was definitely gone. "An infinite sadness took hold of me and I nearly burst into tears. It was the last echo from the bright world out of which I had been jerked by the nose; the last palpitation of its sumptuous and complicated feelings" (297). Sadness for the corpse in one's bed is the last glimmer of emotion. In the camp, living off the dead is strictly forbidden; one must live off one's dwindling bodily resources until one is, like Meier, suspended between death and the appearance of life. Because survivors are stripped of the past, bereavement is an echo of something that happened a long time ago, something perceived from such emotional distance that long extinguished feelings reach conscience from moral years away.

Obeying the law of the camp, the narrator eats his neighbor's soup for as long as possible. Then, the nourishing corpse is gone, and the narrator sinks into *ataraxia* and becomes a Muslim. Loss of hope is quite literally the loss of a horizon. The future is the camp's first casualty. Whenever the narrator dares to think beyond the present, he realizes that he is doomed to live with corpses. If he ever got out of the camp, it seemed to him that "he could only engender children with the enormous eyes of the famished and with the monstrous sex dangling inside the slender arch formed by the legs" (297). Finally, he gave up such thoughts because children are only possible where there is "the love that moves the sun and the other stars" (Dante 297). Many accounts of the Nazi concentration camps allude to the *Divina Commedia*, but always to *Inferno*. Rodoreda quotes instead the last verse from *Paradiso*, the line that perfects the poem and encloses the God-made universe in its overarching law. Recalling the primordial law of life, Rodoreda recuperates the metaphor of the warm, protective uterus as the opposite of the concentrationary universe.

If love moves the universe, the camp paralyzes it. Emotion fuels the cosmos and the camp triumphs when inmates reach absolute apathy. One day, while waiting to unload a truck, the narrator put his hands in his pockets. A young S.S. lifted his fist to strike him in the face. The narrator just looked at him, waiting to be hit. Then the guard lowered his arm and turned aside to shout at others. "I shuddered from shame. First on his account, and then for myself. What did he see in my eyes? If I could only tear them out!" (298). Rodoreda's depiction of shame differs from Antelme's. In Antelme's true story the young Italian turned red when he was pulled from the ranks to be shot. In her tale the narrator is ashamed because he is spared. In both stories shame circulates between an S.S. and a prisoner, as the flare-up of intimacy brought about by violence.

But why does the prisoner feel shame for the guard? Is it because he witnesses the other's degradation? Because the guard is not the master of his own evil? And why is he ashamed of himself? Is violence suffered the ultimate proof of one's humanity? Do blows certify the presence of resistance in the prisoner's eye? But the expected blow never comes. And he asks himself: "What did he see in my eyes?" (298). It is the question about one's identity. But is it really a matter of seeing, of discovering what one is reflected in the other's hatred? Or is it, rather, a matter of not seeing, of the opaqueness of a lurking will, or of the hollowness of inert matter? "To be invisible. Invisible like a thing. Eyes glide over it, tracing its outline" (299). When the S.S. lowers his fist, is it because his gaze meets a moral corpse? In the prisoner, does he see only a shadow of a man? At any rate, one does not strike at shadows.

Rodoreda identifies degradation with the demise of a horizon. Death is the boundary of the subject's investments and the limit to its happiness but also to its unhappiness. But for this to be true, death must remain virtual, the edge of one's being, a line always ahead. Once death installs itself in consciousness, time disappears. And since time is the essence of the human, it is also the condition of futurity. "Here I have been sinking into this unlimited suspension, peacefully" (299). Instinct comes full circle and turns against itself, like the panic-stricken victims trampling each other in the gas chamber, trying to reverse life, to undo birth, to return to the uterus. No image of despair is more powerful than a person struggling to be unborn, and with this unbirthing Rodoreda's character consummates his expiation. Recently, the guards discovered a man hiding in a corner and struck him with shovels until he died like a rat. They now come back every day hoping to find someone else there. In this corner the narrator holes up and waits for the S.S. to find him and erase his conscience. Again, Rodoreda shows at work the psychological law in which Rousset summarized the system of self-immolation that constituted the secret aim of the camps: "Psychologically, it [the deeper nature of the camps] relies on the sadism of forcing the prisoners to secure the instruments of their annihilation" (73).

The victim will always find in himself psychological resources that the Nazi can tap. One of the most striking moments in the story is this characteristically Rodoredian vignette.

> At home, when I was young, we had a fishbowl with three goldfish ... I came up to the bowl and took out one fish. It struggled franticly in my hand ... It had a white spot on the side of his back: the other two were all red. I put it back in the water. When it looked like it had recovered, I took it out again. Then I put it back. I took it out once more and kept doing it until it died. I did it for fun, to see what it would do, not really wanting it to die ... For this reason, at the camp, I was happy not to have a white spot. (295)

An arbitrary mark of difference, a stigma can prove fatal. Six-pointed star, Slavic traits, signs of irretrievable exhaustion, whatever the discriminating gaze of the kapo or the guard fixes on amounts to a death sentence. The main thing is not to be seen, to become transparent, and for that one needs the others. The narrator muses that if he could have made the others walk, it would all have finished quickly. He has discovered the idea of the death march, implemented in the last days of the war. "This mass of men, of silt, would have melted, but then I would have remained alone. And they would have seen me. I would have become visible" (295). To survive, one needs the other fish in the bowl. But, more importantly, concealment is a condition of survival. To stand out, to have volume and relief proves fatal. Individuality is the source of shame, and shame is the body's reaction to the soul's exposure. Hence the question: "What did he see in my eyes?"

Rodoreda's narrator does not survive his shame and thus cannot become a witness, if the witness is he who writes or speaks out of shame. The shame that outlasts the narrator makes him rather a "complete witness," in that it enfolds him in the unsayable, like the uterus of a concealed truth. Paradoxically, it is to the unsayable that we listen through fiction's capacity to produce presence out of silence. But if this is not testimonial literature, then what is it? And, more intriguingly, where did Rodoreda obtain such profound knowledge about the camps? She might have known Rousset's book, she could also have read the fragments of *K.L. Reich* that Joaquim Amat-Piniella published in 1945 in *Per Catalunya*. She could have been informed by Pierre-Louis Berthaud, a survivor of Dachau who had been active in *Revista de Catalunya* and was a friend of many Catalan writers. Or she could have talked to any of the returning prisoners who were lodged in the Hôtel Lutétia in Paris, very near the apartment where she rented a *chambre de bonne* in 1946. Whatever the answer to this small mystery, her grasp of the mission of the camps as laboratories for the testing of biological Darwinism forces us to revise the categorical distinction between witness reports and imaginative accounts of radical evil. It drives home Agamben's claim that bearing witness by proxy means "that there is no one who claims the title of 'witness' by right" (*Remnants of Auschwitz* 120).

CHAPTER TEN

Transatlantic Reversals:
Exile and Anti-History

People often quote the sixth of Benjamin's *Theses on the Philosophy of History*, the one that warns that *"even the dead* will not be safe from the enemy if he wins,"* without fathoming its actuality. The "if" in this sentence is rhetorical, for Benjamin famously added: "And this enemy has not ceased to be victorious" (255). And, although we love that phrase, we rarely remember the one immediately preceding it. The one that calls for something like a permanent epistemic revolution: "In every epoch, the attempt must be made to deliver tradition anew from the conformism which is on the point of overwhelming it." The dead, by which Benjamin clearly does not mean those honored by the victor but those sacrificed for the sake of the tradition, will certainly not be safe if our revolt is merely an excuse to leave things as they are, or, worse yet, to deflect toward conservative goals the sympathetic insight that alone can redeem the past.

Modern Spanish identity has always been a postcolonial identity. The reason for this is that Spain constituted itself as a nation after being severed from its sprawling body across the seas. Decapitated, the crowned head of the empire, the capital addicted to command and an extractive economy, reconstituted itself as the head of a nation state. Not without difficulty or violence. The twin processes of decolonization and nationalization were visualized for the first time in the emergency constitutional assemblies of 1812, the so-called Cortes de Cádiz, which declared the inhabitants of Spain's American possessions free co-nationals of the Europeans, while according them unequal representation (Fradera 66–8). The full-fledged ideological outgrowth of that foundational moment for the nation was the literature of the Generation of '98 and the so-called "problem of Spain" around which it coalesced. Concomitant with this problem was the formulation of the ethnicist doctrine of *Hispanidad* (meaning, roughly, the Hispanic world, or the Hispanic condition), based on the spiritual superiority and defining character of the Castilian language. In Spain, this language was proclaimed the state language in 1902, shortly after the loss of the colonies, and renamed

Spanish in 1923, when the Royal Spanish Academy joined conceptually what had already been legislatively attached, namely state and language. This is how cultural hegemony substituted for political hegemony when the latter was no longer feasible. Then, as the size and weight of a self-conscious Latin America tipped the cultural balance in the second half of the twentieth century, Spain gradually abandoned its ambitions of leadership and began to cultivate a sense of cultural affinity in hopes of participating in a cultural market with great global potential. There is nothing wrong with this effort to define a civilizational space in Samuel Huntington's sense of cultural, not political entities (44). Only, Spain uses this "transnational" extension to crush the other Iberian cultures under the weight of routinely touted numbers of speakers.

But exploitation of linguistic homology need not be an epistemic afterlife for historical violence. It can also be used to recover the alternative histories caught inside the dominant tradition like an insect in the amber drop. An overarching cultural affinity on both sides of the Atlantic Ocean could be an opportunity to retrieve the multiplicity buried under the historically imposed monolingualism, turning the entire area into a richly comparative zone. By changing the cultural representations of the so-called Hispanic world, a multipolar approach to this huge geocultural area has a chance to make the historical violence recede.

A model for a critical postcolonial approach already exists in a novel that Hispanists have studiously ignored, perhaps because it contains a critique capable of delivering the pre-colonial tradition from the claws of postcolonial monolingualism. This novel is *Paraules d'Opòton el vell*, ("Words of Opòton, the Elder") (1968), by Avel·lí Artís-Gener, a writer also known by his penname of "Tísner." After fighting in the Spanish Civil War on the side of the republic, Artís-Gener went into exile with the bulk of Catalan writers in 1939. Unlike the other Spanish exiles, this group could not rely on the continuity of its language or its nation. Publication venues, libraries, the transmission of literacy in schools, everything necessary for the existence of cultural memory had been wiped out after the fall of Catalonia. The Catalan exilic community resembled the Jewish diaspora, of whom Joseph Roth wrote that, after losing the borders that protected them from assimilation, each Jew carried borders around himself (24). Catalan expatriates also took their country with them in the form of memories, an uprooted language, and the consciousness of a defeat that was direr than the loss of a war. For them the Civil War had not been just a clash of ideologies but a verdict of survival or extinction. Although members of the republican community in exile, they were sharply aware of a fate separating them from their Spanish peers. To Spaniards, Mexico seemed a natural extension of their culture.

In some cases, they even fell into a patronizing relation to the former colony. Catalans, however, had no difficulty discerning Mexican difference and engaging this otherness to take distance from the self. In exile they were able to decant a finer awareness of their own experience through the medium of Mexican culture. In his book *Mèxic, una radiografia i un munt de diapositives* ("Mexico, an X-Ray and A Bunch of Slides"), Artís-Gener mentions a family of Spanish refugees who plagued their Mexican maid with excessive demands. On a day when she was more forward than usual, her employer said to her: "Hush, girl. If it were not for us Spaniards, you would still be going around with feathers on your head!" The maid did not bite her tongue and responded: "True enough! It is for this you came, to pluck us!" (*Mèxic, una radiografia* 17).

This attitude can be taken as an illustration of Spanish arrogance, or more generally of postcolonial conceit, but it sheds light on the problem that Artís-Gener works through in his novel. *Paraules d'Opòton el vell* is about overcoming the assimilation of the culturally transcendent into the culturally immanent through historical simplification. In the same book, Artís-Gener remarks: "The simplifying force of the conquerors was extraordinary: the Mexican gods were demons and, therefore, their representations were idols. And that was that, period. Anything derived from this rudimentary principle was considered normal" (*Mèxic, una radiografia* 21).

In Mexico, the republican exiles inherited that simplifying force *qua* Spaniards who, despite their official status as refugees, could not suppress feelings of superiority. Artís-Gener, and this is also true of other exiles, did not derive his sense of reality from pathologizing the Other. He did not experience the country as an extension of the known but as an intriguing exteriority. It was a case of the Levinasian experience of being moved by the face of the Other (in this case, the agony of pre-Columbian cultures), but what moved him was not mortality announced in the face, but concreteness challenging the generality of the received forms of knowledge (*Alterity* 27). Indeed, one question emerging from the encounter with the Other is whether experience that has been previously assimilated and turned into knowledge can retain its concreteness, or whether concreteness is the province of the real, understood as that which transcends the self absolutely. In the presence of an alleged Hispanic culture, the mental operation that represents the Other as similar and assimilates the unknown to the known failed to engage what reality offered to the senses. In Mexico, the Catalan exiles discovered a world bursting at the seams of its representations. On reaching Veracruz, Artís-Gener was "immediately subjugated by the country ... and my impenitent curiosity must have done the rest" (10). Subjugation by and curiosity toward something are the active and passive aspects of reaching out to the Other. They are the subjective epiphenomena of an epistemological breakdown that disturbs the coziness of the *I*. Itwas not the death and neutralization of a non-European Other that Artís-Gener saw in the face of modern Mexico but the transcendence of that death in the *I*'s opening to the non-self, an opening by which the *I* in turn transcends its own death. Fascination exercised by the Other correlated with the self's imperative to fill the gap in its understanding, and this self-transcendence in turn helped a culture in historical extremity, such as the Catalan, to gain insight into its own situation. Here was a "residue," a life on the periphery of world history calling on the vanquished of another history to rescue tradition from the clutch of the victor.

The Mexico that Artís-Gener encountered was brimming with America's millennial character. Far from subsiding into the oneness of Hispanic identity, Mexican difference cried out from its sensuous immediacy. The pre-Hispanic languages, home of pre-Christian gods, were not archaeological traces of the past but a presence refuting historical finality:

> The languages they spoke, a wonder of sounds and inflections, have fortunately survived as proof and confirmation of a phenomenon that we will never tire of proclaiming, because we ourselves have seen it close up. Today, having incorporated the indispensable neologisms, these languages serve for all types of expression, even the most delicate, the most profuse with subtlety. None of the pre-Hispanic languages has disappeared, in some cases despite a chillingly diminished census. On the contrary: regardless of their obstinate official relegation in the past, they retain all their éclat, alive and efficient, spoken by real multitudes. (*Mèxic, una radiografia* 25)

Mexico was not a case of transculturation, in Fernando Ortiz's definition of this term as a process of cultural acquisition simultaneous with the loss of a preceding culture (*Contrapunto* 142). Rather, to Artís-Gener, Spanish culture seemed a superposition that left the deeper layers essentially intact:

> I do not think that in the case of Mexico certain credos were replaced with others, until the new ones were deeply rooted and the ancient ones driven out. What happened was, quite simply, a superposition. It was not the case of a culture being rationally replaced by another; the old, eternal one was simply patched with a piece of new and flashy cloth. (*Mèxic, una radiografia* 31)

To realize the endurance of the indigenous languages while observing their use in the outskirts of Mexico City, must have given Artís-Gener a great deal of hope in the resilience of languages. He voices his feelings in the novel's preamble through an alter ego, a fictitious editor recounting his trove of a sixteenth-century manuscript in Nahuatl. While he was studying this language, the editor says, he found in it "vestiges of fraternity with Catalan" (499). This paradoxical similarity was strengthened by functional affinity. "For me, there was also the pleasure of hearing a language that, in spite of its undeniable validity ... official life considers dead (and now you'll understand why I spoke earlier of linguistic fraternity)" (500). By making the Catalan exiles witness the destruction of their culture, the Civil War sensitized them to the existence of other cultures threatened with extinction. In Mexico, they became sharply aware of a certain interchangeability of roles; the same spirit of conquest that had ruined the Mesoamerican cultures in the sixteenth century was now devastating the Catalan heritage on the Iberian Peninsula.

If success strips the victor of the ability to imagine an ethics beyond the historically given, losers pin their hopes on imagined alternatives to their misfortune. Sympathy assists historical relativism in counterweighing the *élan* of power and humanizes the relation to the Other. Artís-Gener bracketed history by imagining a different narrative, disrupting teleological diachrony with an alternative sequence of events, which, while leaving the outcome unchanged, brought a new optic into play. By showing how things might look from the silenced end of history, Artís-Gener threw the wrench of understanding between victorious subjectivity and a consciousness that has surmounted the illusion of historical destiny.

Paraules d'Opòton el Vell is the chronicle of a voyage undertaken by the Aztecs across the Atlantic a few years before Columbus' first crossing. Through a simple reversal of the chronicles of maritime exploration, Artís-Gener shows that the incorporation of America to world history was a discovery only from the European point of view. Revealing the particularity of so-called universal history punctures the absoluteness of an event whose world-historical status hinges on the epistemological reduction of the Other and its assimilation to the Western logos. Instead of "discovery," Artís-Gener proposed the term "encounter," supporting it with an account of the clash between expectations and experience. His account reveals the consequences of suddenly lifting a culture's epistemic boundaries and the equivocations arising from defective communication. I cannot do justice here to the wealth of a novel for which the author documented himself in chronicles, history, and anthropology, and learned Nahuatl to gain insight into the indigenous culture. The book purports to be the modern edition of the memoirs of an Aztec potter who in 1489 was sent on an expedition across the Atlantic to find the god Quetzalcoatl and convince him to return to Aztlan. Opòton is one of the few survivors of this adventure. In his old age, after the Aztec civilization has been crushed by the Spaniards, he decides to produce a record of the epic voyage and writes it in his native Nahuatl with Latin characters, which he has learned from Franciscan missionaries (682). Opòton's appropriation of writing, which he achieves by fashioning his own writing kit with self-made ink and chicken feathers, emerges as a defiant act of writing history against the grain.

Throughout his adventure, Opòton is aware that sovereignty both requires an account and authorizes it. An official Aztec chronicler accompanies the expedition and produces a codex with the accustomed pictograms in order to inform "Our Great Lord" at the end of their mission. That account is lost, however, along with the other records of pre-Colombian history by the time Opòton decides to write his chronicle of the Aztec discovery of Europe. By then, however, there is no longer an Aztec sovereignty to authorize his account, or a hegemonic worldview to validate his experience, which is reduced to subjective truth: "I am the sole survivor of all who went and it will not be set down on paper to please my vanity but because it is God's honest truth" (513). But this truth that appeals to something beyond humanity for its validation does not introduce new knowledge. Opòton's intimate circle is already familiar with the story through multiple retellings, while the Spaniards would not show any regard for an Indian's story, if they were capable of reading it. Already part of a local tradition, Opòton's memoir has the status of an epic poem, repeated formulaically countless times until it is finally set down in script. Thus, it marks the shift from one type of cultural community to another.

> My cousin from Xalco and others, I do not mean cousins but friends, have told me many times that it would be good if I wrote what happened to us, since I know how to write. I will not say that they wish to read it since they know it by heart and do not understand much about reading and writing because they never went to the padres like me and everything I'll say they know from memory, from all the times they heard me explain it and now I think that maybe they asked me to write it in order to avoid my disturbing them again with my tale. (513)

Julià Guillamon finds the narrator's ego obtrusive, self-centered, and imposing his rhetorical difficulties on the reader. He points out that Opòton departs in this respect from the narrative style of the Spanish chroniclers, although a precedent for authorial intrusion exists in the medieval chronicle of Ramon Muntaner ("La subversió de la crònica" 72). All of this is true, of course, but the criticism is misplaced. As a member of a community deprived of institutional means of authentication, Opòton must rely on his own existence for proof of the veracity of what will henceforth be only signs consigned to paper. Signs, so to speak, cut loose from every social institution. The only way he can endow those signs with semiotic weight is by interposing his own body and making it present in the text. Hence the repeated calls of attention to the writing process, to the fact that it is he, Opòton "of the reedbed and the palm grove" who writes, and that he writes in much the same way as he explored old Aztlan, that is, gropingly, because he is doing something unprecedented for members of his culture.

Through Opòton, Artís-Gener opposes a socially unserviceable truth to official record. This truth may be marginal to the dominant system of thought; even so, it was experienced within hermeneutic categories sanctioned by a religious-political system. At the top of the Aztec social pyramid was the Huey Tlatoani, earthly embodiment of the divinity. His name means literally "the Great One who Speaks," and we are told that he was called this "because speaking was his highest prerogative ... The Lord was the Voice" (*Mèxic, una radiografia* 17). After the conquest snuffs that voice, Opòton does what he would have never dared to do in the ancestral political system: he becomes the voice of his people in an act of substitution as unthinkable as the means he employs are artificial. A member of an oral culture, Opòton resorts to script, turning the enemy's weapon against him. The violence of this move is evident in the strong orality of the manuscript, which lacks an implied reader, but conjures up an audience that reacts to the text while it is being written. Some, like the cousin from Xalco, challenge him on the truth of the tale, the firmness of his memory, or the clarity of his writing. Thus, Opòton's achievement does not lie solely in the perspectival inversion of the center/margin relation (Mas i Sañé 167), but in being able to inscribe his community at the core of the victor's cultural paradigm, symbolized by the primacy accorded to scripture, of which the chronicle is both an instance and a figuration.

Artís-Gener's choice of the sixteenth-century chronicle as generic vehicle serves two purposes. First, as a foil to Opòton's attempt to deliver tradition from the victor, and then as a source of verisimilitude, emphasized with fictitious editorial notes meant to produce the reality effect that, according to Roland Barthes, follows from the merging of two levels of discourse (*S/Z* 108–9). The scholarly patina simulates external corroboration of the manuscript's objective reality, trumping the text's status as fiction. But the gesture of raising a fictional text to the level of history elicits a counterstroke by which historical discourse rejoins fiction. Artís-Gener adapts the chronicles of Indies, the official record of the conquest, to a discourse that narrates military failure and draws lessons from a people's blind encounter with alterity. From Bernal Díaz del Castillo's *Verdadera historia de los sucesos de la conquista de Nueva España*, Artís-Gener drew the idea of an eighty-year-old narrator reminiscing experiences from sixty years earlier (Guillamon "L'experiència"). Into that time gap he inserted the narrative meanderings, hesitations, memory hiatuses, and guessing that humanize Opòton's tale while casting doubt on the chronicler's reliability. Distancing the facts from their articulation in speech weakens the claim to objectivity, showing that, while the events already involved misrecognition, their transcription intervenes in the social construction of reality. As Barthes had explained in an earlier essay, "historical discourse is a fraudulent (*truqué*) performative discourse, in which the apparent constative (the descriptive) is nothing but the speech act's signifier as an act of authority" ("Le discours" 74). As acts of authority premised on the subjugation of indigenous peoples, the chronicles disposed of the complexities of a misunderstood culture, passing simplification for historical truth. Opòton recalls the connection between misrepresentation and violence: "Because they were not acquainted with our wisdom and could not understand it, because they judge based on simple things. Since they saw that we did not read and write like them, which is a simple, unhappy thing ... They did not understand how everything was explained in our papers and they burned them just as they burn people alive" (727).

But if one could read the chronicles in reverse, if it were possible for the subjugated to appropriate the genre and appear in it not as an object of conquest but as a historical subject, the gesture of seizing control of the narrative would undo the relation between master and slave. The same documents would then appear not as the legitimation of foundational violence but as evidence of a mystified encounter with the Other. With one stroke, they would become the record of a cultural shock prior to its debasement into a project of domination. In *Paraules d'Opòton el Vell*, Artís-Gener appropriates the chronicle in the name of the Other and for the Other. His originality lies in the fact that this novel is not an exercise in what Carlos Guzmán Moncada calls "monological alterity," namely the reduction through discourse *about* rather than *by* or *with* the Other (*En el mirall* 156). Reductive objectivizing has been the norm in novels on the conquest written in Spanish. Guzmán Moncada mentions, among others, *La aventura equinoccial de Lope de Aguirre*, by Ramón J. Sender (1962), *La reducción*, by José Tomás Cabot (1963), *El futuro fue ayer*, by Torcuato Luca de Tena (1978), Antonio Benítez Rojo's *El mar de las lentejas*, and Abel Posse's *Daimón* and *Los perros del paraíso* (1983). The difference between these works and Artís-Gener's, according to Guzmán Moncada, is that in the former the Other is always "the object described by the gaze that explains it, not the one that speaks. The narrative voice belongs to the one that "discovers," conquers, and dominates the American native: the latter is the subjugated object, both literarily and historically" (*En el mirall* 88).

If the Other is to become the subject of historical discourse, his voice must be freed not only historically but literarily as well. It was Artís-Gener's feat to let the Other speak through him without ventriloquizing him. Guillamon expresses this fact negatively, saying that Artís-Gener, wishing to step out of his own experience, helped himself to a voice that did not pertain to him ("La subversió" 71). Other-voicedness is in fact so pervasive in the novel that Roser Vernet Anguera considers its linguistic and cultural identity indeterminate. She finds it hard to decide whether "we are faced with a Mexican novel written in Catalan or a Catalan novel written (thought) in Mexican" (78-9). In other words, Artís Gener's identification with Mexico turns the tables on a literary convention that typically pressures marginalized literatures like the Catalan with questions about their definition. Is a literature a linguistic category or a more broadly social one? Is it defined by the hard fact of linguistic affiliation or by an elusive modality of style (in this case a vague Mexicanness)? And, if so, is there a Latin American literature written in Catalan, of which *Paraules d'Opòton el Vell* would be an outstanding though by no means unique example? These are complex questions that will increasingly play a role in the analysis of literary systems, involving not only issues of locality and language but of reception and influence as well.

To return to the novel's other-voicedness: this feature is enacted at such a distance from any dominant position of elocution that it involves no exploitation of otherness but rather a genuine immersion not just in the Other's viewpoint but also in his worldview and the means by which it is transmitted. As Guzmán Moncada states in a recent book, "in *Paraules d'Opòton el Vell* the recognition of alterity is not limited to good intentions, but includes the very conception of the world and of the Language with which Artís-Gener builds this exceptional work" (*Una geografia* 243). Language is indeed the most obvious target of Artís-Gener's defamiliarizing strategy. His Catalan is stuffed with archaisms and expressions directly transposed from Nahuatl, which Artís-Gener culled from Sahagún's *Historia general*, but also from the texts translated by Angel María Garibay and Miguel León Portilla in the 1950s. In addition, Artís-Gener studied Nahuatl and the indigenous culture over a period of sixteen years before completing the novel, if we take as the *ab quo* date 1949, the year he first thought about writing a reverse chronicle (261), and as the *ad quem* date 1965, the year he submitted an earlier draft, *Crònica de Metlesòtxitl*, to a literary contest in Barcelona. But, as Guzmán Moncada points out, the semantic inversion in this novel does not result only from inverting the "discovery" of America, but also from rewriting the commonplaces and the tropes employed by the European witnesses, making the reader aware of the ways in which the unknown is appropriated through various forms of reduction (*En el mirall* 163). This brings Artís-Gener's technique into the compass of parody, producing, in Guillamon's words, a counter image of the Spanish conquest lacking in dignity and essentially ludic ("La subversió" 74).

If the Castilians mistook American reality for fictional passages in chivalric fantasy and biblical myth, the Aztecs mistake Galician women for Amazons and project their legends about Quetzalcoatl's abode in the West onto the land of the Basques, which is the ultimate goal of their journey, just as El Dorado was the vanishing point of the Spaniards' penetration of the American continent. Artís-Gener's relativism gives rise to comic scenes that reveal the arbitrariness and relativity of value. One of these scenes is the (from the Aztec viewpoint) advantageous trading of gold for glass, a material whose rarity entices the Aztec explorers to "cheat" the Galicians of their glass beads and, in a hilarious semi-private joke dedicated to Catalan readers, even of a *porró* (a wine decanter with a drinking spout). The Spaniards' unquenchable passion for gold, Artís-Gener submits, grew in direct proportion to their inability to understand the Aztec symbols or the subtlety of their rituals (*Mèxic, una radiografia* 37). He introduces a Galician equivalent of the Malinche and a symmetrical misrecognition of the Aztec landing on Iberian shores as fulfilling the return of the Apostle Saint James. The confusion draws many Galicians to join the expedition in search of Quetzalcoatl and to fight on the side of the Aztecs against hostile Spaniards. Then again, if the conquistadors destroyed pre-Colombian temples, the Aztecs demolish Christian churches, break religious images, and build pyramids in the villages they take. They try, with little success, to convert Christians to the faith of Quetzalcoatl, but in the end they are defeated, and from defeat emerges not only remorse but also the lesson of human relativity and potential reversal: "Because some of us spoke of conquest … and this was a mistake on our part, because no people has the right to conquer another … and those who did not want to be conquered, it is plain what they have done to Aztlan, says I" (729).

"The greatest difference between the foreigners and ourselves—says Opòton—is the diverse ways of understanding life" (728). Different approaches to life crystalize in different cultures. Particular divinities are but local representations of an absolute that cannot be reached through instrumental reason, in which the Europeans excelled: "They did not know that the more they advanced on the path of tools the farther they were from the gods" (728). Toward the transcendent whole there is no historical, let alone geographical progress. Error is a partial truth subverted by taking it beyond its historical niche.

And now I wish to explain to you what I have reflected all this time and first I must tell you that the Rising Sun is always beyond. No matter how much you travel toward said Rising Sun you're never closer to it because it moves away while you go toward it. And it is the same whether you go to it or you remain where you are, because the earth is round and the Rising Sun goes around it, from which it happens that it is here too, in the same Aztlan that you used to govern so wisely. What Opòton means to say is that said Rising Sun is not a place but a symbol. (726)

Opòton is here combining the discrete times of experience and reflection, of action that cannot be deferred and wisdom arising from the impotence of hindsight. Error accrues with every step taken in pursuit of Quetzalcoatl toward the land of the Rising Sun, with every attempt to close the circle of myth merging the *noumenon* and the *phenomenon*. Roland Barthes observed that historians often employ a rhetorical strategy that he called "organizational shifter." This strategy relies on the "rubbing together of two kinds of time: enunciation time and the time of the enunciated material" ("Le discours" 67). With the benefit of hindsight, the historian can produce the illusion of predictability by introducing references to the enunciation time in his discourse ("Le discours" 68). When Opòton writes his testimony, he already knows the outcome of the Aztec encounter with the Spaniards and realizes the fatal mistake of seeking to endow the partial with the reality of the whole. There is only one sun, but the earth is composed of a plurality of lands with no single myth subtending them all. That is why he resorts to another narrative strategy that Barthes associates with the *effet de réel*, namely the introduction of a historical character into a work of fiction. Opòton's memoir is allegedly historical, but it lacks authority in the absence of socially legitimated countertexts. By means of an organizational shifter, however, he intersects the time of enunciation and the time of the enunciated, endowing his text with a sense of fatality. In a Basque village, where the Aztecs try in vain to understand and be understood by the beret-wearing locals, they use a Galician interpreter to recruit villagers as crew for the return to Aztlan. Only a young child named Fernando Cortés is willing to go with them, but is refused on account of his tender age (732). The pseudo editor writes in a footnote: "The spirit of adventure in a five-year-old child corresponds to the figure of the conquistador and perhaps that first contact with the Aztecs opened his eyes" (732 n. 6).

Opòton does not exactly validate his testimony through recourse to a historical character, but rather through the chance appearance of such a character under the pretense of historical virtuality. A world historical name turns up in an unlikely place (Cortés spent his childhood in Valladolid, the pseudoeditor informs us) but appears forcefully enough to be remembered many years later in the light of decisive events. The irony of the situation is not lost on Opòton, who, imbued with a hard-won understanding of the dialectical nature of all action, suggests that the inclination of Castilians to violent resolutions of the dialectic lies in their inability to grasp the possibility of a harmony between different freedoms: "We showed them the way and here they are, we will never be able to expel them, because I know from experience how stubborn the Castilian Race is and how it never lets go willingly what it has once seized" (726).

Artís-Gener's inversion of the story of the conquest is itself a function of his rubbing of times. From the position of survivor of a society that had been destroyed by Spaniards, he found it easier than other exiles to look at Mexico from the vantage of the subjected peoples, rightful subjects of a history that had been stolen from them. Again, Guzmán Moncada strikes the right critical note when he observes that Artís-Gener rejects not only the genocidal conquest of America by the Spaniards but also the model of domination manifested therein. He also points out that Artís-Gener uses the fable to set up a parallelism between the indigenous peoples who suffered that domination in the past and the Iberian peoples that suffered a similar domination then and again later. And he adds the Benjaminian insight that Artís-Gener's vindication of specific subjects in the past flows into the present and points to the future (*En el mirall* 193).

In the novel we find instances of the linguistic intolerance that led to the imposition of Castilian in the Peninsula and in America. Thus, whereas the Galicians appear as communicatively pragmatic, a Castilian officer angrily forbids Aztec prisoners to speak their language, which defeat has demoted to the level of a dialect: "Are you again speaking in your repugnant dialect?" (735). Thus, through their unexpected acquaintance with the Iberian peoples, the Aztecs get a foretaste of Castilian imperialism, their first contact coinciding with the beginning of the suppression of Iberian diversity on the eve of the overthrow of American autochthonous cultures:

> But there is also the Castilian speech and the Portuguese speech, said to be related to the Galician, and the Arabic speech, and the Catalan speech and the Jewish speech, for these are the names of the diverse tribes that people the earth and there are still many more ... The Old Aztlan, in its totality, is a tangle of diverse languages and if you ask me, in the question form, how they understand each other, Opòton will tell you that they don't. Besides, they have been free some time or other and now they are no longer so because their He Who Speaks,

the above mentioned Tantomontamontatanto, has them totally under his thumb. (691)

Artís-Gener's subversion of the victor's viewpoint works through historical and narrative irony. Historical, in that the projection of Iberian imperialism across the Atlantic recoils and takes the form of internal imperialism. Narrative, in that the very text that under different circumstances would have been a chronicle of discovery and conquest becomes the medium in which tolerance and something like moral wisdom emerge through a subject whom suffering has taught the relativity of identity positions. Guzmán Moncada correctly asserts that the ultimate subject of the novel is not the Indian or the noble savage, for Opòton has, after all, been caught up in imperial desires too. Nor can the Catalan exile be said to organize the novel's meaning. *Paraules d'Opòton* is not a story about a European subject in Aztec garb. Rather, its subject is the opposite of an identity, if by "identity" we understand a monolithic self that defines itself through conflict and domination of an Other (*En el mirall* 194). This remark helps us avoid misrepresenting the novel as a mere refraction of the self on the surface of the Other, as literature depicting a foreign society is liable to be.

Artís-Gener's engagement with Aztec culture is not intended to produce a historical novel or to exploit the past romantically; rather, he uses historical, geographical and anthropological data to produce an anti-history, a chronicle against the grain. His accomplishment, unique among the Civil-War exiles, lies in the fact that he reopened history not by revising it but by revealing its other side, the neglected blind spot of triumphant visions of civilization. That blind spot is the matrix of the linear history that threatens to loop back and destroy both the reasons and the memory of the defeated. Artís-Gener fights back with the weapons of parody and ridicule, but he gains his greatest victory by means of consciousness, which grows apace with the sense of justice. But if justice depends on knowledge, Artís-Gener grasps with unerring intuition that knowledge grows out of sympathy, and sympathy is never adulation of the powerful but respect for the sidelined and downgraded. Not because the latter possess a privileged identity but because, if they are the object of an irreducible responsibility, they may also be the subject of a wisdom that could prove redeeming.

CHAPTER ELEVEN

The Weight of Memory
and the Lightness of Oblivion:
The Dead of the Spanish Civil War

The grave's a fine and private place
Andrew Marvell, "To His Coy Mistress"

Death is the most powerful agent of forgetting. But it is not all-powerful. From time immemorial men have erected barriers against forgetting in death, so that clues suggesting remembrance of the dead are considered by specialists in prehistory and archaeology to be the surest indications of the presence of human culture. The rituals of worship of the dead with their pleas for intercession, sacrificial acts, and burial objects no doubt serve in many cases primarily to ensure that the dead person enjoys a smooth journey into the beyond. But gravestones always also serve as "monuments" warning the living not to forget their dead—and yet people often forget all too easily, for "life goes on." (Weinrich, *Lethe: The Art and Critique of Forgetting* 24)

Thus begins Harald Weinrich's discussion of Dante's restoration of the memory of the dead in his book on forgetting. In this paragraph, Weinrich establishes three basic points that bear on the subject of historical memory. First, the link between memory and the human condition, which comes down, in essence, to the evidence that to be human is to fight not against death (which is a survival strategy common to all living creatures) but against extinction, which only humans are capable of comprehending. To struggle against extinction involves resisting obliteration after the catastrophe of death has taken place. And this is of course what the Dantean characters do in the beyond, when they entreat the Christian poet to remember their stories. Short of undoing death, the poet may hold back their disappearance at the cost of immortalizing their suffering. Thus, they meet their punishment in their own desire to become images of horror for all eternity.

The second point is that the rituals of burial (and, we should add, of mourning) are meant to ensure the smooth departure of the dead; in other words, to sever their emotional entanglement with the living and to secure their status as images in memory. And the third point is the role that certain public acts of memory fulfill in the body politic, warning the living not to forget, or vice versa, stimulating oblivion so that life, a certain quality of life, "can go on."

The Struggle Against Forgetting

The first of these points refers to witnessing, an activity implying some form of presence to the events being witnessed and a moral stance that cannot be dissociated from sympathy with the suffering of victims. In Spain the recent run to open mass graves from the Civil War has given a new twist to the politics of memory, which now appears clearly as an extension of the perpetrators' success. Since the creation in December 2000 of the "Asociación para la Recuperación de la Memoria Histórica" by Emilio Silva and Santiago Macías Pérez, people all over Spain have stepped forward and pointed out the location of unmarked graves, where seventy years ago a sizable number of men and women were hastily buried. They were victims of purges undertaken by the rebel army and Falange death squads with the connivance of the religious authorities. Official support for the retrieval of bodies has not been forthcoming, except in the case of volunteers who fell in the Russian front while fighting alongside the German Wehrmacht in the Second World War. In Catalonia, the Generalitat under the presidency of Jordi Pujol established a pilot program that helped carry out the first exhumations in a region where fifty-four mass graves containing over 4,000 bodies were excavated in the environs of Barcelona alone. And the Basque government provided aid for the forensic activities that are crucial to the identification of bodies. For their part, Spanish governments have remained aloof if not averse to the growing claim for airing the material memory of the repression. The anxiety induced in many Spaniards by those who tenaciously follow the archival trail leading to the exhumation of loved ones, by the renewed debate around the fascist symbols and monuments persisting in many Spanish towns, by high strung incidents like the dispute about the destination of confiscated archives, or by the obstinacy of Basques and Catalans in reasserting their national specificity indicate that the psychological wounds have not healed and the social division created by Franco's unconditional victory continues to shape the collective behavior of Spaniards.

The beginning of the excavations coincided with the high point in a debate about the historical memory that is not exclusively Spanish but global in scope. Nonetheless, it is reasonable to ask: why at this time? The answer to this question bears on the exhaustion of the transition's ethos, a depletion of conviction in the virtues of that political maneuver that is tangible today in many spheres of social life. One of the consequences of this exhaustion has been the appearance of an Antigone complex. The appeals to restore the memory of the dead and the implicit need to recall the circumstances of their disappearance challenge the desire, crucial to the transition's strategy, to historicize the Civil War and its aftermath. By "historicize" I mean here to degrade memories into events that no longer claim the attention, much less arouse the passions, of anyone with the exception of professional historians; events that one is done with.

At odds with the desire for a hasty closure of the past, the exhumation of corpses in the presence of immediate relatives showed the impossibility of establishing a clear distinction between history and memory. This is so because past and present remain interwoven in the emotions of the survivors. When Katherine Verdery writes: "Bodies have the advantage of concreteness that nonetheless transcends time, making past immediately present," she hints at the uncanny feeling that presides over the retrieval of long-concealed graves (28). Uncanny, not in the sense of a gothic manifestation of past violence, but in that of an experience that abolishes the temporal gulf between *that* action and *this* feeling. Uncanny, not because the light and fresh air that flow into the opened grave defamiliarizes the bodies felled by violence and ruined by organic decomposition, but, on the contrary, because the rush of consciousness and the release of contained expectation turn those remains into our contemporaries. Just as long-buried objects can turn to dust when exposed to the slightest aeration, the reemergence of the "secret" dead annihilates at once the meticulous work of mandated amnesia. But it is not only the so-called peace of Francoism that crumbles with the return of the repressed. Those frail vestiges of past violence foul a quarter of a century of cynical democracy.

Dead bodies not only mark a space and localize a claim. They not only ground the assertion "it happened here," but also partake of the present implied by the "hereness." Bodies have the quality of relics, of what is left behind (*relinquere*), but retain the pastness of an event. As a relic, the corpse displays a concrete temporality, and displays it, paradoxically, through the visible corruption of the evidence: fleshless bones, rotten garments, body fragments that cannot be easily matched or identified. The fascination of mass graves nearly three-quarters of a century after their making implies a turning-point in the collective memory with undeniable consequences for historiography. In the wake of the exhumations, it becomes harder to relativize the past, and all that revisionists can do in the face of such evidence is to confront bodies with bodies in a macabre count aimed at crafting a balance without cost to the moral status quo. But although the materiality of bodies cannot be gainsaid, and their identity may be analytically established, they do not for all that resist semantic manipulation. Bodies, says Verdery, present the illusion of having "a single meaning that is solidly 'grounded,' even though in fact they have no such single meaning" (29). This is always the case when dead bodies are mobilized in support of the social body's foundational myth.

The Valley of the Fallen, the postwar massive stonework that serves as Franco and José Antonio Primo de Rivera's mausoleum in the Guadarrama Mountains north of Madrid is a case in point. This granite dream of enduring empire remains a place of fascist pilgrimage through the semantic manipulation of bodies. Hallowed with the body of the Falange's founder and wrapped in the anticipatory aura of Franco's earthly remains, the Valley of the Fallen was conceived as a shrine in advance of its relics. Later, when the regime began to camouflage its ideological origins, bodies were called on again to provide the alibi for the blatant display of power. In this way dozens of bodies from the Republican side, in some cases looted from cemeteries around the Iberian Peninsula, ended up among the nearly 40,000 bodies that turned the monument into a "mass grave" of the fascist crusade. This is how the fiction of a memorial to the sacrifice of both sides arose. The regime never acknowledged that this alleged symbol of reconciliation claimed the lives of thousands of Republican prisoners forced to work on its construction reduced to the condition of slaves.

Calamities like the Civil War retain their divisive potential not only for those directly involved, but also for the groups defined by the institution-alization of the outcome. After a violent settling of differences, societies redistribute social value in ways that determine the potential and restrictions of subsequent generations. One of the serious shortcomings of the Spanish transition was the inability of the parties representing the Republic's legacy to write the history of the democratic state on the tombstones of their dead. The grave of Catalonia's President Lluís Companys, Franco's most illustrious political victim, was officially honored only as late as 15 October 2004, in a ceremony from which the President of the Government and the Head of State were conspicuously absent. To this date, the court martial that sentenced Companys to death in 1940 has not been revised; as a consequence, the post-Franco state *de facto* upholds Franco's liquidation of Catalonia's government in the body of its elected representative. The Civil War continues to be a central referent for the collective self-perception of

Spanish citizens, in part because it was the last extended conflict affecting the entire population, and in part because the values it polarized are set in motion every time the memory of the conflict resurfaces.

The notion of *post-histoire*, mobilized at the end of the Cold War to announce the end of the Hegelian dialectic, had its modest prelude in the Spanish attempt to dam up historical forces with a constitution. Shedding Franco's totalitarianism but retaining the substance of his nationalism, this document soon became a political fetish and, like the crown it legitimizes, an instrument of immobility. But retrenchment behind a constitution conceived as the last station of political evolution requires the dimming of the historical consciousness, which then acquires subversive potential. The deteriorating sense of the past is made worse by the fact that we now live in a post-traditional society. Experience is no longer communicated through widely accepted social rituals or transmitted along with ancient lore, but is fabricated ad hoc and disseminated through a combination of state-sponsored events and the opportunism of the culture industry. Commercial exploitation of the past produces ersatz knowledge. At the same time, real confrontation with the past appears redundant if not downright blameworthy. Never before has there been so much fascination with historical memory and so much resistance to its implications. Our relation to the past has become spectatorial, as if mediated witnessing of the atrocities and injustices of previous generations happened in a different moral planet without any claim on the present.

There is no reason for surprise at the domestication of historical memory: 22 November 1975 does not mark the downfall of a tyranny but the self-transmogrification of a regime that lasted as long as it did thanks to its adaptability, but also to broad support and even broader passivity. It would be wrong to confuse passivity with helplessness. As Saul Friedlander asserts, "in a system whose very core is criminal from the beginning, passivity is, as such, system-supporting" (73).

Widespread complicity accounts for the remarkable tolerance to the censoring of memory well after the Franco era. Such tolerance was often condoned as the price of reconciliation, but the reason cannot really be fear of another conflagration. A more likely cause is the impregnation of society with Francoist values. Although much of the evidence of Francoist crimes was destroyed when police files and records of the civil governments were purged in the 1960s, swift judiciary action during the transition could have prevented further destruction. How, if not by passive complicity, can we account for the general indifference to military and police archives remaining closed to researchers, to files classified until the death of all concerned, to threats against journalists and media, to the rehabilitation of

Falange and of the violent Fuerza Nueva organization as legal contenders in the first democratic elections after Franco's death? Why did the Spanish Parliament, despite recurrent "left-wing" majorities in the 1980s and early 1990s, fail to condemn the dictatorship until 2001, and then only in a lackadaisical manner shorn of practical consequences? The answer to these questions is that the transition was not the much-touted democratic reinvention of the state but an inter-generational overhaul of the institutions calculated to remain in the hands of the same power groups. Few of those institutions were shut, some underwent cosmetic changes, and most remained unchanged. They embodied the Francoist principles at the time. From then on they would channel the evolution of those principles into a diffuse climate of opinion. Repression of memory would make it easier to uphold that opinion without avowing, or even being aware of, its origin.

During the transition, the myth of a consensual re-foundation of the state replaced the myth of the providential Caudillo. "Consensual" implied that a balanced representation of all social groups crafted the new political framework in the course of unhindered debate. Consensus both presupposed and promised national reconciliation. As a token of reconciliation, the regime granted across-the-board amnesty, releasing thousands of people who were serving sentences for political activity considered subversive under Francoist law. But there was a catch, which the crowds clamoring for amnesty in the streets failed to grasp. Amnesty implied amnesia. Both words mean, of course, something different in contemporary English. But the semantic gap is only an effect of the modern distinction between the individual and the social. Amnesty is institution-alized oblivion, the deliberate erasure of a part of the past that otherwise would cling dangerously to the present. Thus, if amnesia is, at least since Freud, disingenuous inability to recall certain chapters from personal history, oblivion is, in the words of Nicole Loraux, "the shadow cast by the political on memory" (83). In the first case, the ego dreads the return of the repressed; in the second, the state is threatened by the relevance of the past to its present organization. Obviously, individuals cannot forget on command, but amnesty ensures that they relegate the proscribed memories to the realm of their private conscience.

Amnesty, then, is amnesia by decree. As a means of surmounting civic strife, it has a long tradition in the West. Regimes based on participation have often availed themselves of this tool. We find the first instance of amnesty in a transition to democracy after a dictatorship, that of the Thirty, in fifth-century B.C. Athens. In 403, the victorious democrats proclaimed a reconciliation involving a ban: *me mnesikakein*, "It is forbidden to recall the misfortunes" (Loraux 87). The ban was implemented through an oath taken by each citizen and enforced with heavy penalties. Isocrates explained its effect: "Since we mutually gave each other pledges ... we govern ourselves in a manner as beautiful as collective ... as if no misfortune had happened to us" (cit. Loraux 91). The intention could not be clearer: to rebuild the state on the fiction that violence in the past left no traces in the present, that it had not befallen the very community on which the ban was imposed. Could there be more explicit proof that politics, as the art of governance, requires the state's custody of the collective memory? An indiscreet peek at its cradle reveals that politics is not the daughter of memory, of Mnemosyne, but of *Lethe*, oblivion.

Amnesty and oblivion are words of Greek and Latin origin meaning the same thing. Once these words entered the political sphere, they took on a prescriptive sense. It is with this sense that a directive of "amnesty and oblivion" (redundant for good measure) featured in peace treaties in seventeenth- and eighteenth-century Europe (Weinrich 171). This clause imposed on the signatories the obligation to renounce all assignment of blame and retribution for acts committed in the course of the previous war. Such obligation was remembered by the Franco officials during the transition and came into play regardless of the hopes or intentions of their victims. By demanding political amnesty, opponents of the dictatorship in effect barred the way to future indictment of the perpetrators, unwittingly granting democratic status to totalitarian individuals and collectives.

A final line had been drawn on the recent past. Soon the Franco decades were no longer seen as a time of exception to be redressed but as a continuum with Spanish history. Nineteen thirty-nine was not, in the emerging view, an interruption of the self-determining tradition inaugurated with the republic, but the beginning of a period of crisis management in line with an overarching nation-building project going back to the fifteenth century, or earlier in the most ardent accounts. It is now possible to understand how the democratization of the regime after Franco's death brought about its normalization. The transition had in fact begun six years earlier, when the Generalissimo proclaimed Juan Carlos his successor on 22 July 1969. The dictator's decision became the cornerstone of the consensus that could be reached after his death. But that consensus implied re-inscribing the Francoist re-foundation of the monarchy through his Law of Succession of 1947.[1] And thus everything was done to obliterate Franco's disruption of the dynastic line, creating in the citizens a sense of historical continuity based on the crown. This manipulation of memory, assisting what was in effect an

---

1 Franco insisted that his resolution of the succession problem was an "instauration" rather than the "restoration" of the monarchy (Carr and Fusi 169).

embezzlement of popular sovereignty, gave Francoism the status of a ripple in the broader stream of the national monarchy.

Cancelling not just the regime's liability but even the memory of its guilt satisfied everyone including outsiders. All remaining international exclusions imposed on Spain since 1939 were repealed after 1975. With the cancellation of the guilt, the social division between victors and vanquished disappeared by enchantment, and with it the distinction between victims and perpetrators. Dissolving the moral certainties of but a few years earlier opened the way to a relativism that would increase in the same proportion as the collective memory declined, making the roles of victims and perpetrators interchangeable. Self-awarded political amnesty permitted Francoists to retain their social and economic privileges, while the opposition, relying on a moral trump card that it had just thrown away, saw in the myth of reconciliation an opportunity for a gradual transformation of the state. Time was on their side, they believed, and Francoism would just wither away. But the myth of the consensual pact threw political culture into a deep freeze, and democratic progress was hindered by a constitution that, instead of adjusting to the country's complexity, proved to be a fetter on the pragmatic evolution of the state.

Images of the Dead

The second point in Weinrich's quotation bears on the process of mourning and the transition of the dead from material presences to mnemonic images. Rituals of remembrance facilitate the disentangling of the living from the departed. Such rituals are at the foundation of culture and at the origin of sedentary society; in other words, of the state. To lie in state is to be placed in public view for honors accorded prior to burial. Public honoring of the deceased sustains the transcendence that the state claims with respect to each subject, lifting bereavement from the private to the social sphere. In ancient Greece, the dead were severed from the family and taken over by the city. The purpose of the public rites, which expressly forbid the presence of female survivors, may have been to curb subjective mourning and bring excess under control, but their long-term effect was to ground the public spirit in the socialization of mourning (Loraux 20). This being the case, the state undergoes a crisis when, neglecting the imperative of ritual justice, it fails to gather the grief of the entire community in its folds.

Antigone's tragedy is often read as a confrontation between the atavistic law of kinship and the higher law of the state; or, alternatively, as the clash between ethics and pragmatics. But she seems more in character as spokesperson for the political legitimacy that Creon's arbitrariness threatens.

Creon's authority rests on the successful deployment of force in civil war and on the threat of further violence made legal by his diktat. His interdiction of burial for his personal enemies undercuts the state's claim to rise above factions, institutionalizes the civil split, and, as Tiresias warns, endangers the city. More fundamentally, it transgresses the limits of humanity by regressing to a pre-cultural stage. Thus, the ruler's inhumanity comes out in his ban on inhumation. Culture is disrupted by the refusal of ritual and the veto on the work of mourning. The tyrant's puffed up identification of his will with the public good contravenes the fundamental principle of culture, namely the sublimation of violence into reassuring mnemonic images. Creon drives out the soothing images associated with the work of mourning by producing alternative images meant to arouse powerful emotions.

> So for the good of Thebes her laws I frame:
> And such the proclamation I set forth
> …
> Therefore to all this city it is proclaimed
> That none may bury, none make moan for him,
> But leave him lying all ghastly where he fell,
> Till fowls o' the air and dogs have picked his bones. (218)

Although mothers were denied participation in the Athenian funerals, they had a right to the bones of the funeral pyre (Loraux, 37). This pledge of the state to return a material trace of the beloved body as proof of the honors rendered to it, is broken by Creon's bequest of Polynices' bones to the beasts. By reinserting the corpse into nature's cycle without ritual mediation, Creon subtracts it from the realm of culture, calling into question the very foundation of the state.

If the state wants to perpetuate itself, Creon's disarticulation of Polynices' body, the scattering and defiling of his bones, calls for a contrasting image of steadfast composure. With such a balancing image, achieved through her own sacrifice, Antigone aspires to repair the breach made by the tyrant in the ritual cycle:

> I'll bury him; doing this, so let me die.
> So with my loved one loved shall I abide,
> My crime a deed most holy: for the dead
> Longer have I to please than these on earth.
> There I shall dwell for ever. (215)

The longer time she reckons with is the time of collective memory; that is, the recurrent time of a cult that Creon may not proscribe or curtail without bringing about his own downfall. It is, in short, the time on which the state is founded. The ancient polis had its origin in ancestor worship, practiced separately by each family or clan. Later, when public worship displaced the penates or household gods, belief in the permanence of the dead through the observance of the rites by the living was transferred to the pantheon and became the foundation of the city.

If the state sublimates death into culture, Creon offends it by organizing a culture of death. Under the aegis of horror, sovereignty is synonymous with the tyrant's death-bringing power, while the images of carnage that he spitefully calls forth become the cornerstones of the new state. Unlike Oedipus, Antigone is not driven by an epistemological passion. When she confronts Creon with the bones of Polynices, the question about the truth (which implicates the state's legitimacy) is not raised. What counts, what is decisive (and the source of renewed tragedy) is her loyalty to the dead. Her justice-rendering act is inevitably tragic because, by turning the scene of horror into one of culture, she not only reasserts humanity but in fact turns the state against itself. And in this way she reinvents it.

The dead who are not granted passage into the cultural beyond remain politically alive. Unable to go on living themselves, the survivors become permanent reminders of a past that no one wants to heed. Their broken lives are evidence that a state that does not bury the dead decomposes alongside the corpses. In this light, the refusal of post-Franco governments to accord symbolic burial to the victims by apologizing for the crimes committed in the name of the state is a fatal avoidance of responsibility. And no pretext will deflect the consequences of denied ritual; certainly not the pretext that the Civil War makes Spanish society both victim and perpetrator, and the state cannot apologize to itself. Such an argument, recurrent in the 1990s, when demands for symbolic restitution were being voiced, willfully dissolves the distinction between state and society, and between society as a whole and the individuals and groups that were victimized, often for the slightest association with the previous structure of governance, for lukewarm adherence to the new axis of values, or simply for belonging to a stigmatized social group. Above all, it ignores that the state *qua* state is the ultimate referent for action undertaken by the institutions.

Of Graveyards and Constitutions

Weinrich's third point referred to the mnemonic role of monuments to the dead. He argues that such monuments are inefficient guarantees of memory, because people are inclined to forget. Nevertheless, gravestones are apt localizations of memory, centers for the organization of the past. Each slice of the past, says Halbwachs, quoting Bergson, is articulated by certain dominant memories, which provide support for secondary ones. To locate a memory means either to recognize it as dominant or to discover another dominant memory, to which the one we want to situate is attached (146). Mass graves dug up with the help of the memory of survivors establish new overriding memories and reorganize the relevance of the past.

Such localizations affect the collective memory more immediately and comprehensively than historiography does. The reason is that memory is bound up with action, whereas analytical discourse relates to knowledge. The more intimately consciousness is involved in the present, the more vivid and compelling memory becomes. According to Halbwachs, "each time we come close to *action*, consciousness adheres more to those memories that resemble our current perception from the viewpoint of the action that we must undertake" (146). Because action relies on memory, the latter is selective and cannot dwell on the totality of past experience or enter into excessive detail. Its inherent tendency to simplification makes memory vulnerable to historical critique, as well as to reversals brought about by a different course of action or an altered pragmatic intent. On the other hand, memory retains the ethical force of witnessing and in this way rises easily to the status of a political factor.

If proximity to action determines that the memories selected by consciousness will resemble our perception of the present situation, the reverse also obtains, and recurrence of a given memory threatens the subject with reiteration of action that is consistent with the pattern of recall. We are not far from the psychoanalytical concept of "acting out," although here the terms are reversed, for it is not repression that leads to a re-composed theater of action, but, on the contrary, it is the fear of certain events that forces memory to recede to the pre-conscious. The Constitution, drenched in tacit memories of the Civil War and the dictatorship, makes it easy to appeal to fear of renewed violence in order to keep history still.[2] Impassioned appeals to the foundational consensus as the supreme argument to keep this political charter shut, betray a troubled awareness that "consensus" on the same terms could no longer be obtained today. But fear depends on images, and the transition's unwillingness to face the horror in its historical basement robbed the dictatorship of its sting in the minds of the young. To compensate for the fading conditioning by fear, affective images are periodically projected on the social imaginary;

2 Not only tacitly, but more overtly in dispositions such as Article 8, outlining the Army's role in preserving the territorial organization of the state, codified as its "territorial integrity."

for instance, warnings about the state's Balkanization, a dire reference to the latest European civil war.[3]

When people denounce the fading of historical memory, this does not mean that historical research or memoirist writing have been lacking. If anything, there is a glut of writing on the Civil War and the dictatorship, but the sheer volume of these studies draws attention away from the central issues, neutralizing their potential impact. The Constitution was, in this regard, a watershed. Rejected by the most obdurate members of the Francoist establishment—among them future premier José María Aznar—it was endorsed by other groups as a limited but potentially adaptable framework by means of which Spain could leave its autocratic tradition behind. It represented an unstable truce between the spirit of change and that of continuity, achieved at the price of substantial forgetting. Even under these conditions, the "consensus-based" Constitution could not prevent conspiracy and military attempts to bring the democratic reforms to a halt; and, less publicized, to produce an involution of the autonomic process in the wake of the coup of 23 February 1981.

Since then the Constitution has changed its sign. No longer symbolizing the spirit of compromise, it has become an emblem of inflexibility and an instrument of regression. H. Rosi Song observes that "this document presents itself as the recipient of mandatory devotion, because it embodies the convention of a national unity and cohesion that precedes the recognition of Spain's plurality" (225-6). In other words, it subordinates the recognition of fact to the prescription of ideology. Song perceptively points out the contradiction inscribed in the Constitution and even its subversion by its putative guardians: "But the loyalty expressed in the concept of 'constitutional patriotism' does not apply to the principles sustained by the Constitution" (225). She refers to the appropriation of this fundamental law by the conservative party, but she could have added that the two dominant parties equally fetishize the document. To judge from the uses to which it is put, it seems that the Constitution's single most important job is to stem the flow of history and to set limits to reality. The Constitution is in effect a screen memory, a displaced metaphor for knowledge that is censored and must be constantly repressed lest it gain admittance to public consciousness. But, of course, what is repressed resurfaces in the form of anxiety and compulsive behavior. The mass graves coming to light all over Spain as on cue are at once a potent image and proof positive of what the transition repressed.

3 In the 1990s, reference to the Balkans in connection with the periphery's demands for territorial reorganization was routinely made in the Spanish political arena, premiers Felipe González and José María Aznar included.

The Historian's Transferential Relation to the Past

It may be appropriate to mention in conclusion that one of the greatest obstacles in mastering the past lies with historians. As self-appointed guardians of historical truth, some of them have been quick to object against the utilitarian appropriation of the past for particular causes in the present. And, while the objection is sound, the persons or professional groups raising it are often blind to their own participation in what they denounce. They too live and act in the present, and their specific way of acting is to re-present the past, that is, to make it comprehensible with respect to the ruling preoccupations of the day and within the consensus of plausibility, which usually means little more than the set of ideas and prejudices currently in force. In Spain, the emergence of competing histories after the reinstatement of the Basque and Catalan statutes of autonomy threatened the hegemonic national discourse. Early on in the post-Franco era, the state institutions and political parties reacted against the, as they saw it, centrifugation of power with a set of schemes that abutted in the coup-d'état of 23 February 1981. A major concern, not only of the conspirators but of other political actors, from the Army to the Socialist Party, was the "autonomic process," that is, devolution to the nationalities, getting out of hand. It was urgent to reign it in. The coup of 23 February was about that, as was the campaign of delegitimation of the cultural and historical claims of the subject nationalities, which, launched around that time, developed in crescendo until today. A central role in this delegitimation fell to historians. On the other side of the national divide, historians too have been at the forefront of the political tug-of-war for the reclamation of historical memory.

Even before the breakup of the Soviet Union and the independence of its satellite republics in Eastern Europe, the Caucasus, and later in the Balkans, Spanish nationalism reacted with "anti-nationalist" frenzy involving the media's creation of a hostile state of opinion, war on the minority languages, fiscal exploitation, and eventually the use of the state apparatuses (such as the judiciary, the Constitutional Court, and the National Intelligence Center) to dispose of political adversaries. A central part of this program of moral and political pressure has been interference in the school curricula, although education is officially an "exclusive competency" consecrated in the statutes of autonomy of the national minorities. On the side of the peripheral nationalities, a contrarian policy has been at work: profuse deployment of national symbols, instruction in Catalan and Euskera in public schools, preferential use of these languages in government-controlled media, hard-ball negotiation of the state budgets to ensure a degree of investment in Catalonia (in the transition the Basque country obtained the right to collect its own taxes), and, not least, reliance on history for the maintenance of their national consciousness, an intellectual effort which the state intelligentsia routinely denounces as fabrication.

As a result of this confrontation of legitimacies in the territories of the national minorities, a battle for the hearts and minds of citizens overshadowed the one-dimensional division of official history along simple class lines (the myth of the two Spains). In this struggle for the hegemonic narrative, reestablishing the central government's control over school programs became an explicit goal for the conservatives after they captured power in 1996. Minister of Education Esperanza Aguirre proposed a curricular reform with the manifest objective of undermining the educational competencies of the historical nationalities. Lacking parliamentary majority at the time, José María Aznar's government was unable to sign the proposal into law. It had to wait until June 2000, when Pilar del Castillo, Aguirre's successor in office, rammed it through Parliament on the strength of her party's newly won absolute majority. By then the soil had been prepared by the centralist media. A typical example of the gestation of the desired climate of opinion was the anonymous article "Controlled Books" ("Libros controlados") published in *El País* on 13 October 1999, in favor of the implementation of one of Aguirre's schemes in the name of market efficiency.

An all-out attack on the limited decentralization of education had started, and history was at the center of the debate. On 27 June 2000, the Real Academia de la Historia launched a campaign under the guise of a survey on the teaching of history in secondary education. Presented as the result of a comprehensive collection of data from all over Spain, this study, of which only an abstract of sixteen pages was made public, denounced the alleged blurring of "the Spanish historical process" by overwhelming it with the "particular vision of the past of this or that Autonomous Community" (Real Academia de la Historia 2000). The results of the study were made available not through an academic publication but through the newspaper with the largest readership, and, although the Academia's officers spoke of a coincidence, it was impossible not to see governmental coordination in the date it had chosen to break the news. The Real Academia never revealed the names of the educators or data gatherers who participated in its survey, but it soon transpired that none had been consulted in Catalonia. Shamed by the evidence of its irresponsible behavior, the Academia then admitted, through an official spokesman, that it had not examined any of the textbooks used in Catalonia and that the study had found nothing to be concerned about with the teaching of history in this autonomous community. At this point one more contradiction did not matter.

Typically, none of the newspapers that had trumpeted the original report publicized the Academia's rectification. In the meantime, evidence that the Academia had submitted to political pressure continued to grow. Within one year, the Fundació Jaume Bofill of Barcelona published a detailed study of the history textbooks used in the different autonomous communities. The researchers, in this case, clearly identified the data and controlled for variables such as programs of study, market share of publishers, textual variations in the books intended for different autonomous communities, and the quantified distribution of the contents. This in-depth study not only exposed the Academia's report as scientifically worthless, but, more importantly, it showed the prevalence of state nationalism in the textbooks currently used in every autonomous community. Furthermore, it revealed that the Real Academia had passed over severe distortions and suppressions of facts in textbooks from autonomous communities governed by the Partido Popular.

As revealing as this affair was concerning the state's tampering with the citizens' understanding of the past, the report's political implications went unnoticed in the first flurry of reactions. University of Barcelona historian Antoni Segura was the first to point them out in his introduction to the study of the Fundació Bofill: "Curiously, the [Real Academia's] report does not mention at any time the context of profound global social change in which the teaching of history is currently immersed, as is, in general, the bulk of education" (31). The report neglected to mention this context because it constituted the repressed horizon of the Academia's waning pertinence. Under the guise of a scientific survey on the teaching of history, the report was an unintended demonstration of the political *raison d'être* of such state institutions and an ominous symptom of the ever deeper conniving between government, media, and scientific foundations.

Fourteen years later, to mark the 300th anniversary of Catalonia's defeat by the joint Castilian and French armies in the War of Spanish Succession, and its ensuing political subjection, the Center for Contemporary History in Barcelona and the Catalan Society for Historical Studies organized a symposium with the title "Spain Against Catalonia: A Historical Look 1714–2014." Participants were highly regarded historians, all with respectable careers and some with international reputations. The mere announcement of the symposium triggered a barrage of criticism in the Spanish media; three of the Spanish nationalist parties, the UPyD, the Citizens party, and the governing Partido Popular announced their intention of suing in order to prevent the celebration of the symposium; and prominent members of the cabinet, among which Minister for Foreign Affairs José García-Margallo, lashed out, calling the organizers pseudo-historians and excluding (i.e. intolerant) nationalists. All of these accusers, which included not a few historians, reacted with farsighted acumen to the content and drift of papers that had not yet been presented. Once again, the alacrity with which political parties, the media, and the judiciary joined the state apparatus to suppress freedom of opinion, or, failing that, to defame dissenters, evinced the profound malaise of Spanish democracy, incapable of countenancing a serene academic debate around the articulation of the past. The explosion of disparagement and contemptuous disrespect intended to silence uncomfortable knowledge bespeaks insecurity. The state dreads a sober account of its territorial policies over the last three centuries, and its swift reaction by means of expletives not only proved the relevance of the conference's theme but showed that this history is still laden with affect. And a past that is shot through with affect is an unresolved past, a past that endures in the present. A past that continues to act in the present, that impressed itself in the memory of a human community with the force of exerted or suffered violence, is by definition a traumatic past. Hence, those who exercised violence remain trapped in violent forms of resolution of present problems, while those who suffered it find it very hard to overcome its intimidating effects.

When dealing with the friable and self-correcting image of the past, it is important to take into account the transferential relation that Dominick LaCapra considers inherent to every analysis of traumatic events. By stepping into the role of secondary witness and coming into indirect contact with the past, the historian undergoes a transferential relation, becoming emotionally involved with the witness, and develops a tendency to act out an affective response (11–12). This response can have either a positive or a negative sign, can be empathetic or hostile, but is always there. Consequently, the historian, says LaCapra, "must work out an acceptable subject-position with respect to the witness and his or her testimony" (12). What is acceptable depends on the ethical or even deontological self-demand of the individual historian and his or her professional community. The transference cannot be avoided, only accounted for, and the absolutely unacceptable subject-position is to deny its existence and to claim pure objectivity with respect to the witness, even or especially when the witness is dead and cannot speak for himself.

CHAPTER TWELVE

Between Testimony and Fiction: Jorge Semprún's Autobiographical Memory

> Germany is not the single European country that has an unresolved
> problem with its collective memory ... Spain also has one, since
> an overwhelming majority rightly decided in favor of a collective,
> desired amnesia in order to achieve the wonder of a peaceful
> transition to democracy. But some day it will also
> have to pay the price for this process.
> Jorge Semprún, Dank. Address on the Awarding of the Freedom
> Prize of the Association of German Booksellers.

Societies do not remember; people do. There is no such thing as group memory prior to or above the individual's precarious retention of the past. This is the reason why cultural memory is transmitted from mind to mind. Social memory is nothing but this exchange. Certainly, material culture contains clues to the past, as do documents of foregone eras; but artifacts no more remember than they speak. Even recorded voice, disembodied and detached from its origin, does not speak; it merely produces sound. Without consciousness there is no language. This trivial though frequently forgotten observation accounts for the seeming paradox that modern society forgets in direct proportion to its accumulation of objects from previous ages. Alienating the past in artistic and technical re-enactments, commodifying the experience of time, staging "history," or museumizing its otherness is the clearest sign of a society's estrangement from its memory. It shows that society not only has forgotten the past but the present also.

Thus, when we speak of collective memory, we refer to the intersubjective constitution of our experience. Personal memory taps into a social fund of memories and modulates itself through them. But even as it does so, it remains anchored in consciousness. Outside of consciousness time does not exist, and memory cannot arise. The collective or "public" dimension means that social memory is not concerned with isolated anecdotes of private life but with events and experiences affecting everyone. As a common denominator of the myriad instances of remembered past, the collective memory cannot but be a convention.

To be compelling, memoirs must be located at the intersection of the personal and the collective. Jorge Semprún's books are for the most part autobiographical recollections whose interest arises from a self-conscious osmosis between the private and the public. Scion of an aristocratic family, son of a diplomat and grandchild of a prime minister, Semprún early on became used to the confluence between family life and the life of the republic. Both merged in his consciousness like two fluids in communicating vessels. The ease with which these spheres intermingle in his life is best dramatized in one of Semprún's most impressive recollections: the death of eminent sociologist Maurice Halbwachs, theorist of the collective consciousness, in the Buchenwald concentration camp, where Semprún was also interned.

Semprún, a former student of Halbwachs at the Sorbonne, says he was present at his professor's agony and, conscious of the need for prayer and without knowing what divinity to turn to, he recited a few verses from Baudelaire's *Le Voyage*: "Oh death, old captain, it is time, let's up anchor..." According to Semprún, Halbwachs appeared surprised; his lips trembled and smiled, giving him a "fraternal" look as he was dying. "Fraternal" is a momentous word. It abolishes the hierarchy between professor and student. But then, the camp had annihilated the past, everyone's past. Previous relations and civilian values, even memories, vanished as soon as deportees passed under the camp's gate.

Equality in abasement and destitution was imposed on all, or nearly all. Jews and Russians were cast to a lower circle of hell than were political deportees. But Halbwachs and Semprún were "political" and, allowing for differences of age and physical condition, on the same rank of degradation and beset by the same risks. Thus, the word "fraternity" would seem to refer to the community of all those who, by virtue of their internment, expected to die in the short term. "This defined our being: to be with the other in the death that approached" (34), says Semprún, and the words are ambiguous. Did "the other" refer to the two of them alone, or did death unite all inmates? But fraternity, in those general terms, did not exist in the camps. Not, if we trust Primo Levi, who early on understood the rule of survival: "I had also deeply assimilated the principal rule of the place, which made it mandatory that you take care of yourself first of all" (*The Drowned and the Saved* 78–9). Or Ella Lingens-Reiner, cited by Levi, who stated: "How was I able to survive in Auschwitz? My principle is: I come first, second, and third. Then nothing, then again I; and then all the others" (cit. Levi 79).

Semprún, then, was likely referring to the death of Halbwachs as the shroud of a spiritual communion between the two of them. But in this scene death was precisely what separated them most. Halbwachs, not Semprún, had entered the tunnel from which, as the block's kapo put it, "your professor will come through the chimney even today" (*L'écriture ou la vie* 32). Was Semprún indulging in metaphysics when he wrote that his Being was defined by the fact that he was *with* Halbwachs *inside* approaching death?

Earlier in the book, he recalls paying several visits to Halbwachs and mentions that another French professor, Henri Maspero, shared the same pallet bed with Halbwachs in block 56 of the small camp. Reading *L'écriture ou la vie*, Maspero's son François also stumbles on the word "fraternal," observing its compulsive repetition. Under the circumstances, he notes, the word could have only two meanings. First, the assertion of an immaterial good constituted by ideas, the aspiration of humanity negated by the camps. And secondly, "the anguish of imminent death— precisely that which cannot be shared" (18). An objection can be raised with respect to the first sense of "fraternal." Semprún does not proclaim the faith in the ideal only for himself. By speaking of a communion, he affirms it also for Maurice Halbwachs. "But of that, he knows nothing: it's *a declaration of faith*, even if they shared equally, not death itself but its presence, its imminence common to all the prisoners—although Semprún's employment in the *Arbeitsstatistik* constituted for him, at the very least, a form of reprieve that, on his pallet bed, Halbwachs (like my father) could not hope for" (Maspero 20).

Against the objection that death was the limit of any conceivable fraternity, Semprún defended himself over the years, asserting his intimacy with the death of Halbwachs and others, such as his friend Diego Morales, who also died of dysentery in Buchenwald. "I had lived Morales's death. I was still living it" (*L'évanouissement* 858). In *L'écriture ou la vie* he discusses at length Wittgenstein's statement in the *Tractatus-Logico-Philosophicus*, "Death is not an event of life, Death is not lived through" (*Tractatus* 185), which he had written in the journal he kept during his eighteenth year. "It is impossible to live death," he claims to have written in the journal, adding that, years later, in *L'évanouissement*, he altered the phrase to "Death is not a lived experience" (181). The verb *erleben* and its substantive *Erlebnis* are, he says, hard to translate into French, and so he corrects the original statement to make it allegedly more rigorous. Wittgenstein should have written instead: "My death is not an event of my life. I do not live through my death" (182). In 2001, in his address for the awarding of the Konrad Adenauer Foundation literary prize to Norbert Gstrein, Semprún insisted in correcting Wittgenstein's "tautological banality" ("Wovon man nicht sprechen kann" 16) and expounded his thought: "Later, in the concentration camp this phrase was confirmed [for me], when I underwent the death of others—pals or unknown ones—as a personal experience. As our Being-with-unto-death [Mitsein-zum-Tode] became the deepest and most intimate experience of that time, I managed to rid myself of the superficiality of Wittgenstein's proposition" ("Wovon man nicht sprechen kann" 16).

His idea is that one experiences other people's deaths in closest immediacy; that their deaths are part of one's life. But it is hard to see how this changes the problem. If Halbwachs did not live through his own death, Semprún's pretense of a communal experience in and of death between the two of them remains misplaced. Dorota Glowacka overinterprets Semprún's phrase, "This carnal distress, which made me uninhabitable to myself. Time passed. Halbwachs was dead. I had lived Halbwachs's death" (53), when she asserts: "He experiences Halbwach's dying in his own body" (99). In the passage, the "carnal distress" does not amount to a co-experience of death. It is the physical reverberation of the other's death, the somatic aspect of bereavement.

In *Le Mort qu'il faut*, Semprún again ministers poetic consolation to a dying inmate (46), this time a young student of approximately his age, whom he calls his brother, perhaps his double (43). Citing Heidegger, whose "Sein-zum-Tode" he had already discussed in his youthful journal (*L'écriture ou la vie* 181), Semprún writes: "There one could experience the death of others as a personal horizon: being-with-for-death, *Mitsein zum Tode*" (*Le Mort qu'il faut* 60). As he had done with Wittgenstein's proposition, he again modified a philosopher's concept to adjust it to his own experience, real or pretended, of partnership in death.

Semprún projects a great deal into Halbwach's silence, forcing the dying man to speak in his own sense. The scene, as told many years later, is fraught with value for the writer he had become in the meantime. He alone among all the inmates at Buchenwald ministered the last rites of the French language to the author of *Les cadres sociaux de la mémoire*. Invoking Baudelaire into the office of ferryman, Semprún reminded the posthumous wayfarer of an ideality that would survive the camp, lifting Halbwachs above the corruption of his body plagued by dysentery—an ideal sphere called out of Semprún's memory of his former education at the Lycée Henri IV in Paris. Here too was a fraternity, a sharing of sorts. But, says Maspero, precisely with regard to the ideal, "if Semprún can speak of sharing, it is because, having sustained Halbwachs, Halbwachs must have sustained him from that moment in the short vigil and continues to support him today" (23). The implication is obvious. Halbwach's "fraternal" look stands for a passing of the relay, and the solemnity of the moment for an initiation. The verbal anointing with

Baudelaire's words served as extreme unction for the departing soul and as consecration and a tacit laying of hands for the aspiring intellectual who would later recollect this moment with the anxiety (hence the iterations) of an heir keen on demonstrating his legitimacy.

This is also Annette Becker's impression. In Semprún's self-styled protagonism at this secular ceremony, she discerns a desire to portray himself as Halbwachs's spiritual son (416), an opinion to which Franziska Augstein, Semprún's sympathetic biographer, objects on the strange grounds that the word "society" had no specific meaning for Semprún (77). Against all evidence, Augstein contends that he could never adopt the notion of a collective consciousness existing outside the individual. Nevertheless, in a footnote, she recalls that in *Autobiografía de Federico Sánchez*, Semprún had written: "You've always been interested in the collective memory, it's a known fact" (13). But she denies any significance to this statement, asserting without substantiation: "nevertheless he never went any closer into Halbwachs's concept of 'collective memory'" (363 n.5). Yet, it is not so much a question of the "collective memory" as of Halbwachs's ideas, and these can be traced in Semprún's work. Monika Neuhofer points out an explicit reference in *Le mort qu'il faut*, when Semprún dreams about the end of the Spanish republic and superposes this event to the death of his mother. "The entire scene," writes Neuhofer, must be read against the background of Maurice Halbwachs's *Les cadres sociaux de la mémoire*" (279). The connection is unmistakable; Semprún mentions this book just before the description of the dream.

It is possible to see in Semprún's literary memoirs a permanent engagement with the processes of memory, insofar as they result from a confrontation between the objects (including the physical co-presence of others) and the spaces that presided over the formation of the subject. In other words, it is reasonable to see in Semprún's work a long-term dialogue with Halbwachs, who, as Maspero fathomed, continued to support Semprún throughout his life. Hence, the consequence of the scene in *L'Écriture ou la vie* for the whole of Semprún's literary career.

Becker accused Semprún of altering the episode for convenience. She alleges that Halbwachs died in block 61, to which Semprún had no access, this being a block where killing of exhausted and terminally ill prisoners took place between January and March 1945 (434–5). Augstein objects to Becker that she cannot have proof of the location. In the final months of the war the small camp was so riddled with infectious diseases that even the S.S. avoided it and no one was keeping accurate records anymore (363 n. 6). That may well be, but Augstein adds that the camp's existing documents show Halbwachs's death to have occurred on 16 March 1945, in block 55.

And while this number is much closer to the one mentioned by Semprún, the date does not bear him out. He says that he visited Halbwachs and Maspero every Sunday in the spring of 1944, and later places Halbwachs's death at the end of spring. But, as François Maspero remarks, his father and Halbwachs did not arrive in the camp until August 1944. And Halbwachs died before the beginning of spring. Where could Semprún have seen the two of them lying on the same pallet bed and week by week witnessed the steady rise of "death's black dawn" in their eyes? Certainly not in block 56, objects Maspero. "Perhaps," he asks, "in the sick bay, during the only week in March when my father was truly dying? Yes, snow in memory" (41).

The scene of Semprún holding the dying Halbwachs in his arms and reciting poetry to him, if not apocryphal, is certainly embellished. François Maspero observes that, earlier in the book, Semprún mentions his father lying next to Halbwachs in block 56, but in the dramatized scene of the poetry recital Maspero has disappeared, and everything happens as if Semprún and Halbwachs were isolated in mutual engagement (24). Someone else has disappeared from the scene: Halbwachs's son, Pierre, himself an inmate at Buchenwald, whom Semprún had included in previously published accounts of his visits to the dying professors. And Maspero rightly asks, with regard to Semprún's assertion of the smile provoked by his recital: "The sight, the presence of the loved child, were they not more powerful than the most beautiful poem in the world?" (25).

Maspero does not dispute the kernel of reality in Semprún's narrative, but expresses reservations about its truth insofar as it could pass for testimony in the strict sense of the word. He settles the matter with an ironical recognition of the novelist's right to take licenses, citing Semprún's own statement: "What's the point of writing books if one does not invent the truth? Or even better, the verisimilitude?" (*Le Mort qu'il faut* 148, cit. Maspero 23). And in turn Becker concludes: "But Semprun does not pretend to offer more than the verisimilitude born of his memories, and what is the writing of history if not another way of restoring this verisimilitude from the available sources?" (417). Monika Neuhofer proposes an interesting approach to this issue. According to her, the introduction of Baudelaire's poem is "a literary strategy to make Halbwach's death narratable" (326 n. 55). "With poetry's help, he has found a form that permits him to speak about death and to give expression to the feeling of 'fraternity'" (330). In view of the impossible witnessing of a death that he did not die himself, it makes sense to speak with Neuhofer of secondary witnessing. She does so in reference to the Polish Jew who, in the wake of his extreme experience as a member of a *Sonderkommando*, could no longer testify, not because of incapacity to speak but because it is not possible to testify the incredible.

This is how Semprún poses the problem: "But there wasn't, there will never be survivors of the Nazi gas chambers. No one will ever be able to say: I was there. One was around, or in front, or on the side, like the guys of the *Sonderkommando* (*L'écriture ou la vie* 60).

Yet, the Polish Jew does in fact speak. He tells the other inmates what he has seen in Auschwitz. Semprún nonetheless interprets the Jew's visible anguish as the distress of someone who is afraid of not being believed, precisely because he has survived. In this paradox—the witness cannot be trusted because he is in a position to witness—did Semprún project his own anguish regarding his own credibility? He says that he can understand the witness's anguish. It stems from the guilt he feels for not having been in the place of those who did not return (60). But did Buchenwald inmates, used to seeing the flames of the crematorium shoot up every evening, find the *Sonderkommando*'s report about the Auschwitz gas chamber really so hard to believe? Was Semprún perhaps retrofitting his memoir with a theme that had by then become commonplace in the literature on the camps?

No one present at the scene displays the least skepticism. Furthermore, on what basis does Semprún identify the prisoner's anguish with remorse caused by his own survival? His likely answer is that he knows through empathy. François Nicoladzé observes: "The Semprunian narrator, like so many other survivors, seems to prowl around this idea: to have left the others in the land of the dead replays, in an even deadlier tone, the first wrenching away from the original soil" (197). Semprún understands the Polish Jew's feelings in light of his own. He was not *there* either when Halbwachs died. He was in front, or around, or next to him, but not in his place. To say that he shared his professor's death amounts to impossible witnessing. Hence the appropriateness of Neuhofer's opinion that "in *L'écriture ou la vie*, Semprún assumes the required secondary witnessing for the testimony of the surviving *Sonderkommando*; with his text he supports the authority of the primary witness" (254-5).

What is persuasive for the *Sonderkommando*'s scene is also valid for the episode of the agonizing Halbwachs. Semprún constructs the situation by describing the witness's physical aspect in detail, conjuring his presence without communicating his testimony. By emphasizing presence and reducing the description to the bare essentials—the look, the bodily position, the voice—he puts in place the conditions for secondary testimony. Again Neuhofer: "Through the repetition of 'Je me souviens' [I remember] Semprún confirms and establishes the evoked image. In this way, Semprún states the relation between him and the Auschwitz survivor: With his 'I,' he guarantees the existence of the witness. The allusion to his own memory in some way doubles the authority of the Auschwitz survivor" (255-6).

Beyond questionable coincidences of time and place, though not of fate, between the young Spanish communist, whose assignation to the *Arbeitsstatistik* ensured his survival, and the septuagenarian French professor who was fated to die in the camp, nothing in the legendary scene, to which Semprún returns time and again, permits us to disentangle the thread of literature from that of life. The tension between fact and fiction announced in the title of *L'écriture ou la vie* pervades a great deal of Semprún's writing. It is this tension, implicit in the conversion of memory into writing, that I would like to consider here with particular attention to *Autobiografía de Federico Sánchez*, the book in which Semprún opposed his private memory to the collective memory of the Spanish Communist Party (PCE), in and through which he had once regarded himself as a historical agent. Tension and interdependence between these two types of memory endow the autobiography with an interest that is lacking in strictly private memoirs.

To be precise, the tension that generates interest in this book is not between extralinguistic facts and narrative strategies, but between divergent orders of discourse: those of fictional and of factual narration. The latter fans out into a range of genres (biography, diary, journalistic story, news, history, legal brief, etc.), while fiction, although divided into subgenres (fairy tale, myth, epic, short story, film script, etc.), tends to be associated with the novel. And while the difference between the two modes of narrative cannot be determined in relation to content (novelists often import real events and characters into their stories, while historians sometimes round up a description with unsubstantiated details, or arrange the facts according to some rhetorical model), one of fiction's defining traits is that it simulates factual discourse. To the extent that the simulation is effective, there is no way to discern the fictional from the factual. Most of the time, though, fictional marks are present, and readers suspend disbelief as on cue. But skillful writers also use the opposite strategy, introducing marks of non-fictionality in order to disarm skeptical readers.

Discriminating between factual and fictional can be impractical, especially in texts written in a confessional or testimonial mode. Käte Hamburger considered narrative in the first person the only genre in which simulation (*Fingiertheit*) remains imperceptible (259). As we will see, her observation is of particular interest to us, because Semprún's testimonial texts are, with the arguable exception of the two Federico Sánchez books, technically conceived as novels. But what Hamburger says of first-person narrative in general can be also asserted of autobiography. This is so much the case that, in the absence of external documentation, first-person narration may be indiscernible from authentic autobiography (261).

Philippe Lejeune, in *L'autobiographie en France*, subscribed to the same opinion, stating that there is no difference between autobiography and the autobiographical novel, so long as one remains on the level of the internal analysis of the text (24). Four years later, in *Le pacte autobiographique*, he pointed out differences of a paratextual nature between what he called an "autobiographical novel" and true autobiography. While the two can be formally identical, they are nonetheless distinguished by the fact that the identity between author and main character is ascertainable for one type of text and merely plausible for the other. In order to ascertain the identity of author and character, Lejeune says that we rely on external information or else on suspicion that the identity may be false. But it is hard to know on what the suspicion might be based, if it arises from internal information alone. In the case of the autobiographical novel, where the identity between author and character is merely apparent, the difference between them is a matter of degree. There is no degree in actual autobiography, says Lejeune: "it's all or nothing" (*Le Pacte autobiographique* 25).

Aside from the fact that readers' suspicion is a subjective category, ranging from credulity to critical distance, the distinction between fictional autobiography and autobiography based on the absolute identity between author and narrator comes to grief in cases like Semprún's *Autobiografía de Federico Sánchez*. The presence of the two names on the cover, one for the person with ownership of the rights to the text, the other for the putative writer of the work, is a paradoxical index of fictionality. Paradoxical because Federico Sánchez was Semprún's assumed name during the years of his militancy in the PCE. It was the name shown in his passport, the name by which he was known to the underground communist network and the Franco police. For years, it was the name Semprún went by in the real world, or in a part of it. Although outlasted by the author's enduring identity, Federico Sánchez was neither a pseudonym in the sense of a penname, nor a heteronym, like Kierkegaard's or Pessoa's alter egos. Assumed for purposes of covert activism on behalf of the Communist Party, this name stands for a specific consciousness and a distinct memory spanning the birth of the communist agent and the death of the party member. This limit is decisive and its eventual overstepping highly significant, as we will see. As a summation of experience, autobiographies are typically written toward the end of their authors' life. And so it is with Federico Sánchez's. This book is the memoir of an identity that unravels with its writing. Federico ceases to exist in order for the autobiography to come into being. It is either writing or life, and the choice of writing reverses Semprún's decision to give up writing for politics in the 1940s and 1950s. As an act of self-transcendence, the autobiography is built on the corpse of the remembering character. A posthumous autobiography means in effect an opposition between what the autobiographer knows and what his former acting self thought that he knew.

An opposition between blindness and insight pervades this political narrative; it is its internal law. Two lines of interpretation vie in the autobiography. One claims command over the order of history, the other over experience. They clash over precedence, each claiming to be the yardstick with which the departures of one discourse with respect to the other must be judged. Opening a gap at the heart of the text, the narrative voice detaches the two orders of discourse, producing a divorce between the fictional (though once historical) character and the historical (though once supplanted) personality that assumes ownership of the text. Whose voice utters the first words from the witness stand? Is it Sánchez who speaks? Or is it Semprún?

"Witness" is no metaphor here. The autobiography opens on the scene of Federico Sánchez's trial by the executive committee of the PCE. And everyone knows that in communist processes, as in Kafka's, guilt is a foregone conclusion. But, in a shrewd reversal, Semprún suspends the pronouncement of the sentence and uses the pause to open another narrative line, whereby it will be he, Sánchez, who indicts the party from the standpoint of his own memory. In this way, the book turns out to be the historical trial of the Spanish Communist Party in which Semprún/Sánchez plays the roles of prosecutor, witness for the accusation, and sitting judge.

The book starts when iconic party leader Pasionaria asks for the floor. Her request is a mere formality; it already announces the sentence, which everyone knows will be without appeal. But at this very instant, a rhetorical strategy suspends her imminent speech, leaving it in abeyance, much as Don Quijote is left holding up his sword and about to attack the man from Biscay at the end of a chapter. In this case, Pasionaria is left open-mouthed at the very beginning of the book, her speech blocked by the flux of Sánchez's memory, which unfolds for the duration of the text, until Pasionaria manages to pronounce her verdict, closing the party's books on Federico Sánchez and Semprún's book withal. His autobiography, therefore, begins not *in medias res* but the instant before it is about to expire. On the brink of extinction, Sánchez's life flashes through his mind, as allegedly happens to dying people.

But is it Sánchez, member of the Spanish Communist Party's politburo, who posthumously recalls his own bureaucratic execution? Or is it Semprún who ventriloquizes the ghost of Federico Sánchez and spins his own memory by means of the latter's? I do not use the word "ghost" in a vague theoretical sense. The word is Semprún's, and he uses it in its ordinary acceptation:

"Ten years later you saw Simón Sánchez Montero again. It was in the summer of 1969, in Madrid. Much had happened since that distant evening of June. You were no longer Federico Sánchez. That ghost had disappeared. You were yourself again: you were me already" (*Autobiografía* 60). Instead of "ghost" he could have said "double." Sánchez's ghost could only arise after his civil disappearance, whereas the double exists alongside the self, projecting the "I" as an "other." *Je est un autre*, Rimbaud said, and the alienation expressed in that phrase is closer to what Sánchez represented for Semprún in the years of his clandestine work for the Communist Party. That *other* was decommissioned, put out of existence by the party's fiat in 1964. It was then that, reabsorbed into the self ("you were me already"), Sánchez became a ghostly memory clamoring to vindicate itself in a ruthless autobiography.

In Sánchez's memoir, Semprún's reminiscences bubble up from the center of his alter ego's traumatic excommunication, as Proust's did from the effect of tea-soaked madeleine on his taste buds. But Semprún was a sophisticated memoirist who knew the usual narratological tricks. One trick he uses time and again is denying the use of intrigue, though it is a form of suspense that organizes the narrative's temporality and allows him constantly to weave in and out of underlying stories as he advances the main narrative flow.

> If you were in a novel, if you were a novelistic character, I am sure that now, looking at Dolores Ibarruri, you would remember other encounters with her. In well-crafted novels, flashes of memory are very nice; they catch the eye. Besides, they provide the narrative with a density that a merely linear development cannot achieve ... It is so, at least in shrewdly constructed novels, those showing know-how. (*Autobiografía* 9)

This rhetorical move is foundational for Sánchez's narrative. Pasionaria's taking the floor not only inaugurates the text but sends the writer's memory searching for origins, as Semprún turns the clock back to 1947, when he was not yet Federico Sánchez. That year he visited the Parisian headquarters of the Spanish Communist Party at Avenue Kleber. Taking us back to Sánchez's proto-memory, the narrator introduces elements that could not possibly be autobiographical in a strict sense. Contributory externalities can have only one purpose: to establish the conditions of writing and provide a sense of objectivity to the life that writes itself. In this way Semprún performs outside the autobiography of his alter ego what he claims not to be doing inside: he remembers previous encounters with Dolores Ibárruri, shaping the narrative by means of a non-linear development that adds density to the account, the very marks that he has just associated with shrewdly constructed fictions.

According to Hamburger and Lejeune, however, these marks do not suffice to distinguish fictional from true autobiography. Paratextual information, not formal decisions, settles that generic ambiguity. But according to Barbara Herrnstein Smith, in historical texts (and Semprún's autobiography styles itself one) we have two narratives at our disposal. One of these can be considered the source of the other, and its chronological order, being the order of history, gives the measure of the distortions and deviations of the second narrative in relation to it (cit. Genette 71). Smith deploys the formalistic distinction between *fabula* (story line) and *sujet* or sequence of events as organized in the narrative. This distinction corresponds to Semprún's contrast between autobiographical chronology (the facts as lived by the narrating character) and novelistic presentation. Only, as Gerard Genette objects, Smith's theory neglects the fact that fictional texts call attention to the anachronisms by means of various verbal markers. Although these markers can be implicit, says Genette, we recognize them through our knowledge of causal relations. Hence, the distortion of the narrative order does not appear to the reader in relation to an absolute order of the events that would be independent from all renderings, but in relation to what the narrative in question says the order of events to have been (Genette 72-3). And, indeed, we only know the chronology of Sánchez's memories through the autobiography, as told by a narrator who alerts us to the deliberate analepses and prolepses incurred in relation to a linear discourse whose form Semprún attributes to the divinity.

> But I have not written this story in chronological order, perhaps because I am not God, perhaps because biblical models and the false reconstruction of a life from beginning to end bore me, perhaps because life has no beginning and no end, although it has beginnings and ends. Be that as it may, I have started to write this story by the end, at the very moment in which the diatribe that Pasionaria is about to pronounce will expel Federico Sánchez to the dark oblivion of outer darkness. (*Autobiografía* 162)

Semprún's choice of temporality is consonant with the autobiographical genre. By starting at the end of the tale, he not only acknowledges that there are indeed a beginning and an end, if not to life (which is a metaphysical assertion) certainly in narrative. And because there is an end that closes the circle and turns into a recuperation of the origin, he abjures the party's ever-postponed utopian future and decides to write retrospectively, by dint of memory rather than of faith. Furthermore, the act of memory by which he conjures the ghost of Federico Sánchez and makes him walk again is a reaction to the speech act with which Pasionaria, like a cruel mother, once cast him from under her wing and out of the communist family. Narratologically, then, the memory anticipates the event out of which it grows, the action follows the reaction.

But Semprún's claim that he is not reconstructing Sánchez's life must be nuanced. Reconstructing a life is what an autobiography does, and if there is no infancy in Sánchez's, this is because he was born as an adult out of Semprún's political convictions, like Minerva from the head of Zeus. And Pasionaria helped with the delivery. Sánchez has a story to tell, even if that story is not told in biblical fashion, from Genesis to Apocalypse, but in Augustinian fashion, as a tension of temporalities in the narrator's consciousness. Sánchez's autobiography arises from his (or Semprún's) need to rescue his memory from the oblivion decreed by Pasionaria. Her words are the big bang that sets his memory in motion and expands it into an autobiography. But the resulting universe exists in a different, subjective temporality, as in Borges's story "The Secret Miracle." It is indeed Pasionaria's words that propel his memory, but the autobiography develops in the timeless space between her asking for the floor and the words she pronounces immediately after. And this bifurcation of time stands for the clash between official party history and individual memory.

When Pasionaria asks to take the floor, what had been a simple tactical disagreement within the leadership of the PCE becomes a gaping abyss between the party line and the wayward intellectual. Twelve years later, Semprún steps into this void to write the story of his communist activism, pitting his memory against the party's claims of historical perspicuity:

> It leaves me cold that those who were wrong in '64 and have been wrong since then continue to lead the party: those who have never seen a forecast or prediction of theirs come true; those who have no other merit than surviving all their mistakes: pushed forward by the flow of a history that they neither properly understand nor command: those who nevertheless continue to believe that they are reality's demiurges and will end up convinced that Franco's death was the result of their strategy. (*Autobiografía* 35–6)

Neither the Judeo-Christian God nor its Hegelian reincarnations correlate their stories with individual experience. The biblical God, because, as master of the beginning and the end, He connects both by means of a line, otherwise known as His providential plan, that is at odds with human deviations, otherwise known as sin, which entangle individuals in particular stories with their own beginnings and ends. And communists, because they twist reality to fit their dialectic. But since reality does not have the good sense to ratify their prophecies, communists subsequently twist their interpretations to neutralize the facts.

> A system of this kind [the Stalinist] constantly needs to remake history, rewriting it to adjust it to the tactical needs of the political moment. For this reason, the worst enemy of that system is the truthful testimony. A lucid, critical memory is the worst enemy of that pragmatic, arbitrary history of the forgetful. (*Autobiografía* 173–4)

Truthful testimony based on personal memory challenges the Communist Party's claim to scientific objectivity. Semprún's critical use of chiasmus turns the tables on his judges. It is they, not the intellectualized Sánchez—"harebrained intellectuals," Pasionaria had called him and Fernando Claudín (*Autobiografía* 303)—who are guilty of the bourgeois sin of subjectivity: "One could even say, I think, that subjectivity has been a specific malady of Spanish communism" (*Autobiografía* 73). This may well be, but subjectivity goes hand in hand with the novelist's license to organize fictional plots. By making subjectivity an inherent trait of Spanish communism, Semprún lays the charge of fictionality, indeed of myth making, at the Party's doorstep.

In light of his recurring defense of the writer's license to walk on the razor's edge of verisimilar memory, what does he gain by denying time and again that he is writing the autobiography in the form of a novel? Charging the Communist Party with chronic subjectivity is tantamount to denouncing an idealization gone awry. The communist worldview is a failed theoretical paradigm, all the more scandalous for its self-described materialism. On the opposite side of the party/individual dichotomy, he, Sánchez/Semprún, remains committed not to the theory but to the link between the past and its representation in consciousness, to memory, that is. And faithfulness to memory implies the existence of what Paul Ricœur called "prenarrative quality of experience" (74). Any rendering of past events must be continuous with this quality if it aspires to the status of "truthful testimony." According to this view, there are narrative pulsations at the core of events, something like a skeletal or spectral arrangement of the facts demanding to be recounted before they can be comprehended. Ricœur uses the example of the patient who tells his psychoanalyst bits and pieces of experiences, dreams, mental representations and associations. "We may rightfully say of such analytic sessions that their goal and effect is for the analysand to draw from these bits and pieces a narrative that will be both more supportable and more intelligible" (74). What is true for a patient's fragments of consciousness applies equally to a writer's memory. And, indeed, Semprún's non-linear, associational, story-within-a-story method of narration renders visible the entanglements of the subject with strains of previously untold narrative, which memory keeps in isolated seclusion until writing braids them together into a cogent tale.

> I suddenly remembered that other Sunday, thirty years earlier. Memory, as everyone knows, is like a *babushka,* one of those Russian dolls made of painted wood, which can be opened to find inside an identical though smaller doll, and another, and yet another, until one reaches the last, teeny one, which cannot be opened. (*Autobiografía* 200)

That last tale tucked away in the deepest recesses of memory is of course what the psychoanalyst tries to tease out by probing in the patient's subconscious. Although he is incomparably closer to his own memory than an external analyst could ever be, the self-scrutinizing autobiographer is interpretatively disadvantaged through his own resistance to self-knowledge. Only by opening that last, seemingly inaccessible box would the author be able to complete his self-portrait and organize the story from beginning to end. Short of illuminating this blind spot, the autobiography remains patchwork, the author suturing pieces and fragments of narrative into a meandering story that claims to correspond to the contents of an individual consciousness, and these to the facts of a life, Federico Sánchez's.

Here the tension between fictional and factual narrative comes again into play. To be engaging, an autobiography must not only entice the reader with the external details of a life, but also, and more fundamentally, with the inner movement of that life, with its subjectivity. Semprún is aware of this requirement when he writes, apropos his private meeting with Pasionaria in her exclusive coach in a train traveling between Prague and Bucharest:

> You boarded that especial train; remember it.
> How could I not remember it! If I were writing a novel instead of a merely testimonial report, with only the facts and what was said, the minute details, heads and tails of the naked truth, I would doubtless use the opportunity for literary showcasing. I could write a brilliant chapter about that journey, just by letting the resources of the novelistic imagination settle in and proliferate. (*Autobiografía* 194)

The difference between enriching the scene with imaginary accessories and giving a sober but detailed (blow-by-blow) rendering of the event should not be mistaken for the antinomy of fiction and fact, imagination and the object. The key word in the passage is "remember it." The scene of the meeting in the railway car does not reproduce life as it happened but as it is remembered.

More precisely, as remembered in 1977 by the disenchanted anti-communist that Semprún had become in the meantime. In his post-Second World War journal, Ernst Jünger warned about the interference of after-knowledge with memory: "One imports the consequences much too easily [into hindsight], not to speak of simple interest" (*Jahre der Okkupation* 40). Semprún admits as much, but, unlike Jünger, he does not extrapolate from this generalization to his own memory. Harboring no suspicions about his motives, he does not suspect ambiguity in his autobiographical settling of accounts with the ideology he had once mistaken for historical truth. It is the party's memory that is tainted with pragmatism, not his:

> Once more you are astonished to realize how selective the memory of communists is. They remember certain things and forget others. Still others they expel from memory. Communist memory is actually a form of forgetfulness; it does not consist in remembering the past but in censoring it. The memory of the communist leaders works pragmatically, according to their interests and current political objectives. It is not historical, testimonial memory; it is ideological memory. (*Autobiografía* 213)

Semprún's astonishment underscores the interval between himself and Federico Sánchez, between the man with a communist memory and the writer that imports the consequences of his break with the party into his retrospection. The man who boarded Pasionaria's reserved railcar in the Prague station was a committed Stalinist. His fealty to the party had led him earlier to report members of his own cell, practicing the same ideological censorship that he was to denounce years later. In the late 1940s, he attended the meetings of cell 722 of the French Communist Party, corresponding to the district of Saint Germain-des-Pres, where he lived at the time. Members of this unit included, besides Semprún, Robert Antelme, Daniel Antelme, Marguerite Duras, Edgar Morin, Dionys Mascolo, Claude Roy, Jacques-Francis Rolland, Roger Vaillant, Pierre Hervé, Pierre Courtade, Clara Malraux, Michel Leiris, Georges Bataille, Dominique and Jean-Toussaint Desanti. In 1950, this cell was the object of a Stalinist process resulting in sanctions being applied to several of its members, some of whom resigned from the party. The occasion had been when, at one of their meetings, members of the cell, especially Antelme, Duras, and Mascolo, had defended literature's autonomy from political ideology and *en passant* they had mocked the criteria with which the party's cultural mandarins—Louis Aragon, Jean Kanapa, or Laurent Casanova—condemned writers like Malraux and Faulkner.

Antelme, Duras, Mascolo, and Regnier denounced Semprún as an informer, a *mouchard*, who had betrayed their friendship. They accused him of having put an end to a modality of militancy based on intellectual freedom and plurality of opinion rather than on the narrow guidelines issued by the party's central authority. When Antelme's and Mascolo's letters to the party in protest at their expulsion were published in 1998, and Semprún's name was revealed by an article in *Le Monde* on 16 June, he sought to refute the accusations in an article published ten days later ("Non, je n'ai pas 'denoncé' Marguerite Duras," *Le Monde* 26 June 1998) in which he flatly denied having been present at the trial of Robert Antelme. Unfortunately for his disavowal, Edgar Morin affirmed in a television program of Canal Plus that Semprún had indeed been the author of the report accusing Duras, Mascolo, Antelme, and others. And, on 8 July, Antelme's widow, Monique Antelme, replied with an article of her own in *Le Monde*, titled "Jorge Semprún n'a pas dit la verité," in which she asserted that Semprún had been present at the meeting in which the secretary of the 6th district section of the French Communist Party, Perlican, had read an injurious report, mostly against Robert Antelme, that was presented as having been prepared by Jorge Semprún (Semprún Maura 142–4).

Historian of the Spanish Communist Party Felipe Nieto advances the thesis that Semprún's decision to become a "vigilante" vis-à-vis ideological deviations could have been a precautionary reaction to potential accusations of Titoism by association with his brother-in-law, Jean-Marie Soutou, a diplomat in Belgrade who was suspected of the heresy in communist circles (76). Semprún's brother Carlos offers a more scathing explanation. According to him, in 1950, Santiago Carrillo had offered Semprún a promising career in the Spanish Communist Party, and Jorge was not willing to endanger that prospect by going into the party with the ballast of a friendship with a bunch of petty bourgeois intellectuals who, after being expelled, had become class enemies and objective enemies of the USSR. "Instead," writes Carlos, "he could brag—he did it in my presence—about having expelled them. It was a plus" (129).

But this was in 1950. Fourteen years later, it would be Semprún's turn to be accused of deviationism by the leaders of the PCE. And ten years after his own exclusion, twenty-five after the affair of cell 722, he resuscitated the ghost of his former communist self in the role of Clémence, Albert Camus's penitent judge in *The Fall*. He began this full-blown attack on the party to which he had been unreservedly devoted by admitting what he could not suppress because it was widely known, namely his former Stalinism. The contrition accompanying this self-denunciation was more damaging to the party than any outsider's attack. As for the penitent judge, well, he was not really to blame; he had been drawn into the totalitarian ideology through the sheen of genuine virtues and noble philosophical reasons. And just as he had denied any wrongdoing in the Antelme–Duras affair, now he placed the responsibility for his indoctrination not on his own political blindness but on the shoulders of Benigno Rodríguez, a communist agent with "a Stalinist superego that worked without fail or truce," whom he admired (22). It was to this man that Semprún traced his communist orthodoxy. And lest this fascinated induction seemed questionable for a hyper-educated intellectual, Semprún added a predisposition stemming from more distinguished motifs: "I belong to the generation that still reached Marxism through reading Hegel, and more specifically, through Lukács's reading of Hegel in *History and Class Consciousness*, a key book in my eighteenth year of age" (25).

The philosophical origin of his militancy distinguished him from other members of the Spanish cadre. Thus, merely by recalling his intellectual provenance, he could turn the accusation of illegitimate origins against the party's leadership. In his mind, it was the inexpiable sin of bourgeois birth that accounted for his expulsion. "It's the Origins. Don't think about it anymore. They come from the working class and you don't. They speak in the name of the Origins, condemn you in the name of the Origins, expel you to the hell of your own unspeakable Origins" (*Autobiografía* 299). Perhaps. But Semprún had been a member of the executive committee for years. He belonged to the inner circle. He was entrusted with a position of responsibility: organizing the underground network in Spain during the halcyon years of the dictatorship. And everything suggests that he was given that responsibility not in spite but because of his cultural background.

Whether or not his expulsion had been a matter of social origins, he reacted by taking refuge in those origins. Since he had been de-realized, erased from communist memory, and cast into "the hell of outer darkness" (*Autobiografía* 298), he could only climb out of that hell by recalling his intellectual origins. Like Dante led by Virgil, Semprún could call on his psychopomps to claim a more exalted lineage than the one the party denied him. His Marxism drew from the authentic sources—Hegel, Marx, and Lukács—whereas his comrades had perverted the doctrine by importing the themes of a peasant-Catholic culture (*Autobiografía* 22). Kindled by faith in the coming world order, the fire of the party spirit glowed in their primitive faces. "A Pentecostal tongue hovers over their heads. They're all of working class origin and that origin sanctifies and apostolizes them, making them worthy of proclaiming the virtues of the Party-Spirit, of singing its praises and casting you into the hell of outer darkness" (*Autobiografía* 298).

He had no place in their communion. They preached the triumph of the universal class; yet it was social origins that decided one's destiny. But even their inverted nobility was deceitful. "You look at your comrades of working class origin and you see the tongues of Pentecostal fire dancing over their baldness. Actually, they have not worked for decades and many of them have only been workers by origin, never real workers" (*Autobiografía* 299). Re-classed into a privileged bureaucracy and tucked away in comfortable exile, the party's leadership makes its message, its rhetoric, incomprehensible to the masses: "Carrillo not only speaks from outside but also from afar, and the workers to whom he speaks not only cannot listen to him but would not even understand him if they could hear his calling" (*Autobiografía* 81).

To this rhetoric plagued with jargon Semprún opposes a straightforward discourse, allegedly avoiding the temptation of literary exhibitionism. In this context, the repeated mantra that he is not writing a novel means that he, unlike Carrillo, speaks to the militancy in a language they can understand, because it is Federico Sánchez's, the comrade who lived among them, went to the same bars, the same soccer stadium, the same demonstrations in police-surveyed Madrid. Never mind that Semprún is back in Paris and Carrillo is by now back in Spain. It is not Semprún but the old, reliable comrade Sánchez who now speaks out against the party and confronts the leadership's fantasies with his harsh revelations. But who is really speaking? Earlier, it had been the Party spirit that spoke through Federico Sánchez. A tongue of fire had lingered above his head.

Semprún's self-exhortation to remember—"remember it!" he says to his alter ego—indicates the gradual construction of a character from inside. Autobiography is a means of access to a character's subjectivity. But the fact that something, an elusive memory, a tiny doll, cannot be opened and referred to a previous one, makes of autobiography a limited self-disclosure. Inasmuch as the self is an "other" to itself, self-writing yields no more than the partial reflection of a subjectivity. Only in fiction is an unobstructed glimpse into someone else's subjectivity possible, and that is, according to Genette, because this "other" is a fictional character or someone who is treated as such (in this instance, Sánchez by Semprún); treated, in other words, as someone whose thoughts the author imagines while pretending to report them. We can only guess infallibly what we invent, says Genette (76). And this applies as much to an author's insight into characters of his own designing as to what someone remembers by casting it in the mold of language.

Semprún's iterations of the disclaimer that he is not writing a novel are unmistakable marks of artificiality. In ordinary communication, people do not feel compelled to reassure their interlocutors that what they say is not invented, unless one is somehow aware that they are spinning their words. Suspension of disbelief is in order not just in poetry but also in social intercourse. It belongs to the conventions that make communication possible. On the contrary, in the *Autobiografía* we have already noted instances when

Semprún finds it necessary to warn the reader that he has left the fictional form behind and stepped into the austere precincts of truth. Looking closer, though, his departure from novelistic *poiesis* is hardly in evidence, since he has recourse to rhetorical techniques that, taken by themselves, do not help us discriminate between factual and fictional autobiography. There are moments when he is aware of this and settles the issue by means of simple negation. "If we were in a novel, one could tell me that Vicens's sudden appearance is a skillful narrative gimmick. But we are not in a novel" (*Autobiografía* 162). Or: "And of course I could write a dazzling chapter of a novel, if I were writing a novel" (*Autobiografía* 195). But since these assertions are intradiegetic (given the identity between character and narrative voice), they cannot be considered a guarantee of factuality.

Genette sees no reason why factual discourse should deprive itself of iteration, any more than fictional discourse does. As proof of this, he points to autobiography's use of it. But when speaking of iteration he has in mind marks of frequency (such as "every Sunday...") that operate by means of syllepsis (the use of one word applied to two or several others) identifying events considered similar or treated as such (75). The iterations of which it is a question here, though, are of a different kind. They are not borrowed from a type of fictional discourse (pseudo-autobiography) for a type of factual discourse (authentic autobiography); rather, they are what we might call marks of autobiographical false consciousness. Denying that he is writing a novel, Semprún not only stakes a truth claim; he also endows Sánchez with ontological status in the real world, builds him up as someone whose autobiography, if not his life (futile like the action of the party he served), produces historical effects by bringing testimony against the party's leadership.

Sánchez's autobiography, staged as an act of memory, of recollection, as a mobilization of language and of narrative techniques with referential intentionality, is the story of a retrospective enlightenment produced by his traumatic severance from the inner circle, the sancta sanctorum, of the Spanish Communist Party. I do not resort to religious language arbitrarily. Semprún deploys it when summarizing the epithets apportioned to Pasionaria in the hagiographic literature as "our mother, who art in heaven" (*Autobiografía* 21). In his autobiographical recollections, Semprún mines his memory to reveal levels within levels of language, like Russian babushka dolls stacked inside each other. Moving between the different levels, the subject progresses from myth to enlightenment, from delusion to self-discovery and anagnorisis, which the text describes as the transition from novel to testimony. "In other words, Dolores [Ibarruri] is both daughter and mother of the people. Her own daughter and mother, after all. The family romance of the neurotic poets from the personality cult era, among whom I must count myself, is, as can be seen, rather transparent in its melodramatic plot. Let Oedipus come and see" (*Autobiografía* 21). Oedipus, the blind seer of tragic myth, but also the Freudian transgressor of the elementary taboos. Sánchez is pictured here as a son who denies his mother after having made her the object of desire, just as Oedipus denied motherhood by taking Jocasta for a wife and turning himself into his own stepfather. Semprún's lingering Oedipal pulsation (killing Carrillo and denying the political mother) is the reversal of his infatuation with Pasionaria, to whom he had once dedicated abject poetry.

Liliana Soto-Fernández is probably right in seeing Ibarruri as a substitute for the mother Semprún had lost early on (132). A mother substitute who, as so often in fairy tales, turns out to be a cruel stepmother. Unless one prefers a less charitable, non-psychoanalytical interpretation and concludes that Semprún, like so many others in the party, engaged in leader adoration out of calculated desire for advancement. This coarser but more natural explanation ties with one of Semprún's black holes in his multiple variations on his own autobiography. I refer to the affair of the communist cell that met at the apartment of Marguerite Duras in Rue Saint-Benoît. "What is striking—says Alain Brossat—is the way Semprún organizes in his various books the disappearance of the activity that, in the years after Liberation, took him to the leadership of the French Communist Party as a militant active in intellectual circles" (200). What this dubious episode suggests is not the fragility of memory, its inconsistency and friable edges, but the deliberate occultation of that which the remembering subject cannot assume or afford in his objectivized self-projection in the world. "Everything happens as if Semprún, whose usual weakness is the gusto with which he mentions his acquaintance with famous people, had tried to erase from his multi-faceted, often redundant account, everything that led to the famous unacceptable scene in which he played the role of informer" (Brossat 200).

A few years before his death, in a colloquy celebrated in Girona in April 2003, Semprún, in the presence of his old friend Javier Pradera, recalled an episode in which he had also played an unglamorous role on behalf of the party. In 1960, twenty-six-year-old Pradera had sent a critical analysis of the situation in Spain to the party's leadership in Paris. The Spanish masses, he said, were not ripe for a general strike, which the party was intent on organizing as an infallible method to topple the dictatorship. The committee, presided by Secretary General Santiago Carrillo, interpreted Pradera's tactical advice as insubordination and instructed Federico Sánchez to report the content of Pradera's letter to the executive committee. One week later, Sánchez was asked to write the official response rebuking the young comrade for daring to disagree with official policy. This letter must have been harsh, because Semprún acknowledged in Girona: "The one who had to send Pradera to the jail of the Politburo in order to let him know that he had gone astray and lost perspective ... I was the one in charge of [writing] that letter" ("Palabras de apertura" in Pla, *Jorge Semprún* 8–9). A confession, no doubt, but one that he immediately mitigated: "I tried to do it in a way that he could understand the sympathy inside that critique, but in the end the fact was—it is probably kept in the archives—that the critique to the most lucid interpretation of the situation made in 1960 in a letter from Javier Pradera to the political bureau was made by Federico Sánchez. This is for history in small caps" ("Palabras de apertura" 9).

Self-exculpation characterizes Semprún's confessional method. Mitigating qualifications occur at every critical point in his career. It is a normal defense mechanism, but it grinds in the middle of his merciless attack on the party's memory. Although plausible, his claim that he was forced to write the letter is more damaging than his silence. Why did he now disclose this incident, which he had failed to remember twenty-six years earlier, as he was pitting Federico Sánchez's memory against the party's? He claims to be providing negligible information, merely a footnote lost in dusty party archives, an inessential truth "for history in small caps" ("Palabras de apertura" 9). Perhaps the circumstantial presence of the victim of his "typical Leninist exercise," as he himself described his action ("Palabras de apertura" 8), had something to do with it. Even if Pradera had no intention of reminding the former apparatchik about his inglorious performance forty-three years earlier, the incriminating document was indeed in the PCE archives, and Semprún knew it ("Palabras de apertura" 9). Much better then to volunteer the information, wrapped in protests of goodwill, for "history in small caps" before an indiscreet historian fished out the incriminating document and brought it to light. This possibility materialized ten years later in Felipe Nieto's detailed history of Semprún's communist career.

Under these conditions, Federico Sánchez's reply was a piece of nonsense. We cannot know if he really believed anything in that jumble of lessons typical of a condescending teacher, seasoned in the Marxist-scholastic jargon and exclusive owner of a dialectical vision about which, he intimates, his disciple is largely ignorant. At the same time, he cautioned him not to go over the cliff of an evanescent leftism or to be seduced by the paralyzing defeatism of a bourgeois intellectual. The truth is that Semprún's document, affectionate and with paternal overtones at times, addressed to the "long loved one" with whom, he says, he has discussed so much and wants to continue discussing in Madrid as in Paris, did not respond in a straightforward way to any of Pradera's objections to the party's policy, or to the question of the oligarchic exiting from the dictatorship, or to the conditions of possibility in the past or in the future, or to the forecasts, even if born out of rumors, about a possible monarchic solution with European integration as a backdrop. Federico Sánchez is the leader invested with authority who denies any hypothesis that the party has not foreseen. (Nieto 382)

Pradera's opinion about *Autobiografía de Federico Sánchez* was severe, notwithstanding the fact that it was dedicated to him. "The book seems to me excessive in tone and written from the low rather than the lofty passions" (cit. Canal 71). Still, his judgment merits consideration not just in relation to Semprún's arraignment of the Spanish Communist Party—which Pradera had also left shortly after Fernando Claudín's and Semprún's expulsion—but also for the light it sheds on the latter's method of assembling true bits and pieces from memory into inaccurate or misleading self-images.

Now, with these real facts Jorge has put together a story in which the accumulation of partial truths paradoxically does not yield a truthful book as its final product. Most of the things he says and of which I am cognizant are true, but his memory is exceedingly selective and confers a unilateral character to the book. When one complains about the others' lack of memory, one must be very scrupulous with one's own. (cit. Canal 71)

In his brilliant analysis of the twists and turns that Semprún called "the dizzying motionless spiral of my memory" (*Autobiografía de Federico Sánchez* 296), Brossat asserts that this writing technique, focused on the displaced, revised, ever more detailed repetition of the same episodes, parodies the confessional practice of the Stalinist parties. Mandating full disclosure from party members, this "spiritual exercise" precluded transparency, because the individual knew that not everything could be said. Brossat finds in Semprún's literature the same tension between the reader's demand for truth and the "right" to modulate the truth after his own fashion, which the subject of his novels and essays commandeers, "claiming for himself an unlimited credit of invention, selection, 're-writing'" (192). In Semprún's denial of his role in the expulsion of his friends from the French Communist Party converge, according to Brossat, the limits to Stalinist confessions (one simply does not tell it all) with the shame of the former member of Buchenwald's *Prominenten* vis-à-vis a survivor of one of the harshest commandos in the same camp. Robert Antelme, who never forgave Semprún for his part in the cell 722 affair, was such a rare survivor, and Brossat writes in this regard:

> From this moment one will better understand the unmentionable feeling of guilt and shame ... established between someone who did not know the worst circles of hell and someone who came very close to the Gorgon's eye, that the unavowable takes form when the former, in a later sequence, becomes the informer of the latter's political incorrectness. At that moment, the full weight of the unpayable debt of the one who declares that he went through the suffering of the concentration camp "with insatiable intellectual curiosity" ... in the place of the one who came within a hair's breadth of succumbing in it ... comes back in force and arrests the confession's machine, substituting wicked silence for the story's infinite noise. (201)

Although the notion of intellectual curiosity in face of the horror may revolt readers who have been taught to look on the extermination camps as places off limits for the understanding, curiosity seems to have been a common disposition among inmates. Viktor Frankl has written:

> Cold curiosity predominated even in Auschwitz, somehow detaching the mind from its surroundings, which came to be regarded with a kind of objectivity. At that time one cultivated this state of mind as a means of protection. We were anxious to know what would happen next; and what would be the consequence, for example, of our standing in the open air, in the chill of late autumn, stark naked, and still wet from the showers. In the next few days our curiosity evolved into surprise; surprise that we did not catch cold. (Frankl 14–15)

There is nothing irreverent about experiencing mental detachment in face of the physical suffering of oneself and others. It is not the temporary dissociation of the mind from the senses that is shocking, but the adaptability revealed by an otherwise unexceptional remark that escaped Brossat's scrutiny. This is the full citation: "You bore, without much difficulty, with insatiable intellectual curiosity, the experience of the concentration camp, in Buchenwald" (*Autobiografía de Federico Sánchez* 11). These three words—"without much difficulty"—expose the difference between Semprún's experience of the camp and the experiences of inmates like Antelme and Halbwachs.

In *L'écriture ou la vie*, the author associates his longing to forget to the feeling of "almost indecency" caused by "having spent eighteen months in Buchenwald without one single minute of anguish, one single nightmare,

carried by ever renewed curiosity, sustained by an insatiable lust for living"
(171). Compared to the condition of the average prisoner, whom Primo Levi
described as "an 'impeded' man ... and therefore profoundly downcast," and
as "a rag of a man" (*The Drowned and the Saved* 160), the absence of anguish,
even of nightmares, during the full time of his internment, suggests a
privileged situation. He would play it down, asserting that he belonged
to the "plebs" for all ordinary purposes (*Le Mort qu'il faut* 174), but his
advantage, only an edge perhaps but decisive in the dire conditions of the
camp, emerged in other places, as in the description of his showering with
hot water at chosen times and in small groups, as opposed to the weekly cold
shower in a crowded room that was mandatory for ordinary prisoners (165).
Or in his disclosing to Frank Appréderis in 2010, the year before his death,
that the clandestine communist organization in Buchenwald distributed an
extra ration of soup to its members (*Le langage est ma patrie* 46).

Necessarily, this double dipping came at the expense of the other prisoners.
There was no way to ignore it. "These combatants," says Semprún, as if he
were not speaking about himself, "were therefore a little better nourished
than the others" (46). "A little" may have been an understatement, if one
believes Semprún's brother Carlos's remark that, when Jorge came home
from Buchenwald, he looked just a little leaner than before but nothing
compared with their younger brother Paco, who had spent the war at home
and was emaciated from the restrictions. Later, continues Carlos, he could see
the difference between Jorge's healthy appearance and the images of camp
survivors, "true walking corpses, dressed in rags or in the striped 'uniform'
that U.S. Army documentaries and the press published every day" (120).

Such unconcealable privilege, rarely admitted by Semprún, and then only
after paring it down, suggests that in his case the shame of surviving, about
which Levi wrote unforgettably and Bettelheim described as a paradoxical
dissociation between mind and feeling (297),[1] could have rational causes.
By cooperating with the S.S. in the bureaucratic running of Buchenwald,
Semprún had become a tool of the death machine, no different in any
essential way from the millions of Germans who, without necessarily
adhering to Hitlerism, went on with their ordinary work inside the spiritual
trap that Nazi Germany had become after 1933.

In a published dialogue that took place late in Semprún's life, Jean
Lacouture raised the question of objective complicity in the role the

---

1 "The survivor as a thinking being knows very well that he is not guilty, as I,
for one, know about myself, but that this does not change the fact that the humanity
of such a person, as a feeling being, requires that he *feel* guilty, and he does"
(Bettelheim 297).

clandestine communist organization had played in the functioning of the camp (*Si la vie continue …* 75). Semprún's answer, though probably realistic, smacks of copout. If it hadn't been the communists, he says, someone else would have done it. "In any case, the factories would have continued to produce," he says, referring to the prisoners' production of war material for the German army (75). Semprún's justification was pragmatic, if also self-serving. By infiltrating the camp's bureaucratic apparatus, the communists were able to save the leadership of the resistance, the future leaders of the Western countries (*Si la vie continue …* 76–7). In other words, they looked after themselves for the higher motives. He allows that he came as close as possible to collaborating without falling into the moral abyss. Others, a minority, were more incautious and imitated the Nazis: "Why have I talked about the razor's edge? Because the least inadvertence, the least weakness suffices to transform this into complicity. And some have done it, German communist kapos who collaborated with the system. Some, a minority, even adopted Nazi habits; that is to say that they hit" (*Si la vie continue …* 77).

Although these protestations of decency are credible, still he fielded Lacouture's question by avoiding the point. Accepting some, perhaps unavoidable, degree of cooperation and adopting the behavior of the S.S. are widely different things. One could have cooperated with the intention of helping others, even unaware of any advantages to oneself, but even then it would remain true that without the cooperation the machinery of death would have ground to a halt. To deny this by saying that others would have done the job is probably realistic but morally evasive. It transfers one's responsibility to others who were not put to the test. It assumes universal corruptibility as extenuating circumstance. A comprehensible position, which can under circumstances be vindicated on historical but not on moral grounds, as Semprún came to understand with regard to communism. To the end of his life, however, he reduced moral freedom in the camps to the choice between fatalism (letting the Nazis, or the divinity, or chance decide) and determining oneself the fate of others.

Listening to a postwar discussion about the resistance in the camps, Gerard, Semprún's alias in the French resistance and self-narrating character of *Quel beau dimanche*, thinks his friends' arguments abstract, without any basis in experience. He dives into his memory and explains to them: "The single choice that presents itself is the following: does one let chance take over or does one intervene to modify chance, minimally in any case? On the other hand, perhaps it is not chance but fate. Or God. As you wish. But there is no other choice: to let God, fate, or chance decide, or to intervene with the force that we have, with the power at our disposal" (*Quel beau dimanche* 211).

In reality, the choice is not between God (or destiny, or fate) and human powers, but between letting an omniscient God (or blind fate) decide and impersonating God (or playing fate) and choosing according to one's lights, at the risk of serving one's interest or ideology. It means transforming Kantian law (the universal validity of the moral imperative) into a relativistic morality based on one's incidental values.

> At Buchenwald, all men do not weigh the same. A resistance fighter does not have the same weight as a guy who has been pinched in a neighborhood that has been sealed off after an attempt, or who has been busted for black marketeering. They may be equal before God, they certainly wear the same red triangle of political deportee that the S.S. give indistinctly to all the French, but at Buchenwald they do not weigh the same with regard to a strategy of resistance. (*Quel beau dimanche* 212)

Semprún's privileged situation in Buchenwald begs the question of the witness. Or the questions. Xavier Antich asks several. "What should one witness? Where is that *there* which the witness occupied and from which he ought to witness, if he can? Only about that which is *his*, that which he lived, which he experienced in the first person? ... About what horror can the surviving witness give testimony?" (162). His complex attempt at a reply by way of Blanchot, Levinas, and Agamben is a fascinating attempt to balance the proposition of an unspeakable horror without possible witness with Semprún's ventriloquizing of death by virtue of his claim to having been *there*. On the touchy issue of Semprún's years of silence, which he justified by the world's unwillingness to listen as soon as death entered the picture (*Écriture ou la vie* 146), Antich glosses: "And it was not only the presence of death in the story. It was death speaking. Speaking, of course, through the one who had passed through it" (177). Metaphorically, perhaps. But in reality Semprún had not passed through death. Had he done so, he could never have declared, except with utter cynicism, that he had endured the camp "without much difficulty." The answer seems to be, again, that Semprún, who was not actually *there* and who did not live his own death, let alone that of others, but did experience the camps as an extension of the communist struggle against Nazism, eventually took upon himself the responsibility of secondary witnessing. He would then witness for others, for the real witnesses, for those who had been *there* but were inexorably sucked into the "silence of death," the only thing, says Semprún, that "could have expressed the suffering" (*L'écriture ou la vie* 169).

Once he has assumed the task of secondary witnessing, Semprún relentlessly returns in his books to the places where the suffering lies buried in memory. There he lays siege to the silence with the gyrations of memory, sounding the depths of suffering by means of words. For this reason, his clash with Claude Lanzmann apropos the role of the document versus imagination was somewhat disconcerting. Like Lanzmann, Semprún vindicates empathy and practices the imaginative or affective "rounding" of the mnemonic traces of the past. But it is easy to understand why he would object to Lanzmann's "extreme, fundamentalist formulation" ("L'art contre l'oubli" 11). As a testimonial novelist who relies on the authority of his narrator, Semprún could never accept Lanzmann's dogmatic mysticism. The latter's conjuring of suffering and of ultimate evil through the negative dialectic of the unrepresentable collides with Semprún's practice of excavating his memory by means of representation. In his first book, *Le grand voyage*, he invented the Jew Hans Freiberg not merely in order to have a Jewish companion, as he would later say in *L'écriture ou la vie* (46), but above all to give a place in the narrative to all those other Jewish companions whom he claims to have had in real life. Ostensibly at odds with Lanzmann's puritanical crusade against the idolatry of the archive (and his provocative statement that, if there were a film documenting the gassing of prisoners, he would destroy it), Semprún had this to say about the filmic materials showing the camps:

> When I saw appearing on the cinema screen, under an April sun that was so near and yet so far, the muster ground of Buchenwald, where cohorts of deportees wandered in the distress of their recovered freedom, I saw myself brought back to reality, reinstalled in the truth of an indisputable experience. It had all been true, then, and everything still was: none of it had been a dream. (210)

Semprún resorts to archival documentation, or at least he mentions it as an objective witness and indispensable means to knowledge. It helps him to ground the imagination of the horror in ascertainable fact: "My work at the central archive of the camp, the *Arbeitsstatistik*, permitted me to know fairly exactly to what the numerical sections assigned to the arriving convoys corresponded: to what origin, what period of Buchenwald" (*L'écriture ou la vie* 53). Against archival work of this sort neither Lanzmann nor his converts can reasonably object, because, as Georges Didi-Huberman points out, by opposing the archive to the film *Shoa*, "Lanzmann does not see that he is opposing a type of historical objects *in general* to a filmic work *in particular*, which is already a contradiction by 'excess'" (146). For some, patient reconstruction of the scene of the crime by filling in the details can never satisfy the mystical duty to share in the awe of the unspeakable. Even so, it remains true that we can know—to the limited extent covered by the word "know"—the face of the horror *in history* only if we consent to "trivialize" it by attending to the empirical evidence. In the end, it is the humble detail—grisly or commonplace—that authorizes the witness's account. Another camp survivor, the psychologist Bruno Bettelheim, saw in the declaration that the holocaust was unimaginable and unspeakable a defense mechanism to avoid facing what it had been like in its gruesome detail (91).

Notwithstanding the anathemas hurled against those who dare relate horror to the commonplace, history presents an ordinary face even in the midst of extraordinary evil. Everyone knows with what abhorrence Hannah Arendt's realization of the incommensurability between the crime and the criminal in the figure of Eichmann was met. The relatives of the drowned required that the perpetrator should be nothing less than the ponderous embodiment of evil. An outsized monster was needed, not just for psychological reasons but also, as Bruno Bettelheim believed (264), to avoid the legal complications of trying him as a stand-in for the German people. The problem was that, if the system of which he had been a cog was indeed monstrous, the sneezing, cliché-dependent, nearly obsequious Eichmann did not measure up. His mediocrity and obvious paucity of character were perhaps the most appalling revelation of the Jerusalem trial. The horror, as remembered and as imagined, clashed with the figure of a colorless, punctilious functionary, an *Angestellte*, who could do no better than try to deflect responsibility by referring to his actions as "duty" (*Pflicht*).

Before Arendt, Ernst Jünger had already commented on the banality of Nazi figures in his little-read postwar reflections. Speaking of Himmler, he wrote:

> What has always moved me strangely about this man was his pervasive bourgeois nature. One could think that someone who sends many thousands to death would visibly distinguish himself from all others, and Luciferian glory would glow around him with terrifying glare. Instead, one meets these faces that one finds in every town when one is looking for a furnished room and a prematurely retired inspector opens the door. (*Jahre der Okkupation* 68)

Jünger saw what others, following in Kant's footsteps, have called "radical evil" as an advanced stage in the long-term increase in abstraction. His insight merits quoting at some length:

> Here, on the other hand, the extent to which evil has pervaded our institutions becomes clear: the progress of abstraction. Our hangman may turn up behind the next desk. Today he hands us a registered letter

and tomorrow the death sentence. Today he punches our ticket and tomorrow he shoots a hole in the back of our head. He executes both with the same pedantry, the same feeling of duty. Whoever does not already perceive it in the train station halls and in the keep-smiling of the saleswomen goes color-blind through our world. This world not only has terrifying zones and periods; it is terrifying from the ground up. (68)

Bettelheim agrees with Arendt on the banality of evil, while warning us not to put the accent on the banal. "But what must concern us primarily is that evil is evil; we must not permit its banality to detract from this fact" (280). Eichmann was not personally a monster, but he, along with millions of others, served a monstrous will and in doing so brought an evil system into being. The same is true of communism, the other twentieth-century totalitarian system that held millions in thrall. Communism's radical evil is disputed, perhaps because, unlike fascism and Nazism, it was not militarily defeated and many intellectuals were caught in its ideological tangles long after its crimes had come to light. As a result of the embarrassed or fanatic denial of so many intellectuals in the West, communism has benefited from significant indulgence: its proclaimed universalism, egalitarian promises, and sublime intentions raised it above the crude political facts. While Nazi *pentiti* found no sympathy anywhere, communist apostates generally met with understanding and esteem, even those who hung on long after the revelation of communist crimes on a massive scale.

Semprún is a case in point, and *Autobiografía de Federico Sánchez* the record of his strategic "debriefing." As critics remarked at the time of its publication, the book is a political vendetta. But this was possibly a side effect and not its true motivation. Semprún was pitiless with the party, because this text constituted his formal revocation of allegiance. It was the convert's repudiation of his former idol in the court of liberal democracy, the system that was to rule world history for the foreseeable future. Asked by Lacouture what made him revise his ideas about communism, he replied: "The crucial factor is the discovery of the Gulag. For me, old deportee to a Nazi camp, it has been truly impossible to pass the Gulag through the dialectical mill that always manages to understand and accept everything" (*Si la vie continue ...* 68). There is, of course, the question of timing. When did Semprún first learn of the Gulag's existence? Did he really have to wait until the 1970s before he reacted to what had been broadly known since the mid-1950s?

In 1949, David Rousset, also a Buchenwald survivor, denounced that, while the Nazi camps had been shut, there were still concentration camps in the Soviet Union. He was the first to use the word "Goulag" in French. He appealed to former deportees to Nazi camps to form a commission of inquiry to investigate the conditions in Soviet camps. The appeal concerned Semprún as a former deportee, and it is inconceivable that he did not learn about it, either directly or through its public repercussions. For his proposal, Rousset was attacked by Pierre Daix, the editor of the communist weekly *Les lettres françaises*. A former resistance fighter and Mauthausen prisoner, Daix denied any similarity between the Soviet "reeducation camps" and the Nazi camps, and accused Rousset of being an agent of the United States and slandering the Soviet Union as part of the capitalist plan to continue the Nazi war effort against the one country that worked for peace and justice ("Pierre Daix, matricule 59.807 à Mauthausen" 4). Rousset sued, and this led to a famous court case, which he won on 25 November 1950 (Verger 134), wreaking havoc with the credibility of the editor of *Les lettres françaises* and, by extension, the methods of the French Communist Party. But Semprún's memory did not register this first of numerous ground shakes.

Being a Stalinist and Rousset a Trotskyite, Semprún probably found it easy to ignore his denunciations of the Soviet penal system. But not long after the Rousset-Daix confrontation, Daix himself had to recognize the existence of Soviet camps in a *Letter to Maurice Nadeau* published in *La nouvelle critique* in April 1957. Although he reaffirmed his communist faith and sought to excuse Stalin's penal system, he could no longer skirt the issue when pressed to take a stand regarding Soviet crimes.

> I did not doubt that the repression could be directed against the revolutionists themselves. I continue to think that a revolutionary power has the right and the duty to defend itself against its enemies. The drama concerns the innocent victims, the proportion of innocent victims. And even those who lived in the U.S.S.R. in 1950, what did they know then about this drama? (38)

The excuses are lame. It would have been appropriate to send counter-revolutionaries to Siberia. But that is what most of the deportees were accused of being or of having "objectively" become. The drama of the camps (notice the avoidance of the word "crime") is reduced to a drama for the innocents only, without explaining what innocence consisted in under Soviet law. This limitation is further shrunk by the assertion that the whole question of drama hinged on the proportion of innocents, obviously suggesting that the proportion must have been small, a thesis supported by Daix's extensive report on the functioning of the Soviet courts. And if all of this is not mitigation enough, he adds that in 1950, not coincidentally the year his bluff against Rousset was called out in court, even Soviet citizens, let alone French ones, could not have known about the camps. If these half admissions sound like German false consciousness regarding knowledge about the Nazi camps and the sort of people interned in them, the reason may not be all that mysterious. But the point here is that grudging admission is admission nonetheless, and all the stronger for being made in the tones and with the circumlocutions of zealous militancy.

Around this time, Daix began publishing dissident Soviet authors in *Les lettres françaises*, and in 1963 he wrote a preface for the French translation of Solzhenitsyn's *One Day in the Life of Ivan Denisovich*. Semprún not only failed to take stock of the mounting evidence about the existence and nature of the Soviet camps, but even after *The Gulag Archipelago* was published in France in 1973, he continued to consider himself a communist and defined himself as Marxist at least until the publication of *Autobiografía de Federico Sánchez* four years later.

This would make of the *Autobiografía* the official record of his apostasy, putting the publication in a different light from just being an ill-humored reaction to his disciplining by the party. In this new light, his answer to the question of why he waited so long to publish it is hardly convincing: "I did not want to publish a book against the Communist Party, against some of its leaders, while it was engaged in the clandestine struggle against Franco. It was not possible. The members would not have understood" (*Si la vie continue* ... 127). When one repudiates a totalitarian creed, one does not hesitate to denounce it out of concern that its members may not understand.

A certain pattern of deferment emerges. Things happen with regard to *Autobiografía de Federico Sánchez* in a way that is reminiscent of what happened with his writing about Buchenwald. In *L'écriture ou la vie* he explained that after the Liberation he had started to write about his captivity but gave up his attempts soon after because "Like a luminous cancer, the narrative that I tore from my memory, piece by piece, phrase after phrase, devoured my life" (204). He repeated this explanation, with slight variations, in his reception speech of the Peace Price of the Association of German Booksellers in October 1994 in Weimar: "In Fall 1945, at twenty-two years of age, I started to work literarily with that life experience: that memory of death. But I found it impossible. Please understand: it was not impossible to write—it would have been impossible to survive the writing" ("Wovon man nicht sprechen kann" 36). His brother Carlos refuted this explanation, offering a more trivial one: "But it just happens that I read the first version of *The Long Voyage*; what happened is that he was unable to get it published then, around 1947–8. And it was Primo Levi that committed suicide" (Semprún Maura 124).

Anxiety about prodding in his memory may or may not be the true reason for his postponement. Others did not find it impossible to write about their internment; in fact, the determination to bear witness helped many to stay alive. Not only Primo Levi, David Rousset, Robert Antelme, or Joaquim Amat-Piniella—whose gripping novel *K.L. Reich* Semprún never mentioned in his texts or public speeches—wrote shortly after their release; others too found writing about the camps an urgent task and an obligation. In time, Semprún came to feel that way as well. In his late novel *Quel beau dimanche*, he inserted the following dialogue between Gerard, Semprún's *nom de guerre* in the resistance, and Pierre Courtade:

> —And you, asked Pierre Courtade at a certain moment in this confused end of the night, are you not going to write about the camps?
> I shook my head.
> —No, I replied. It's too early.
> Courtade chuckled sarcastically.
> —What are you waiting for? That it is too late? That the whole world forgets? (228)

In the meantime, though, it was he who forgot, or rather repressed his memory of the camps: "I have chosen to forget, I have put in place ... the strategy of voluntary amnesia," he wrote in *L'écriture ou la vie*" (236). There is no escaping this conclusion, if we believe what he says about the occasion that brought it all back and sparked his decision to write *Le grand voyage*. It was in Madrid, in 1960, in the apartment of Manolo Azaustre and his wife, both members of the Communist Party. Listening to his host's account of the executions in Mauthausen, Semprún says that he was put in mind of his own experience of the camps (*Autobiografía de Federico Sánchez* 212). Struck by the poor narrative skill of his comrade, he felt that he could do a better job of it (216).

And now, having inaugurated his life as a writer, it happened again that Semprún came to feel the duty to write about his immediate past but was prevented from doing so, this time for political reasons. This was in 1965, the year he was expelled from the Spanish Communist Party (*Si la vie continue* ... 127). Political reasons also had something to do with his decision not to write about Buchenwald in the Fall of 1945, or so it would seem from Semprún's declaring in his Peace Prize speech: "In part that [i.e. his decision to put writing in abeyance] explains my decision for politics" (37). The Buchenwald books and *Autobiografía de Federico Sánchez* are thus intimately connected, and not only through a moratorium awkwardly explained. They are related, in the first place, because, if Semprún had not joined the Communist Party, he would not have wound up in Buchenwald. Secondly, because without the party he might not have survived the camp. And thirdly, because, if he had inaugurated his literary career in 1945, he may never have become Federico Sánchez.

His strategic silence makes it not just possible but rather probable that his belated enlightenment concerning the evils of Stalinism was less a question of ignorance than of repression—something similar to his voluntary amnesia in 1945. Pressed by Lacouture, he admitted the obvious, but again offered a face-saving explanation, this time the Spanish dictatorship.

> All right, historically one could have known earlier. My personal biography is that of a member obsessed with the struggle in Spain, where the clandestine communist instrument fights effectively against the fascist power. This is why I became conscious of the reality of the Soviet camps so late, and the shock of this consciousness made everything swing, leading me to a pitiless analysis of communism, and thus of my own past. (*Si la vie continue ...* 68-9)

Such "confession" is embarrassing for a Paris-based intellectual. Even if Semprún had failed to take stock of the significance of the German–Soviet pact of 1939—which led a Paul Nizan to abandon the party—because he was only sixteen at the time (*Si la vie continue ...* 65-6), and even if he could—less understandably—dismiss Rousset's denunciations of the Soviet camps in 1950, by 1953, the year Semprún entered Spain as a clandestine communist agent, he could not have been unaware of the falling-out between Sartre and Camus, France's foremost living writers, one year earlier. In his response to Sartre (over Francis Jeanson's captious review of *The Rebel* in *Les Temps Modernes*), Camus had written: "If one is of the opinion that authoritarian socialism is the principal revolutionary experience of our time, it seems to me difficult not to come to terms with the terror that it presupposes, particularly today—and, for example, so as to remain close to reality, with the fact of concentration camps" ("Letter to the Editor" 121).

Camus, who had been expelled from the Algerian Communist Party in 1937, shared with Semprún a past in the Resistance and a present as an irreconcilable critic of the Franco regime. Yet, he did not hesitate to denounce the communist barbarity, even though, in the Parisian climate of the 1950s, such moral independence entailed isolation and hostility from the dominant intellectual milieu. In contrast, Semprún's claim that he had not heard about the Soviet camps until twenty years later defies belief. As does his inability to draw any consequences from his discovery, in the course of three visits to the Soviet Union in the 1950s, that it was the most unjust society he had ever known (*Si la vie continue ...* 145). This is what makes so pathetic his assertion that the timing of his break with communism was inconsequential and what really counted was the extent of the break. "What is important is not that I broke quite late, in 1964, but that I broke and how far I went ..." (*Si la vie continue ...* 148).

A Marxist, of all people, should know that, if the timing of a decision is of no account in eternity, it is everything in history. To the strange notion that the moment of his egress from the party was irrelevant, he added that he broke with it in 1964. But the facts do not bear this out. Not only did he not leave the party voluntarily, but, when he did, he did not make a clean break with communism and Marxism, as he asserted on occasion (Canal 66). In fact, he considered himself a better Marxist than the party's leadership, since, unlike Santiago Carrillo or Pasionaria, he was baptized in the waters of Georg Lukács' *History and Class Consciousness*, which Semprún claims to have read at eighteen, the year of his political coming of age: "From this moment, by virtue of that book, I consider myself a Marxist" (45).

For a long time, he was an ambitious party member, climbing the ladder all the way up to the narrowest circle in the hierarchy. "Soon I was nothing but a member of the Spanish Communist Party," he confessed to Lacouture. In 1954, two years after he started working full time for the party, he ascended to the Central Committee and then on to the Executive Committee in 1956. But his meteoric advancement did not happen because his profile casually responded to what the Party needed at the moment (*Si la vie continue* ... 93). It happened, and it could not have been otherwise, because he proved himself ideologically reliable, paying his dues to the cult of the leader with adulating odes to Pasionaria, not shrinking from denouncing comrades (the cell 722 affair), and, when the occasion called for it, disciplining a friend in abject obedience to the party (his letter to Pradera).

There can be little doubt that his former comrades would not have understood, let alone appreciated, his sweeping invective against the party in 1964, but to think that they would have looked more kindly on it in 1977 was self-deluding. When it finally came out, the autobiography elicited a spate of negative reviews and a relatively noisy in-house controversy.[2] Far from proving a desire to strengthen the left through debate, as he claimed in an article in *El País* of 8 January 1978 (cit. Canal 72), his "patient" wait of fourteen years until the party's legalization entailed, on the contrary, a devastating attack on the party precisely when its democratic legitimation was at stake, namely at the start of post-Franco parliamentary politics. Much later, he would admit, indirectly, his awareness back in the 1970s that the Communist Party had no future in the restored monarchy: "One had truly to be blind about oneself, as the communist leaders were at this moment,

---

2 The articles around the debate were compiled in a book, *Semprún-PCE. Historia de una polémica*, and published the following year as a follow-up to *Autobiografía de Federico Sánchez*.

not to understand that Spain had chosen to turn democratically toward its future. For Spain, when it was able to vote freely, the Communist Party, even if heroic, was the past" (*Le langage est ma patrie* 67). In other words, the left Semprún had wished to strengthen with his book no longer included the communists. "Left" was becoming an antonomasia term, a blanket designation for the post-Marxist Spanish Workers Socialist Party, the PSOE, the party that was visibly wresting the hegemony of the left from the PCE. Perhaps he did not even aim to strengthen this up-and-coming political formation, which was fast becoming a haven for communists fleeing their sinking boat, as much as to bolster his own prospects by recanting his "misguided though justifiable" allegiance and vilifying former comrades in the process.

Since 1965, the official date of his expulsion from the PCE, Semprún had been building up his friendship with Felipe González, the PSOE's leader. González was, for Semprún, "the political man that suited me" (*Le langage est ma patrie* 77). In July 1988, he would become Minister of Culture in the cabinet of Felipe González, and after his dismissal in March 1991 he would bring back Federico Sánchez one last time in another autobiographical book, *Federico Sanchez vous salue bien* (1993).

The fact that Semprún retained the name of his communist alias until his definitive departure from Spanish politics suggests a certain continuity between his clandestine activity in the 1950s and 1960s and the glamorous role he now played as arbiter of Spain's cultural policies. This second installment of the autobiography of his political alias was again, partly, a critique of the party apparatus, the PSOE's this time. But now Semprún spared the party's Secretary General from his critique, which centered on González's friend, the despotic vice-president of the Government, Alfonso Guerra. Even after González personally removed him from his cabinet, Semprún wrote that his expulsion could not "change anything to their long mutual trust, to the grateful generosity of our reciprocal feelings, to the intellectual esteem that had not ceased to grow during the years spent working together, in the tutorial clarity of his friendship" (*Federico Sanchez vous salue bien* 321).

"Tutorial" is a subservient adjective for an intellectual of Semprún's stature. Proof perhaps that, in 1993, he did not yet know (or did not wish to know) his friend's implication in the dirty war against Basque nationalists and ETA members between 1983 and 1987, which had come to light the year before Semprún accepted a post in González's cabinet. Nevertheless, the convictions of José Barrionuevo, the PSOE's minister of Interior, and of director of state security Rafael Vera, as well as the revelations pointing to González as the ultimate level of command in the counterterrorist organization, should have put Semprún on his guard. Nothing, however, reveals his awareness of González's responsibility in state terrorism, let alone that he harbored any suspicions of criminality or corruption in his "tutor."

In his account of the years when he held a position of responsibility in González's government, memory, even the memory of the very recent past, proved unreliable, if not downright inconvenient. In any case, in his description of the tension between the two of them during their final encounter, he revealed and denied something in the same breath: "And the tension between us, which did not originate in disagreement, in manifest discord, which came from the consciousness of having reached a limit, a breaking point between the extraordinary private complicity and the obligations of the public charge" (*Federico Sanchez vous salue bien* 321). How far did their private complicity go? How much did it excuse? How long would it take Semprún to "remember" what everyone in Spain knew? In the end, Semprún would never muster the courage to denounce his friend's cynical exercise of power, as he had Santiago Carrillo's or Pasionaria's. In his conversations with Lacouture five years after leaving office, Semprún still maintained: "It is not with Felipe González that I had political conflicts, but with the apparatus of the socialist party" (114). And so, the question of denial forces itself on us, leading back through his very late "realization" of communism's crimes to his vague admission of the implications of his role as a *Prominent* in Buchenwald.

These lapses of memory—let us call them such—are rarely mentioned in the largely hagiographic studies of Semprún, who, as a writer, profited from his status as a Resistance fighter, a political deportee, a prominent member of the PCE in the anti-Franco opposition, a more or less opportune Stalinist dissenter and a vehement detractor after the party had initiated its unmistakable decline, and finally a cabinet member of the, at the time, still prestigious government of Felipe González. All of these phases in his biography are meritorious, even admirable considering the context, but in each of them a kernel of darkness remained at the center of the memory that grew around it like the flesh of a peach around the pit. Such selective darkness compels us to ask whether the narrative *epiformations*, the compulsive, spiraling gyrations around the centers of memory in his autobiographical texts were not the means to protect delicate kernels of amnesia. Those dark centers of un-narrated memory caused not just blind spots in his autobiographical stories but also distortions in what he chose to bring to light. To point to their influence on the iterative strategy in Semprún's texts is not to accuse him of lying. "It must be remembered," said Bettelheim, "that denial, even when it begins as a conscious process, soon becomes an unconscious one; otherwise it could never work so well, and so completely" (85).

The chiaroscuro resulting from the convergence between two kinds of narrative, the factual and the fictional, and two kinds of memory, the personal and the collective, makes of Semprún's texts ambiguous documents for the history of the second half of the twentieth century. In these texts, the status of truth responds to a Kantian inner perception of experience rather than a Hegelian focus on the universal significance of the concrete. The most explicitly autobiographical of these texts, Federico Sánchez's autobiography, cultivates the semblance of a novel under the permanent denial of its novelistic structure. It proceeds in a constant see-saw between recourse to novelistic techniques (placed under erasure) and the affirmation of a "truthful memory" that will make it possible to reconstruct historical truth against the biographical distortions of communist memoirs (as in Carrillo's *Mañana España*) (*Autobiografía de Federico Sánchez* 174).

What he says about this book is, to a considerable extent, valid also for his other texts, since the greater part of Semprún's biographical canvases are continuations of the legendary "dialog" between the lyrical (and thus subjective) reciter of Baudelaire's *Le Voyage* and the theorist of the collective memory. "Federico Sánchez is a book written like a novel, but in which nothing is novelized. It's for this reason that it is very novelistic. One could almost say about it what Boris Vian wrote about his: 'In this book everything is true because everything is invented.' But one could equally say the opposite. 'In this book everything is invented because everything is true'" (*Si la vie continue …*129).

The reason why these texts are important for the historical memory is not that the writer's heteronyms (Gerard, Juan Larrea, Federico Sánchez) have symbolic value for a history of the present. To a great extent, Semprún's life differed from the lives of most Spaniards during the Civil War and Francoism. There is no justification for the idea that the adoption of the Stalinist confessional exercise as a template for his arraignment of the party added precision to his account or endowed it with historical concreteness. After all, turning the model into its own antithesis does not "sublate" the silences and concealments that characterized the "self-critical" exercises mandated by the Communist Party. Where Semprún's texts are emblematic, or, if this sounds too figurative, then at least redolent of the historical memory of this period, is in corroborating what one might call the social praxis of this memory.

Semprún occupies a liminal position as a witness to the historical memory of Spain's Civil War and Francoist era. He did not participate in the war, except from the distance of a privileged exile while attending the best public schools in Paris, the Henri IV and the Saint Louis, usual gateways to the *Grandes Écoles*. But he immersed himself in the clandestine opposition to Franco, taking a leading role in the expansion of the Communist Party among students and intellectuals in the 1950s. This participation tinges his memory with the shades of an ideology in which freedom and totalitarianism were confused. Later he tried to disentangle these antithetical ideals by narrating from personal memory against the party's collective narrative. From the shipwreck of the ideology that spanned his political life from 1942, when he first contacted the Spanish Communist Party (*Si la vie continue ... 46*), until 1965, the year of his expulsion, he not only drew important consequences for his political biography, but also attempted to salvage the legend of the party's heroism as the only significant anti-Franco opposition, with all the implications for his courageous commitment and his no less courageous dissent.

His liminal position with respect to the historical memory of this period can also be looked upon as representative in its skepticism toward witness accounts of the Civil War and its blindness regarding the historical narratives in which he played a part. Hence, what he says about the memories of Civil War combatants crystallizing in irreconcilable mythologies applies also to the often inflated and self-congratulatory memories of the anti-Franco heroes.

> It was there, in Cordón's house, hearing Líster tell his military exploits against, let us say, the confederal forces of the Council of Aragon, when I began to understand that the civil war would only be mythology so long as it remained their thing, of those who made it, and unmade us, by doing it so badly; that it would only be history, finally, only a practical knowledge that would permit us to live with it, assuming it critically instead of expending ourselves in its deceitful labyrinths, when it became our thing: of those who did not make it, of those who were overwhelmed by the ideological weight of such a long legend with contradictory signification ... (*Autobiografía de Federico Sánchez* 92)

Semprún's liminality is representative not so much in the sense that, as the Civil War protagonists disappeared, Spain gained a more objective understanding of the conflict, but in the sense that their heirs have indeed appropriated its "memory" and put it to pragmatic uses of their own. These include blurring as a way of "living with" the war's ideological legacy. Above all, Semprún's method of alternating fiction with fact to create a subjectively viable and objectively livable truth about the past seems representative of contemporary Spaniards' penchant for secondary witnessing. Ardent demands for the "recovery" of the historical memory mean in effect that, although no one can any longer tell "it" as it was, because the past belongs to the dead, people feel the need to fashion a view of the past for themselves. Such "pragmatic knowledge" can only be a collectively endorsed narrative in which ethics trumps epistemology. At such historical remove from the experience of the primary witnesses, the formula for indirect, or in Semprún's words, "spiraling" memory (*Autobiografía de Federico Sánchez* 296) is that of his own autobiographical narrative: a *poietic* history in which invention is the guarantee of truth.

But this, of course, threatens to be no longer memory in the strict, neurological sense of the term, but idealization in the form of "educated mythology": "We are reaching the end of the age of memory. And if people continue to write about the camps, about deportation, it will be more and more in the form of fiction" ("L'art contre l'oubli" 11). Semprún was not disturbed by this development—"mixing testimony with fiction does not pose a problem for me" (11)—perhaps because he recognized his own method in it. The objection to this inexorable distancing from life toward writing is, of course, that there is a limit to the romanticization of the facts. One may, like Semprún, consider that the truth suffers, in his case, from insufficient "elaboration" (*Le langage est ma patrie* 32), or consider with his brother Carlos that Semprún shamelessly misrepresented the truth about his life. Such polarization regarding the memory of a concrete past within the narrow circle of a family is striking evidence that, in Spain, the historical memory of the period inaugurated by the Civil War remains torn between contrary interpretations, and still distant its dispassionate appropriation by the curators of inert history.

CHAPTER THIRTEEN

It Wasn't This:
Latency and Epiphenomenon
of the Transition

All you want, after forty years of repression and frustration,
is not years of pleasure and elation, but the simple
horizontal rest in a luxuriant field of marjoram ...
Antoni Serra

It wasn't this, my friends, it wasn't this that so many flowers
died for, that we wept for with such yearning.
Lluís Llach

S paniards have now lived in democracy as long as they did under Franco's
dictatorship. Forty years have elapsed since the first post-Franco elections.
That amounts to two and a half generations by traditional assessments of
the time of public influence of an age group. And the fact is that recent
generations of Spaniards know about the Civil War roughly as much as
their parents knew about the Republic: very little, if anything. And the little
they know, they know it filtered through a precarious, uncertain memory.
Memory deficiency, in this collective sense, means above all insufficient
information, but the problem cannot be ascribed merely to a low flow of
information but rather to lack of criteria in sifting and putting the pieces
together. The filters were already in place and the censorship was much
stronger when the transition was taking place. For the most part, those
who tried to explain the transition against the grain of official discourses
interpreted the events with the help of theories that were standard in
left-wing political analyses at the time. Theories that seduced more than
they explained; legitimated more than they clarified.

The transition, like the Civil War or Francoism, was not the solution of the
previous conflicts but the synthesis of the historical dialectic, which became
the new thesis, to put it in the Hegelian terms then in fashion. Expressed

without the sepia color: contemporary analyses of the transition could not really be historicizing exercises, since they were steeped in the conflict they claimed to explicate. One of the best books on the subject, Jaume Lorés's *La Transició a Catalunya* (1985), suffered from the overvaluation of Marxism common at that time, while severely underestimating the importance of national identity that was to become hegemonic in Catalan politics over the following decades. Only four years after the publication of this book, Marxism was thrown on history's heap of discarded ideas.

Even the concept of transition as harmonious resolution was flawed. The dictatorship had been structured on a new idea of time. For it, a new era began in 1939, the "first year of Victory," and a new, fascist calendar was established to brand the memory of the conflict in the minds of the losers. Victory implied defeat, and those who basked in its glory could do so only against a background of humiliation among the vanquished. In its early phase, the Franco regime was a tacit prolongation of the war; it relaxed its grip in the 1960s but it continued to execute its political enemies right up to the end. Franco signed five death sentences shortly before his own death in 1975. This continuation of war by other means meant that the transition was the real postwar. It is to this period, rather than the so-called postwar of the 1940s, that Peter Sloterdijk's observation concerning postwar times applies. According to him, at the end of armed conflicts the resulting balance between the historical forces leads both winners and losers to inspect their cultural premises in light of the outcome in the field of battle. In general, says Sloterdijk, winners interpret their victory as confirmation of the rightness of their outlook and disposition, which are thus reinforced, whereas the defeated—insofar as they do not delude themselves or rationalize their errors—must try to ascertain the reasons for their failure. In this way, they can reach the conclusion that their defeat was not caused only by the enemy's military superiority but also by weaknesses of their own, such as poor behavioral adaptation to the objective situation or a fatally wrong position toward the world (17–18).

There is no doubt that Francoism bolstered Spanish traditionalism and the transition consolidated its sway under a facade of modernity. The political arrangement after Franco's death not only reversed the demise of the monarchy on 14 April 1931, but strengthened the legitimacy of the traditional powers that had tottered under the Republic, attempted to recapture the state in the summer of 1936, and consolidated their victory by physically eliminating the opposition in the 1940s and crushing any outbreaks of subversion in the following decades. In 1975, the opposition, aware of its weakness, yielded to the military blackmail accepting a transition that merely accommodated the regime to the requirements of membership in the European Community. Neither that weakness nor the population's conformism at this foundational moment can be explained without the years of soul searching by the defeated and their quiet revision of the ideas they had fought for in the war. The virtual extinction of anarchism as a political doctrine cannot be accounted for solely by repression. Its fall from its former position as the predominant working-class ideology in the 1920s and 1930s to absolute marginality bespeaks massive reorientation of the vanquished with regard to the objective conditions not only in Spain but in the world at large during the second half of the twentieth century.

The transition was the true postwar in the sense that only then did the government put an end to the hostilities, demilitarize the police, and free political prisoners. Spanish society was then reorganized not on the basis of naked violence, as in 1939, but of the implications, now metabolized, of the outcome of the Civil War and of the Second World War. After the death of the dictator, it became possible at last to underwrite a social peace, which, while guaranteeing the privileges of the winners, opened the way to participation by the parties that emerged from the underground and represented various strains of political sentiment. So, when the constitution was ratified in a referendum, the hostilities finally came to an end. It was year thirty-six of the Victory. Even so, the wounds did not heal and the old conflicts remained latent throughout the following decades. Despite the general amnesty and much talk of reconciliation, the magnitude of the crimes and the perpetrators' unwillingness to admit responsibility hindered the definitive settlement of the past. In fact, reconciliation was not sought; it was imposed. It was the byword, the dogma used to blackmail those who alone could endow the new scheme of power with the much-needed legitimacy: the defeated and their heirs. These were cowed into conceding it, relinquishing all claims to a different settlement.

Euphoric visions of a new dawn, couched in extravagant praise for the political maturity of Spaniards—counterintuitive after four decades of radical depoliticization—underlie many narratives about the transition. This fantasy is found, for instance, in Raymond Carr's and Juan Pablo Fusi's influential history of the transition, where the authors write approvingly about an opposition that sensibly sacrificed its political objectives for the higher good of an inclusive democracy (227). For all the talk about inclusiveness, one looks in vain in their book, furnished with a long glossary of acronyms of political organizations, for any mention of ERC, Catalonia's government party during the Second Republic and the Civil War. This was also the party of Josep Tarradellas, Catalan president in exile and a crucial figure of the transition, unaccountably forgotten in their book. The reason for this absence may well be that ERC had been excluded from the first elections, ensuring its marginality for a long time thereafter. Carr and Fusi were not exceptional in their bias. In general, Spanish historians of the transition obscured the social and cultural advances of Republican Catalonia before 1936, omitting an image of a past that remained alive in many people's memories as a horizon of aspiration.

The hostilities may have ended formally in 1975, but influential sectors of the establishment did not see things that way. Reconciliation was not in their agenda, as shown by the violence unleashed to intimidate the opposition after Franco's death. Its primary vehicles were paramilitary groups like Fuerza Joven, with more than 4,500 militants in 1978; or the Basque-Spanish Battalion, an ultra-right organization composed of members of the Civil Guard, the Spanish police, army officers, and civilian thugs. Between the mid-1970s and the early 1980s, its commandos crossed the French border to murder people suspected of Basque nationalist sympathies in actions financed and possibly planned by the state information services (the Spanish version of the CIA). In Barcelona, a group calling itself the Guard of Franco was responsible for shootings in a music store and in a concert by Lluís Llach (an action testifying to the political significance of the Catalan song), for throwing Molotov cocktails in various locales, for beatings at the university of Barcelona, setting off a bomb at the Villarroel theater, and planting another at the office of the satirical magazine *El Papus* with the intention of blowing up the building and killing the editor.

That same year of 1977, on 24 January, a right-wing commando entered the law office on 55 Atocha Street in Madrid and shot five labor lawyers. The killers were members of Fuerza Nueva, Falange Española de las JONS, the Brotherhood of the Guard of Franco, and the National Union of Transportation and Communication Services, a public organization with great influence in the Franco regime. Its president, Vicente García Ribes, was a Falangist and one of the few *procuradores* (a Francoist version of the state representatives) who voted against the Law of Political Reform that initiated the transition to democracy (Sánchez Soler 75). Some were collaborators of the social-political brigade of the Spanish police. Supporters of the murderers attended the trial wearing the Falangist blue shirt, interrupted the witnesses, and several times bellowed the Falange anthem "Cara al Sol." During the trial, which elicited criticism of the judge's leniency against the accused, the state prosecutor did not attempt to investigate the political links of the killers, but well-known ultra-right elements declared to the press that the Atocha murders had been instigated by the police. The spate of violent actions in that ominous year of 1977 could not have been coincidental. Important elements of the Francoist apparatus utilized small right-wing groups, always ready for violence, to destabilize society, justify a *coup d'état*, and block the incipient liberalization.

Although this violence was explained as the desperate reaction of marginal extremists, it was rooted in the sociological Francoism that pervaded Spanish society at the time and reflected the immobility of the state apparatus. While political parties were legalized, schools dismissed teachers who joined the left-wing ones. The Council of Rectors of Spanish Universities refused to appoint as chairs faculty who had fought against the dictatorship and had been punished for it. In the first three years of the transition, 600 journalists went on trial and 400 administrative sanctions were imposed on media and art groups. Penalties could be stiff. Francisco García Salve was sentenced to six years and two months in prison for "insulting the authorities" in an article published in the newspaper *El Imparcial*, in which he demanded amnesty for trade unionists who had been arrested (Krasikov 132–3). In 1981, Catalan journalist Xavier Vinader became an icon of the struggle for freedom of the press after he was sentenced to seven years and had his professional credentials suspended for writing three articles about the actions of violent far-right groups in Euzkadi. ETA had subsequently killed two of the people mentioned by Vinader, and the judge estimated that the journalist had imprudently signaled the targets to the terrorist organization. In the meantime, right-wing extremists rampaged through Vinader's house, wreaking extensive damage and painting threatening messages on the walls. It was not the first time he was unceremoniously told to let off his investigations. In 1974, he started denouncing the impunity with which ultra-right groups terrorized the population, and the following year someone in the orbit of these groups placed a firebomb in his home.

Far-right violence evoked sympathy and often complicity among the army and security forces, as it soon transpired in multiple conspiracies to derail the reform of the state. Roughly around the time when Vinader obtained his journalism degree, fascist youth, under the gaze of a conniving police force, unleashed full-scale terrorism in Spain's major cities, bombing cinemas, restaurants, neighborhood associations, attacking bookstores and setting them on fire, or beating people in the streets and forcing them to sing the fascist anthem or repeat fascist slogans. The squads of fascist youth were not a spontaneous burst of compressed ideology. They were managed by seasoned Francoist hardliners such as Generals Tomás García Rebull (a Falangist military officer, Blue Division volunteer, and iron cross laureate with a street to his name in the provincial capital of Jaén) and Carlos Iniesta Cano (director of the General Military Academy in the 1960s and director general of the Guardia Civil in the last years of Franco), the lawyer Blas Piñar López (founder of the far-right organization Fuerza Nueva and self-styled political heir of Franco), or former ministers José Utrera Molina (Falangist lawyer and secretary general of the National Movement—the name for the fascist rebellion leading to the Civil War), José Antonio Girón de Velasco (Falangist lawyer, co-founder of the fascist party JONS, who had been responsible for the Ministry of Labor in the 1940s and 1950s, and part of the network of the February 1981 coup), Francisco Ruiz-Jarabo Baquero (minister of justice in the cabinet of Franco-designated acting president Carlos Arias Navarro), and Raimundo Fernández Cuesta (member of the Army's judiciary corps, secretary general of Falange and minister of justice under Franco, then founder of the Spanish National Front, renamed Falange Española de las JONS, after the Caudillo's death). Taking provocation to the streets, these Francoist diehards, collectively known as "the Bunker," tried to elicit riots that would give them a pretext to block the reform of the state. Franco's long political life had created the illusion that his regime was eternal. For them history had stopped in 1939. It was now merely a question of ensuring it would remain at a standstill.

Far from being the gratuitous expression of impotence, the Bunker and its assault troops effectively conditioned the crafting of the constitution, as did the sabre rattling in the army barracks. Several attempts to turn the clock back demonstrate that a part of the Franco establishment believed in the mirage of immobility. Jealous of the authority derived from their victory in the Civil War, these sectors staked their future on a crumbling political structure. Their last important gamble, the *coup d'état* of 23 February 1981, provides a clue to the depth and breadth of the reaction. This event showed that the fate of the transition was not predicated on amnesia but on keeping alive the memory, and hence the fear, of the powers that had ruled Spain with an iron fist for forty years—powers that could rise again to smash the tender shoots of democracy at the slightest provocation.

If one could speak of trauma in this context, reactions like the coup of February 1981 would fall under the category of a return to the primal scene. Consistent with this interpretation, Lieutenant General Jaime Milans del Bosch, Captain General of Valencia, prepared an edict for the coup modeled on the one General Emilio Mola, leader of the rebellion that started the Civil War, proclaimed in July 1936. In 1981, the attempt to revert to military rule came very close to succeeding, and the possibility of a bloodbath was real. According to J.F.F., a senior army office who conceded an interview on the twenty-eighth anniversary of the coup, an order had been issued that evening to execute several deputies and high-ranking members of the government that were being held in Congress. The officer who received the order decided to wait, and for this reason it was not carried out (T.P.F.). Nearly three decades after the event, use of initials by both the interviewer and the interviewee suggests ongoing concern for the consequences of revealing the facts about the evening in which a coordinated regression to dictatorship nearly succeeded. Rather than unconscious regression to the primal scene of trauma, fears and in some cases nostalgia of the Francoist past justify our speaking of latency of archaic elements in post-Franco Spanish society. Those elements emerged forcefully in February of 1981, but cordoned off by secrecy and compressed into the opera buffa character of Civil Guard Lieutenant Colonel Antonio Tejero Molina, they were trivialized and thus allowed to infect the new democratic order. The coup of 1981, while ostensibly failing in its brasher theatrical version, achieved a significant triumph for the reaction: the reform of the state was brought to a halt and in some aspects reversed. The coup had instantly forged a consensus around the traditional institutions, strengthening the monarchy; and it established a paralyzing prudence that arrested the transformation of the state and set the stage for future conflict.

Historians and political scientists contributed their fair share to the myth of a sensible, voluntary choice for moderation, cooperation, and goodwill. Carr and Fusi, for instance, applauded the "sacrifice" freely accepted by the communists, who, according to these historians, would have paid a hefty price for the patriotic gesture of accepting the monarchy and facilitating the reform. Leaving aside the fact that it was never in the communist agenda to be patriotic, Carr and Fusi did not grasp that communists "sacrificing" their revolutionary strategy presupposed that this strategy had real possibilities; presupposed, in other words, that a complete break with the dictatorship was conceivable. The truth, however, is that a revolutionary strategy had no future, and sacrificing the republican ideals to embrace an archaic institution like the monarchy was one more opportunistic about turn for the communists.

By 1976, communism was no longer a credible power alternative in Western Europe, not even under the guise of Santiago Carrillo's "Eurocommunism." Nor did Carrillo's fantasy of a democratic revolution led by the Spanish Communist Party gain any traction (*Mañana España*, 207–8). In order to gauge the potential for a clean break with the Franco regime, it suffices to consider that the elections of 15 June 1977, the first since the Civil War, were amply won by the newly founded Union of Democratic Center of the reformist Francoists. They took the majority of votes throughout Spain with the exceptions of Catalonia and Euzkadi. The Spanish Communist Party, the most active underground organization during the dictatorship, obtained 10 percent of the vote. Although Carrillo, ever the tactician, later affirmed that Adolfo Suárez, president of the transition government and head of the Union of Democratic Center, carried out the "rupture" planned by the Communist Party (Satué 323–4). In 1977, Jorge Semprún, a disaffected former member of the party's politburo, ridiculed Carrillo's smug pragmatism: "he might tell us that the fact that he is the leader of a parliamentary microminority is itself a true revolution. But how are we to classify the fact that Mr. Roberto Conesa is still the chief of the political police?" (*Autobiografía de Federico Sánchez* 206).

Given the correlation of forces, a transition without rupture was inevitable. But the price paid for the failure to give Spain an honest democratic bill of health was its remaining hostage to Francoist ideology and subject to reflexes learned during that long period of social conditioning. Nostalgia for the old ways did not bode well for the future. Tolerance for backsliders reached the heights of scandal with the leniency shown to the conspirators that had brought democracy to heel. Of the twenty-nine defendants in the trial for the events of 23 February who received jail sentences, not one served the full time. The coup's civil network was never investigated, nor were its masterminds José Luis Cortina, commander of the AOME, the operations group of the CESID, the Spanish Intelligence Agency, and his superior, Lieutenant Colonel Javier Calderón, brought to trial (Palacios 199–203). Also hushed was the collusion of the United States Embassy and of the papal nuncio, Antonio Innocenti.

According to Juan Alberto Perote, Cortina's successor at the head of the AOME, forty-eight hours before the coup started, Cortina met with U.S. ambassador Terence Todman and with the Vatican's nuncio (Medina 302). On 23 February, the U.S. bases in Spain, as well as the embassy and consulates, were on high alert since early morning. The long shape of a U.S. carrier could be seen outside the Barcelona harbor, as if standing sentry. Secretary of State Alexander Haig's comment that the coup had been "an internal Spanish affair" signaled, at the very least, that the United States did not frown on a military assault on the budding Spanish democracy. The Reagan government, eager to incorporate Spain into NATO, had been impatient with President Suárez's approaching the non-aligned countries. Ambassador Todman is said to have discussed with Cortina various schemes to remove Suárez from the presidency of the Spanish government. The Vatican, for its part, fretted about the new government passing "anti-Christian laws," such as the legalization of divorce, the reform of school curricula (eliminating the mandatory teaching of Catholic doctrine), and the possible legalization of abortion, all indicative of a gradual separation of Church and state (422). In those heady days, many people from different institutions seemed to agree that the democratic experiment had failed, that Spaniards were not yet ready for democracy.

It may have been from a shared sense of inopportune historical acceleration that conspirators received unusually benign treatment in court and, especially, after their sentencing. A more likely reason, though, was the strong hold that Francoist powers retained on the state apparatus. The focal figure and ostensible beneficiary of the coup, General Alfonso Armada, was sentenced to thirty years in prison, but was paroled after six. General Jaime Milans del Bosch, who sent the tanks into the streets and declared the state of emergency in Valencia, received a penalty of twenty-six years and eight months but served only ten. Colonel Antonio Tejero Molina, recidivist conspirator and fanatic Francoist, was given thirty years, but was put on open prison after twelve and was paroled after fifteen. They all remained in active service, with pay and the right to military honors until 1983. After the socialist victory, a royal decree took them off the list of service and stripped them of rank, pay, and military status, although they retained their pensions. In their case, "prison" is a misnomer. A journalist who interviewed Tejero described his "cell." An entire floor was at his disposal. He received some of his visitors in a room adjoining his private quarters, a hall of 60 square meters, with fireplace, a bar, fine furniture, television, telephone permanently connected to the outside world, and even a portrait of Franco. This room became a pilgrimage site. According to Tejero, in the first twenty months after his arrest, he received 32,000 visits. Friends and admirers brought him wines, fine foods, and flowers. In his "cell," he received a committee that presented him with the draft for the creation of a new fascist party, the leadership of which they offered to him, and he accepted the honor. They even planned to present his candidacy for the next election and discussed the appropriate name for the new party: Spanish Solidarity (Krasikov 148). Not a single one of the men condemned for attempting against democracy ever expressed remorse (Riego 16). On the contrary, they held conversations with the planners of the next coup, operation Cervantes, before it was aborted in October 1982.

The coup of 23 February, or 23-F, as it is commonly referred to in Spain, showed the persistence of military intervention in politics well after the end of the Franco regime. It was a wake-up call, all the louder in that the assault of Congress was captured on television, and the images of the Civil Guard holding the deputies at gunpoint circulated widely. The sensational images of gunshots fired at the ceiling of the chamber broke the silence of Spanish television on the army's restiveness and recent military conspiracies. The previous year, a so-called Galaxy operation had been organized by the same man who now held the world's attention standing at the presidential podium with a three-cornered hat on his head and a gun in his hand (Rueda Laffond 87).

While the coup reinforced King Juan Carlos's reputation, historians of the 23-F often fail to point out that, without his ambiguous conversations with Alfonso Armada and Jaime Milans del Bosch, and his consent to create an emergency "government of national salvation" after removing president Adolfo Suaréz from office, the coup would never have got off the ground. If it came very close to succeeding, it was on the misunderstanding (later blamed on Armada) that Juan Carlos had given it his blessing. Perhaps it was Jesús Palacios who best captured the balancing act between the army and the monarch that long evening when Spain held its breath: "On 23 February 1981, power was wholly in the hands of the army, and the officers waited calmly for the king to make up his mind ... All of them, without exception, were at his command" (419). In the end, Juan Carlos decided in favor of legality. But it bears remembering that it was not the ultimate purpose of the military action that he rejected but the grotesque manner in which it was carried out. The undisciplined, ultra-reactionary Tejero was the wrench thrown in the works.

It took a long time and serious blunders on the part of Juan Carlos for the tale of a heroic monarch thwarting the infamous protagonists of the coup to subside. Until 2011, the press ignored any views that might cast doubt on the hegemonic account of the events. That year alternative lines of interpretation began to appear, some questioning the image of a king fully ignorant of the plan and firmly on the side of existing legality (Capdevila 51). As the ethos of the transition began to wear off, the possibility of a scheme to strengthen the figure of Juan Carlos, while controlling what many perceived as a runaway autonomic process, began to emerge. Before the coup, the crown had been vulnerable. Juan Carlos was Franco's chosen heir, and the army respected him to that extent. For the generals, all of whom had served under Franco, the reform initiated by Adolfo Suárez had gone too far. In the creation of autonomic administrations, the Armed Forces saw only fragmentation of national unity. To make things worse, the reforms coincided with a severe economic crisis and high unemployment; it was easy to use the general malaise as a political weapon. And there was the violent activity of Basque activists, which the army, the Civil Guard, and other right-wing sectors linked to the Francoist apparatus blamed on the government's torpor. For months, discrete meetings among multiple players had been taking place, and a plan had been hatched to replace the government with a coalition that would modify the constitution and change the course of the state. The idea of putting the brakes on the reform found broad support across the political spectrum, including Felipe González, leader of the opposition and proposed candidate to the vice-presidency of an emergency cabinet presided by General Armada (Palacios 413). González himself seemed perfectly aware of these plans when he stated at a meeting of the executive committee of the socialist party on 18 October 1980: "There are times when the [political] parties do not have any idea of where things are happening" (Medina 240).

Although at the time only 4 percent of those polled declared that they sympathized with the military attempt, this figure would probably have been much larger if the coup had succeeded. Extensive apathy—José Maravall called it "political cynicism" (116)—toward political decisions and institutional changes was another form of continuity. Some 20 percent did not answer or said they did not care. Although a hefty 76 percent were opposed to the coup, the fact that it came very close to succeeding suggests that the authoritarian temptation was strong in the institutions and did not lack support among the population. Thereafter Francoism, or rather, the tradition it represented, entered a state of latency that has since revived in antidemocratic attitudes, setting Spanish political life apart from the European mainstream.

Unable to sustain the principle of accountability, the Spanish transition compromised the new regime's possibility of genuinely embracing the rule of law. Spain entered into European modernity burdened with the archaism of absolute politics. Spanish parties are hierarchical organizations with top down decisions, unable to compromise, so that short of obtaining absolute majority of deputies, they flounder in verbal skirmishes and inefficiency. The separation of powers is cosmetic and the judiciary was never reformed. The transition was an epiphenomenon of the historical process originating in the need to manage the essence of Francoism by updating the political legitimacy of the traditional interests it had safeguarded at the time of need. Staging the regime's self-abolition and re-foundation followed Tancredi's logic in *Il Gatopardo* when he supports the taking of the Kingdom of Naples by Garibaldi's troops: "Se vogliamo che tutto rimanga come è, bisogna che tutto cambi" (If we wish everything to remain as it is, then everything must change) (Lampedusa 42). To what degree the transition was a conservative maneuver can be grasped by comparing the strength of dissident culture before and after.

The oppositional power of song, for instance. It has been said, quite plausibly, that "more than the underground work of the political organizations and clandestine unions, combative anti-Francoism was led in by a group of singers and bands that were on the front line" (Batista and Casas 269). Unlike political slogans and rallying cries, songs express sentiment, mitigate judgments, insensibly modify dispositions; in a word, they transform life. With good reason, the dictatorship feared an enemy that came armed with songs and it fought this enemy with censorship and the prohibition of performances. Frequently, members of the political police, the infamous "Social Brigade," showed up at the concerts to make sure the censorship was observed. If it wasn't, they could fine the organizers or shut down the venue. Vigilance was stricter in the Catalan-speaking lands

(Catalonia, Valencia, and the Balearic Islands), where the *Nova Cançó* (the New Song) had arisen as a form of cultural resistance. Miquel López Crespí recalls that in October 1967, during Raimon's recital in cinema Born, in Palma de Mallorca, members of the Social Brigade were reading the lyrics to make sure the singer complied with the text authorized by the police (*L'antifranquisme a Mallorca*, 32).

In the 1960s, singing in Catalan was an act of defiance that everyone understood. Due to this aura of revolt, some Spanish and even a few Italian singers produced Catalan versions of their hits. From a Gramscian perspective, there is no doubt that the Nova Cançó mobilized and assembled the anti-fascist movement in the Catalan-speaking lands and inspired oppositional groups throughout Spain. In the late 1970s, political parties were legalized and professional politicians took to the stage, while the people demobilized and the song was marginalized along with other forms of protest. Official histories of the transition do not mention this popular disarming, but Núria Feliu, one of the protagonists of Catalan song in the 1960s and 1970s, spoke of an attempt emotionally to neutralize the force of Catalonia (cit. Strubell 140). Singers from that era denounced their betrayal by the politicians. Many of these came out of the blue and, like Hamelin's piper, carried off the masses that had been politically educated in the trenches of popular culture, where the song exerted the broadest appeal.

Such was the prestige of the Catalan song in the 1960s that it could be used as an opportunity for self-promotion. Joan Manuel Serrat, an emergent singer in 1968, accumulated symbolic capital by refusing to sing in Spanish as Spain's official representative in the thirteenth Eurovision Song Contest. Broadly seen as a gesture of defiance, no one noticed that the no-show at the Royal Albert Hall had no international repercussions. The Spanish government replaced Serrat with the mediocre Massiel, a twenty-one-year-old Madrid singer who made news by winning. Although there were rumors that Spanish Television, TVE, had bribed judges, these allegations were never proven. Officially, therefore, Europe, far from chastising Franco for persecuting Catalan, acclaimed the new, perky image of Spain represented by a young, short-skirted woman singing a trivial lyric ("La, la, la") to cheery music. If Massiel was a propaganda success for the regime, Serrat's defiance was an empty gesture for internal consumption. But it raised his status. Unperturbed by any sense of contradiction, the Barcelona singer went on to perform almost exclusively in Spanish, obtaining popularity and revenue throughout Spain and Latin America. In Catalonia, his ship-jumping was often contrasted to the cultural and political integrity of Catalan song mainstays like the Valencian Raimon, the Mallorcan Maria del Mar Bonet, and the Catalan Lluís Llach. Once again, Serrat showed political opportunism by his explicit support of the socialists in the halcyon days of their absolute majorities. After this party tried to block the development of Catalan autonomy by passing the LOAPA law for "harmonizing autonomy processes," and even after the socialist government's dirty war on Basque militants exploded in its face, and with the party riddled with corruption scandals, Serrat continued to cheer socialist president Felipe González in the 1993 electoral campaign, asking him to provide "more of the same." Later, when the Catalan Parliament was debating a permanent ban on bullfights, Serrat accompanied Spain's Minister of Culture to Barcelona's Monumental bullring in support of this gory spectacle.

The twilight of the transition allowed for a great deal of ambiguity. In time, as attitudes became clearer through the evidence of political choices, personal reputations gained more definition. The cynical slogan "we were better off against Franco," coined as a response to the nostalgic "we were better off with Franco," implied that the generic opposition to the regime had given way to concrete, more precise, and often local struggles, which divided the former allies into irreconcilable interest groups. The broad anti-Franco opposition had been commandeered by civil society. But in the 1980s that civic front began to unravel in a wave of hedonistic socialization of egotism. The *Movida* had displaced the protest movements of the 1970s. It was by no means an isolated development. Spain had abandoned its specificity as the last remaining dictatorship in Europe and was reflecting broader developments in the Western world.

In Catalonia, demobilization of civil society began when the Assemblea de Catalunya was dissolved after the historic demonstration of 11 September 1977. As the political parties confronted each other at the polls, they began to monopolize the popular representation, fragmenting the anti-Francoist unity with their rivalries. Breaking up the hitherto united front strengthened the state's centralism at a time when it was ideologically in retreat. The army plots intended to reverse the transition were the jerks of a collective body that had entered the post-Franco era dragging its feet. Shortly after the sounding line that was 23 February 1981, the Socialist party proposed the LOAPA, a law intended to check the development of the autonomic process. Simultaneously, the first post-Franco attack on the Catalan language took place when 2,300 allegedly leftist intellectuals signed a manifesto attacking the reemergence of Catalan in education and in public life. The Francoists had attacked Catalan as the language of a red-separatist amalgam. Now a pseudo-progressive front attacked it as the badge of the bourgeoisie.

The Catalan response to the "Manifesto of the 2300" was the *Crida a la Solidaritat*, the Call to Solidarity. The *Crida* was a movement of peaceful resistance to the continuation of the policies against Catalan language and culture in the post-Franco era. Initially numbering 3,000 participants, the *Crida* soon became a broad movement supported by institutions with experience in the defense of Catalan culture during the dictatorship: Omnium Cultural, Unió Excursionista de Catalunya (Catalonia's Hikers Union), Orfeó Català (the Catalan Choral Society), and the CIEMEN (Escarré International Center for Ethnic Minorities and Nations). On 24 June 1981, it was able to fill up the Camp Nou, the stadium of the Barcelona Football Club, for an event held under the motto "We are a nation." The Spanish ultra-right had planned a massacre at the stadium. But the *Crida* not only infuriated the right; it also irritated the Socialist Party by concentrating 350,000 protesters on Passeig de Gràcia, Barcelona's swanky avenue, to demand the repeal of the LOAPA.

Taking the political stage, the former anti-Franco activists were insensibly becoming party bureaucrats and alienating many of the people that had fought the regime. But the new political parties had no institutional model other than the Francoist one, and adapting to it was easier than remaking the institutions from the ground up. Ministries, provincial councils, municipal governments, these were the tools of politics, and they were occupied by the same functionaries that had made them places of privilege and authority for decades.

Among the most significant events of the transition was the appearance of new dailies. Madrid's *El País* became for some time a gauge of the country's political transformation, replacing Barcelona's *La Vanguardia* as Spain's international newspaper of choice. But the most noteworthy journalistic event of the transition was the appearance of the daily *Avui*, the first daily to appear in Catalan since the Civil War. Under the Franco regime, publication of news in Catalan had been forbidden. Permission to publish *Avui* had been applied for and rejected. But Francoists knew that they could not maintain the prohibition, since no liberalization of the regime would be credible without allowing a Catalan press. Josep Faulí was right when he considered *Avui* a "symbol, representation, and sample of the great problem that had to be resolved, the Catalan problem" (Faulí 117). *Avui* appeared on 23 April 1976, four months before schedule, because Josep Espar Ticó, the paper's promoter, doubted that the political conditions were ripe for a democracy and considered that "if *Avui* had to die as a result of political involution in Spain, it was better that it be killed rather than stillborn" (Cadena 106).

Thus, the Catalan press reemerged after four decades of silence fully aware that it could soon disappear again; aware, in other words, that the set of interests loosely identified as Francoism, torn between reinvesting themselves in a formal democracy or extending the dictatorship, would only concede the minimal amount of freedom compatible with their hegemony.

As a result, what had once been a thriving press in Catalan would remain limited to *Avui* and a few local newspapers for decades. It was not until October 1997, twenty-one years after the publication of *Avui*, that *El Periódico*, the mouthpiece of the socialist party in Catalonia, started publishing a Catalan edition. And Barcelona's principal daily, *La Vanguardia*, only began printing a Catalan edition on 3 May 2011, in response to the appearance of *Ara*, a competitor for the representation of liberal opinion in the Catalan language.

Literature's social relevance pales next to the symbolic impact of an emergent press. Even so, literature is the medium that best reflects the evolution of the language and society's level of sophistication. In this area, too, every inch of ground had to be painfully regained for the Catalan language. Regular publication of modern literature in Catalan only began with the so-called "aperture" of the 1960s. Rapid increase in publication in the decade after Franco's death struck fear in authors who had renounced the inconveniences of the cultural resistance in exchange for the attentions of the Spanish media and institutions. Surprised by the renewed prestige of Catalan, some Spanish-language authors in Catalonia considered themselves ignored by the autonomous cultural institutions and disguised their resentment and a good deal of bad conscience with intemperate attacks on the language's precarious comeback. These authors had taken for granted the dictatorship's sense of normality, and were indifferent to the fact that Catalan literature had been hegemonic before the Civil War and that it had a preferential claim to institutional support in the autonomous region. It had taken full-scale repression of the Catalan language for a "Catalan literature in Spanish" to emerge in the 1940s. The period from the 1940s to the 1980s was the "golden" age of Spanish literature produced in Catalonia, some of it by Catalans, much by relocated Spaniards who profited from the political constraints on the Catalan cultural industry.

Begrudging the promotion of literature in Catalan by the Catalan government and institutions, Spanish-language authors in Catalonia replicated in their own sphere the demand of the Francoist elites for confirmation of the privileges obtained through repression. Among the privileges that Spanish writers had enjoyed for decades was their monopoly on the Catalan literary market, obtained through the prohibition of the language and, more decisively, through the schooling of multiple generations of Catalans in a language different from their mother tongue. After the prohibition was lifted with the Statute of Autonomy of 1979, a subtler policy of constraint came into play not only through the Spanish language near monopoly on the media and most of the market, but also through emotional pressure on speakers and by a plethora of laws requiring the use of Spanish.

Francoist policies of frank eradication had been "democratized" by turning them into policies of circumstantial coercion and gradual suffocation.

Within the Catalan area of influence, the case of Mallorca is of special interest, because the Balearic Islands exemplify to a very high degree the sociological changes that turned the Catalan-speaking lands into something completely different from what they had been before the Civil War. The case of Mallorca is particularly poignant not only because there the Falangist pressure was exerted implacably from the beginning of the Civil War, as George Bernanos described in his testimonial *Les grans cimetières sous la lune*, but also because the transformation of the island's economy through massive tourism after the 1960s broke down the traditional form of life, altering the island's demography and sweeping away its cultural referents. Some Mallorca writers—Baltasar Porcel, Maria Antònia Oliver, Miquel Bauçà, or Carme Riera—settled in Barcelona during the dictatorship, as others had earlier in the century—Gabriel Alomar, Miquel dels Sants Oliver, or Joan Estelrich—and as others would in the post-Franco era—Sebastià Alzamora, Arnau Pons. But although most of these have written about Mallorca, it is mostly those residing on the island that took up the task of describing its transformation through the tourist industry. Gabriel Janer Manila, Biel Mesquida, Maria Antònia Oliver, Antònia Vicens, and Guillem Frontera, among others, described the cultural shock brought on by the rapid change that took place in the second half of the twentieth century. The tourism boom affected the manners, morality, and way of life on the island, making a whole new class appear, a tourism bourgeoisie and its necessary counterpart: a hotel and restaurant working class made up of migrants from the Spanish mainland and of Mallorca farming hands, who left behind the rough work in the countryside for the promise of steady wages.

According to Pilar Arnau, these authors capture the impotence of a generation of Mallorcan men and women in face of the rigidities of Catholic and petit bourgeois morality in the island, while they critique authoritarianism and denounce the exploitation of the new working class (103). As time passed, it became clear that the immigrated working class not only failed to develop a class-consciousness but also neglected to rise to solidarity with the autochthonous population's persecuted language and culture. In the 1970s, the majority of Mallorca intellectuals did not recognize that this moral failure amounted to unconscious transmission of Francoism's plans of cultural substitution. Marxism, the dominant frame of social analysis at the time, created a blind spot for the national question, and this blind spot prevented solidarity among the Catalan-speaking peoples. Despite the island's spectacular transfiguration, accompanied by a dramatic reversal of the value of land—the traditionally lowly valued coast rising much higher than the arable interior—and notwithstanding the swift emergence of a powerful hotel bourgeoisie, the situation described by Josep Melià regarding the Mallorcan elite of the eighteenth and the early twentieth centuries persisted: "An incomplete society, a half-baked country about to unravel, Mallorca did not admit of the dialectic patterns of normal societies. Both, the right and the left were equally colonized by the structures of real power. It is not even fitting to say that economic power translated into political power" (Melià 207).

To a great extent this description applies also to Catalonia. Here the ruling class was also Castilianized and the urban areas profoundly transformed by a flood of migrants from all the provinces of rural Spain. Large swaths of the most populated towns in Catalonia became home to people with little or no connection to the territory, its language, or its history. Also applicable is Melià's description of a post-Franco right and left that were profoundly colonized, representing the return of the dynastic parties of the Restoration, expelled from Catalan politics by the irruption of the Catalan national agenda at the beginning of the twentieth century. Despite the similarities, however, there was a substantial difference in the degree of historical awareness and political will between the Catalan and Mallorcan elites. In Catalonia, memory of the republican interim and, above all, the long history of struggles for Catalonia's political identity, was decisive for rebuilding the national consciousness that Melià missed in his native Mallorca. In his own words, on the island there was, "instead of a liberating culture ... a semi-culture, a degree of semi-information, that reflects alien ideas and inflates reputations" (Melià 285–6).

Subjected to the Spanish ideological grid without the possibility of opposing a national principle of its own, Mallorca's culture was far more exposed to assimilation than Catalonia's. Absent a liberal bourgeoisie committed to democratic reform, the mediation between conformity and rebellion that had been possible in Catalonia failed to materialize in Mallorca. A young generation of anti-fascists responded to Mallorca's provincialization as the forced appendix of an alien Spanish culture by idealizing world revolution and importing the theories of decolonization through armed struggle prevalent in left-wing European circles at the time. Miquel López Crespí captured the ideological fervor of the anti-Franco opposition in 1960s and 70s Mallorca, recalling the movement of young people who were "ready to sacrifice their lives, if necessary, in the attempt to free their people from the oppression of capitalist exploitation—salaried work—and imperialism—the oppression of nations" (*Cultura i antifranquisme*, 152). Whereas they shared the first objective—anti-capitalism—with Marxist militants throughout Spain, the second objective—the struggle for national liberation—was exclusive of the Catalan-speaking lands and, more earnestly, the Basque country.

The excess of these objectives (to eliminate all at once fascism, capitalism, and imperialism) could only lead to disappointment. This is how Antoni Serra, a Mallorca journalist and writer, appraised the failure of the anti-Franco opposition to transform the regime:

> Most of what I observed was deplorable but very real and pathetically cruel: the continuation of Francoism within apparently democratic structures, no matter how hard they tried to disguise it ... Between cynicism, opportunism, climbers, sudden conversions, cronyism, this is the Mallorca that we have been shaping in the democratic era, a Mallorca of failed autonomous politics and inexistence. (Serra 192)

Serra speaks of the latency of Francoism within the democratic structures put in place during the transition and about a politically overridden Mallorca. Francoism inspired, designed, and implemented Spanish democracy; it inhabits the very form democracy took in Spain. Mallorca's inessentiality as a heteronomous region of Spain, its inexistence as part of nationally cohesive Catalan-speaking lands, does not stem from ontological deficit but from confining the island's national energies to a state of latency. Mallorca society retains a strain of its identity without for all that investing it in the common Catalan culture. As a consequence, it is unable to activate this identity in politically meaningful ways. A collective consciousness wary of more capacious political units (Melià 229), Balearic society affirms itself through dialect and localism, sapping its strength in a delusive pursuit of its own insularity, encouraged in this by the Spanish state as the surest way of reducing the former political rival to the sectarian ruins of the province. "A person who knows the confederate tradition of the kingdoms of the Catalan–Aragonese crown—wrote Melià—knows also that we should not fear belonging to the same political community [as the Catalans]" (230). Then, as now, Mallorca is torn between assimilating to Spain and remaining in historical limbo. But even in limbo the existence that Serra missed in post-Franco Mallorca endures in a state of latency, ready to be activated when conditions are ripe.

I have argued that the transition was the actual postwar period. Postwar times are typical latency times, during which the defeated ideals live on in a laconic state of circumspection. As happens with energy, ideals do not disappear but change state. Far from liquidating Francoism, the transition consolidated its gains. The reorganization of the state during that period defused the oppositional energies that had built up during the long dictatorship, permitting the ruling ideas of Spanish nationalism to germinate and to spread under cover of democratic normality. It would be a mistake to think that this posthumous victory of Franco was determined solely by his long incumbency in power. In 1975, his regime was as illegitimate as it had been in 1945. The Cold War had kept him in office. But by 1975 the Cold War was no longer a significant horizon for European politics (it was a different matter for the United States, which was soon to make a right turn by electing Ronald Reagan to office), and communism no longer was a serious alternative to the consumer society that Spain had become in the 1960s.

That was the reason for Santiago Carrillo's strategic turn to Eurocommunism, stirring the Spanish Communist Party away from its Stalinist past and exchanging the goal of revolution for parliamentary strife in a democracy that he was not the only one to describe as "bourgeois" (Carrillo, *Mañana España*, 207–8). The international situation was the prime mover of the changes occurring in Spain. The Spanish Communist Party had to negotiate with the Crown to become a legitimate political player, while Francoism needed to shed its own skin and could not do it without the opposition's cooperation. Hence, just as an old Stalinist could embrace democracy without inducing excessive incredulity, hard-core Francoists like Manuel Fraga Iribarne and Rodolfo Martín Villa tiptoed the line between their former roles as repressors and their new roles as politicians with important responsibilities in the post-Franco administration.

The word "transition," firmly established to designate the years immediately following the death of Franco and the beginning of the restored constitutional monarchy, is deceptive as a descriptor of the events following the demise of the personal regime of General Franco. The term "transmission" would be more adequate to designate the mechanism for the renewal of power. Carefully engineered to retrofit an aging state apparatus, the transmission remodeled the institutions, shaping the period with the myth of a progressive society that had finally broken with its dark legacy and struck a new path of integration to the West through respectable democratic government. The myth did not fool everyone, and the evidence of the transmission caused people who had fought Francoism in hopes of founding a radically different country to cross the threshold of old age with the feeling of having got nowhere. In their case, at least the past was not a foreign country.

CHAPTER FOURTEEN

Window of Opportunity:
The Television Documentary
as After-Image of the War

Traumatic experiences are events that resist being articulated as memories and instead emerge in the present through their aftereffects. In the case of the Spanish Civil War and, especially, the long postwar that was the dictatorship, official history and social memory failed to articulate a convincing representation of those traumatic decades. In the absence of thick description that brings to consciousness the magnitude and intensity of the events, the character of the trauma must be inferred from social symptoms and traced back to the events themselves. But symptoms have great potential for distortion of the original affect and, as time passes, for grave misinterpretation and even erasure of the association with the past. The dissipation of the liberal and libertarian traditions, the intimidation of several generations of losers, the massive conformism and scapegoating mechanisms, and the low public awareness of the historical facts are some of those symptoms. Although not dealing strictly with the subjective dimension but with social processes of repression and distortion, the problem of the historical memory can use the psychoanalytic notions of trauma, resistance, and substitute formations to understand collective behavior and to explain the difficulties experienced by Spaniards in coming to grips with the facts that confront them as victims and perpetrators of an unreconciled past.

No other medium has brought the historical memory to the focus of public attention as television has, and no other genre has delved so much in the misrecognized and often unknown recent past as the television documentary. For years, the documentary has been the principal means for working through the resistance to memory of the majority of the population. The effectiveness of television relates to its popularity, intimacy, and loose conditions of reception, which need not be passive but may include a certain degree of interaction between viewers and programmers. These features, combined with the low level of attention demanded from the viewer, make the television screen a projective surface onto which psychic formations are transferred on a large scale. While it would be farfetched to compare the viewer's couch with the psychoanalyst's, television can nonetheless help to objectify inarticulate emotions and unconscious reflexes.

Simmering emotion keeps the memories of the Civil War and the dictatorship from becoming mere historical knowledge. People in Spain are not capable yet of looking on that period with indifference. This melancholic attachment to the past, confirmed by a spate of novels and films on the war and the early years of the dictatorship, is consistent with the failure to engage in collective mourning during the transition. That irretrievable moment should have been an occasion for the conscious confrontation with the pain inflicted and suffered, an exercise in genuine acceptance of responsibility on one side and of magnanimity on the other, understood as a prelude, but only a prelude, to letting go of the past. As it was, the difficulty in historicizing this particular past relates to the emotional side of intelligence, to passionate attachments that keep an ethical conflict alive. Under these conditions, engaging in pure recollection is quite challenging, as the history wars discussed in Chapter 11 demonstrate.

Political changes have much to do with the ways history is coded and re-coded, and with the territories opened to memory or sunk into oblivion. A gaping hole affects the past, which, like the hole in the ozone layer, grows apace with human activity. The world political climate has changed since 1989, and therewith the perspectives on the Spanish Civil War. With the Cold War paradigm gone, the "two sides" of the Spanish Civil War began to be disentangled from the old Manichean readings and considered in their complexity. Softening of the frame of reference made it possible to re-float some images of the past. This promised a more nuanced understanding. However, a more limber ideological frame also encouraged revisionism. On the right of the political spectrum, the Franco era was being cleansed of its barbarous aspects and rationalized. As this operation advanced, a gray area developed, blurring the distinction between victim and perpetrator, with incalculable consequences for Spanish democracy and the coexistence among Spaniards.

Traumatic experiences overpower the psyche's rational defenses and are internalized without benefit of cognition or understanding. Being unprocessed, these experiences leave behind no available memory, although, as Freud emphasized, there are often retrospective explanations and interpretations made up to account for the symptoms. The unavailability of the memory to consciousness does not imply that the memory does not exist or that it is inactive. As Freud explained in his fundamental study, *Erinnern, Wiederholen und Durcharbeiten* (1914), although the patient does not remember the traumatic events, he or she acts them out, unwittingly repeating the repressed scene. The past is rehearsed through symptoms that may appear inconsistent with the context in which they surface, but are fully intelligible in reference to the repression (*Erinnern* 520). The traumatic event is reproduced, then, not as memory (that is, not in the sphere of representation) but as deed. Although, strictly speaking, it is always the individual psyche that somatizes a trauma, some collective dramas seem to mimic this psychic mechanism, multiplying its effects and incorporating them into the culture. From this analogy it seems possible to infer the existence of a collective unconscious, at least as a working hypothesis. By "collective unconscious" I only mean the reverse of the "collective memory," a term borrowed from the sociology of Maurice Halbwachs and used here in the sense of a pattern of inter-subjective memory shared by a group and maintained through the ordinary exchanges of social life. The collective unconscious would stand, then, for the darkened area of the public memory, where the causes of social reflexes and collective attitudes have fallen out of view for reasons that are also social in nature.

The full experience of the war and the postwar repression is irretrievable. No representation can express the horror of the first experiments in carpet bombing on a market day in Guernica, General Yagüe's machine-gunning of the prisoners massed in the bull-fighting ring in Badajoz, or the thousands of nightly executions in Mallorca wrenchingly denounced by George Bernanos, who anticipated the incredulity of his conservative French readers even as he wrote: "Evidently, you find that hard to read. It is also hard for me to write it. It was harder to see, to hear" (132). Because of the difficulty in seeing and hearing, any account of the war and the repression must remain inadequately abstract. How could a witness transmit in symbolic language the impression produced by the "sacas," the routine shooting of prisoners without trial; the slave labor of Republican POWs; the rounding-up of republican fugitives by Nazis in occupied France; the months and years spent in prison fearing the nightly executions; the intimidation of entire populations? A witness is someone whose eyes are full and whose mouth jams as he attempts to articulate private images into common language.

Although historical novels and films never transcend their fictional status, they serve an important function by structuring the garbled grammar of the emotions and introducing sense into the erratic logic of experience. But that sense is made ambiguous by the fact that these cultural products often replace, and so displace, the reader's and viewer's experience of the content of the past with "screen images" in the Freudian as well as the literal sense. Furthermore, while fictionalized accounts may be effective vehicles of emotion, they lack the force of the reports by historical actors themselves or by those with a valid claim to presence. Witnessing is more than acting as a medium; the witness must consciously recollect the origin of the present reflexes and dispositions. It is not enough to convey a memory in the rough or embellished with romantic detail; the witness must lay bare the primal scene of victimization, which alone explains society's compulsion to repeat it disguised in symptoms. Fiction's failure to do so is one reason why survivors are rarely pleased with films allegedly made in their honor. Vicente Aranda's *Libertarias*, for example, met with the disapproval of the real militia women it allegedly portrayed.

What feeds the debates about the historical memory in post-Franco Spain is not so much lack of knowledge about the past as unwillingness to draw practical consequences from it. If we agree that violence is socially transmitted, as I argue in Chapter 4, then we have to admit that some of the diffuse violence in contemporary Spain originates in the aggressive energies unleashed during the war and the postwar. Having seeped into the ground of collective life, that violence reemerged through a transformation-neurosis not only in the reactive violence of terrorism and the readiness with which Spanish society countenances state counterterrorism and police torture,[1] but also in violence with a clear scapegoating component. Such diffuse violence ranges from the symbolic and discriminatory violence against minorities, and the spectacular rise in domestic violence, to neo-fascist attacks against immigrants and paupers. Freud remarked that the stronger the resistance to confront the past, the more thoroughly will remembrance be substituted through action that repeats the aim of the repressed memory (*Erinnern* 521). In the same way, the transition's refusal to face up to the past by lifting it to public consciousness abetted the symbolic violence directed against the victims of the fascist uprising and confined them to their longstanding humiliation. Symptomatic manifestations of the continued force of the original aggression were the refusal to compensate individuals and groups for violations of their physical integrity and to return property impounded during or after the war; the legalized plundering of the "enemy" regions through fiscal imbalance; rejection of motions to invalidate military trials without guarantees responsible for many executions in the 1930s and 1940s; and the rehabilitation of the dictator and of the doctrines promoted by his dictatorship, simultaneously with the return of the Francoist clans and families to the summit of political, media, and economic power.

Inadvertently, the victims may have contributed to the veil of silence thrown over the crimes. Traumatic events produce discontinuous memories.

---

1 In 2002, Eric Sottas, director of the World Organization Against Torture, was alarmed at the growing approval of torture as an antiterrorist method among Spanish and Basque citizens (Arbós).

The events fester in the background while new memories intervene, modifying the representation of the original experiences or even putting them beyond reach. Because the Franco regime continued to kill, torture, and abuse until the end, the intimidation hindered the naming of the terror. In July 2002, the country was shocked when a mass grave was excavated in the province of León, at the site where thirty-seven republican militia men had been shot on the night of 5 November 1937. The villagers had known of the existence of the grave for sixty-five years, but no one had dared to speak about it. Other mass graves have been found since then, and others will probably turn up as more people "remember" crimes from three-quarters of a century ago. Difficulties of all kinds explain that it took almost the same amount of time to establish the number of people killed in the fascist repression. Historians now set the number of victims at 150,000.

During the transition, the suppression of facts and the eradication of memories were rationalized as necessary for the consolidation of a democratic regime. Calling for reconciliation, politicians turned to the task of refashioning the "truth" about the nation, a task that included refashioning the "truth" about the dictatorship as well. If, as Jane Jacobs claims, "[r]econciliation is an official entry into the process of disclosing previously repressed aspects of the nation's history and setting these 'secrets' into a national framework of 'truth'" (207–8), the Spanish transition offers a case-book example of deceitful reconciliation, with the consequence that the resulting "national truth" became rife with tensions. It is true, as Jacobs warns, that "[w]hat can and cannot be said in the emerging truth of the reconciled nation will not of course transcend existing power relations" (208). Precisely for this reason, the continued repression of certain voices and viewpoints, the impossibility of saying, and even of excavating the full truth about the past, exposed the power relations that presided over the transition, set its limits, established its course, and coordinated its objectives. Construed as the demise of Francoism, the transition was, at heart, a timely sloughing of the outer tissues without loss to the vital organs: a facelift.[2]

---

2 Many political analysts deny the continuity between the two regimes. This too was part of the transition's scenario. Paloma Aguilar, for example, asserted: "Today, it is evident that in the end there was a break with the past, since the current Spanish democracy is, without doubt, consolidated and the [political] balance is comparable to that of many other European countries" (*Justicia, política y memoria* 13). Significantly, Aguilar grounded her opinion in the fact that the new democracy did not exact political or juridical responsibilities for the fascist crimes (14). Thus, she inadvertently confirmed the link between impunity, continued repression of the facts, and the less than immaculate nature of the political pact and the regime that evolved from it.

One of the obstacles to the determination of the truth was the continuation of censorship by barring access to the official documents of the repression. Even so, if those sources were, for the most part, inaccessible, there was a wealth of information waiting to be tapped in the memory of the survivors who had been silenced for decades. But despite a few efforts in the line of oral history, such as Ronald Fraser's, this source was rarely mined before the 1990s. Beginning in that decade, there was a surge of interest in the documentary of historical memory. The new interest in oral testimony benefited from newfound fascination with traumatic memory, a concern that was heightened, if not inspired, by Claude Lanzmann's film *Shoa* (1985). It is difficult to ascertain if *Shoa* directly influenced the vogue of testimonial documentaries in Spain, since that film was not shown there until 2002. It is not farfetched to speculate that this long delay had to do with the local taboo on memory. Be that as it may, it remains true that the presentational techniques differ considerably. Lanzmann's obtrusive intervention and his strong transferential drive are absent from the Spanish documentaries on the historical memory, which studiously avoid Lanzmann's aggressive pressure on witnesses and his obdurate stance against "understanding."

One of the earliest documentaries on the historical memory was *In Memoriam*, produced by Dolors Genovès for Televisió de Catalunya, the Catalan public television channel, in 1986. The novelty of her approach was that, instead of focusing on well-known political personalities, as Jaime Camino had done in *La vieja memoria* (1979), she interviewed ordinary working class people in their familial setting. Her attempt to reconstruct the experience of the war for ordinary people contributed to socialize memories that had remained private. During the interviews, the deterioration of the public memory of the war became evident in the gap between the family's transmission of the past to the younger generations and the formal teaching of history at school. Six years later Genovès produced another documentary on the Civil War, *Operació Nikolai* (1993). Drawing information from hitherto inaccessible Soviet files, this film traced the abduction and assassination of the POUM leader Andreu Nin in 1937 all the way back to Stalin. Then, in 1994, she struck closer to home with *Sumaríssim 477*. In this new documentary, she probed into the memory of a Francoist crime in which Catalan Falangists had been implicated. Making use of classified materials, Genovès reconstructed the summary court martial and execution of Manuel Carrasco i Formiguera, a member of the Catalan government, in Burgos in 1938.

Genovès was not the first journalist to break the taboo on revealing fascist crimes. In 1989, Francesc Escribano had produced, also for TVC, a documentary on the final hours of Salvador Puig Antich, a young Catalan libertarian who was court-martialed for allegedly slaying one policeman, condemned without evidence, and executed in 1974 after the sentence was confirmed by the Council of Ministers presided by General Franco. But *Sumaríssim 477* disturbed a tacit compact between the media and the powerful. During the transition, Francoists had offered political participation in exchange for immunity that extended to their reputations. When Genovès was permitted to consult the files of Carrasco's trial, all those implicated were already dead. Even so, the transition's pact of silence lay so heavily on the previous half-century that vice-president of the Socialist government Narcís Serra required TVC not to reveal the names of the witnesses for the prosecution. Genovès, however, insisted on full disclosure, and, after some hesitation, TVC let her have her way.

As might have been expected, the program rankled in a society that made peace conditional on the dissimulation of responsibilities. The perpetrators were all dead, but they had left families behind, and some of the offspring were well placed. *Sumaríssim 477* ended with the statement that Carrasco was condemned on the testimony of the eight witnesses for the prosecution. This statement became the centerpiece of a lawsuit brought by the family of one of the witnesses, Carlos Trías Bertran, against Genovès and TVC for traducing the honor of this former Falangist. The controversy was Byzantine, because there is no question that the court martial, however predetermined its outcome, drew its spurious legitimacy from the formalities, and the protocol required the connivance of the witnesses. This was, in different words, the conclusion reached by the Supreme Court when it overturned two previous sentences by lower courts that had ruled in favor of the plaintiff. In its Sentence No. 216/1999, the Supreme Court stated that "[t]he truthfulness [of the facts] is indisputable," refining its criterion of truthfulness to distinguish between documented facts and acceptable inferences: "The documentary narrates truthful facts and value judgments befitting a historian's [use of] scientific freedom."[3] The value judgments referred to the documentary's assumption that the witnesses volunteered their attestations, to the description of their testimony as "pitiless," to the use of the word "exclusively" in assessing the significance of the witnesses' depositions for the trial's outcome, and to the arguably implied suggestion of a link between the witnesses' conduct and the official privileges they enjoyed under the dictatorship.

Genovès was also criticized for dramatizing the court martial.[4] But the main objection was to Carrasco's dignified last words to the court, denouncing

3 The daily *El País* reported the sentence on 18 March 1999 ("El Tribunal Supremo" 15).

4 Journalist Arcadi Espada called it "a cheap stylistic exercise" (189).

its vindictiveness. Not only are those words not in the proceedings, but the record suggests that, at the last moment, the defendant pledged his allegiance to the "National Movement" in an effort to save his life.[5] Had Genovès falsified the record in order to show an unbroken martyr who goes down accusing his judges? To the charge that she had forged the evidence, Genovès retorted that she had merely reproduced a statement from the counsel's declaration in court, whose author, she believes, was the lawyer Manuel Carrasco himself. Her decision raises a delicate question concerning the status of historical truth. Is this truth enshrined in literalism? Or does it call for judgment, and thus for an ethical choice in the use of the available documents?

The question is relevant not only with regard to the historian's sense of the priorities in the face of conflicting data, but also with regard to her sense of the facts in dealing with documentary ambiguity or downright mendacity. Was Genovès right or wrong to represent Carrasco proffering words, which, although extracted literally from the defense's declaration, may not have been uttered by the defendant in court? Were those words actually spoken by Carrasco, and did the judges replace his statement in the record of the proceedings with a cowardly adherence in extremis to the military coup? Carrasco's plea for clemency in the name of an ad hoc political conversion is formulaic and appears to have been used routinely by the defense in court martials. Should it be given more credibility than the defense's carefully prepared allegation, which doubtlessly reflects Carrasco's position? Which is historically truer: the statement Carrasco deliberately prepared either by himself or with the aid of his counsel, or the ritual words he might have uttered when all was lost and the murderous nature of the process stared him in the face? These are valid questions with no verifiable answers. The audience must decide, and it can do so only through a transferential working out of the material, considering the facts and their internal relation against the background of what it already knows.

There is no doubt that Genovès aimed for effect. There is nothing unusual in this. Historians' use of rhetorical features in the retrieval of the past is hardly remarkable; why should it be in a documentary for mass consumption? Her dramatized reconstruction of the court martial may be compared to the docudrama, a film form that helps audiences come to terms with a difficult past through mimetic dramatizations. Apropos of the docudrama, Marita Sturken observes that "[i]n the cultural reenactment of the original drama,

---

5 According to the proceedings, Carrasco, upon being asked by the president of the court if he had anything to declare, appealed to the court for leniency on the grounds of his being Catholic, married, and father of eight children, and of his being "today a supporter of Spain's Salvation Movement or desiring its triumph."

coherence and narrative structure emerge, and fragments of memory are made whole" (85). This is also true of Genovès' retrospection of Carrasco's life to the moment of his execution, but whereas docudramas constitute "a site for healing and redemption" (Sturken 89), *Sumaríssim 477* created a situation in which, ironically, the perpetrators could be portrayed as the victims of a vendetta. The general director of TVC, Joan Granados, apologized to the witnesses' families, faulting Genovès for her obsession to "get to the bottom of things."[6]

To criticize the dramatization of a trial is to miss the point about the nature of the documentary in the absence of historical footage. It is not just that Carrasco's plight was inherently dramatic, but drama is inherent to television. Even in a direct situation such as an interview, says Martin Esslin, the main interest falls not on the facts but on the emotional impact (27). Television, the most intimate medium (30), makes us witnesses by proxy, and therefore contemporaneous with the emotions of the "in real time" witnesses. In a sense, viewers occasion the emotion. It is for their sake that the witness struggles with the failure of language, the loss of composure, and irrepressible pain and anguish.

Orality is the interview's inner law, and plausibility the touchstone of its evidential value. This value is contingent on the interviewing techniques and the interviewer's choices and emphases. When the interview is incorporated into a visual medium like television, new factors come into play that can affect the status of the evidence. The problem is compounded when the televised interview is interspersed with a different visual sequence, as often happens in the testimonial documentary. Under these conditions, the verbal message loses its linearity, increasing in symbolic value with the help of the visuals. Television makes the verbal messages more ambiguous than a purely verbal medium would. Even the images are more ambiguous than in other media. Whereas the cinema establishes regular conditions of viewing for limited audiences, television establishes communication with an indeterminate audience in indefinable pragmatic settings. The variability in interplay between the image and its conditions of reception gives television messages a somewhat random or haphazard meaning (Wolton 66). But television also brings forth an immediacy unavailable to verbal media. For example, it can contextualize interviews by furnishing the informants' physical environment (Thompson 235).

In *Sumaríssim 447*, Genovès used a mixed technique to great effect. The interviews were conducted in a nearly abstract manner, framing the

6 A chronicle of this episode was provided by one of its instigators, Arcadi Espada, in *Contra Catalunya*.

informants to isolate them from their ordinary surroundings so that the voice would carry the full weight of the past. In this way, the past evoked by the interspersed visuals emerges as the witnesses' relevant environment, and indeed as the moral environment that, drifting from the past, envelopes the viewers in the present. It is the covert past that entices Genovès and focuses her attention on the assassination of an innocent man on whom a fascist court placed an inordinate symbolic onus. "Carrasco is everything: he is Catalonia and he is the Republic," reads the sentence. Genovès contrasts this grandiloquent paranoia with the immediacy conveyed by the historical visuals about the man and his private as well as public life and, to a certain extent, by the dramatized court martial, inviting the viewers' emotional transference through their mediated proximity to the victim.

Techniques like editing and framing can smooth out the tension between the visuals and the discourse, while depriving witnesses of their agency. One instance of this method was the interview program *Mujeres del 36*, produced by TV2, a Spanish government channel, in 1999. Republican women from various parties and political associations were invited to reminisce about their experiences during the war. While some of them described harsh social conditions before the war, they were surprisingly silent about the fate of politicized women in the postwar. Furthermore, their memories were strikingly free from any traces of trauma. Concha Liano, a member of the anarchist organization Mujeres Libres, described her participation in the revolution in the eager tone of a schoolboy recounting a field day. The heavy editing of the interviews may account for the fact that Liano's more jovial presence intensified toward the end of the program, outweighing the other testimonies, especially through the closural force given to her elated remark: "The things one can now say in Spain!" Ending on this note, Spanish Television deactivated memory's potential for indictment, sublimating history in the status quo.

After *Sumaríssim 447*, TVC continued to produce documentaries about the Civil War, but it was some time before it returned to the Francoist repression. In November 2000, it broadcast *Els últims morts de Franco* (Franco's last killings), a documentary about the last executions of the regime. In September 1975, three members of the Patriotic and Anti-Fascist Revolutionary Front (FRAP) and two ETA militants had been court-martialed without procedural guarantees, without witnesses, and at one point without defense. A terminally ill General Franco confirmed their death sentences. Then, in March 2002, TVC launched a series of three documentaries under the title *Oblidar o recordar?* ("Forget or Remember?"). These programs deserve special attention, because, with the framing rhetorical question, TVC was laying bare the dilemma bequeathed by the transition.

The first installment was *Veus ofegades. Cartes d'un exili a França* ("Smothered Voices. Letters of Exile in France"). This film, directed by Montserrat Bessess, focused on the fate of the 500,000 republican exiles (about half of whom were Catalan) who crossed the Pyrenees between February and March 1939. The film grips the viewer as it relates the conditions of internment in the camps of Argelès sur-Mer, Saint Cyprien, Ribes Altes, or Agde. Confined without shelter, sanitation, or adequate food supplies in enclosed stretches of the beach, interns huddled together or buried themselves in the sand to retain body heat during the cold winter nights. Their detention was aggravated by arbitrary family separations, isolation, and forced labor for the men. Some, considered "dangerous elements" on account of their political militancy, were incarcerated. And after the German occupation, many men were handed over to the Germans and dispatched to Mauthausen, while women and children were sent to Franco's Spain. In unoccupied France, the Vichy government also "repatriated" republican women and children, drafting the men into the infamous foreign labor corps. There, conditions were so bad that the men missed the concentration camps and some even escaped to occupied France, preferring to work for the Germans, who, needing to build their Atlantic defenses, paid the refugees for their work. Vichy, in the meantime, shipped unwilling Spanish workers to Germany as part of "la relève," a prisoners-for-workers tradeoff between the two governments.

The documentary centers on the letters written by refugees: letters describing the conditions in the camps, begging political, or, most often, economic assistance, and also letters from the families left behind in Catalonia, where hungry relatives deprived themselves in order to send some ounces of flour, a handful of worm-eaten beans, or a few eggs to their loved ones in wealthier France. But the letters that provide both the title and the pathos of this documentary are 300 letters written between February and August 1939 and intercepted by the prefect of the district. Letters bespeaking affection and nostalgia, a wife's longed-for intimacy, the desperate pain of a mother who reports the death of a young daughter to an unsuspecting father, the unbearable hardship in the camp. Unread by their addressees, the letters were kept in the archives of the *département* of Haute-Garonne until 1998, when they were casually discovered. Smothered for sixty years, these spectral voices from the past sound in this documentary for the first time.

Next in the series was a documentary about the armed resistance to Franco during the 1940s. Inspired by Ferran Sànchez's book, *El Maquis a Catalunya*, Enric Calpena produced this two-part documentary, balancing the testimonies of former resistance fighters, *Guardia Civil* officers, and villagers who had been accidental spectators of the skirmishes. But in spite of the neutral tone the emotional dissonance inherent in the subject matter occasionally breaks through the civil, unimpassioned reporting, as when a former resistance fighter, after relating his interrogation by the army, explains that his disfigured face was smashed on that occasion. Such moments bear out Dai Vaughan's definition of the documentary as "the attempt at a materialist reading of film" (108). The documentary is materialist in the sense that the resistance fighter's composed signaling to his broken face anchors the viewer's response in a past that is not reducible to fancy. The body underwrites the emotion that the image elicits from viewers. Thus, although the interviews synthesize a historical memory for reflection, the memory's overwhelming power stems from the transference of an emotional undercurrent that the witnesses' composed words can hardly conceal. This is as true for the pain of the broken and defeated as for the spite of the Francoist veteran, who, sixty years on, still remembers the unpaid meat and bread requisitioned by the Maquis during their failed incursion in Franco territory. Transference, as LaCapra observes, is inevitable as long as trauma is not inert. To the extent that the past is still with us, it implicates us in events we would rather inspect as impartial bystanders (40).

The third and last program in the series was *Els nens perduts del franquisme* ("Francoism's Lost Children"). In this documentary, Montse Armengou and Ricard Belis tackled one of the least known episodes of the dictatorship: the fate of imprisoned children. The film begins with the origins of fascist social experimentation, recalling the establishment, during the war, of the *Gabinete de investigaciones psicológicas* on direct orders from General Franco. At this center, Dr. Antonio Vallejo Nágera, an apologist for the doctrine of racial purification,[7] experimented with POWs, hoping to prove that Marxism was a disease to which mentally retarded individuals were particularly vulnerable. Women, being intellectually feeble, were especially responsible for the revolutionary excesses on the republican side. These were the "scientific" origins of a policy of preemptive education of republican children, which few Spaniards knew about or cared to remember.

Next, women are given the floor in front of the camera. Several of them recall their capture and transportation to prison. Suffocating in closed wagons, in the stench of excrement and the decaying bodies of dead children, they slowly made their way across Spain to their appointed places of captivity. Many of these women and children were arrested when the fascists failed to capture their menfolk. Some of them lost their lives in

---

7 In *Eugenesia de la hispanidad*, a book on racial eugenics, Vallejo-Nágera pathologized the poor and working classes and laid out the politics of segregation, sexual control, and indoctrination later implemented by the Franco regime.

lieu of their husbands and fathers. Others were children refugees who had been living in foreign countries until they were "repatriated" against their parents' wishes or the host countries' consent. The Gestapo aided Franco in the abduction of children residing in countries occupied by the Germans. Back in Spain, the children were renamed to prevent their being claimed by their families, confined to special asylums, and raised in stern disciplinary conditions. The purpose of this scheme was to preclude the emergence of a new generation of republican-minded individuals, and to punish Franco's enemies at the same time.

In the documentary, mothers describe how, in the appalling conditions of the prison, they tried to keep their infected children from being taken to the infirmary, from which none ever returned. One of the informants had been a captive at the age of four. She remembers a child suckling from a breast on which the bow and arrows, the fascist symbol, had been branded. Another remembers a fellow prisoner calling to her child, who was named after Lenin, and the guards, infuriated by the name, smashing the child's head against a wall. One priest recalls the women's despair at being separated from their children moments before their execution and begging their butchers to kill the children along with them. Nuns serving as prison wardens ate the children's rations. They did not succor dying children, but praised God because the children went to Heaven.

In 1936, shortly after the outset of the war, the Franco government had created Auxilio de invierno, a copy of Nazi Germany's *Winterhilfe*. Renamed Auxilio Social, it was placed under the direction of Mercedes Sanz Bachiller, the widow of Onésimo Redondo, one of the earliest fascist leaders and a Nazi admirer. After 1943, Auxilio Social placed 12,000 children in state or religious institutions. Asked about this compulsory tutelage in the documentary, Sanz denied having any knowledge of it. She also denied that mothers or children were abused in these institutions. Through skillful editing, her statements are interlaced with the counter-statements of witnesses, former wards of Auxilio Social who recount a chilling tale of inhumanity. By collating the witnesses' testimony with the perpetrators' denials, the documentary brings them face to face in the virtual courtroom where the viewers will pronounce their ethical verdict. Furthermore, testifying against the deniers, the witnesses raise grave objections to the character of the democracy that supervened. Teresa Martín, who was incarcerated as a child, denounces society's culpable oblivion:

> After forty years of dictatorship and twenty-five of democracy, people still don't know anything about what happened ... Not one of us has been given a voice; not in the TV channels, not in the radio or the

press; not one of us. A couple of books, two dozen books. Much has disappeared, but when someone wants memory to endure, memory is there. All that person needs to do is ask, and I am speaking. We have not been given a voice. I am sixty-two and it's the first time that I have spoken out. It's the first time that someone asks me.

Although the state's practice of taking children away from their mothers and turning them over to institutions and regime-approved families began as a "humane" alternative to killing the children of imprisoned women, it soon developed into a profitable business involving doctors, nurses, functionaries, and religious orders. These networks, operating under the protection of the government, trafficked with babies born out of wedlock to single mothers, who gave birth anonymously in apartments or convents set up for the purpose. These "institutions" charged for the women's confinement and then again for the adoption of the child by childless couples who often simulated a pregnancy. Like so much else from the Franco era, this arrangement continued to operate well into the post-Franco period, often by the same people who had been active in this line of business during the dictatorship. The amnesty law of 1977 not only exonerated them of their past involvement but made it impossible to investigate their subsequent activities perpetrated under the mantle of the same, unaltered legislation. When the constitutional state finally reformed the law regulating adoptions in 1987, and then again in 1996, it relinquished the right to investigate any cases before 1996 (Roig Pruñonosa 631–2). It added, therefore, twenty years to the impunity granted under the amnesty law of 1977, in addition making it extremely difficult and in most cases impossible for the affected people to recover their original identities.

To denounce the perpetrators after a shameful pact of silence requires courage and the willingness to compromise a professional aloofness that may be disgraceful under certain circumstances. In *Sumaríssim 447*, Genovès had relinquished the position of onlooker, a safe position that LaCapra considers "particularly questionable in the case of the Holocaust and other extreme or limit-events" (41). The real question, of course, is how extreme Spanish fascism was, how brutal and inexorable its sadism against the class enemy, the national minorities, and other resisters. The answers to this question fall along a spectrum of projective positions, some of which are anchored in compulsory forgetting. Genovès' attempt to crack the silence that protects the perpetrators had been impugned under the pretext of rebuking her professional ethics. But no one could refuse an incarnate victim the right to turn memory to account. In *Els nens perduts del franquisme*, Soledad Real, a frail old lady, proclaims with considered ardor: "I want to talk about this, because I want people to know that something must be done. We may not weep. We must do, we must do something." And who could take exception at her exhortation?

Immediately after airing *Els nens perduts del franquisme*, TVC staged a two-tier debate, one in the television studio, featuring intellectuals and politicians, and the other in a bar, where young people born after the death of Franco gathered to talk about the convenience of forgetting or remembering. Although the debate among the seniors was undistinguished, the young people's discussion was memorable. Half of them expressed their impatience with a past that, in the words of German historian Ernst Nolte, "will not go away." That past seemed too discontinuous with their lives to have any real claim on them. They argued in favor of letting the Civil War dwindle into an academic subject. They also felt that fascination with the past paralyzes, and attention to past injustices deflects attention from present issues. Although conventional, these arguments stated the case for turning the page and letting the older generation bury their dead.

The other half of the youngsters retorted that the world is not a virginal place or Francoism something from which one can skip and move on. Without knowledge of the dictatorship, said twenty-one-year-old Montse Dalmau, much of what is happening today is incomprehensible, the return of neo-Francoists to power, for instance. "You just have to look at the present government ... They are all the legacy of new generations [of Francoists] and some old ones who stayed on." Marta Vallejo, nineteen years old, understood that information is not enough, and that the intergenerational transmission of traumatic memory is crucial to historical evolution. Grief and anguish, the inevitable byproducts of mourning, must be accepted in order to apprehend the—in her words—"hallucinating historical moment" lived by previous generations. That moment is hallucinating for the young, who must confront its ghosts in the twilight of the historical imaginary, but it is, or was, real enough for the witnesses; real in the psychoanalytical sense of something that shatters the ego's defenses. There is nothing surprising in young people's refusal to allow the real to shatter the defenses built to protect them from an uncomfortable memory.

Joan Rota, a young man of twenty-four, also understood the inter-subjective transmission of the scars of the past: "We must be fully aware of our situation and [of the fact] that it has inherited this entire process. They [the previous generation] were educated in fear, and we ought to consider if our parents did not somehow educate us with the consciousness of all they have lived through." Rota raises the important question whether it is possible, or even desirable, to approach the past without analyzing one's own relation to it. The fear of the vanquished and of the victims is loose upon the historical scene, as is the arrogance of the victors and the impunity of the perpetrators.

If grief and anguish, or even anger, are the unpalatable affections experienced by those who try to cope with the past, anxiety may well be the emotion lurking behind the refusal to probe the past. Rota suggests as much when he asks: "Does the lack of mobilization among the young play any role in the subject we are discussing?" In other words, what is the relation between conformity and forgetting? Replying to Juan Reguera, a twenty-six-year-old man who had earlier derided the notion of trying to discern among old people those who were victims from those who were perpetrators, he goes on to say: "We cannot afford to have people walking around who were directly implicated in death penalties, in executing whoever they found annoying at that time." Rota understands that only if memory is hitched to action can the compulsion to repeat be curbed. Freud had pointed out that a traumatic disorder cannot be healed by treating it as a historical matter, but must be viewed as an actual power in the present (*Erinnern* 521). For the young man, it is urgent that people discern that the traumatic experience of the past lives on in the social forces that oppress us in the present. In this light, the transition's "pact of silence" appears as a counter-therapeutic procedure leading to the return of the repressed.

Freud believed that the way to control the drive to repeat was to transform it into a source of memory. But to accomplish this, first the anxieties must be displaced to a safer ground where they can unfold without harm. Only then can the drives working at the root of trauma be recognized for what they are. I suggest that, in the social sphere, television is such a symbolic outlet for the processing of traumatic memory. By staging the anxiety that goes unacknowledged in everyday life, television creates an opportunity to scrutinize the traumatic past. Coupling the medium's intimacy with the detachment brought by the intervening screen, television provides a transferential space where the drives can unfold as on a playground. The viewers who discharge their emotions through the phone line during the program's intermissions bring this potential home. Released from liability, their faceless voices move freely over the range of subject positions, from the neo-fascist who provocatively asserts that Franco raised Spain to its historical zenith, to the outraged caller who, with a quivering voice, denounces the flaunting of portraits of Francisco Franco and José Antonio Primo de Rivera in certain homes in Barcelona.

Televisió de Catalunya's historical memory documentaries did not attempt to suture the past. They did not resolve the viewers' anxieties by means of a structured narrative or other reassuring devices. On the contrary, the montage of historical photographs and film, bonded by re-constructive sequences, points to the elusive nature of a memory in ruins. Each image proclaims its symptomatic value and calls for exegetic action on the part of the viewer. Thus, the images' instability foregrounds their semantic displacement. Not only are they objects of interpretation, but their truth does not depend only on their anchorage in *something* that was actually *there*, but also on a retina that can no longer behold that *something* except by means of transference and illumined by the pale light that comes from another time somewhere beyond the screen. Images, seen in this way, are after-images,[8] windows of opportunity to trace the passage of the real over the surface of the eye.

8 For a discussion of the concept of "after-image," see chapter 1 in Resina, *After-Images of the City.*

CHAPTER FIFTEEN

Anachronism and Latency in Spanish Democracy

Why Latency?

A s a biological metaphor that draws on theories of vitalism, latency presents an advantage over the psychoanalytic metaphor of repression, now trivialized to the point of meaninglessness. "Repression" implies an underworld of compacted experience that takes its cue from social space distribution: the lower suburbs and out-of-view districts and ghettos of modern cities, or, pushing the metaphor, the "closeted" lives of pre-twentieth-century sexual minorities. Whereas the term is helpful in suggesting the relation between memory and space, it has difficulty accounting for temporal discontinuities and the anachronistic reappearance of phenomena. To explain leaps in time the theory of repression multiplies the psychic containers (subconscious, preconscious, consciousness) and resorts to another metaphor from the realm of physics, that of communicating vases: what the ego represses from consciousness reappears in the form of neuroses and manifests itself through various somatic outlets. In this view, the unconscious is like an everglade, with the fluid element seeping through apparently solid ground. Repression tends to ignore time, because the theory relies on the eternity of the unconscious, or what amounts to the same thing, the contemporaneity of memories.

It is not surprising, therefore, that Freud resorted to the concept of latency to explain the paradox between the delay between the onset of the cause and the manifestation of the effects, in other words, to bridge the conceptual gap opened in the mechanical idea of repression by the phenomenon of traumatic neuroses. Freud introduced the idea of latency in *Moses and Monotheism*, where he attempts to explain the long delay between the murder of Moses by the Jews and the ritualization of guilt feelings in Judaism and Christianity. Trying to find comparable phenomena, he turns to the traumatic accident with belated onset of psychic and motor symptoms, which he explains as follows: "The time that elapsed between the accident and the first appearance of the symptoms is called the 'incubation period,' a transparent allusion to the pathology of infectious disease ... It is the feature one might term *latency*" (109–10). Later in the same essay he posits the notion that such processes as can be observed in the life of individuals with regard to the formation of neurosis must also have developed in the human species. "That is to say, mankind as a whole also passed through conflicts of a sexual-aggressive nature, which left permanent traces, but which were for the most part warded off and forgotten; later, after a long period of latency, they came to life again and created phenomena similar in structure and tendency to neurotic symptoms" (129). As one can readily see, Freud has recourse to the idea of repression, that is, defensive forgetfulness, even where he resorts to latency and to the notion of traces that become active much later in distorted ways.

Freud's interest lies not so much with latency per se as with the origin of the neuroses in an ur-violent act of an oedipal nature, an act, that is, elicited by the threat of castration. And because the symptoms he discusses are the result of *traces* having gone through processes of symbolization, his theory retains the metaphor of the unconscious, i.e. a semantically transformative space inaugurated by the repression. But because he derives both the act and its repression from his interpretation of individual cases, he must take a leap in order to link the individual neuroses to large-scale historical developments. And he does, by assuming the correspondence of philogenetic and ontogenetic processes.

For all its "biological" underpinnings, psychoanalysis veered toward mentalism and the autonomous region of the imaginary, with the concept of time attaching to abstract "stages" (like Lacan's famous mirror stage) that are removed from the concrete time of social and organic processes. Latency avoids this pitfall by resorting to a biology-based notion of time. The term refers to the suspension of an organism's external functions, while the internal functions retain all their energies and potentialities. Latency relates to the heartbeat, to the minimal degree of life in concrete organic form. By alluding to what exists fully and yet independently of its manifestations, the concept can be useful when extrapolated to the social sciences in general and historical analysis in particular. There it can throw light on transitional phenomena that befuddle assumptions of epistemic changes, historical watersheds, and theories of discontinuity.

An example of this application, without explicit reference to the term latency, is found in Maurice Halbwachs' concept of collective memory, his term for the continuity of custom and sentiment below the historical threshold of awareness. After speaking of a certain delay between the moment when experience is registered as a memory and the time when it yields its historical meaning to consciousness (a delay formally reminiscent of Freud's use of the term latency for the breakthrough of the neurosis), Halbwachs goes on to establish his famous distinction between history and collective memory:

> History is not all of the past, but it isn't all that remains from the past either. Or, if one prefers, next to a written history there is a living history that perpetuates or renews itself through time and in which it is possible to find again a great number of those ancient currents that had vanished only apparently. (113)

There is a past, then, that remains outside the scope of historical consciousness, and it is an active past, "a living history," which spans long periods and produces the repetitions that psychoanalysis attributes to neuroses and unresolved traumas. Only, Halbwachs does not presuppose a psychic unconscious but merely a historical one—what is temporarily inaccessible for history remains active in the ancestral flow of the collective memory of a people.

Latency versus the Event

Simplistically, theories are often classified as progressive or conservative. Leaving aside the fact that these valuations tend to oscillate, so that what is progressive today may appear as the acme of conservatism tomorrow, it is generally the case that so-called progressive theory has tended to emphasize discontinuities, revolutionary breaks, the metaphysical or messianic irruption of the event, and so on, while so-called conservative theory has privileged permanence, development, recurrence, and spatiality. From this point of view, a theory based on the idea of latency would be unequivocally conservative, because it would seek to explain economy and conservation, like the first law of thermodynamics. But this is precisely what is needed in an intellectual environment that has become wary of theories governed by horizons of rupture and is no longer willing to give unlimited credit to all things utopian.

In the early 1990s, the explosion of criticism attendant on Francis Fukuyama's proclamation of the end of Hegelianism signaled widespread blindness to the exhaustion of the future as a repository for social dreams. The fact that critics were quick to ideologize a description of the new state of the world that left capitalism—itself immersed in a receding horizon of progress—as the single form of the world economy, proved that ideologies are more resilient in the cultural sphere than they are in the economy. In capitalist countries the fall of communism produced a surge of intellectual nostalgia related to the loss of the biggest alibi of social democracy. Western utopianism had been folded into a rising standard of living paid for by the masses that inhabited the socialist paradises. Now the revolutionary horizon was gone with one stroke, leaving a shattered economy and wrecked societies in its wake. That reality was incontestable, but Western intellectuals soon found an outlet for their frustrated dreams: heaping scorn on the burning conflicts left exposed by the ebbing utopianism. Post-Cold-War conflicts were not really new. They had been festering all along, while intellectuals remained fixated on the chiliastic thrills of world revolution. Suddenly, the unresolved issues caught their attention without, however, bringing them out of the comfortable moral dualism that underpinned their worldview. By and large, the intellectual class still judged historical matters with the nineteenth-century yardstick of progressive versus reactionary. Yet, national and ethnic tensions, religious fundamentalism, urban fractures along cultural fault lines, these and similar phenomena had not appeared out of the blue. They were not the reactionary reflection of a progressive agenda gone awry. Nor were they new creatures spawned by globalization, although they had been unquestionably exacerbated by modernization. The reemergence of national conflicts after the era of international brotherhood behind the iron curtain called for some form of exegesis other than the theory of default, according to which abeyance of utopian ambition equals political entropy.

To account for the carry over of historical energies through periods of low intensity, the concept of latency could prove more useful than the theory of downright suppression with a lapse from consciousness. In place of universal class struggle as the key to social change, latency would show that, on the whole, the struggles of the last century were driven by the dialectic between globalizing nations, on the one hand, and forms of sociality considered as grist for the mill of the master peoples, on the other. Latency can also show that the modernizing impulse, based on an ever-expanding notion of the future, paralleled the ever-larger territorial influence of the modern nations. Modernity was, in effect, the most discriminating feature in the world's distribution of power.

That pattern of domination has not run its course, but it appears to have exhausted its legitimation by reference to the future, much as first-century Christians had to come to terms with the non-return of Christ within their lifetimes. Similarly, the end of history, as befallen in the 1990s, was not the termination of change and the conclusion of social struggles but the grand finale of the kind of change that had been theorized under the rubric of the event. By event I mean a world-shattering phenomenon that interrupts the concatenation of everyday moments, intersecting an atemporal category into the historical chain. A sort of *deus ex machina*, the

event presumes the existence of a time outside of time, yet another version
of the unconscious from which the future is supposed to emerge in the
garb of the absolute unknown, generally through the midwifery of violence.
But with the exception of a few diehard revolutionaries, people today no
longer privilege apocalyptic versions of the future, and even our worst
nightmares—the overheating of the earth, the population explosion, water
and food scarcity, the depletion of non-renewable resources, the destruction
of Western culture and the demise of liberal regimes through unwieldy
migratory pressure—are experienced as already part of the landscape. It is as
if we had survived our human condition and had to live henceforth beyond
our mortality. It is exactly as if we existed in a state of latency.[1]

Postwar Times

Peter Sloterdijk begins his *Theory of Postwar Times* with the claim that we
live in an age of surrogates. Our ability to make do with the semblance
of things places us beyond Marx's observation about modernity as the
time in which "all that is solid melts into air" (83). If it can be defined in
any way, then postmodernity is surely the age of mass-produced placebos.
Instead of republican democracy we have teledemocracy. Instead of society,
multiculturalism. Instead of events we have appointments. Instead of
indentity, consumption. Instead of learning, education. Sloterdijk names two
expressions of surrogate culture: the ubiquity of the staging principle in the
contemporary event-culture, and the substitution of occurrences through
memory-events, which has led to a "jubilee's industry," an *haute cuisine* in
which only what has been warmed up counts anymore (10). Certainly, the
celebration culture is a vicarious reenactment of historical events that are
perpetuated—so the theory goes—through public commemoration. Such
staging in the form of public rituals offers evidence of the exhaustion of
history as a horizon of action. We seem to commemorate selected fragments
of the past out of an intuition that memory is the last remaining point of
contact with historical realities. Nothing else seems capable of bringing us
into situations that provide us with the sense of historical agency. Pierre
Nora's distinction between memory and history arises from the impression
that history is now a commodity to consume in places designated for the
purpose, the so-called memory places. Towns and countries cultivate a
selected memory in direct proportion to the stability they wish to promote;
that is, the more active the celebratory culture, the less the collective subject

1 See, for instance, Walter Laqueur's sobering analysis of the demographic
change in Europe, and the eloquent book's subtitle: "Epitaph for an Old Continent."

looks to the future as a blank page on which to write one more chapter in the history books. I will not go here into the reasons for the exhaustion of the future. But it bears saying that the rampant "jubilee's industry" is not a form of latency. On the contrary, the popular emphasis on memory, which may well signal nostalgia for memory, draws attention away from the past's actual manifestations in the present.

Such genuine manifestations can take the form of a revision of attitudes after dramatic periods; those, for instance, that were marked by the wars of the previous century. Sloterdijk considers it a basic law of postwar times that cultures draw conclusions from the outcome of the conflict and anchor that hard-won knowledge in their cultural memory (16). Ordinarily, the winner culture sees its cultural premises reinforced through their practical confirmation in the battlefields. Conversely, when losers reflect on the causes of their defeat, their self-criticism often leads to deep changes in the cultural mindset. Sloterdijk calls such soul-searching and the ensuing transformation of the cultural norms into more innocuous and less risky patterns "metanoia" (18).

While undoubtedly the losing side is more goaded by the circumstances to undertake a metanoic evaluation of its culture, sometimes it is the winner that reforms its cultural decorum the better to retain the advantages it has accrued in combat. Sloterdijk is centrally concerned with a century and a half (1806 to 1945) of conflictive French–German history. However, analysis of those particular relations, which have been twice at the core of European wars and remain at the core of the current peace, does not exhaust the theory's usefulness. The theory of postwar times can also tell us something about the outcomes of civil wars, and thus about the long-term effects of the Spanish Civil War of 1936–39.

The theory explains the hardening of the winning side's culture in the 1940s and 1950s, with a stress on ultramontane Catholicism and Castile's imperial mission. These forces had been challenged by the Republic through the separation of Church and State and by incipient devolution represented by the new statutes of autonomy for Catalonia (effective) and Euzkadi (in process). The economic interests of those traditional sectors had been further challenged by plans for land reform, and, after the war started, by the social revolution led by the anarchists and soon harnessed to the geopolitics of the Comintern by the Spanish Communist Party. On the losing side self-scrutiny was precluded at first by the eruption of the Second World War, which kept alive the hope for a vindication of the Spanish republic through defeat of the Axis. Ideological values were thus put on hold. The hope for the instauration of the Republic was dashed by the support given to the Franco regime by Great Britain and the United States, but then, for some people, it was maintained during the thick of the Cold War by the active and well-organized Communist Party. The relative inconclusiveness of the ideological struggle in Spain meant that the self-critical disposition diagnosed by Sloterdijk as typical of losing sides—with obvious attention to the post 1945 German experience—was missing. To be sure, republicans of different stripe recriminated each other for losing the war, but this is hardly representative of the self-analysis posited by the theory of postwar times. Still, instances of self-criticism existed, but they were not general enough to build upon them in the way that Sloterdijk does for post-Second World War Germany. Members of the Catalan upper classes (regardless of whether they had sided with Franco, against, or kept above the fray) tended to conclude that the struggle for devolution they had followed since the beginning of the century had been wrong, because it had led to catastrophic results. After the war many members of this class renounced their cultural heritage in a metanoic effort to avoid similar catastrophes in the future. But this means, quite simply, that they considered themselves losers regardless of the side they had supported in the war, or, conversely, that victory for them did not reinforce their cultural premises, but instead brought about a metanoic dismissal of those premises that was more unfavorable and uncompromising than any modification of cultural viewpoint undertaken by the losers.

Metanoic reflection became apparent long after the war, when both winners and losers found that their cultural premises no longer applied. By 1975, the year Franco died, the ideology of the Cold War was nearly spent. This ideology had permitted him to remain in power long after the demise of the other fascist regimes. Franco had risen to power with the help of Hitler and Mussolini. In 1945, when he seemed about to be ousted by the armies of the democracies, the Allies unexpectedly allowed him to remain in power. They had come to consider him an ally in the Cold War. But, by 1975, with the Cold War spinning toward the end of Soviet Power, his regime had become a liability to the economic forces that had profited from it. Aware of their historical obsolescence, the more astute Francoists became increasingly critical of the government—"disillusioned" was their term. This was a time of revised memoirs, edited diaries, and doctored autobiographies designed to cast a favorable light on former Falangists by staging their metanoic sentiments as retrospectively as possible.

A similar reconstruction took place among the losers—for instance, Stalinists who exchanged their erstwhile fundamentalism for critical detachment from the Soviet authorities. Their belated and always suspect independence, however, did not go much further than circumspect recognition that traditional class objectives had to be mediated by the provisional acceptance of liberal democracy. On both sides of the ideological spectrum, metanoic readjustments to the cultural decorum were made for the purpose of salvaging the substance of the wartime struggle. Such repositioning undoubtedly involved a degree of reconciliation with the adversary, a move widely understood as a patriotic requirement. But uppermost in the minds of the proponents of reconciliation was the intention to preserve essential values in a state of latency.

The Spanish Transition to Democracy as Postwar Times

I do not mean it as a provocation when I assert that Spain did not have a true postwar until thirty-five years after the end of combat. The regime of exceptionality resulting from the 1936–39 Civil War did not resolve the conflicts that had plagued Spain with internal wars and military coups since the eighteenth century. Franco chose to conduct a war of attrition in order to mop up every shred of resistance. As a result, most of the casualties took place in the rearguard in the form of assassinations and wholesale massacres. For Franco, victory was not enough if it did not entail the absolute subjection of the adversary. Consequently, the ideological clean up continued after the end of the military operations in the Year of Victory, as 1939 became enshrined in the annals of the dictatorship. Franco's peace was a continuation of the war by other means. And his justice consisted of summary court martials lasting minutes and often processing whole groups of prisoners at a time. After the war, thousands of people were executed to weed out the enormous prison population. As time went by, the social-political brigade, a Spanish police force modeled on the Gestapo, kept the pressure on all forms of political organization other than the Falange. When communist militant Julián Grimau was executed on 20 April 1963, former high-ranking Falangist Dionisio Ridruejo sent a letter to *Le Monde* criticizing Franco's cruelty and stating that "such actions were evidence of the attempt to perpetuate the state of civil war" (Krasikov 55).

Franco's permanence was predicated on fear, and fear meant a high degree of social immobility. His regime was incomprehensible without keen awareness of the simple hierarchy of winners and losers, institutionalized in the form of social rifts of a class and cultural nature. Franco's genocidal attempt to exterminate the Catalan and Basque cultures was far reaching. He did everything to prevent the social reproduction of their languages and to ensure that cultural practices associated with them would fall into oblivion. But to speak of these policies as the product of one mind is to misrepresent history. In this sense Franco was merely the executor of a deep, widespread cultural hatred.

When Franco died there was a staged unraveling of his regime, orchestrated by its most prescient members. Often conceived of as a Rousseauian contract based on a political *tabula rasa*, Spain's transition to democracy—*the transition* for short—can be thought more precisely as the medium for various latency phenomena. Most visible among these was the restoration of the monarchy after forty-four years. Retrospectively, it is easy to show that the crown's current popularity is the result of successful propaganda. In the 1970s, few in Spain believed that the monarchy was going to last. However, skepticism does not prove that support was lacking. We must assume the existence of latent monarchical sentiment if we are to explain how readily the monarchical idea took hold of Spaniards' imaginations. It did so in spite of the fact that Juan Carlos de Borbón represented not only national continuity but also Francoist legitimacy. To accede to the throne Juan Carlos swore the Principios Fundamentales del Movimiento, the Francoist code of law, before the full assembly of the Francoist Cortes. This is the reason why hard-core Francoists later accused him of perjury; by endorsing the self-liquidation of the dictatorship, the monarchy had lifted itself to democratic legitimacy by its own undemocratic bootstraps.

So explicit was the connection between the monarchy and the fundamental principles of Francoism that the officers who participated in the coup of 23 February 1981 were convinced that they acted with the King's blessing. Five years after the change of regime, the conspiracy revealed the same military unruliness that had brought on the Civil War—and for much the same reasons. Through the 1978 constitution, Spain had become a composite "state of autonomies," and in the early 1980s the territorial reform was beginning to unfold with the reinstatement of Catalonia's and Euzkadi's statutes. The army, however, was still incapable of accepting a modest decentralization. In the barracks the sentiment was strongly in favor of restoring "Spain's unity" by force. Many years later, a retired officer, who had found himself in the midst of the action in February 1981, recalled that in the months before the coup the army was restless on account of the new autonomic arrangements. The same witness admitted that, if plans for the coup had been shared more extensively, many military regions would have supported the rebellion (T.P.F.).

Spain's justice system never followed the lead from the 1981 coup back to the right-wing violence of the 1970s. The bands of youngsters who terrorized the population in the largest cities were never brought to justice. Nor were their leaders. If the transition had come to pass by the strength of the opposition, Spanish democracy would not have legalized the Falange. Yet, despite its paramilitary structure and violent tactics, the historical fascist party was never the object of attention by the law of political parties, which was designed to interdict political groups that endorse violence.

From the point of view of a theory of postwar times, Falange's legality is normative: winners see their ideology confirmed. Nevertheless, this conclusion clashes with the fact that Falange has remained electorally marginal and today none of its members occupies a position of responsibility in government (although many former members are or have been in high office, including the presidency). It would be wrong to speak of latency in this context. The concept is irrelevant to explain the programmatic continuity of the fraction that inflamed the Civil War, led the repression, and became the single legal party in the dictatorship, with Franco himself as its leader. If the single party became a marginal alternative after 1976, this can only be attributed to the fact that Falange cannot thrive in a democratic environment. Conversely, the quality of Spanish democracy can be measured by the currency of Falange's principles. Such continuity, regardless of whether the principles are traced back to Falange or adopted by other political formations, does call forth the idea of latency. "Latent" in this sense does not mean "dormant." We can hardly grasp the deterioration of Spanish democracy without positing something like an active agent working through official and unofficial channels of opinion formation.

In his classic study *Public Opinion*, Walter Lippmann showed how political rhetoric becomes vague when superficial harmony is the goal in an environment riddled with conflict. "Almost always vagueness at a crucial point in public debate is a symptom of cross-purposes" (178). The celebrated consensus of the transition relied on a wholesale emptying of words like "freedom," "justice," "autonomy," "nationality," and "democracy." The vagueness of these terms facilitated a superficial conciliation of interests without the players conceding any of their long-term goals. Mental reservation guaranteed the permanence of the issues and the eventual return of conflict. Connected with this permanence is the belabored question of the historical memory. How, to put the matter bluntly, is it possible to reconcile the claim that the transition was based on a compact of silence with the notion that it preserved the historical contradictions? How could it, on the one hand, release the accumulated tensions and, on the other, store massive pent-up feelings? The acrimony of contemporary Spanish politics owes a great deal to the fact that the words on which the transition proceeded as on slippery stones meant different things to different people and different things to the same people at various times. The consequence of the failure to come to terms with the conflicts at the rhetorical level, the failure, that is, to narrativize the recent past, was that the inherited affects, locked up in the irreducible dimensions of aspiration on the one hand and defensiveness on the other, retained all their explosive potential. This retention of historical energy is what I mean by "latency." The vocabulary on which the consensus of the transition was built was out of touch with the facts and could not work with them to transcend the past; nor could it use its energy to bring about the only acceptable kind of closure, namely the one that integrates what has been as well as what could have been, i.e. actuality and potential, into what will be. With the word "reconciliation" many people matched up images of Falange thugs; with the word "freedom," images of police brutality; with the word "justice," memories of lengthy prison terms, torture, and executions; with the word "democracy," evidence of rigid authoritarianism.

Certainly, reconciliation was intended to produce coherence of sentiment where there was a heterogeneous array of feelings. But the semantic stoppers that sealed (or dressed up) the transition staged a narrative of historical surmounting, while letting the meaning leak out of the words. The rhetoric guaranteed legibility but paled in comparison with the images of recent struggles in people's minds. Hence, it was urgent to replace those images with imageless ideas, and this was done, rather successfully, for the new generations. Today young people have only a faint idea of the dictatorship. Franco himself has become an avuncular figure, perhaps overly stern and certainly outmoded, but on the whole good-natured: a provider of peace and economic recovery, whose name and image are honored in many a Spanish village and town. Words can always be made to mean other things, or nothing at all. What was tacitly clear at the time of his death gradually blurred in the convoluted language of the law, becoming subject to interpretation. Such codification of the past agrees with the theory of controlled forgetfulness. Even so, affects that had thickened during the Franco era are still felt today, even if they not always have a clear object or seek release through substitute ones. An unmistakable emotional pitch attaches to ungrounded words and ideas, to the point that many people experience animosity against certain social groups, their symbols, and cultural products without being able to substantiate their feelings or even to know why they experience them.

The instinctive behavior of entire groups may be explained through semantic displacement, as Lippmann does with regard to the formation of public opinion. He believes that, if a stimulus can be found that arouses the same emotion as another, it can be substituted for the original stimulus to produce the desired emotional response. We are all familiar with this basic publicity trick. An example in the political sphere is scapegoating, a tragic *quid pro quo*, as René Girard has abundantly shown. In scapegoating it is the mechanism that counts; the victim is irrelevant. Hence, it can be replaced through semantic slippage. This maneuver can be seen at work in the replacement of anti-Semitism with anti-Catalanism in the fascist discourse of the 1930s.

Displacement and replacement mechanisms are undoubtedly at work in the crudest manifestations of propaganda used by certain media. The temptation to substitute schematic models for painstaking empirical observation is universal and to some extent unavoidable, if thinking must take place at all, but its deliberate, systematic deployment is the mark of propaganda. In Spain it has led to an excess of verbalism, the habit of quarreling about names rather than things. Beyond semantic displacement, the persistence of dispositions that were primary themes for the outbreak of the Civil War suggests an archaism of emotion that can shock rational thinking as it moves through different phases of the symbolic and crystallizes in public policy.

The theory of hauntology, of ghosts running amuck among the living, has been proposed as a metaphor for something as paradoxical as amnesiac memory. Under the aegis of postmodernity, Marx's metaphor of the specter (a gothic figure of speech for the menace of communism) gave way to something much more ethereal or banal. In this "theoretical" use, ghosts either refer to unwanted memories from the past (a trite use of the gothic tale) or to an invisible (or unknowable) range of causes for ascertainable effects, as in the spectrality of light. Says Avery Gordon: "The way of the ghost is haunting, and haunting is a very particular way of knowing what has happened or is happening. Being haunted draws us affectively, sometimes against our will and always a bit magically, into the structure of feeling of a reality we come to experience, not as cold knowledge, but as transformative recognition" (8). This hypothesis squares rather lyrically with the semantic displacement that retains feeling while making its original causes indiscernible. "Transformative recognition" is, like "magically," mystifying language. It means nothing precise. But the point about such processes is that, by engaging in them, we circumvent rationality (Gordon's "cold knowledge"). In essence, hauntology purports to account for unacknowledged presences. It draws whatever empirical strength it has from a sensual reality (the ghosts are seen after all) that is ratified by the emotions. But why speak about ghosts and not, more pragmatically, of latency, that is, of observable reality that appears momentarily muted or inactive, yet remains animate and ready to stir at the first sign of a propitious environment?

Latent Anti-Semitism

To conclude, I propose a strong thesis, which admittedly depends on the practical demonstration of the theory of latency. Spanish fascism was the 1930s and 1940s fulfillment of long-standing Castilian authoritarianism. Italian inspiration and German assistance were contributing factors, but

Spaniards could rummage in their own traditions to find the totalitarian impulses that became murderous during the Civil War and its aftermath. In fact, reverse inspiration is possible. In an interview with Adolf Hitler published by Josep Pla and Eugeni Xammar in the early 1920s, the Führer acknowledged Spanish anti-Semitism as the great precedent for his own project of racial cleansing. "We have a precedent in what Spain did with the Jews. Nevertheless, we will correct the Spanish solution. We will not give the Jews the option between conversion and expulsion. No. We are for expulsion pure and simple. For Spain, the Jewish problem was a religious problem. For us it is a problem of race" (Xammar 203). The interview may be apocryphal, a prank of two young foreign correspondents, neither of whom mentioned this interview in their respective memoirs. But, even if the meeting never took place, their observation of the rise of Nazism in Germany was astonishingly accurate, and, short of predicting the final solution, focused on Hitler's racial obsession at the core of his political program. Whether apocryphal or genuine, the interview furnishes a striking example of latency, where after four and a quarter centuries Hitler's plan to eradicate European Jewry echoes the world-historical expulsion of Jews from the Iberian Peninsula. There is, of course, a long line of pogroms linking 1492 and 1923, but the power of the expulsion to radiate ethnic hatred through the centuries is neither magic nor ghostly. The hatred survived periods of subdued activity to come back in force with the newly pulsing ideology.

The reasons for Spanish anti-Semitism were not religious any more than German anti-Semitism was racial. Religion and race were the local ideologies used to justify group hatred. They were, circumstantially, the official and so to speak legitimate doctrines that no one was likely to contest. Given the specificity of time and place, they were likely to be put at the service of the collective passions. Anti-Semitism had been lethal long before it discovered the race motif. Throughout Europe pogroms often took place when gentile debt to Jewish lenders had reached dangerously high levels. Any pretext was good to smite a minority that came to be hated for concrete reasons of group loyalty, competition, and envy. Thus, paltry hatred against Jews could be re-signified as collective defense of religious or racial purity. And when the Jews were already disposed of, the hatred could be tapped to semiticize peoples whose economic eminence combined with political marginality to make them at once threatening and vulnerable. The equivalence of Catalans and Jews, nurtured in the Spanish imaginary since the nineteenth century, made the social environment ripe for agitation. As soon as the emotional transfer was complete, Catalans could be scapegoated in the Civil War and blamed for it too. And just as anti-Semitism outlasted the presence of Jews, the affect that attached itself to Catalans did not dissipate with the destruction of their culture and institutions. It continued unabated into the democratic period, at first under the relatively inconspicuous form of economic suffocation, and later as barefaced attacks on the region's political and cultural specificity.

Screening out of Catalans from high office, positions of influence, and public opportunities did not stop with Francoism. At first, the practice was stealthy, but as years passed and Spaniards felt their new regime increasingly legitimated, discrimination and assault on civil rights became unabashed once again. Discrimination takes many forms, from unequal public investment to blocking Catalan companies from fair competition and deliberately peripheralizing the region through puny expansion and inadequate maintenance of its communications system, effectively hindering its competitiveness and international projection.[2] But these are only abstract descriptions, which do not convey the emotions that alone explain the effect of those practices on those who suffer them. Such behavior is not from yesterday. It is the current expression of a past that will not go away but remains misrecognized in the present. If anti-Semitism is, as some claim, the original form of racism, it is also the historical source of Spain's most intractable social rift. A society that achieves self-awareness in the act of self-mutilation creates a paradigm for conflict resolution and repeats it over time until, having come to grief, that society either revises its premises or ceases to exist. The unmitigated catastrophe of the Civil War did not serve this purpose, though. Insofar as it produced winners and losers, it did not force everyone to acknowledge the universal scope of the losses. And the winners found it reassuring to buttress their myths with affects that had, from their point of view, been rewarded by their superior use of violence.

The anachronistic view of national unity achieved under the Catholic monarchs, Falange's dearest myth, hinged on anti-Semitism. Fourteen ninety-two, the year when the last Moorish enclave in the Iberian Peninsula fell to the Christian armies, was also the year of the expulsion of the Jews. This conjunction—military conquest and ethnic cleansing—marked the Spanish national identity indelibly, so that the Spanish idea of unity has

2 An example of this behavior is found in Endesa's president, Manuel Pizarro, brandishing the Spanish constitution to prevent the purchase of the company by the Catalan Gas Natural. Tapping the anti-Catalanism that flared up in 2005 as Catalans were negotiating the Statute of Autonomy, Pizarro maneuvered to sell the company's stock to the German E.ON, proclaiming that German ownership was preferable to Catalan control. Pizarro presided Endesa as an appointee of the Partido Popular, whose leader, José María Aznar, had used his stint as President of the government to privatize the state company in 1998. Endesa had been created in 1944 as a state agency to invest in and regulate the energy industry.

since been inseparable from ideological orthodoxy, and both unity and orthodoxy have been enforced with real or symbolic autos-da-fé. National mythology traces back the cleansing of the social body to Castile's fabled queen, Isabel I. The queen's alleged zeal for cleanness as a metaphor for her intolerance turns up in Eugenio d'Ors' Falangist portrait of the Castilian queen as an unmistakable precursor of the party's leader. Her passion was "to clean Spain of factions and bandits. Of Moors and Moriscos. Of Jews and heretics. Of particularist leprosy, of monastic scum" (54). In ominous anticipation, d'Ors outlines the agenda for the new inquisitors after a war that will be kindled two years later. And, again, the path is traced in advance by the queen's foundational politics:

> To achieve the work that the conquest of Granada permits and initiates, years and years will be necessary. One day it is the Morisco question. The Landlady intervenes with her passion for order, tidiness and cleanness. The Moriscos are expelled. Later, the Jews as well. Spain will remain smooth like the palm of a hand. It will be smoothed further, after the Queen's death, by Cisneros and the Inquisition. (80)

After his "war of unification," Franco was not satisfied with military victory. He too saw conquest as the opportunity to eradicate the undesirables that d'Ors had presented as warts on the surface of Spain in 1492 and, implicitly, in 1934. Jews and the particularist leprosy, Moors and Moriscos, objectionable identities to be rubbed off, along with other socially offensive categories, until the country was unified and the leader held it in the palm of his hand.

The loathing had persisted for four and a half centuries. It would last longer. Franco supported Isabel's beatification, initiated in 1958 by the Bishop of Valladolid, José García Goldáraz. Her devotees have been seeking her canonization for decades. It is blocked, it seems, by the inconvenience of the two feats for which d'Ors and the Falange had praised her, namely the institution of the Spanish Inquisition and the expulsion of the Jews. It is hard to avoid the suspicion that, rather than religious devotion, which would need to be fabricated around the new saint, what Isabel's champions are really promoting is the canonization of a political modality. If the Vatican concedes, a particular conception of the state would be raised, at least for Catholics, above the fray of political discussion. Elevated to the altars, that is, to perpetuity, the unitary state would enter the ultimate stage of latency. It would become an article of faith. And the expulsion of Jews a mere accident in the process of state building, a cleaning, an ordering, a tidying up that could be renewed ad libitum with or without Jews. For the Jew is ultimately a metaphor for all forms of the particularist leprosy.

The emotions that anti-Semitism once stirred can always be conjured in the absence of the original object. All that is needed is another object that evokes similar emotions. The murderous disposition once exercised against Jews, of a gravity that is hardly mitigated by invoking the reason of state, as proponents of Isabel's canonization do, has proved its capacity to flare up again after long periods of latency. And so has the violence against objects that have once served as placeholders for its original target.

CHAPTER SIXTEEN

Negationism and Freedom of Speech

On 27 November 2007, Spain's Constitutional Court ruled, in reference to genocide, that to penalize "negationist" behavior is "an attack against the right to freedom of expression" (Panyella 32). The sentence modified an article of the penal code that made negationism punishable, and it came in the wake of a trial against well-known neo-Nazi Pedro Varela. The high court justified its decision by arguing that "[it cannot] be stated that all denial of conduct legally defined as a crime of genocide objectively pursues the creation of a social climate of hostility against those persons who belong to the same groups ... who in their day were victims of a specific crime of genocide" (Constitutional Court Judgment No. 235/2007, of 7 November).[1] The Spanish magistrates' ruling was laden with implications for jurisprudence and for the relation between law and history. It is worthy of attention for what it can tell us about the conditions for democracy, and indeed the very conception of democracy, in post-transition Spain.

The key question, in every legal settlement, is whom does the sentence favor? If the parties directly affected by the change in the penal code are deniers on the one hand and the victims of genocide on the other, then the question has an unequivocal answer: deniers win. And they win big for linking their cause to a democratic freedom, to freedom in short. Unquestionably, democracy protects negationists as much as anyone else, but one can reasonably ask if it must protect negationism as well. If democracy includes respect for the truth (that is, a certain adequation of legislation to a social consensus based on unimpeded and undistorted access to facts) and protection of minorities' physical and social wellbeing, then it is possible to ask whether the Spanish Constitutional Court's decision was not a setback to democracy under the pretext of a principled defense of the democratic right to freedom of expression. We shall come back to the nature

---

1 Unofficial translation. <www.tribunalconstitucional.es/gl/jurisprudencia/ ResolucionTraducida/235-2007,%20of%20November%207.pdf>.

of this freedom. For now, we should remark that the sentence is offensive because negationism is, in and of itself, an aggravation of the original crime.

Negation of crimes and thus of the truth flourishes where perpetrators enjoy social esteem or at the very least rely on passive indifference, and where the political and juridical arrangement is pervaded by consciousness of the lingering effects of crimes that are negated. Negation, in other words, does not occur in abstract academic space but in social terrain, where leniency furnishes a protective umbrella for crimes that often remain unstated. The move by Spain's Constitutional Court constitutes an event of great significance, in that it abrogates not just the consequences of historical judgment but the notion of historical truth as such. One clarification is in order. I do not suggest that a court of law has jurisdiction on epistemological matters. In a post-Nuremberg environment, however, a court of law is bound by historical truth when the latter has become foundational for the juridical situation. Currently, legislation in democratic societies incorporates concepts such as "hate crime," "crime against humanity," "racist aggravation," or "racial discrimination" that only came into existence or were substantially reinforced after the Nuremberg trials. To excise the historical fact of genocide from the sphere of law deprives the law of an empirical basis for its definition and sanction of those crimes. Similarly, and this is what makes the Constitutional Court's decision ominous, post-1975 Spanish legislation cannot sap the social knowledge about Francoism without eroding its own democratic legitimacy. If Francoism was not, or was not what a majority of people in the 1970s knew it to be, then the constitution that was crafted to transcend the impasse between institutional power and popular truth is voided of historical meaning.

What was so eventful in the ruling to decriminalize negationism? First, its pioneering character, which made this decision precedent setting. Spain, the last country in Europe to give up fascist political traits, became the first, among those that have laws against negationism,[2] to depenalize attempts to erase social awareness of crimes against humanity, committing the fact of genocide to the freeplay of social discourses. Such move ran afoul of the European Court of Human Rights, which in a decision of 2003, stated that:

Disputing the existence of crimes against humanity was, therefore, one of the most severe forms of racial defamation and of incitement

---

2 Some of these are the Belgian Holocaust denial law or the 1990 French *Gayssot Act*, which prohibits any "racist, anti-Semitic or xenophobic" speech. Switzerland also outlawed the denial of the Holocaust (Article 261bis of the Penal Code), as did Germany (§ 130(3) of the penal code), Austria (Article 3h Verbotsgesetz 1947), Romania, Slovakia, the Czech Republic, Lithuania, and Poland (Article 55 of the law creating the Institute of National Remembrance 1998).

> to hatred of Jews. The denial or rewriting of this type of historical fact undermined the values on which the fight against racism and anti-Semitism was based and constituted a serious threat to public order. It was incompatible with democracy and human rights and its proponents indisputably had designs that fell into the category of prohibited aims under Article 17 of the Convention. (Inadmissibility Decision in the Case of *Garaudy* v. *France*)

ECHR concluded that in application of Article 17 of its Convention (which provides that no one may use the rights guaranteed therein to seek the abolition or limitation of those same rights), the plaintiff cannot appeal to the protection of Article 10 (the right to freedom of expression) insofar as he wants to use it to dispute crimes against humanity. The following year, the ECHR reiterated this exclusion for "the category of clearly established historical facts—such as the Holocaust—whose negation or revision is removed from the protection of Article 10 by Article 17 of the Convention (*Chauvy and Others* v. *France* 20). Freedom of expression was thus explicitly subordinated to historical truth and respect for the rights of others.

This decision disturbs fundamentalists for whom freedom of speech is context free and unlimitable. Even if it functions as a cover for assailing other fundamental rights, its abuse, so the argument goes, can always and everywhere be restrained by the free marketplace of ideas. Redolent of the laissez-faire argument about the ultimate fairness of the market, freedom of speech fundamentalism does not consider that this right emerged as a guarantee against governments' irrepressible tendency to muffle opposition rather than as a sanctuary for symbolic aggression against defenseless individuals or minorities. Such untrammeled liberalism dispenses with the "harm principle" recognized by John Stuart Mill and invoked (although to deny its applicability) by the Spanish Constitutional Court. Much less does legal fundamentalism concede the claims of the "offense principle" introduced by Joel Feinberg in 1985, or sufficiently weigh the evidence that, in a context of latent or explicit aggression, "symbolic" easily slips into effective violence, as in child pornography, sexual exploitation of women, hate speech, and other forms of actual and not merely hypothetical degradation of people. If some countries have incorporated anti-defamation laws and racist aggravation to ordinary crimes into their legal systems, it is because their legislative bodies contextualize the limits to freedom of expression.

Negationism cannot take cover behind freedom of expression, because it is not a matter of expression. Negationists do not opine about or interpret past experience; they erase it. In place of indubitable experience, experience that preceded not only its enunciation but even the possibility of enunciating, they introduce ideology that is rooted in the motives that led to the original crime. And yet this shrill ideology works by playing down the importance of ideology: yes, there were some casualties, perhaps even concentration camps, but there was never a master plan to exterminate a human group. If one can relativize something as horrific as the Holocaust, then every denial becomes possible, including acts of domestic persecution that are so much more easily hidden among the casualties of a Civil War. From the victims' point of view, though, the genocidal intent is never in doubt. They know that they were chosen on account not of their acts but of their identity. And since that identity has become inextricable from the experience of persecution, nothing jeopardizes it as much as denying its experience.

In robbing victims of their experience, negationism kills them all over again; it wants a world without witnesses, and thus it seeks to undo the legacy of victimhood. Negationism is fed by the same prejudices that were lethal in the past; within its scope a historical hatred transmutes into hatred of history. Negationists act as if they could dull the self-hatred arising from identification with the perpetrators. Nothing is more puerile than the belief that, if the crime could only be thought out of existence, then the denier's pathos would become less criminal. Negationists continue to hate and to justify the hatred, but their shoddy reasons show them wearing their hearts on their sleeves. If they deny genocide in the past, it is in order to perpetuate its pathos into the future. In their perverse logic, acknowledged genocide is an obstacle to unfettered racism. This is why its negation amounts to ongoing aggression. Negating the substance of the crime, namely the targeting of the victims for who they are, downgrades victimhood to victimism, lifting the protection afforded by society's bad conscience. Were there not other inmates in the camps? Gypsies, Slavs, Frenchmen, other Germans? Then, by what right do the Jews claim centrality for anti-Semitism in the course of a world war? Targeting the Jews out of anti-Semitism is not only far more dramatic than attributing their murder to accidentalism and, above all, is the only reason that squares with the facts of their systematic rounding up, careful separation from other populations, dehumanization, and ultimate transformation into *Lebensunwertes Leben* ("life unworthy of life").

The paradox of negationism is that it relies on the memory of persecution. Deniers are not in the grip of skepticism but of the desire to enhance the offense through fear and intimidation. They operate on a split front: the crime must and must not have taken place. It must remain an inarticulate memory, a traumatic specter casting a pall of fear over the targeted category of people without crystalizing into an image of horror, because horror that is revealed places the victim off limits.

The Spanish Constitutional Court's decision to decriminalize negationism is ominous in that it presents as an act of justice the freedom to annihilate public consensus about experience that can never be righted by an act of jurisprudence. Such a decision constitutes, in effect, a prolegomenon to renewed violence. The Court's justification of its ruling through recourse to freedom of expression clashes with the narrow limits of this very freedom when it bears on the symbols of the state. Swift and harsh application of laws against whatever may be construed as apology of terrorism, the severity with which offenses against the monarchy or disrespect toward the flag are penalized, speedy translation of an insufficiently meek response to a judge or a police officer into punishable defiance of authority, pre-electoral banning of political parties, judicial harassment, barring from office, and even incarceration of political enemies, closing of newspapers and shutting down television broadcasting stations: these actions do not bespeak ingrained reverence for freedom of speech, and yet they have all occurred under the mantel of legality in post-Franco Spain. If freedom of speech is not the cornerstone of Spanish democracy, why does its alleged inviolability trump the positive damage done by negationism?

Negationism shares with pornography an addiction to pleasure obtained from denigrating a subject that stands for an entire class of people. But while pornography predicates its denigration of women on the graphic humiliation of an individual, negationism erases the representation of generic terror in order to humiliate individuals who are singled out because of their identity. Questioning pornography's protection by the First Amendment to the United States constitution, Catherine A. MacKinnon stresses the performative modality of discriminatory language, pointing out that social inequality is created and enforced largely through words and images. In respect to denigration, "saying it is doing it" (13). Her remarks apropos pornography ought to serve as a red flag to the Spanish Constitutional Court's treatment of negationism. What is particularly noxious about the court's ruling is that it anticipates the denier's obvious line of defense, namely that his words do not produce a social effect but merely lay out an "intellectual" position. When did aggression become a matter of opinion? Like pornography, what hatred does, "it does in the real world, not only in the mind" (15).

There is no greater hostility toward a victimized group than to deny its victimization. Doing so naturalizes the history of abuse and allows the denigration to go unchecked by moral sentiment or positive law. The surge of power experienced by the denier, when he disarticulates knowledge that was painful to acquire, is neither an opinion nor a subjective sentiment but the proceeds of social action. The point here is not that the Spanish judiciary is remarkably partial when it comes to protecting freedom of speech, which it is, but that it undoes the relation between history and justice, treating a sensitive ethical matter as if the issues at stake were an abstract problem of law. The fact that the Constitutional Court modified the Penal Code to exclude negationism from the list of punishable offenses shows that the judges did not deliberate within the scope of interpretable law, but assumed political agency in a step of incalculable moral consequence. What was hitherto codified as an injustice (and thus socially perceived as such) blurred into the gray area of indifferent acts. Furthermore, by keeping history in abeyance, the court assumed the garb of a historical subject. If negationism is a crime elsewhere in Western democratic states, it is because the relation between history and jurisprudence is understood, and the consequences of negationism are perceived to threaten not only the social stability but also the ethical foundations of the state. The question then arises whether a non-representative, non-elected body at the service of the state may legitimately adopt the prerogatives of sovereignty and lift the legal sanction on attempting against the crucial link between ethical awareness of the past and the rule of law.

The Constitutional Court acted as if it operated in an abstract juridical sphere, where freedom of speech is merely a principle and negationism a concept. In doing so it harked back to tradition. Until the middle of the twentieth century, law was considered ahistorical. This was especially the case where the doctrine of natural right (or divine right) prevailed, but also where right was held to be inseparable from positive acts of legislation. Shoshana Felman argues that this state of affairs changed at the Nuremberg trials, when the court, by indicting the representatives of the Nazi regime, "for the first time called history itself into a court of justice" (11). Since then, "it has become part of the function of trials to repair judicially not only private but also collective historical injustices" (12). The Spanish Constitutional Court ruled as if the atrocities of the twentieth century had not intervened and jurisprudence enacted since Nuremberg, including the Universal Declaration of Human Rights, had no bearing on Spanish law. Its position raises important questions regarding the nature and scope of human rights, national sovereignty, and the limits to the autonomy of states.

The first of these questions bears on the distinction drawn by the court between genocide and its negation. Is it really true that denying the historical fact of genocide does not contribute to a climate of hostility against the group that was victimized in the past? Such questions cannot be answered philosophically. In order to answer this one meaningfully, society must be scanned for signs of hostility against the group. If they are present, then one must ask to what degree negationists participate in the hostility, and what might be the correlation between group-directed hostility and tolerance of negationism. This means that the Spanish court's decision would come under scrutiny as a possible symptom of deteriorating democracy. Furthermore, one such symptom would be the state's refusal to countenance collective rights, or, what amounts to the same thing, its failure to look beyond the denier's individual right to freedom of expression to the collective stigmatizing of an entire group. There is little doubt that the court's decision to waive the denier's accountability had less to do with a meditated reconsideration of the legal process than with the objective defenselessness of groups that are hurt by denial.

This question also bears on the court's invocation of a human right (freedom of speech, recognized under Article 19 of the Universal Declaration of Human Rights) to suspend the application of another human right (the inherent dignity of all human beings) that is recognized in the preamble to the Declaration. Disregard for the dignity of the victims of genocide takes the form of suspending the right to know, thus lifting an important safeguard against recurrence. And with the legal guarantee of the truth also goes the right to freedom from fear. A step at a time, victims of genocide are divested of rights and dignity until the threshold of physical violence is crossed again. Thus, the first question leads to the related question about priorities among rights. While it is true that human rights are folded into the civil rights of liberal democracies, they are also recognized by some non-liberal states. Such states remain in good standing within the international community to the extent that they respect and are willing to enforce respect of human rights. Human rights are thus more basic and general, and therefore more universally binding, than civil rights. They are the litmus test for a state's progress toward full-fledged liberal democracy, and when infringed they are the first sign that a state is regressing from liberalism's principles of division of powers and equality before the law. Hence, it is contradictory to position freedom of speech, a human right that emanates from civil rights, ahead of a more fundamental human right such as freedom from harm and the concomitant obligation to prevent genocide, which hinges on its detection, as the ECHR acknowledges when it warns signatory states against allowing freedom of expression to outdo the recognition of crimes against humanity.

John Rawls defines human rights as constitutive of a Law of Peoples, which "applies to how peoples treat each other as *peoples*" (83). This law differs from cosmopolitan liberal justice in that it concerns all societies, even hierarchical ones, that comply with his definition of a decent society, namely one that complies with the Law of Peoples. Because this law concerns the way *groups* treat each other, states that deny the existence of collective rights risk falling below the threshold of decency. Furthermore, this law is not reducible to a set of regulatory principles with jurisdiction over a specific society only, as the Spanish constitutional law clearly is. On the contrary, according to Rawls, "How peoples treat each other and how they treat their own members are, it is important to recognize, two different things. A decent hierarchical society honors a reasonable and just Law of Peoples even though it does not treat its own members reasonably or justly as free and equal citizens, since it lacks the liberal idea of citizenship" (83).

No matter that Rawls confuses peoples with citizens and thus with states, the thrust of his argument is clear: a people organized as a state, to remain "decent" and thus a "*bona fide* member of a reasonable Society of Peoples" (84), is not free to subject other peoples to demeaning conditions, regardless of whether the subjected peoples live within the borders or enjoy citizenship in that state. Rogue states typically persecute internal peoples, euphemistically (and disparagingly) called minorities, and states that degrade or persecute their minorities risk becoming rogue states. Rawls' confusion between peoples and citizens stems from his belief in democracy as the free exercise of public reason, a condition he extends to his transnational Society of Peoples, the central defining trait of which is to be reasonable. But because democracy cannot be attributed to each and every member of this Society, Rawls replaces this unfeasible unifying feature with decency, the lowest common denominator of what he deems "reasonable." And since, in the political realm, states are the ultimate referent of "reasonableness," the bar is set rather low for states to accede to the Society of Peoples. Short of exterminating populations deemed undesirable, fellow states in this Society do not as a rule object to domestic hierarchies or similar processes of differentiation, which in the absence of ethnic homogeneity often involve marginalization and/or assimilation of internal others.

Paradoxically, liberalism sometimes relies on a weak definition of human rights. For Michael Walzer, "majorities have no obligation to guarantee the survival of minority cultures" (74). In his own version of the decent society, minorities "have a claim, indeed, to physical but not to cultural security" (74). This is another version of the notion that individuals, not groups, are the bearers of rights, a position that brings Walzer into ethical proximity with the Spanish Constitutional Court, which ruled, in effect, that in the absence of a demonstrable link between negationism and a climate of hostility against the group that was victimized, the individual right of the denier to his opinion prevails over the minority's moral and cultural security. But is not this very opinion evidence of the existence of a climate of hostility against the victimized, who are first scapegoated and then deprived of the social recognition of their defining (and in some cases determining) experience?

With regard to culture, Walzerian liberalism is neocon. It does not actively promote the destruction of minority cultures, but by legitimizing indifference it signals that a passive climate attends on social decisions to rout out a minority culture. By denying the obligation to protect minority cultures, Walzer pulls the plug on them. At the limit, this way of thinking rejoins negationism. By reducing the understanding of genocide to the destruction of individual bodies, it passes over the reasons why precisely those bodies and not others were massacred. And, vice versa, it is blind to genocidal actions so long as wholesale massacres are not in the perpetrators' agendas, just as some judges refuse to acknowledge torture when police employ methods that leave no traces on their victims' bodies. So long as corpses are not on the scene, liberalism remains unperturbed when states persecute minority cultures or when the market finishes them off after they have been weakened by colonialism or dictatorship.

It will be objected that Walzer does not condone aggression against minority cultures, and the objection carries. Yet, exempting majorities from obligation toward these cultures fails to take into account the fact that the threat against them is constitutive of the social relation that establishes the minority as such. His argument for ethical indifference seems acceptable only in the case of accidental minorities, namely fractions of majority groups located outside the areas where they are hegemonic but still drawing support from those areas. Although numerically a minority in relation to its contingent majority, such a group is not a minority in an absolute sense. Absolute minorities lack hegemony in their own sphere and consequently cannot draw it from anywhere else. Absolute minorities are usually locked in states with potentially unfriendly majorities; lacking a diplomatic corps to protect them and sovereign institutions to grant them their specific rights, they are the historical targets of genocide.

Relations between majorities and minorities are often the outcome of long-term patterns of domination, sometimes including genocidal episodes. It is difficult to settle these relations "reasonably" through "arrangements that satisfy the members (not the militants) of this or that minority" (Walzer 75). Part of the difficulty is in the language (and hence the concepts) deployed by liberalism. The distinction between member and militant is untenable, unless membership is defined to exclude militancy; but then the definition would beg the question of what settlement could satisfy a minority that represses its most conscious and vocal members? A minority purged of militants, even when satisfied by a particular arrangement with the majority, would reconstruct the unhappy minority *en abîme*. In other words, it would always recreate militancy.

Walzer's distinction is based on the liberal prejudice that political problems are always susceptible of rational solutions, but when this prejudice comes up against an intractable clash of wills, it concludes, quite illogically, that militancy is opposed to rationality. According to this prejudice, membership and militancy converge only outside the sphere of reason. Or to put it differently, inside a minority one can be either democratic or liberal, but not both. Liberalism would insist on the minority's attainment of the full universality of rights (which the majority denies it) thus leaning toward militancy, while democracy would settle for the path favored by the greatest number (the members). We end up with the paradox of a self-cancelling liberalism; or, what amounts to the same thing, with an overlap between liberalism and militancy, or, yet again, a liberalism outside the sphere of "reasonableness." One need only turn Walzer's distinction inside out to see that it endows the majority with rationality: that the majority becomes in fact the standard of rationality and the litmus test for what counts as membership in the minority and what is excluded from it.

Walzer's position suffers from confusion between morality and politics, a confusion exposed by Chantal Mouffe in *The Democratic Paradox*. The Aristotelian identification between the good and the rational, espoused by liberals, fatally neglects the role of the affects in securing allegiance to a polity. Politics is, as Mouffe insists, intrinsically agonistic, and the violence inherent in power relations cannot be extracted from political transactions, not even those that allegedly satisfy the members of a minority, where "satisfy" has undertones of resignation. The full meaning of consensus is undermined not by circumstantial but by intrinsic authority, which no amount of participation will dispel. This is so because the subject of consensus is not this or that individual as such but an always already political subject.

To put it differently, the "I" that speaks politically (and this might be the primordial "I") is, like the enunciatory "I" described by Émile Benveniste, not a referent outside of speech but the elocutory possibility of enunciation, of language realizing itself. As such, however, it is a pronoun devoid of experience, and, paradoxically, that lack is what prevents it from "saying" anything. The "I" that comes into being in political discourse participates in consensus formation from a systemic position codified as dominant or subaltern. Either it inflicts its will or obeys an alien will; either way it renews the foundational violence of politics. Consensus is a face-saving piety, a syllogism codifying the relative strengths in the majority/minority binary. More to the point, the "I" representing the reasonable member of a minority (unlike the militant who is a militant *because* excluded from consensus formation) has given up reference to experience outside the political frame that authorizes him or her to speak for the minority.

With this we come to the political meaning of the Spanish Constitutional Court's decision to strike down negationism from the roster of punishable crimes. This decision redrew the boundaries between minority and majority, admitting previously excluded discourse into the language of consensus formation. As a consequence, it narrowed the circle of "just members" of the minority and widened the experience that is excluded from any arrangement that could satisfy that minority. By allowing negation into the mainstream of political discourse, the court put pressure on the experience of the victims, changing it from indubitable to debatable. Given the relatively small size and inconspicuousness of the Jewish community in Spain, the court's decision resonated with political meaning beyond the scope of the Holocaust, just as neo-Nazism in Spain adopts anti-Semitism as a code for hatred against other minorities. At a time when debate about the historical memory had transcended the academic compound and spilled over into the public arena, a verdict protecting negationism had unmistakable political implications.

There is nothing intrinsically democratic in a high court's decision, but if the court responds to growing public indifference to the experiential shape of the past, then its decision would have to be regarded as democratic. It would be extending the right to be free from the consequences of action undertaken in the past, and even from knowledge of that past, to a community of equals whose equality materializes before the law. Mnemonic equality among the members of a group is not only the basis of national identity but also the condition making legislation passed in the name of the group democratic. This is so whether the group retains what Dan Diner calls a mnemonic canon, the requirement for the emergence of a "community of solidarity," an *ethnos*, or throws it away in order to practice only the kind of memory that produces "ad hoc cohesion" (184). Far from paradoxical, the desire to break with the mnemonic canon is powerful in democracies, which favor ad hoc cohesion over intergenerational transmission of foundational memories.

Democracy, says Mouffe, developing an argument made by Carl Schmitt in *The Crisis of Parliamentary Democracy* (1926), can exist only for a people, a *demos*, and therefore the equality of rights it postulates at the political level requires other kinds of equality, requires, in short, the homogenization of the citizens (40–1). It requires, that is, that majority rule be guaranteed by the progressive elimination or assimilation of the minority. And this can be done most expeditiously by destroying the minority's mnemonic canon and luring it toward the kind of memory that produces ad hoc cohesion. Liberalism, on the other hand, has its reference not in a *demos*, a people, but in humanity, the subject of abstract universal rights. Liberal democracy confuses both, mistaking a particular national subject for the universal subject that a nation, by definition, cannot be.

Human rights are the expression of a universalistic ethics. But, like all rights, human rights need states to define and enforce them, and historical contingencies to emerge and to mature to the point where they are implemented. The Universal Declaration of Human Rights on 10 December 1948 was the result neither of philosophical refinement nor of divine revelation, nor yet of new insight into the nature of law. It was an ethical breakthrough caused by unprecedented human catastrophes. If rights are, in the words of Alan Dershowitz, "quintessentially undemocratic, since they constrain the state from enforcing certain majoritarian preferences" (16), universal human rights are the single most powerful constraint on states and their majorities, whose interests at certain times have proven genocidal. States often pay lip service to such rights but tend to resist them, because a right is always a limit on sovereignty.

It may be asked whether rights should trump the will of the majority, and the answer to this question, when issued by a government, will give a reliable measure of the degree of liberty tolerated by a state. But the existence since 1948 of universally embraced human rights binds every state and is therefore the single most powerful check on sovereignty. This means that sovereignty is no longer based, as Carl Schmidt thought before the Second World War, on the sovereign's power to decide over the life of subjects. World courts, such as The Hague, now supplement, and in certain cases replace, national courts in the trial of the worst violations of human rights. Universal human rights entail world jurisdiction and thus a court that is aloof from the interests of any one state. World courts are undemocratic in Dershowitz's sense. Being independent from any existing polity, they do not rely on a political majority for their legitimacy. And this raises the question of what kind of consensus they rely on. The answer is that they rely on widely accepted standards of decency. These standards are not inherent in any transcendent category of consciousness; they are shaped by world historical events, and are thus relatively shielded from political oscillations in any given state.

Human rights are not natural; otherwise they would have been discovered long before they were formulated. Even so, they are assumed to be part of human nature in the same performative act that established them. In the preamble of the Universal Declaration of Human Rights one can read: "disregard and contempt for human rights have resulted in barbarous acts which have outraged the conscience of mankind..." But the truth is that rights are recognized in the breach; they are the remedial response to severe moral outrage. They are not a positive finding but the idealized image of a world made whole again by human goodwill. Rights belong to the realm of the "ought," not of the "are." These two realms can only be confused by fatalism, which moves within the sphere of tragedy. But tragedy, as Giorgio Agamben remarks, is precisely what genocide in general and the Holocaust in particular lifted from the historical scene. "After Auschwitz," he says, "it is not possible to use a tragic paradigm in ethics" (99). Tragedy relies on fate and the concomitant embodiment of heroism, which is the expression of unknowingly incurred guilt. However, if the tragic hero pays for excess *objectively* incurred, the essence of genocide is that the victims are innocent—nothing they have done individually can ever justify their collective murder. Rather, they are ontological prey, sacrificed not for what they do but for who they are. And yet that sacrifice is not inscribed in the laws of history. So undetermined is it that the final solution, any final solution, evokes incredulity. Negationism misuses the spontaneous refusal to believe, the unprompted "it cannot be" by taking advantage of the victim's untragic essence. Nor is the perpetrator a tragic figure either. The adverb "unknowingly" does not qualify the guilt incurred by a society that nurtures genocide. Even when the camps are out of sight, the degrading of the victim started in the public realm and was always already murderous.

Genocide issues from resentment, and so does its denial. If this is accurate, how can we explain the paradox that the twentieth century witnessed several genocides, including the yardstick for them all, if it was not driven by resentment? Agamben argues that the ethics of the twentieth century began with Nietzsche's overcoming of resentment. Against the impotence of the desire to undo the past, Zarathustra teaches joy in the recurrence of everything that has once taken place, repeated down to the slightest detail. Superior love of life would reveal itself in the active affirmation of the immutability of the past. Nietzsche's is an ethics diametrically opposed to denial, and yet equally unacceptable in that it involves subjective freedom (the courage to say "yes" to all of the past) in objective determination (the inevitability of recurrence of all causal sequences in eternity). This superior love of life is that of a subject who has made himself the sovereign of every event by assimilating chance into self-willed determination. If it is a heroic ethics, then it is voided by the enormity of the crimes it would joyfully countenance.

This ethics certainly pervades the perpetrators' sense of their self-overcoming through contempt for every human consideration. In his 1943 Posen speech to high-ranking S.S. officers, Heinrich Himmler came as close as anyone ever did to heroizing the extermination of Jews: "To have stuck this out, and—excepting cases of human weakness—to have kept our integrity, that is what has made us hard" (cit. LaCapra 28). Dominick LaCapra is undoubtedly right in arguing that Himmler "alludes to a kind of initiatory, radically transgressive limit-experience for Nazi perpetrators—

an unspeakable rite of passage involving quasi-sacrifice, victimization, and regeneration through violence" (28–9 n. 19). And I would argue that the rite of passage, imagined as a rite of elevation, is linked to the experience of the negative sublime invoked by LaCapra in relation to the spectacle of piled up corpses. The Nazi grows in self-perceived stature in proportion to the Jew's descent into sub-humanness. Overcoming resentment, under the ethical circumstances inaugurated by the camps, is possible only by dehumanizing both the resented and the resenter. A god does not resent an insect.

But an anti-Nietzschean ethics that refuses to accept the amorality of the past need not be slated to the morality of resentment. There is no compelling reason to accept Nietzsche's characterization of morality as impotent revenge, as Agamben does in taking Jean Améry's self-ascription to the world of resentment at face value. Améry's refusal to let crime flatten to mere historical fact is not steeped in the impotence of unfeasible revenge. He explicitly foregoes all hope of redress as long as the crime comes into its truth and the criminal remains stuck to his fate along with the victim. "My resentments are there in order that the crime become a moral reality for the criminal, in order that he be swept into the truth of his atrocity" (cit. Agamben 100). In this resentment, there is hope neither of human justice nor of divine punishment. This is not the resentment that Nietzsche detected at the root of Christianity. Justice in the wake of the Holocaust has become necessarily epistemological, a matter of consciousness squaring with the facts.

An affirmation of the past altogether different from Nietzsche's can be found in Walter Benjamin's *Theses on the Philosophy of History*, in the famous passage about a future historian who will fan a spark of hope in the past, because he is convinced that not even the dead will be safe from the enemy if he wins (*Illuminations* 254). Here, Nietzsche's desperate redemption of all suffering through the joy of superior vitalism is met by a historicism capable of gathering strength from the past for struggles in the present. Benjamin's historian in dark times turns to the past for a spark of hope and says "yes" *in extremis* to the suffering of the dead, thus redeeming it from the barbarism of a history that drains it of significance. For Benjamin, the Hegelian theory of history as rational teleology gave way, under the barrages of the First World War and the Nazi conquest of power, to a broken chain of devastation—the ruins gazed upon by the angel of history as he regresses along an infinitely appalling trauma.

Inspired by Benjamin's view of history as trauma, Shoshana Felman turns her attention to the actual subjects of history: the traumatized, who are deprived of speech and thus rendered incapable of bearing witness to their victimization. The aporia in this theory of history is evident. History is a record of articulated experiences, a matter of speech. But if the relation between history and trauma is speechless (Felman 33), then testimony dissolves into aphasia. With witnesses as the aphasiacs of history, to guarantee the negationist's freedom of speech is to abjure history twice, to remove its traumatic embodiment in favor of articulated language—which is the prerogative of the victors. The reverse of the Führer's "inspired" speeches is the inarticulateness of the Muslim: a body surviving biologically after the spirit has fled. Underpinning the charisma of power is the aversion experienced even by fellow inmates vis-à-vis the Muslim. Life so brutalized that it no longer reacted to stimuli, this life-beyond life was the nether point in the Nazi organization of history. Less than human, the Muslim was the abject counterimage of the Führer's transcendence of humanity from above.

The Nazis' tragic concept of history is the opposite of Benjamin's idea of history as constituted by the silence of the victimized. In Felman's words:

> History ... is thus inhabited by a historical unconscious related to—
> and founded on—a double silence: the silence of "the tradition of the
> oppressed," who are by definition deprived of voice and whose story
> (or whose narrative perspective) is always systematically reduced to
> silence; and the silence of official history—the victor's history—with
> respect to the tradition of the oppressed. (34)

Where can one turn to recognize and honor this tradition of the voiceless? What official history silences, trauma reveals in bodies that struggle to break the stranglehold of language on what aims to be said. If "history becomes equal to signification in human language" (Benjamin, "The Role of Language" 60), then witnessing trauma demands something that language cannot convey, the evidence of experience, and this can only be produced by the body in which experience is inscribed. To put it differently, Benjamin's idea of history's unconscious merges with Hans Ulrich Gumbrecht's observation that meaning cultures (as opposed to presence cultures) repress the spatial or material side of signification, giving rise to a metaphysics of meaning (81).

Gumbrecht's observation helps us to understand the Spanish Constitutional Court's decision to liberalize the area of meaning at the expense of traumatic history. To rule in favor of freedom of speech when speech is known to run counter to experience is to declare meaning insubstantial, free-floating, and spectral—a *flatus vocis*. Under those conditions, experience's inarticulateness succumbs to the noise of undecidable opinion. Presence, on the other hand, makes it immediately apparent that power—the power to lift the traumatic constraints on speech—relies on violence to organize relations among bodies. According to Gumbrecht, the more a culture imagines itself as a meaning culture, the more it will disguise violence in its power relations. This camouflage, he says, explains the confusion in recent decades between power relations and relations defined by the distribution of knowledge. "But the lines along which knowledge is distributed will only coincide with the lines of power relations as long as the stability of the lines of knowledge distribution is ultimately covered, even in a meaning culture, by the potential and the threat of physical violence" (84). In the case of Spain, such coverage is now guaranteed by the ostensible link between the negation of genocide, whose stakes are ultimately not the accumulation of epistemological capital but the raw assertion of power, and the redistribution of social certainties at the foundation of the present Spanish state. The chartering of negationism on the back of freedom of speech not only separates witnessing (an experience linked to presence) from speaking, body from meaning, it also secures the convergence of knowledge toward power relations, paradoxically, by abstracting discourse from its effect on bodies and, whenever it is convenient, excepting it from the constraints of the law.

CHAPTER SEVENTEEN

Exhaustion of the Transition Pact: Revisionism and Symbolic Violence

Around the turn of the century, coinciding with the foundation in December 2000 of the "Association for the Recovery of the Historical Memory," people all over Spain came forward to point out the location of unmarked graves, where seventy years earlier a sizable number of men and women had been hastily buried. They were victims of purges undertaken by the rebel army and Falange death squads, often with the connivance and blessing of the religious authorities. These excavations were the high-water mark in the debate about the historical memory. In the absence of that debate, they may never have taken place. It is safe to surmise that, by stirring the public consciousness, the intellectual context created the opportunity. Nonetheless, it is reasonable to ask: why then? The answer to this question bears on the exhaustion of the transition ethos. A quarter of a century after the end of the dictatorship, faith in the breakthrough supposedly accomplished by the transition had dwindled, and the consequences of that loss of confidence were tangible in many spheres of life.

Leaving aside the frills, the transition was calculated to legitimize a state that had never been legitimate in the eyes of other states. Part of the legitimation strategy was to historicize the Civil War and the dictatorship. By "historicize" I do not mean to delve into the causes and contexts of the past, but to degrade memories into events that no longer claimed the attention, let alone aroused the passion, of anyone other than professional historians. Painful personal memories had to be replaced with events that people felt were remote and done with. And this had to be achieved without resorting to blatant censorship. Defusing the political implications of a collective memory that was still alert in the mid-1970s could be defended as a control strategy in a context of social volatility at the end of the Franco regime. This was a time of routine mass demonstrations and strikes in the largest cities, which the right met with overt provocations and violent episodes. There were also violent incidents on the left. Between 1968 and 1982, the actions of the Groups of Anti-Fascist Resistance First of October

(GRAPO) claimed the lives of more than eighty people. In May 1977, Barcelona businessman José María Bultó was murdered by a self-named Popular Catalan Army, and Joaquín Viola, former mayor of this city, was killed by the same group the following year. ETA, a better organized and more experienced organization, stepped up its actions in the years following Franco's death. It became acutely clear that, if the violence spread and became endemic, it would give Francoist hardliners the pretext they were looking for to derail the political reforms. The moderates who were committed to advancing the constitutional model, people like president Adolfo Suárez and Communist Party leader Santiago Carrillo, worked hard to avoid a polarization that would have torn the transition to pieces. They must be commended for it. But in the absence of a timely confrontation with the past and of symbolic redressing, historicization, the treatment of the past as specialized, irrelevant knowledge, took the form of occultation, of turning an unread page in the history books.

There is nothing surprising about the state's domestication of the historical memory. This is something that all states do on occasion. Totalitarian states do it all the time. The date 22 November 1975 did not mark the downfall of a tyranny but the transmogrification of a regime that could last as long as it did thanks to its adaptability to a varying international context and to the fact that it enjoyed broad support and even broader passivity. Briefly stated: Franco was condoned internationally and tolerated at home. Passivity of such duration borders on complicity. As Saul Friedlander asserts, "in a system whose very core is criminal from the beginning, passivity is, as such, system-supporting" (73). And the Franco regime not only originated in a treacherous assault on the legally constituted government; it based its longevity on extended crime, much of it committed after Franco became Spain's absolute master.

The passivity did not end with the regime. Spaniards had been conditioned to a state of historical ignorance and political indifference. Only by positing a rhizomatic spreading of the complicity throughout society is it possible to account for the indifference, lasting well into the 1980s and 1990s, to military archives remaining closed to researchers; to files being classified until the death of all concerned; to threats proffered against journalists and the media until this very day; to official rebuff of petitions for the return of confiscated documents, buildings, and other assets to their legitimate owners; to the rehabilitation of Falange as a legal contender in democratic elections; and to the governing conservatives' rejection—until 2002—of parliamentary propositions to condemn the dictatorship. In 2013, the conservatives voted in Congress against a motion to make 18 July—the anniversary of the *coup d'état*—a day of condemnation of the dictatorship on the pretext that it would saddle the younger generations with the intolerable weight of the Civil War (Ruiz Sierra).

How could a society that still had to prove its new democratic conviction tolerate such restrictions on justice and the deliberate dimming of the recent past? However unpopular, the only answer concordant with the facts is that the transition was not a truly democratic re-foundation of the state, but its outward transfiguration. The regime changed as much and no more than was strictly required to consolidate the power of the ruling elites. The transition was, in effect, an inter-generational transfer of the institutions. Some of the staff was rejuvenated without putting at risk the institutions' purpose. Few institutions were shut, some underwent cosmetic changes, and most remained unchanged. Jesús Fueyo—a Franco-appointed National Counselor of the National Movement—had anticipated that they would survive the dictator: "after Franco, the institutions," he replied to the frequently asked question: "after Franco, what?" And certainly the institutions embodied the principles of the National Movement, ensuring their continuity by creating a diffuse climate of opinion. If Francoist opinion was to remain unchallenged, it was essential for it to be naturalized, made invisible like the air Spaniards breathe. To accomplish this, the origins of the present had to be muddled and forgotten.

During the transition, the myth of a consensual re-foundation of the state replaced the myth of the providential Caudillo. A ruler "by God's grace," as the legend in Spanish money reminded everyone, now became a government by universal consent. "Consensual" suggested that a balanced representation of all social groups had crafted the new political framework in the course of unhindered deliberation. The word implied that the nature of the new regime had been arrived at as a result of a free decision. Yet the choice between republic or monarchy was never contemplated, much less brought up for referendum by the people. If Franco ruled by the grace of God, Juan Carlos became monarch by the favor of Franco. "Consensus" never was the end point of rational deliberation. It was the given out of which the framework of the state had to be produced within predetermined limits. "Consensus" both presupposed and promised national reconciliation. As a token of reconciliation, the regime granted across-the-board amnesty, releasing thousands of people who were serving sentences for activity considered subversive under Francoist law. But there was a catch, which the crowds clamoring for amnesty in the streets failed to grasp. Amnesty implied amnesia. By accepting blanket political amnesty, opponents of the dictatorship in effect barred the way to future indictment of the perpetrators, unwittingly granting democratic status to totalitarian individuals and groups.

A final line had been drawn on the recent past. As a consequence, the Franco decades came to be seen not as a deviation to be redressed and corrected but as a continuum with Spanish history. Officially, 1939 was emblazoned in people's minds not as an unlawful interruption of the popular sovereignty reappropriated with the Second Spanish Republic but as the beginning of a period of crisis management consonant with the overarching national history and continuous with the new restoration. The transition had in fact begun six years before Franco's death, when the Generalissimo proclaimed Juan Carlos his successor on 22 July 1969. The dictator's decision to reinstate the monarchy thus became the cornerstone of the only consensus that could be reached after his death. But that consensus implied re-inscribing as democratic the Francoist re-establishment of the Monarchy, under conditions specified in his Law of Succession of 1947.[1] By arrogating the power to generate a new legitimacy and skipping one dynastic generation, Franco in effect created a new monarchical regime based on Francoist principles and law (the Ley de Principios del Movimiento Nacional of 1958). After his death, everything was done to forget his disruption of the dynastic line, creating a false sense of historical continuity by obscuring the fact that the king was an interloper. Dissimulating the king's political origins and manipulating the popular memory through a false sense of rupture with the dictatorship reduced Francoism to the status of a ripple in the broader stream of traditional Spanish history.

Anchoring the Francoist state in the Bourbon monarchy had been Franco's plan. Thus, when Juan Carlos gradually began stirring the state toward a constitutional democracy, the hardliners considered this maneuver a betrayal of the Fundamental Principles he had sworn to uphold. However, the more pragmatic among Franco's supporters understood that taking cover under the mantle of change had the advantage of canceling their historical liability without loss of wealth or status. And, indeed, the maneuver succeeded brilliantly. All remaining international exclusions imposed on Spain since 1939 were repealed after 1975. The Western democracies were only too happy to endorse the myth of the country's long trek toward democracy. They too had uncomfortable memories with regard to Spain, which they had abandoned to the fascist powers in 1936 and again, with even less justification, in 1945. Great Britain and the United States in particular had reasons for remorse. They claimed freedom and democracy as the supreme values for which they had fought in the Second World War. They had vowed to rid Europe of fascist dictators; yet both had agreed to leave Franco in

---

1 As noted above, Franco saw his resolution of the succession problem as an "instauration" rather than the "restoration" of the monarchy.

power, no matter the cost to Spanish democrats. Through an ironic reversal, the fascist ally of Hitler and Mussolini had become NATO's reliable ally in the Cold War, itself fought in the name of freedom and democracy.

For the Western powers, the legend of a country inherently unfit for democracy finding its way to the European Promised Land was a most convenient clean-up story. In 1936, England's non-intervention policy had effectively handed the Spanish Republic over to the communists and sealed the fate of Spain. Great Britain's unconcealed preference for Spain's anti-democratic forces over the loyalists was conveniently sunk into oblivion. As was Churchill's betrayal of Spanish democracy in 1945, when, breaking previous commitments broadcast from the BBC, he praised Franco during a session of the British Parliament, clearing the way for transforming him from an enemy of democracy into a strategic ally. Truman would make Churchill's policy his own, and the House of Representatives voted in March 1948 to include Spain in the Marshall Plan, a prelude to the defense treaty signed between both countries on 26 September 1953. By supporting Franco, the United States began its shameful policy of subverting democratic values in exchange for strategic advantages, to the lasting damage of the democratic principles on which its long-term hegemony rests.

The multilateral cancellation of guilt charmed away the division between victors and vanquished, and with it the distinction between victims and perpetrators. Dissolving the moral certainties opened the way to relativism, which would increase in proportion as the collective memory declined. Eventually, it would permit perpetrators to assume the role of victims. Across-the-board amnesty insulated Francoists against indictment, allowing them to retain their privileges. Anti-Francoists, settling for the freedom of political prisoners, did not immediately realize that, by acquiescing, they had granted immunity to those responsible for state crimes. The majority looked forward to a gradual transformation of the state. Time was on their side, they thought, and Francoism would eventually wither away. But the myth of a consensual pact sent democratic culture into a skid. Power remained out of balance, and Francoists used the state levers to impose their will in a virtually un-amendable constitution that soon proved to be less a tool of democracy than a fetter on progress.

Despite its inherent conservatism, the most obdurate members of the Francoist establishment, among them the future president José María Aznar, rejected the constitution. Pragmatists, however, saw in it an opportunity to retain control of the state while leaving the autocratic tradition behind. The constitution of 1978 represented an unstable truce between the spirit of reform and that of continuity, at the price of substantial forgetting. Since then, the constitution has changed its sign. An emblem of inflexibility, it no longer symbolizes the spirit of compromise that brought it into being. Used as a wall of contention against the pressing demands for territorial reform, it no longer serves the purpose of conciliating political wills. Conceived as a vault for the safekeeping of power, it subordinates the recognition of fact to the prescription of ideology. The constitution is in effect a screen memory, a displaced metaphor for knowledge that is censored and must be constantly repressed, lest it gain admittance into public consciousness.

Historians' slow and grudging admission that the transition was the last and possibly the greatest triumph of the Francoist establishment since the end of the Civil War, suggests that they maintain a transferential relation to a past that was and remains traumatic. As an example of this unconscious disposition, I will examine one instance of "historicizing" the living memory of the past, to show how the historian replicates the transition's rejection of a polygonal memory of the civil war and Francoism. In an essay on the subject of memory and institutionalization during the transition, Paloma Aguilar, a Madrid-based historian,[2] denounces "the use and abuse of the past" in the practices of "nationalist movements, which tend to legitimize current grievances with reference to historical events" ("Institutional Legacies" 128). The expression is telling. It is not clear that grievances can be legitimized or why they should be. Grievances must be addressed. And if they are sustained in time, as discrimination, racism, and related practices tend to be, then they form a historical continuum and are not so much "legitimized" as revealed by historical events. Jim Crow laws are continuous with present-day housing and job discrimination, the latter hardly needing "legitimation."

What Aguilar implies with this poorly worded but revealing sentence is that national minorities that denounce their discrimination are not entitled to complain, since their allegations of historical abuse is itself an abuse of history. The deviousness of the argument is apparent from her question-begging premise. Although she generalizes the attribution of a problematic recourse to history to all "nationalist movements," the butt of her attack is obvious in that she adopts the insidious Spanish convention of reserving the term "nationalist" for the subject nationalities,[3] neglecting

2 She is also a member of the Institute Juan March, a research center founded under the dictatorship by the tycoon who helped finance Franco's *coup d'état*. Neither this nor other foundations were scrutinized in the transition, the links between private funding and public power being simply taken over by the constitutional regime.

3 Aguilar is guilty of this rhetorical abuse when she opposes "national Spanish parties" to "Basque nationalist parties" ("Institutional Legacies" 140), and when further on in her essay she refers to the former as "non-nationalist parliamentary groups" ("Institutional Legacies" 141–2).

to mention that historically the term "national movement" applies only to the aggressive Castilian nationalism that, monopolizing the demonym "Spanish," captured and transformed the state after 1939 and legitimized its conquest after 1977.[4] As Hannah Arendt explains, the name "movement" alluded to the profound distrust for political parties that reached decisive proportions in the years of the Weimar Republic (131). Thus, Aguilar's first inaccuracy is to designate as movements conventional parties with stakes in parliamentary democracy. My point, though, is not to take issue with a disingenuous palming off of political tactics as epistemic categories, but to challenge the wisdom of contesting the connection between current grievances and historical events, especially when the former are denied validity by calling the latter into question.

Aguilar's pretense of steering clear of the pragmatic use of history would seem naive if it were not fraudulent. No less than the discourses she attacks, her account of memory is determined by a set of values which are hardly divisible from that "use and abuse of the past" that she attributes to the national minorities she patently disapproves of. Unwittingly or not, she participates in the organized denial of a well-attested history of abuse. From the evidence that the Franco army killed fewer people in the Basque provinces than elsewhere, she seeks to delegitimize Basque (and implicitly Catalan) political struggles. There is no reason to question the numbers she brandishes, but whereas documenting aspects of the past contributes to historical knowledge, resorting to historical data to make a political statement about the present makes her guilty of the same strategy that she castigates. Such lack of restraint in a historian is all the more troubling in that it took place at the height of the conservative Spanish government's ideological war on the Basque national parties. In other words, the objectivity predicated on the data was compromised by the researcher's ulterior goal. And this makes it an interesting case for the thesis that I defend throughout this book, namely that it is impossible to achieve a consensual view on the Civil War and Francoism due to the transition's failure to settle the issues and to the distortions this failure induced in Spanish democracy.

---

4 The Spanish National Movement was a reaction to the emergence of non-Spanish national parties after the demise of the Spanish empire, precisely when the dominant nationality—the Castilian—launched a compensatory program of nationalization of the peninsular territories. It was accompanied by a staunch though illusory effort to reassert empire through a pan-Hispanic movement. With respect to early twentieth-century pan-movements, Hannah Arendt observed, "While overseas imperialism had offered real enough panaceas for the residues of all classes, continental imperialism had nothing to offer except an ideology and a movement" (105). This remark applies to Spain no less than to the other empires Arendt had in mind.

The past is always debatable. So are its documents. And so is memory. At the moment when actions enter into the symbolic domain, they are consigned to interpretation and made consistent with values that, being anchored in the interpreter's social context, are not falsifiable the way scientific statements are. One instance of semantic dependence on values would be Aguilar's claim that the republican Basque government "betrayed" the Spanish republic by negotiating its surrender to the Italians rather than to the Spanish rebels. The nationalist subtext in this assertion does not require explication. Why should the Basque authorities surrender to Mola, who had threatened to raze the entire province of Biscay, rather than to General Roatta, a less brutal commander, in exchange for permission to evacuate the people most at risk of reprisals? Also revealing is Aguilar's characterization of the Basques' refusal to destroy Bilbao's industry as a "betrayal" of the republican cause. These are value judgments that cannot be resolved in the sphere of fact. The facts are indisputable, but they do not necessarily substantiate Aguilar's judgment. It is not obvious, except perhaps to a Spanish nationalist, that the Basque government should have prioritized Spanish honor over Basque lives and surrendered to Mola. The same is true about the notion that Basques should have destroyed their industry for the sake of a doomed republic that had first begrudged them autonomy and then failed to defend their country.[5] For the Basques, the republic had passed away, but industry would continue to supply their

---

5 Juan Manuel Epalza, who on PNV (Basque Nationalist Party) orders deposed the Santoña military commander, has explained: "We had asked the central government to send warships to transport our army to Catalonia; we had been refused (Fraser 410). This fact belies Aguilar's denunciation of the PNV's unwillingness to continue the war effort. And Pedro Basabilotra, speaking of the resentment among Basque troops, points out: "They felt betrayed by the republic which had constantly promised and failed to deliver weapons. While in Madrid we heard they had arms and planes..." (Fraser 412). This information is credible. Madrid's government failed to support the Catalan expedition to take Mallorca, thus allowing the island to remain in fascist hands and become the base from which the Italian aviation could bomb Barcelona for the remainder of the war. The Republican government preferred to send Spain's gold reserves to the Soviet Union and buy weapons from Stalin at inflated prices and at the cost of giving executive power to the Communist Party rather than send the resources to Catalonia in order to buy materials for its war industry. George Orwell remarked on the contrast between the poorly equipped militias fighting in Aragon and the good-looking, well-armed troops sent from Valencia to fight the CNT and the POUM in the rear (143-4). He did not fail to remark, accurately: "The Barcelona fighting had given the Valencia Government the long-wanted excuse to assume fuller control of Catalonia" (144).

livelihood after defeat.[6] Republican or fascist, Madrid would always live off its traditional business.

Ultimately, the question of betrayal does not lie in the facts but in the historian's loyalties. Basque nationalism has its reasons as well as its myths, at variance from those of Spanish nationalism. Questions of value entailing different loyalties cannot be settled by pitting rational historiography (ours) against mythical memory (theirs). The dichotomy is devious because most of those concerned with the Civil War and the Franco period are sucked into its maelstrom. This is not to say that documentation is irrelevant, or that some accounts are more objective than others. It is to say that data does not speak for itself; that the historian makes it speak, and sometimes ventriloquizes it. On this matter, it is important to reckon with the transferential relation to the past that Dominick LaCapra considers unavoidable in every epistemic relation to traumatic events. What he says about witnesses applies to archival work when the documents are taken as testimony of collective trauma: "[Testimony] raises the issue of the way in which the historian or other analyst becomes a secondary witness, undergoes a transferential relation, and must work out an acceptable subject-position with respect to the witness and his or her testimony. Transference here implies the tendency to become emotionally implicated in the witness and his or her testimony with the inclination to act out an affective response to them" (11–12). Needless to say, transference does not necessarily entail positive emotion; it merely concerns the response, in that it is easily charged with affect and requires the working out of what LaCapra calls an acceptable subject-position and we could translate as a position of subjective awareness.

Historicization, Friedlander warned, may be misused as a pretext for collapsing the distinction between a more-nuanced interpretation of the past and "increasingly apologetic readings of the events" (99). Aguilar does not overstep the facts but perilously approaches apologetic terrain when she candidly admits to seeking a particular result from the data. "What we are seeking to demonstrate," she says, "is that, contrary to what Basque nationalism has maintained, first clandestinely and then openly, the overall situation in the Basque country (at least during the war years and immediately after) was not clearly worse than in the rest of Spain but, in terms of certain indicators, substantially better" ("Institutional Legacies"

---

6 The argument that Basque factories should have been destroyed to keep them from falling into Franco's hands ignores the fact that Franco could count on virtually unlimited supplies from his allies. Furthermore, it is to ignore that destroying the industries, besides eliminating the Basque economic base, would have triggered reprisals.

148). In other words, she *wishes* for confirmation of a thesis. With the help of comparative data, she points out that the number of trials initiated in 1939 in the Basque Provinces is below the "national average." From this she infers a milder repression in Euzkadi. The problems with this *modus operandi* are obvious. Nineteen thirty-nine is a late date for the Basque Country, which fell to the rebels in August of 1937. The harshest moments of the repression would have occurred shortly after. In the early days of the war, and immediately after Franco's army captured a city or region, executions often followed without trial. As a result, court proceedings are an unreliable benchmark of the cruelty visited on the population of conquered territory. Furthermore, relying on official records for assessing the repression's intensity must be further qualified by the extensive destruction of documents.

Looking at the available evidence, Francisco Espinosa Maestre also reaches the conclusion that the repression in Euzkadi was less severe than in other places of the Iberian Peninsula. More circumspect, however, he uses the evidence within premises that he knows cannot be fully demonstrated. For instance, he believes that, unlike repression in the areas immediately taken by the rebels, all murders committed by the Franco troops after February 1937 must be on record, because, he asserts, they were mostly executions of death sentences passed by the Prosecution of the Occupation Army (60). If this assumption were correct, the repression in Euzkadi would indeed have been less severe than in other provinces. But Espinosa Maestre cautiously invokes probability, not certainty, when he believes that the repression would have been registered in the courthouses and in the graveyards (60).

In passing, he mentions that, unlike people in other regions, Basques could cross the border into France to escape repression, but, surprisingly, he does not accord much weight to this geographic advantage (70). Nor does he concede much credence to the theory that Euzkadi was spared a harsher repression by the fact that its population was generally conservative and intensely Catholic. And yet, the fact that the Vatican tried (unsuccessfully, because the telegram was intercepted and did not reach its destination) to negotiate a separate peace with the Basque government, suggests that the Catholic hierarchy was interested in curbing the reprisals. The prosecutor of the Occupation Army, Felipe Acedo Colunga, may have had in mind the Church's interest in avoiding bloodshed in a devout region that could not pass for red, or he may have been thinking of Franco's concern not to feed world opinion with news about his army's brutality in the wake of the bombing of Guernica, when he hinted at "political reasons of the [military] campaign" for muting the repression in Bilbao (*Memoire of the Prosecutor of the Occupation Army*, cit. Espinosa Maestre, "Sobre la represión franquista"

71). Espinosa Maestre admits that there may have been political reasons for the restraint, but declares himself unable to imagine what those might be.

Another reason Acedo Colunga mentioned was lack of witnesses willing to come forward against those indicted. Such atypical dearth of witnesses for the prosecution cannot be explained by supposing that the military authorities had lifted the ban on the intervention of guarantors that was enforced elsewhere. Acedo Colunga does not mention an abundance of guarantors but rather a lack of witnesses as the reason for insufficient evidence to support death sentences. Such general holding back, forfeiting the opportunity for revenge or for ingratiating oneself with the new authorities, suggests that we are in presence of an interclass solidarity not found anywhere else in the peninsula. That difference can only be explained by the existence of deeply rooted national solidarity that operated in the face of the invader.

This difference may also explain the relatively more benign treatment of the Basque population after the fall of Bilbao and San Sebastian. Espinosa Maestre rejects the idea that the Basque government's protection of right-wing prisoners and relative absence of persecution of the Church by the republicans could have mollified the fascist authorities. He points out that in places such as Huelva, where the republican authorities protected right-wing residents and one single priest was killed before the city fell to the fascists, the military repression surpassed that of Euzkadi (73). He admits that there was serious economic penalization through impounding of property by the fascists, but he does not believe that this form of legalized theft affected Basques more than others (73). His theory for the milder repression in Euzkadi is that Franco needed to preserve the Basque industry and could not afford a carnage that would have eliminated qualified labor and middle management. He adds that, in Euzkadi, the Catholic Church, which elsewhere guided and even participated in the repression, was a moderating factor, due to the conservative, religious character of the Basques (74). This squares with the Vatican's interest in brokering a Basque surrender to the Spanish nationalists as a way of preserving Catholic life in the region.

The possibility that Franco understood the importance of keeping the Basque industrial infrastructure working after the capture of Biscay is somewhat diminished by the fact that Basque industrial installations were heavily bombed during the war, without apparent concern for the postwar economy. A more likely reason for the relative respect of life and limb in Euzkadi was the presence of influential Basques on Franco's side. They would not only have been interested in salvaging their property and the region's economic potential, but would have retained a modicum of ethnic solidarity cutting across the social classes. Unusual reluctance on the part of Basque

Francoists to come forward as witnesses for the prosecution in the trial of Basque nationalists supports this possibility. Espinosa Maestre himself mentions the existence of a pro-Franco Basque bourgeoisie that assisted in the military coup and fought for the Spanish nationalists in the war (73), without, however, drawing the legitimate conclusion that, even after casting their lots on different sides of the war, a strong Basque solidarity buffered the fascist appetite for retaliation.

The available figures from the military trials bespeak a certain restraint on the part of the authorities when compared with the numbers from other regions. Espinosa Maestre is right in saying that repression in Bilbao cannot be isolated from what happened in other cities, like Málaga, that had been taken before (64). But it is wrong, or at least useless, to gauge the harshness of the repression by exclusively quantitative measures. As Conxita Mir points out:

> to pay attention to the non-quantifiable effects of repression, such as fear, silence, social control, humiliation, or the participation in civil society through denunciations, reports, endorsements, etc., is a good reflection of the new pathways toward a better understanding of violence, by giving to progressively systematized popular knowledge a new academic dimension. Oral sources played a key role in this change ... as much as court records, because all together has contributed to visualizing the extremes of collaboration with the repressive practices employed, allowing us to grasp a new vision of violence which does not appear as a mere imposition "from above" by the rebel army but also as something encouraged "from below," making the interpretation of the memory of the war and the postwar more complex. (270)

Although death is the absolute measure of repression at the individual level, it is not the only or even the best indicator of repression at the social level. How does one quantify fear and humiliation? How intensive are these controls on a population for whom deeply ingrained social traits such as language were primary factors of marginalization and put it at risk of reprisals? This was without any doubt the experience of Catalans of all classes and it seems to have been also the experience of many Basques. How does one measure the degree of humiliation by virtue of ethnic or national identification? Or the pain of being forcibly torn from one's cultural habits? Sensing that death sentences do not tell the whole story, Espinosa Maestre follows Aguilar in trying to prove the privileged treatment of Basques by pointing to their higher postwar economic wellbeing. Aguilar even compares infant mortality rates in the Basque Country with the national average, inferring a higher standard of living, which would belie Basque allegations of having suffered especial duress. But the argument is flawed by her failure to take prewar conditions into account. Comparing the postwar and prewar levels of wellbeing for the same community would provide a more reliable picture of the degree of social injury. And wellbeing cannot be measured by a single variable. Had she taken prewar conditions into account, Aguilar would have had to admit that, long before the war, the Basque country outstripped most Spanish regions in material standard of living.

But beyond the pitfalls of interpreting data, there is a methodological problem with estimating political repression solely or primarily through economic indicators.[7] Mob psychology has often justified the oppression of certain groups by pointing the finger at their perceived superior comfort. A more versatile analysis would show that health and economic standards taken by themselves are not a reliable gauge of the degree of political wellbeing a social group enjoys, or of the level of suffering inflicted on it. A more refined analysis would reckon with group-specific variables, which are ultimately those that tend to decide the fate of minorities in the midst of intolerant majorities. And it would try to estimate, however qualitatively, the cost of subtraction, of the violently imposed regression from the previous social and cultural status, and of its immediate and long-term repercussions throughout the social body. It would, that is, recognize the pain of the missing limb, of the empirical specter of the would-have-been, and factor in the costs of the decapitated future. Such subjective but real pain does not

---

7 One non-trivial indicator is the extent to which groups are included or shut out of political representation (and thus given equal opportunity to influence their own future through the legal channels of the state). The electoral law in force today in Spain was designed to guarantee the subordination of the national minorities. By privileging an obsolete territorial representation based on the province (itself an artificial centralizing design created in 1833 to break down historical identities) rather than on population, it ensures the periphery's under-representation. Each deputy from the province of Barcelona requires 129,268 votes, whereas one from the province of Soria requires only 26,177 votes, that is more than 103,000 fewer. In other words, Soria is represented on a five to one ratio with respect to Barcelona. If instead of Soria we compare Toledo, the most populated province of Castilla-La Mancha, we find that, with 90,064 votes for each deputy, Toledo's representation is 1.4 that of Barcelona. Even worse is the marginalization of Basques and Catalans in the Senate, where each province has four representatives regardless of population, Furthermore, Basques and Catalans have, as such, no representation in the Supreme Court, with the result that the Constitution is systematically interpreted against their interests. Elections are regulated by an Organic Law of 19 July 1985. Since the Socialists enjoyed an absolute majority in the Parliament that year, this law cannot be attributed to Francoism. Nevertheless, its approval and permanence suggest the extent to which naturalized Francoist attitudes pervaded Spain's political culture during the transition.

transpire from comparisons of flat social data. By "flat" I mean data analyzed without benefit of temporal coordinates that would permit one to estimate the degree of truncation a society undergoes during the crisis that is the object of evaluation.

Aguilar's "demystifying" project with regard to the historical—but in reality present—claims of the national minorities aims to achieve some form of mnemonic homeostasis. She takes exception to the existence of different memories of what for her are national, i.e. essentially homogeneous events. Different memories tend to underwrite diverging narratives, and diverging narratives imply a divided social body. In other words, they call into question the myth of unity underlying the nation state and threaten to delegitimize the territorial asymmetry of power. Aguilar subscribes to an entirely different legend and pits myth against myth, endorsing the fiction that the transition was the "recognition of collective culpability for crimes committed during the war" ("Institutional Legacies" 129). Victims and perpetrators are thus homogenized in the baseness of universally shared criminality.

In this view, there is no room for redressing or even for apologies. The nationalization of guilt protects each and every perpetrator. As a result, no one need suffer from a public bad conscience. Aguilar is a respectable historian who cannot be lumped together with deniers such as Pío Moa and Nicolás Salas, but who, distressed by the political stirrings of national identities different from her own, comes perilously close to supporting the state's organized denial of the attempted razing of a people's existence as such. The discourse of some historians about the two nationalities that fought against Spanish nationalist aggression in the Civil War matches some of the templates proposed by Israel Charny to recognize deniers of genocide:

- Do not acknowledge that the genocide took place.

- Direct denials should not be attributed to the government or high leaders, only to functionaries and anonymous spokesmen.

- Deny the facts of the genocide by transforming them into other kinds of events.

- Represent the perpetrators as victims and the victims as perpetrators (or as lesser victims than the others were).

- Not only deny the facts of the genocide outright, but advance counter-claims that the victims were treated well.

- Insist as long as possible that all the data are not available, that allegations are forgeries and hoaxes, and that further research is needed and/or that new research disproves the claims of genocide.

- Question the statistics, so that the number of dead victims is smaller than usually stated.

- Move from the facts of the genocide to some kind of relativist comparison that mitigates the horror of these events.

- Distance the event in time—it all happened so long ago, there is a new generation of the (perpetrator) people today, why not let the wounds heal? (cit. Cohen 133-4)

These markers of denial are not restricted to genocide in the narrow sense of physical extermination. They apply equally to other forms of repression, targeting groups by virtue of their intrinsic characteristics, and they certainly apply to severe instances of cultural genocide, such as the attempted eradication of a people's identity, language, and culture. With regard to this form of repression, which has no equivalent in the rest of Spain, historians outside the affected communities have been remiss to admit the facts or have trivialized their significance.[8] Some have engaged in full-fledged denial.

The transition's consensus on artificially distancing the events in time came to grief when the dead started to surface and cast their shadows over the uneasy peace made of fear and silence. When television channels finally broadcast the stories of survivors who ventured to pit their isolated memories against a regime that exists by purloining the past, the so-called transition pact and the constitution on which it rested were clearly exhausted. Even, or perhaps especially, when driven by private pain and intimate emotion, the recovery of the dead showed that in the long run regimes of oblivion cannot be normalized, despite explications that seek to reallocate responsibility by making the victims shoulder the guilt all over again.

8 The repression in Catalonia is amply documented. For an insightful discussion about the "deconstruction" of memory in recent Spanish historiography, see Colomines, "La deconstrucción de la memoria. El argumento perverso sobre la represión franquista."

Bibliography

Abad Nebot, Francisco. "Sobre el concepto literario de 'Siglo de Oro': Su origen y su crisis." *Anuario de Estudios Filológicos* 9 (1986): 13–22.

Abel, Olivier. "The Religious Rationale of Violence." *Violence and Its Causes: A Stocktaking.* Paris: UNESCO Publishing, 2005: 73–8.

Abella, Rafael. *Semprún-PCE. Historia de una polémica.* Barcelona: Planeta, 1978.

Adam, Heribert. "How Emerging Democracies Deal with the Crimes of Previous Regimes." In *Legal Institutions and Collective Memories.* Ed. Susanne Karstedt. Oxford: Hart Publishing, 2009.

Agamben, Giorgio. *Means without End: Notes on Politics.* Trans. Vincenzo Binetti and Cesare Casarino. Minneapolis: University of Minnesota Press, 2000.

—. *Remnants of Auschwitz: The Witness and the Archive.* Trans. Daniel Heller-Roazen. New York: Zone Books, 1999.

Aguilar, Paloma. "Institutional Legacies and Collective Memories: The Case of the Spanish Transition to Democracy." In *States of Memory: Continuities, Conflicts, and Transformations in National Retrospection.* Ed. Jeffrey K. Olick. Durham, N.C.: Duke University Press, 2003: 128–60.

—. *Justicia, política y memoria: Los legados del franquismo en la Transición española.* Estudio/Working Paper 2001/163. Madrid: Instituto Juan March de Estudios e Investigaciones, 2001.

Alonso, Martín. "Estructuras retóricas de la violencia política." In *Violencia y política: Historia, memoria y víctimas.* Eds. Antonio Rivera and Carlos Carnicero Herreros. Madrid: Maia, 2010: 101–65.

Alvaro, Francesc-Marc. *Els assassins de Franco.* Barcelona: l'Esfera dels llibres, 2005.

Amat-Piniella, Joaquim. *K.L. Reich: novel·la.* Barcelona: Edicions 62 (2001).

Ametlla, Claudi. *Catalunya, paradís perdut: La Guerra civil i la revolució anarco-comunista.* Barcelona: Selecta, 1984.

Antich, Xavier. "La cuestión del testimonio. Notas para un diálogo a cuatro voces y una impugnación. La de Jorge Semprún, a Martin Heidegger." In *Jorge Semprún o las espirales de la memoria.* Ed. Xavier Pla. Kassel: Reichenberger, 2010: 161–89.

Aparicio, Juan (ed.) *JONS: Antología.* Barcelona: Editora Nacional, 1939.

Arbós, Montserrat. "Entrevista: Eric Sottas, Director de l'Organització Mundial Contra la Tortura (OMTC)." *Avui Digital.* 2 November 2002.

Arendt, Hannah. *The Human Condition.* New York: Harper & Row, 1958.

—. *Imperialism.* New York: Harcourt, Brace and World, 1968.

—. *On Violence.* New York: Harvest, 1970.

Armengou, Montserrat, and Ricard Belis (dir.) *Els nens perduts del franquisme*. Televisió de Catalunya, 2002.

—. *Polio. Crònica d'una negligència*. Televisió de Catalunya, 2013.

—. *Ramon Perera, l'home dels refugis*. Barcelona: Rosa dels Vents, 2008.

Arnau, Pilar. *Narrativa i turisme a Mallorca (1968-1980)*. Palma: Edicions Documenta Balear, 1999.

Aróstegui, Julio. "Violencia, sociedad y política: la definición de la violencia." In *Violencia y política en España*. Ed. Julio Aróstegui. Madrid: Marcial Pons, 1994: 17–55.

Artís-Gener, Avel·lí. *Mèxic, una radiografia i un munt de diapositives. Obres Completes de Tísner*. vol. 6. Barcelona: Editorial Pòrtic, 1995: 5–199.

—. *Paraules d'Opòton el Vell. Crònica mexicana del segle XVI*. In *Narrativa catalana de l'exili*. Ed. Julià Guillamon. Barcelona: Galaxia Gutenberg/Cercle de Lectors, 2005: 491–752.

—. *Viure i veure*. 4 vols. Barcelona: Editorial Pòrtic, 1989–96.

Assmann, Jan. *Das kulturelle Gedächtnis. Schrift, Erinnerung und politische Identität in frühen Hochkulturen*. Munich: C.H. Beck, 2007.

—. *Monotheismus und die Sprache der Gewalt*. Vienna: Picus Verlag, 2006.

Associació Catalana d'Expresos Polítics. *Notícia de la negra nit: Vides i veus a les presons franquistes (1939-1959)*. Ed. Ignasi Riera. Barcelona: Diputació de Barcelona, 2001.

Augstein, Franziska. *Von Treue und Verrat: Jorge Semprún und sein Jahrhundert*. Munich: C.H. Beck, 2008.

Avni, Haim. *Spain, the Jews, and Franco*. Trans. Emanuel Shimoni. Philadelphia: The Jewish Publication Society of America, 1982.

Bahrani, Zainab. *Rituals of War: The Body and Violence in Mesopotamia*. New York: Zone Books, 2008.

Balcells, Albert. "Manuel Azaña i Catalunya durant la guerra civil." *Violència social i poder polític: Sis estudis històrics sobre la Catalunya contemporània*. Barcelona: Pòrtic, 2001: 163–86.

—. "Violència i terrorisme en la lluita de classes a Barcelona del 1913 al 1923." *Violència social i poder polític. Sis estudis històrics sobre la Catalunya contemporània*. Barcelona: Pòrtic, 2001: 11–118.

Barrera, Heribert. "Els agents socials." In *Memòria de la Transició a Espanya i a Catalunya*. Eds. Rafael Aracil and Antoni Segura. vol 1. Barcelona: Publicacions de la Universitat de Barcelona i Centre d'Estudis Històrics Internacionals, 2000: 245–61.

Barthes, Roland. "Le discours de l'histoire." *Social Science Information* 6(4) (1967): 65–75.

—. *S/Z*. Paris: Seuil, 1970.

Bartra, Agustí. *Crist de 200.000 braços*. In *Narrativa catalana de l'exili*. Ed. Julià Guillamon. Barcelona: Galàxia Gutenberg/Cercle de Lectors, 2005: 55–164.

Batista, Antoni, and Àngel Casas. "Les cançons de la Transició." In *Memòria de la transició a Espanya i a Catalunya*. Eds. Rafael Aracil, Andreu Mayayo, and Antoni Segura. vol. 4. *Els joves de la transició*. Barcelona: Publicacions de la Universitat de Barcelona i Centre d'Estudis Històrics Internacionals, 2003: 265–79.

Beaulac, Willard L. *Franco: Silent Ally in World War II*. Carbondale: Southern Illinois Press, 1986.

Beauvoir, Simone. "Œil pour œil." *Les Temps Modernes* 5 (February 1946): 813–30. Trans. Mary McCarthy in *Politics* (July–August 1947): 134–40.

Becker, Annette. *Maurice Halbwachs: Un intellectuel en guerres mondiales, 1914-1945.* Paris: Agnès Viénot, 2003.

Benet, Josep. *Cataluña bajo el régimen franquista. Informe sobre la persecución de la lengua y la cultura catalana por el régimen del general Franco (1a. parte).* Barcelona: Editorial Blume, 1979.

—. *Desfeta i redreçament de Catalunya.* Barcelona: Editorial Crítica, 1978.

—. "20 anys d'ajuntaments democràtics." In *Memòria de la transició a Espanya i a Catalunya.* Eds. Rafael Aracil and Antoni Segura. vol 1. Barcelona: Publicacions de la Universitat de Barcelona i Centre d'Estudis Històrics Internacionals, 2000: 199-220.

Benguerel, Xavier. *Els fugitius.* Barcelona: Selecta, 1956.

—. *Els vençuts.* Madrid and Barcelona: Alfaguara, 1969.

—. *Memòries 1905-1940.* Madrid and Barcelona: Alfaguara, 1971.

Benjamin, Walter. *Illuminations.* New York: Schocken Books, 1969.

—. "The Role of Language in *Trauerspiel* and Tragedy." In *Selected Writings*, vol. 1. *1913-1926.* Eds. Marcus Bullock and Michael W. Jennings. Cambridge, MA: Harvard University Press, 1996: 59-61.

—. "Theses on the Philosophy of History." *Illuminations.* Ed. Hannah Arendt. Trans. Harry Zohn. New York: Schocken, 1969: 253-64.

Benveniste, Émile. *Problems in General Linguistics.* Trans. Mary Elizabeth Meek. Coral Gables, FL: University of Miami Press, 1971.

Bergson, Henri. *La pensée et le mouvant.* Paris: Félix Alcan, 1934.

Bernanos, Georges. *Les grands cimetières sous la lune.* Paris: Plon, 1938.

Bernardot, Marc. *Camps d'étrangers.* Broissieux: Éditions du Croquant, 2008.

Bernstein, Richard J. *Radical Evil: A Philosophical Interrogation.* Cambridge: Polity Press, 2002.

Besses, Montserrat. *Veus ofegades. Cartes d'un exili a França.* Televisió de Catalunya, 2002.

Bettelheim, Bruno. *Surviving and Other Essays.* New York: Alfred A. Knopf, 1979.

Beumelburg, Werner. *Kampf um Spanien. Die Geschichte der Legion Condor.* Oldenburg/Berlin: Gerhard Stalling Verlagsbuchhandlung, 1939.

Bierce, Ambrose. "An Occurrence at Owl Creek Bridge." *Tales of Soldiers and Civilians.* Kent, OH: Kent State University Press, 2004.

Boitel, Anne. *Le camp de Rivesaltes, 1941-1942: Du centre d'hébergement au "Drancy de la zone libre."* Perpignan: Presses universitaires de Perpignan/Mare nostrum, 2001.

Borges, Jorge Luis. "El milagro secreto." *Ficciones.* Buenos Aires: Emecé, 1956.

Bowen, Wayne H. *Spain During World War II.* Columbia: University of Missouri Press, 2006.

Boyd, Carolyn P. "Violencia pretoriana: del Cu-Cut! al 23-F." In *Violencia política en la España del siglo XX.* Ed. Santos Juliá. Madrid: Taurus, 2000: 289-325.

Brieden, Hubert, Heidi Dettinger, and Marion Hirschfeld. *"Ein voller Erfolg der Luftwaffe." Die Vernichtung Guernicas und deutsche Traditionspflege: Wunstorf-Pforzheim-Bonn.* Neustadt: Verlag Region und Geschichte, 1997.

Brossat, Alain. "Retórica de la sinceridad y 'mentir vrai' en la obra de Jorge Semprún." In *Jorge Semprún o las espirales de la memoria.* Ed. Xavier Pla. Kassel: Reichenberger, 2010: 190-201.

Burgess, Greg. *Refuge in the Land of Liberty: France and its Refugees, from the Revolution to the End of Asylum, 1787-1939.* New York: Palgrave Macmillan, 2008.

Butler, Judith. *Precarious Life: The Powers of Mourning and Violence.* London: Verso, 2004.

Cadé, Michel. Preface to Anne Boitel, *Le camp de Rivesaltes, 1941–1942: Du centre d'hébergement au "Drancy de la zone libre."* Perpignan: Presses universitaires de Perpignan/Mare Nostrum, 2001: 15–17.

Cadena, Josep Maria. "El projecte editorial de l'*Avui*." In *Memòria de la transició a Espanya i a Catalunya.* Eds. Rafael Aracil, Andreu Mayayo, and Antoni Segura. vol. 5. *Els mitjans de comunicació.* Barcelona: Publicacions de la Universitat de Barcelona i Centre d'Estudis Històrics Internacionals, 2004: 91–109.

Caillois, Roger. *The Edge of Surrealism: A Roger Caillois Reader.* Ed. Claudine Frank. Trans. Claudine Frank and Camille Naish. Durham, N.C.: Duke University Press, 2003.

Calpena, Enric (dir.) *El Maquis: La guerra silenciada.* Televisió de Catalunya and Mercuri S.G.P., 2001.

Camus, Albert. "A Letter to the Editor of *Les Temps Modernes*." In *Sartre and Camus: A Historic Confrontation.* Eds. and Trans. David A. Sprintzen and Adrian van den Hoven. Amherst, N.Y.: Humanity Books, 2004.

Canal, Jordi. "La verdad de las mentiras, las mentiras de la verdad: Jorge Semprún, Federico Sánchez y el comunismo." In *Jorge Semprún o las espirales de la memoria.* Ed. Xavier Pla. Kassel: Reichenberger, 2010: 53–83.

Capdevila, Arantxa. "La disolución de un consenso: el 23-F en la prensa." In *Cartografías del 23-F: representaciones en la prensa, la televisión, la novela, el cine y la cultura popular.* Eds. Francisca López and Enric Castelló. Barcelona: Laertes, 2014: 33–52.

Carr, Raymond, and Juan Pablo Fusi. *Spain: Dictatorship to Democracy.* 2nd edn. London: George Allen & Unwin, 1981.

Carrillo, Santiago. *La crispación en España. De la Guerra civil a nuestros días.* Barcelona: Planeta, 2008.

—. *Mañana España. Conversaciones con Régis Debray y Max Gallo.* Madrid: Akal, 1976.

"Carta colectiva de los obispos españoles a los obispos de todo el mundo con motivo de la guerra en España." <http://imagenes.publico.es/resources/archivos/2011/8/1 5/1313407861676Cartaobisposguerracivil.pdf>.

Casanova, Julián. *The Spanish Republic and Civil War.* Cambridge: Cambridge University Press, 2010.

Casassas, Jordi (ed.) *Els intel·lectuals i el poder a Catalunya (1808–1975).* Barcelona: Pòrtic, 1999.

Cate-Arries, Francie. *Spanish Culture behind Barbed Wire: Memory and Representation of the French Concentration Camps, 1939–1945.* Lewisburg, PA: Bucknell University Press, 2004.

Cenarro, Angela. "Violence, Surveillance, and Denunciation: Social Cleavage in the Spanish Civil War and Francoism, 1936–1950." In *Social Control in Europe: 1800–2000.* Eds. Clive Emsley, Eric Johnson, and Pieter Spierenburg. Columbus: Ohio State University Press, 2004: 281–300.

Centelles, Agustí. *The Concentration Camp at Bram, 1939.* Barcelona: Actar i Arts Santa Mònica, 2009.

Centro de Investigaciones Sociológicas [CIS], *Veinticinco años después.* Estudio 2401. Madrid: Ministerio de la Presidencia, 2000.

Clastres, Pierre. *Archaeology of Violence.* New York: Semiotext(e), 2010.

Cohen, Stanley. *States of Denial: Knowing about Atrocities and Suffering.* Cambridge: Polity Press, 2001.

Colomines, Agustí. "La deconstrucción de la memoria. El argumento perverso sobre la represión franquista." In *Casa encantada. Lugares de memoria en la España constitucional (1978–2004)*. Eds. Joan Ramon Resina and Ulrich Winter. Frankfurt am Main: Vervuert, 2005: 207–21.

Conde, Francisco Javier. *Teoría y sistema de las formas políticas*. Madrid: Instituto de Estudios Políticos, 1944.

Coronado Ruiz, Carlota, and José Carlos Rueda Laffond. "The Television of the Past: History, Remembrance and Representation of Franco's Spain." *Catalan Journal of Communication and Cultural Studies* 4.1 (2012): 43–56.

Costa, Lluís. *Premsa i societat a la Girona franquista*. Barcelona: Diputació Col·legi de Periodistes de Catalunya, 1989.

Cruz González, Antonio. *Las víctimas de Negrín: reivindicación del POUM*. Malaga: SEPHA, 2008.

D'Ors, Eugenio. *La vida de Fernando e Isabel*. Barcelona: Editorial Juventud, 1982.

Daix, Pierre. "Lettre à Maurice Nadeau sur les intellectuels et le communisme." *La nouvelle critique* 84 (April 1957): 9–184.

—. "Pierre Daix, matricule 59.807 à Mauthausen: Pourquoi David Rousset a-t-il inventé les camps soviétiques." *Les lettres françaises* (November 1949).

Dante. *La Divina Commedia*. Milan: Ulrico Hoepli, 1965.

Derrida, Jacques. "On Forgiveness." *On Cosmopolitanism and Forgiveness*. Trans. Mark Dooley and Michael Hughes. London: Routledge, 2001.

Didi-Huberman, Georges. *Imágenes pese a todo. Memoria visual del Holocausto*. Trans. Mariana Miracle. Barcelona: Paidós, 2004.

Diner, Dan. *Cataclysms: A History of the Twentieth Century from Europe's Edge*. Trans. William Templer with Joe Golb. Madison: University of Wisconsin Press, 2008.

Donoso Cortés, Juan. "Discurso sobre la dictadura." *Obras Completas*. vol. 2. Ed. Juan Juretschke. Madrid: Biblioteca de Autores Cristianos, 1946: 187–204.

Eliade, Mircea. *The Sacred and the Profane: The Nature of Religion*. Trans. Willard R. Trask. New York: Harvest, 1959.

Ellwood, Sheelagh M. "Falange Española, 1933–9: from Fascism to Francoism." *Spain in Conflict 1931–1939. Democracy and Its Enemies*. Ed. Martin Blinkhorn. London: Sage, 1986: 206–23.

Escribano, Francesc. *Puig Antich: Les últimes hores*. Televisió de Catalunya, 1989.

Espada, Arcadi. *Contra Catalunya*. Trans. Jaume Boix Angelats. Barcelona: Flor del Viento, 1997.

Espinosa Maestre, Francisco. *Contra el olvido: historia y memoria de la guerra civil*. Barcelona: Crítica, 2006.

—. "Sobre la represión franquista en el País Vasco." *Historia Social* 63 (2009): 59–75.

Esslin, Martin. *The Age of Television*. San Francisco: W.H. Freeman, 1982.

European Court of Human Rights. Case of *Chauvy and Others* v. *France* (Application no. 64915/01) 29 June 2004.

—. Inadmissibility Decision in the Case of *Garaudy* v. *France* (no. 65831/01) 7 July 2003. Press release issued by the Registrar. <http://hudoc.echr.coe.int/app/conversion/pdf/?library=ECHR&id=003-788339-805233&filename=003-788339-805233.pdf>.

Fabre, Jaume, Josep M. Huertas, and Antoni Ribas, *Vint anys de resistència catalana (1939–1959)*. Barcelona: La Magrana, 1978.

Farràs, Andreu, and Pere Cullell. *El 23-F a Catalunya*. Barcelona: Planeta, 1998.

Faulí, Josep. "Els diaris de la Transició." In *Memòria de la transició a Espanya i a Catalunya*. Eds. Rafael Aracil, Andreu Mayayo, and Antoni Segura. vol. 5. *Els mitjans de comunicació*. Barcelona: Publicacions de la Universitat de Barcelona i Centre d'Estudis Històrics Internacionals, 2004: 116–18.

Feinberg, Joel. *The Moral Limits of the Criminal Law: Offense to Others*. New York: Oxford University Press, 1985.

Felman, Shoshana. *The Juridical Unconscious: Trials and Traumas in the Twentieth Century*. Cambridge, MA: Harvard University Press, 2002.

Ferran de Pol, Lluís. *Campo de concentración* (1939). Barcelona: Publicacions de l'Abadia de Montserrat, 2003.

Ferrer i Gironès, Francesc. *La persecució política de la llengua catalana*. Barcelona: Edicions 62, 1986.

Fontana, José María. *Los catalanes en la guerra de España*. 2nd rev. edn. Barcelona: Acervo, 1977.

Fontana, Josep. "Reflexiones sobre la naturaleza y las consecuencias del franquismo." In *España bajo el franquismo*. Barcelona: Crítica, 1986: 9–38.

Fradera, Josep Maria. *Colonias para después de un imperio*. Barcelona: Edicions Bellaterra, 2005.

Frankl, Viktor E. *Man's Search for Meaning: An Introduction to Logotherapy*. Trans. Ilse Lasch. rev. edn. New York: Simon and Schuster, 1962.

Fraser, Ronald. *Blood of Spain: An Oral History of the Spanish Civil War*. New York: Pantheon, 1979.

Friedland, Amos. "Evil and Forgiveness: Transitions." *Perspectives on Evil and Human Wickedness* 1.4 (2004): 24–47.

Friedlander, Saul. *Memory, History, and the Extermination of the Jews of Europe*. Bloomington: Indiana University Press, 1993.

Freud, Sigmund. *Erinnern, Wiederholen und Durcharbeiten*. In *Werkausgabe in zwei bänden*. vol. 1, *Elemente der Psychoanalyse*. Eds. Anna Freud and Ilse Grubrich-Simitis. Frankfurt am Main: S. Fischer Verlag, 1978: 518–25.

—. *Group Psychology and the Analysis of the Ego*. Trans. James Strachey. New York: Norton, 1959.

—. *Moses and Monotheism*. Trans. Katherine Jones. London: The Hogarth Press and the Institute of Psycho-Analysis, 1939.

—. *Die Verneinung* (1925). *Gesammelte Werke*, vol. 14. London: Imago Publishing Co.: 11–15.

Fukuyama, Francis. *The End of History and the Last Man*. New York: Avon, 1993.

Fuster, Joan, *Dos quaderns inèdits*. Alzira: Bromera, 2004.

Galimberti, Umberto. *I vizi capitali e i nuovi vizi*. Universale Economica. Milan: Feltrinelli, 2007.

Gallagher, Susan Vanzanten. "'I Want to Say:/Forgive Me': South African Discourse and Forgiveness." *PMLA* 117.2 (2002): 303–6.

Genette, Gérard. *Fiction et diction*. Paris: Seuil, 1991.

Genovès, Dolors, and Llorenç Soler. *In Memoriam*. Televisió de Catalunya, 1986.

Genovès, Dolors, and Lluís Montserrat. *Sumaríssim 447*. Televisió de Catalunya, 1994.

Genovès, Dolors, and Ricard Belis. *Operació Nikolai*. Televisió de Catalunya, 1992.

Glowacka, Dorota. "'Don't Leave Me, Pal': Witnessing Death in Semprún's Buchenwald Narratives." In *A Critical Companion to Jorge Semprún*. Eds. Ofelia Ferran and Gina Herrmann. New York: Palgrave Macmillan, 2014: 91–106.

Goldhagen, Daniel. *A Moral Reckoning: The Role of the Catholic Church in the Holocaust and Its Unfulfilled Duty of Repair.* New York: Alfred A. Knopf, 2002.

González Calleja, Eduardo. *Contrarrevolucionarios: Radicalización violenta de las derechas durante la Segunda República 1931–1936.* Madrid: Alianza Editorial, 2011.

—. "La razón de la fuerza. Una perspectiva de la violencia política en la España de la Restauración." In *Violencia y política en España.* Ed. Julio Aróstegui. Madrid: Marcial Pons, 1994: 85–113.

González Calleja, Eduardo, and Fredes Limón Nevado. *La hispanidad como instrumento de combate: Raza e imperio en la Prensa franquista durante la Guerra Civil española.* Madrid: Consejo Superior de Investigaciones Científicas. Centro de Estudios Históricos, 1988.

González Cuevas, Pedro Carlos. "Ledesma Ramos o el imposible fascismo español." "Introducción" to Ramiro Ledesma Ramos. *Discurso a las juventudes de España.* Madrid: Biblioteca Nueva, 2003: 11–34.

—. "Política de lo sublime y teología de la violencia en la derecha española." In *Violencia política en la España del siglo XX.* Ed. Santos Juliá. Madrid: Taurus, 2000: 105–44.

Gonzalo, Julio A. "Prólogo" to *Si España quiere suicidarse nosotros lo impediremos.* 2nd edn. Madrid: Ciencia y Cultura, 2006: vii–ix.

Gordon, Avery F. *Ghostly Matters: Haunting and the Sociological Imagination.* Minneapolis: University of Minnesota Press, 1997.

Goytisolo, Juan. *Reivindicación del conde don Julián.* [1970]. Barcelona: Seix Barral, 1976.

Grunebaum, Heidi. "Talking to Ourselves 'Among the Innocent Dead': On Reconciliation, Forgiveness, and Mourning." *PMLA* 117.2 (2002): 306–10.

Guernica. Being the Official Report of a Commission Appointed by the Spanish National Government to Investigate the Causes of the Destruction of Guernica on April 26–28, 1937. London: Eyre & Spottiswoode, 1938.

Guillamon, Julià. "L'experiència viscuda." *Avui* (30 December 1984).

—. "La subversion de la crònica: 'Paraules d'Opòton el Vell.'" *Serra d'Or* 338 (December 1997): 71–5.

Guilleminault, Gilbert. *Prélude à la belle époque.* Paris: Denoël, 1956.

Gumbrecht, Hans Ulrich. *Production of Presence: What Meaning Cannot Convey.* Stanford: Stanford University Press, 2004.

Guzmán Moncada, Carlos. *En el mirall de l'altre: "Paraules d'Opòton el vell," l'escriptura dialògica d'Avel·lí Artís-Gener.* Barcelona: Publicacions de l'Abadia de Montserrat, 2004.

—. *Una geografia imaginària: Mèxic i la narrativa catalana de l'exili.* Valencia: Tres i Quatre, 2008.

—. "*Paraules d'Opòton el Vell/Palabras de Opoton el Viejo*: el problema de l'altre/l'altre com a problema." *Literatures. Revista de l'AELC* 1–2 (1998): 89–109.

Hacking, Ian. *Rewriting the Soul: Multiple Personality and the Sciences of Memory.* Princeton, N.J.: Princeton University Press.

Halbwachs, Maurice. *La mémoire collective.* Ed. Gérard Namer. Paris: Albin Michel, 1997.

Hamburger, Käte. *Die Logik der Dichtung.* 4th ed. Stuttgart: Klett-Cotta, 1994.

Herzberger, David. *Narrating the Past: Fiction and Historiography in Postwar Spain.* Durham, N.C.: Duke University Press, 1995.

Hirschman, Albert O. *The Passions and the Interests: Political Arguments for Capitalism before Its Triumph*. Princeton, N.J.: Princeton University Press, 1977.

Hobsbawm, Eric, and Terence Ranger. *The Invention of Tradition*. Cambridge: Cambridge University Press, 1983.

Hoffman, Karen D. "Reflections on the Unforgivable." *Perspectives on Evil and Human Wickedness* 1.4 (2004): 13–23.

Huntington, Samuel P. *The Clash of Civilizations and the Remaking of World Order*. New York: Simon & Schuster, 1996.

Hurtado, Amadeu. *Quaranta anys d'advocat: història del meu temps, 1894–1936*. Esplugues de Llobregat: Ariel, 1969.

Irla, Josep. "Memorándum de Cataluña a la U.N." *Galeuzka* 2 (1946): 523–7.

Jacobs, Jane M. "Resisting Reconciliation: The Secret Geographies of (Post)colonial Australia." In *Geographies of Resistance*. Eds. Steve Pile and Michael Keith. London and New York: Routledge, 1997: 203–18.

Jefatura del Estado. "Ley 16/1985, de 25 de junio, del Patrimonio Histórico Español." *BOE* No. 155, 29 June 1985. <www.boe.es/buscar/act.php?id=BOE-A-1985-12534&tn =1&vd=&p=19850629>.

Jünger, Ernst. *Jahre der Okkupation*. Stuttgart: Ernst Klett Verlag, 1958.

—. *Über die Linie*. Frankfurt am Main: Vittorio Klostermann, 1950.

Kant, Immanuel. *The Conflict of the Faculties*. Trans. Mary J. Gregor. Lincoln: University of Nebraska Press, 1992.

Kierkegaard, Søren. *Philosophical Fragments*. Trans. David F. Swenson. Princeton, N.J.: Princeton University Press, 1962.

Kluger, Ruth. "Forgiving and Remembering." *PMLA* 117.2 (2002): 311–13.

Koestler, Arthur. *Dialogue with Death: The Journal of a Prisoner of the Fascists in the Spanish Civil War*. Trans. Trevor Blewitt and Phyllis Blewitt. Chicago: University of Chicago Press, 2011.

Köhler, Wolfgang. *The Place of Value in a World of Facts*. [1938]. New York: Meridian, 1959.

Koselleck, Reinhart. *Futures Past: On the Semantics of Historical Time*. Trans. Keith Tribe. Cambridge, MA: MIT Press, 1985.

Krasikov, Anatoly. *From Dictatorship to Democracy: Spanish Reportage*. Trans. N. Shartse. Oxford: Pergamon Press, 1984.

Kristeva, Julia, and Alison Rice. "Forgiveness: An Interview." *PMLA* 117.2 (2002): 281–7.

—. "Diversité dans la tempête." *Libération* (1 January 2000). <www.liberation.fr/ tribune/2000/01/01/diversite-dans-la-tempete_315573>.

Kuper, Leo. *Genocide: Its Political Use in the Twentieth Century*. New Haven, CT: Yale University Press, 1981.

LaCapra, Dominick. *History and Memory After Auschwitz*. Ithaca, N.Y.: Cornell University Press, 1998.

Lacroix, Michel. *De la beauté comme violence: l'esthétique du fascisme français, 1919–1939*. Montreal: Presses de l'Université de Montréal, 2004.

Laín Entralgo, Pedro. *Descargo de conciencia (1930–1960)*. Barcelona: Barral, 1976.

Lampedusa, Giuseppe Tomasi di. *Il Gatopardo*. Milan: Feltrinelli, 1961.

Laqueur, Walter. *The Last Days of Europe: Epitaph for an Old Continent*. New York: St. Martin's Press, 2007.

Ledesma Ramos, Ramiro. *Discurso a las juventudes de España*. Madrid: Biblioteca Nueva, 2003.

Lee, Adrian. "Death Railway PoW Who Forgave His Torturer." *Daily Express* (28 December 2013): 37.

Legaz y Lecambra, Luis. *Introducción a la teoría del estado nacionalsindicalista.* Barcelona: Bosch, 1940.

Legion Condor, Einsatz und Heimkehr. Reichspropagandaleitung. Munich: Zentralverlag der NSDAP, Franz Eher Nachfolger, n.d.

Lejeune, Philippe. *L'autobiographie en France.* Paris: Armand Colin, 1971.

—. *Le pacte autobiographique.* Paris: Seuil, 1975.

Levi, Primo. *The Drowned and the Saved.* Trans. Raymond Rosenthal. New York: Summit, 1988.

—. *Survival in Auschwitz.* Trans. Stuart Woolf. New York: Touchstone, 1996.

Levinas, Emmanuel. *Alterity and Transcendence.* Trans. Michael B. Smith. New York: Columbia University Press, 1999.

"Libros controlados." *El País Digital* (13 October 1999).

Lippmann, Walter. *Public Opinion.* Charleston, S.C.: BiblioBazaar, n.d.

—. *The Public Philosophy.* Boston: Little, Brown, 1955.

López Campillo, Evelyne, Hervé Poutet, and Anna Rémis. "Una cruzada para una nueva tierra santa. ¡Fraternidad, libertad, igualdad!" *Norba* 14 (1997): 137–46.

López Crespí, Miquel. *L'antifranquisme a Mallorca (1950–1970).* Palma: El Tall, 1994.

—. *Cultura i antifranquisme.* Barcelona: Edicions de 1984, 2000.

Loraux, Nicole. *Mothers in Mourning: with the Essay of Amnesty and its Opposite.* Trans. Corinne Pache. Ithaca, N.Y.: Cornell University Press, 1998.

Lorés, Jaume. *La Transició a Catalunya (1977–1984). El pujolisme i els altres.* Barcelona: Empúries, 1985.

Lyotard, Jean-François. "The Sign of History." Trans. Geoff Bennington. *Post-Structuralism and the Question of History.* Eds. Derek Attridge, Geoff Bennington, and Robert Young. Cambridge: Cambridge University Press, 1987: 162–80.

MacKinnon, Catharine A. *Only Words.* Cambridge, MA: Harvard University Press, 1996.

Maier, Charles. "A Surfeit of Memory?" *History and Memory* 5.2 (1993): 136–51.

Mamdani, Mahmood. "Amnesty or Impunity? A Preliminary Critique of the Report of the Truth and Reconciliation Commission of South Africa (TRC)." *Diacritics* 32.3–4 (2002): 33–59.

Maravall, José Antonio. *Carlos V y el pensamiento político del Renacimiento.* Madrid: Instituto de Estudios Políticos, 1960.

—. The *Transition to Democracy in Spain.* New York: St. Martin's Press, 1982.

Martínez, Ana, and Llum Quiñonero (dir.) *Mujeres del 36.* Televisión Española, 1999.

Marx, Karl. *The Communist Manifesto.* Trans. Samuel Moore. Harmondsworth: Penguin, 1985.

Mas i Sañe, Sílvia. *Les novel·les d'exili d'Avel·lí Artís-Gener.* Barcelona: Publicacions de l'Abadia de Montserrat, 2008.

Maspero, François. *Les abeilles & la guêpe.* Paris: Seuil, 2002.

McNamara, Vincent. "The Hegelianism of Young Donoso Cortés." *Saints, Sovereigns, and Scholars: Studies in Honor of Frederick D. Wilhelmsen.* New York: Peter Lang, 1993: 337–43.

Medina, Francisco. *23F, La Verdad.* Barcelona: Plaza Janés, 2006.

Melià, Josep. *La nació dels mallorquins.* Barcelona: Selecta, 1977.

Mercier, Vivian. *The New Novel: From Queneau to Pinget*. New York: Farrar, Straus and Giroux, 1971.

Mill, John Stuart. *On Liberty*. Harmondsworth: Penguin, 1985.

Mir, Conxita. "Construyendo el pasado. La investigación del pasado incómodo." In Lourenzao Fernández Prieto and Nomes e Voces (eds.) *Memoria de guerra y cultura de paz en el siglo XX de España a América, debates para una historiografía*. Gijón: Ediciones Trea, 2012: 263–73.

Mommsen, Wolfgang J. "Die Vergangenheit, die nicht vergehen will." *Gegen den Versuch, Vergangenheit zu verbiegen*. Ed. Hilmar Hoffmann. Frankfurt am Main: Athenäum, 1987: 83–93.

Moreno, Javier. Interview with José Luis Rodríguez Zapatero. *El País* (15 January 2007). <http://elpais.com/diario/2007/01/15/espana/1168815614_850215.html>.

Mosse, George. *Fallen Soldiers: Reshaping the Memory of the World Wars*. Oxford: Oxford University Press, 1990.

Mouffe, Chantal. *The Democratic Paradox*. London: Verso, 2000.

Neuhofer, Monika. *"Écrire un seul livre, sans cesse renouvelé." Jorge Sempruns literarische Auseinandersetzung mit Buchenwald*. Analecta Romanica 72. Frankfurt am Main: Vittorio Klostermann, 2006.

Nicoladzé, Françoise. *La deuxième vie de Jorge Semprún: une écriture tressée aux spirales de l'histoire*. Castelnau-le-Lez: Climats, 1997.

Nieto, Felipe. *La aventura comunista de Jorge Semprún*. Barcelona: Tusquets, 2014.

Nietzsche, Friedrich. *Werke*. Ed. Karl Schlechta. 3 vols. Munich: Carl Hanser, 1954.

Nolte, Ernst. "Vergangenheit, die nicht vergehen will." *Frankfurter Allgemeine Zeitung* (6 June 1986).

Nora, Pierre. "Between Memory and History." In *Realms of Memory: The Construction of the French Past*. Trans. Arthur Goldhammer. Ed. Pierre Nora. vol. 1. New York: Columbia University Press, 1996: 1–20.

Oliver i Fontanet, Joan. *El 20-N a Catalunya: els catalans i els últims dies del franquisme*. Barcelona: Planeta, 2000.

Ortega y Gasset, José. *España invertebrada. Obras completas*. vol. 3. Madrid: Revista de Occidente, 1957: 35–128.

Ortiz, Fernando. *Contrapunto cubano del tabaco y el azúcar*. Havana: Jesús Montero, 1940.

Ortiz Heras, Manuel. *Violencia política en la II República y el primer Franquismo: Albacete, 1936-1950*. Madrid: Siglo XXI, 1996.

Orwell, George. *Homage to Catalonia*. Boston: The Beacon Press, 1952.

Pagès i Blanch, Pelai. "Juan Negrín o la reinvindicación de la derrota." Prologue to Antonio Cruz González. *Las víctimas de Negrín: reivindicación del POUM*. Malaga: SEPHA, 2008: 11–16.

Palacios, Jesús. *23-F: el golpe del CESID*. Barcelona: Planeta, 2001.

Panyella, Jordi. "El TC diu que negar el genocidi és un exercici de lliure expressió." *AVUI* (17 November 2007): 32.

Patterson, Ian. *Guernica and Total War*. London: Profile Books, 2007.

Payne, Stanley. *Fascism in Spain, 1923-1977*. Madison: University of Wisconsin Press, 1999.

Péguy, Charles. *Œuvres en prose (1909-1914)*. Bibliothèque de la Pléiade. Paris: Gallimard, 1961.

Pellicani, Luciano. "Was Fascism Revolutionary?" *Telos* 122 (2002): 59–79.

Pla, Josep. *Escrits empordanesos. Obra Completa*. vol. 38. Barcelona: Destino, 1980.

—. *Historia de la Segunda República*. 4 vols. Barcelona: Destino, 1940.

—. "El liberalisme fictici i el liberalisme real." *Polèmica. Obra Completa*. vol. 40. Barcelona: Destino, 1982: 35-9.

Pla y Deniel, Enrique. *Las dos ciudades: carta pastoral que dirige a sus diocesanos el Excmo. y Rvdmo. Sr. Dr. D. Enrique Pla y Deniel, obispo de Salamanca, en 30 de septiembre de 1936*. Salamanca: Establecimiento Tipográfico de Calatrava, 1936.

Pla, Xavier (ed.) *Jorge Semprún o las espirales de la memoria*. Kassel: Reichenberger, 2010.

Pons, Damià. *El jonc i l'aritja. País, cultura, política*. Palma: Lleonard Muntaner, 2006.

Pons Prades, Eduardo. *Los años oscuros de la transición española: la crónica negra de 1975 a 1985*. Barcelona: Belacqva, 2005.

Pradera, Javier. "Semprún y los cuatro modelos de intelectual." In *Jorge Semprún o las espirales de la memoria*. Ed. Xavier Pla. Kassel: Reichenberger, 2010: 13-18.

Preston, Paul. *¡Comrades! Portraits from the Spanish Civil War*. London: HarperCollins, 1999.

—. *The Spanish Holocaust. Inquisition and Extermination in Twentieth-Century Spain*. New York: W.W. Norton & Company, 2012.

Primo de Rivera, José Antonio. "España y Cataluña." Discourse in the Spanish Parliament. 30 November 1934. <www.rumbos.net/ocja/jaoc0079.html>.

—. *Si España quiere suicidarse nosotros lo impediremos*. 2nd edn. Ed. Julio A. Gonzalo. Madrid: Ciencia y Cultura, 2006.

Proctor, Raymond L. *Hitler's Luftwaffe in the Spanish Civil War*. Westport, CT: Greenwood Press, 1983.

Quevedo, Francisco de. *La rebelión de Barcelona ni es por el güevo ni es por el fuero* [1641]. *Obras completas en prosa*. vol. 3. Madrid: Castalia, 2005: 445-79.

Quintana, Lluís. *Més enllà de tot càstig: reflexions sobre la transició democràtica*. Barcelona: Icària, 2004.

Raguer, Hilari. *La pólvora y el incienso: la Iglesia y la Guerra Civil española (1936-1939)*. Barcelona: Península, 2001.

Rawls, John. *The Law of Peoples*. Cambridge, MA: Harvard University Press, 1999.

Real Academia de la Historia. "Informe sobre los textos y cursos de historia en los centros de enseñanza media." *El País Digital* (28 June 2000).

Redondo, Onésimo. "Ideario." <http://web.archive.org/web/20081006214248/http://www.luceros.es/onesimoredondo/ideario.htm>.

Resina, Joan Ramon. "The Concept of After-Image and the Scopic Apprehension of the City." In *After-Images of the City*. Eds. Joan Ramon Resina and Dieter Ingenschay. Ithaca, N.Y.: Cornell University Press, 2003: 1-22.

—. "El dilema de la modernidad: ¿historia o mito?" In *Mythopoesis: literatura, totalidad, ideología*. Eds. Joan Ramon Resina, Enric Bou, Joseph J. Duggan, et al. Barcelona: Anthropos, 1992: 251-79.

—. "From Rose of Fire to City of Ivory." *After-Images of the City*. Eds. Joan Ramon Resina and Dieter Ingenschay. Ithaca, N.Y.: Cornell University Press, 2003: 75-122.

—. "Short of Memory: The Reclamation of the Past since the Spanish Transition to Democracy." *Disremembering the Dictatorship: The Politics of Memory in the Spanish Transition to Democracy*. Amsterdam: Rodopi, 2000: 83-126.

Rey, Fernando del. "La Segunda República y la violencia. Entre la cultura política y la acción revolucionaria." In *Violencia y política: historia, memoria y víctimas*. Eds. Antonio Rivera and Carlos Carnicero Herreros. Madrid: Maia, 2010: 63-99.

Ricœur, Paul. *Critique and Conviction: Conversations with François Azouvi and Marc de Launay.* Trans. Kathleen Blamey. New York: Columbia University Press, 1998.

—. *The Just.* Trans. David Pellauer. Chicago: University of Chicago Press, 2000.

—. *Time and Narrative.* Translated by Kathleen McLaughlin and David Pellauer. vol. 1. Chicago: University of Chicago Press, 1984.

Rieff, David. *Against Remembrance.* Victoria: Melbourne University Press, 2011.

Riego, Carmen del. "Los protagonistas del golpe disfrutan de sus retiros." *La Vanguardia* (20 February 2006): 16.

Robbe-Grillet, Alain. *Pour un nouveau roman.* Paris: Gallimard, 1963.

Roberts, Stephen G. H. "Miguel de Unamuno y su relación con el socialismo entre 1914 y 1924: una primera aproximación." *Cuadernos de la Cátedra Miguel de Unamuno* 43 (2007): 89–98.

Rodoreda, Mercè. "Nit i boira." *La nostra revista* 18 (1947): 294–9.

—. *Quanta, quanta guerra...* Barcelona: Club Editor, 1980.

Rodrigues-Moura, Enrique. "Políticas culturales en torno a la lengua española." *Lingüística hispánica: la gran riqueza del español, la variedad dentro de la unidad.* Ed. José María Santos Rovira. Bogota: Instituto Caro y Cuervo, 2013: 157–87.

Roig, Montserrat. *Els catalans als camps nazis.* Barcelona: Edicions 62, 1977.

Roig Pruñonosa, Neus. "La búsqueda de la filiación biológica: La detención ilegal de recién nacidos y la usurpación de su identidad en España (1938–1996)." Doctoral dissertation. University of Almería (2016).

Roth, Joseph. *Juden auf Wanderschaft.* Cologne: Kiepenheuer & Witsch, 1985.

Rother, Bernd. "Franco und die deutsche Judenverfolgung." *Vierteljahrshefte für Zeitgeschichte* 46 (1998): 189–220.

Rothenberg Gritz, Jennie. "The Guilt of the Church." *Atlantic* (Jan.–Feb. 2003).

Rousset, David. *L'univers concentrationnaire.* Paris: Les Éditions de Minuit, 1965.

Rovira i Virgili, Antoni. *Els darrers dies de la Catalunya republicana: memòries sobre l'èxode català.* Barcelona: Proa, 1999.

Rueda Laffond, José Carlos. "El 23-F como recuerdo-destello: prácticas de memoria en el documental televisivo nacional." In *Cartografías del 23-F: representaciones en la prensa, la televisión, la novela, el cine y la cultura popular.* Eds. Francisca López and Enric Castelló. Barcelona: Laertes, 2014: 81–105.

Ruiz Sierra, Juan. "El PP elude condenar el franquismo en el Congreso." *El Periódico* (21 May 2013). <www.elperiodico.com/es/noticias/politica/partido-popular-elude-condenar-fransquismo-congreso-2396297>.

Salas, Nicolás. *La "otra" memoria histórica.* Cordoba: Almuzara, 2006.

Salvat, Joan, and Lluís Montserrat. *Els últims morts de Franco.* Televisió de Catalunya, 2000.

Sànchez, Jordi. "De la marxa de la llibertat a la crida per la solidaritat." In *Memòria de la transició a Espanya i a Catalunya.* Eds. Rafael Aracil, Andreu Mayayo, and Antoni Segura. vol. 4. *Els joves de la transició.* Barcelona: Publicacions de la Universitat de Barcelona i Centre d'Estudis Històrics Internacionals, 2003: 205–18.

Sánchez Pérez, Francisco (ed.) *Los mitos del 18 de julio.* Barcelona: Crítica, 2013.

Sánchez Soler, Mariano. *La transición sangrienta: una historia violenta del proceso democrático en España (1975–1983).* Barcelona: Península, 2010.

Santacana i Torres, Carles. *El franquisme i els catalans: els informes del Consejo Nacional del Movimiento (1962–1971).* Catarroja: Editorial Afers, 2000.

Sarraute, Nathalie. *L'Ère du soupçon: essais sur le roman.* Lagny-sur-Marne: Impr. de E. Grevin et fils, 1956.

Sartre, Jean-Paul. *Being and Nothingness.* Trans. Hazel E. Barnes. London: Methuen, 1957.

Satué, Francisco J. *Los secretos de la Transición: Del Batallón Vasco Español al proceso de los GAL.* Madrid: La Esfera de los Libros, 2005.

Schmitt, Carl. *Donoso Cortés in gesamteuropäischer Interpretation.* Plettenberg: Peiran Verlag, 1988.

—. *Political Theology: Four Chapters on the Concept of Sovereignty.* Trans. George Schwab. Cambridge, MA: MIT Press, 1985.

Sebald, W. G. *On the Natural History of Destruction.* Trans. Anthea Bell. London: Hamish Hamilton, 2003.

Segura, Antoni (ed.) *Els llibres d'història, l'ensenyament de la història i altres històries.* Barcelona: Fundació Jaume Bofill, 2001.

Semprún, Jorge. "L'art contre l'oubli." *Le Monde des débats* (May 2000): 11–13.

—. *Autobiografía de Federico Sánchez.* Barcelona: Planeta, 1995.

—. *L'écriture ou la vie.* Paris: Gallimard, 1994.

—. *L'évanouissement.* Paris: Gallimard, 1967.

—. *Federico Sanchez vous salue bien.* Paris: Grasset, 1993.

—. *Le grand voyage.* Paris: Gallimard, 1963.

—. *Le langage est ma patrie: entretiens avec Franck Appréderis.* Paris: Libella, 2013.

—. *Le Mort qu'il faut.* Paris: Gallimard, 2001.

—. *Quel beau dimanche.* Paris: Grasset, 1980.

—. *Si la vie continue ... entretiens avec Jean Lacouture.* Paris: Grasset, 2012.

—. "Wovon man nicht sprechen kann." In Norbert Gstrein and Jorge Semprún. *Was war und was ist. Reden zur Verleihung des Literaturpreises der Konrad-Adenauer-Stiftung am 13. Mai 2001 in Weimar.* Frankfurt am Main: Suhrkamp, 2001.

Semprún Maura, Carlos. *A orillas del Sena, un español...* Madrid: Libertad Digital, 2006.

Serra, Antoni. *No hi ha quart poder. Memòries periodístiques del meu temps de glòria.* Palma: Editorial Moll, 2002.

Severino, Emanuele. *Téchne. Le radici della violenza.* Milan: Rizzoli, 2002.

Sloterdijk, Peter. *Theorie der Nachkriegszeiten: Bemerkungen zu den deutsch-französischen Bezihungen seit 1945.* Frankfurt am Main: Suhrkamp, 2008.

Sofsky, Wolfgang. *The Order of Terror: The Concentration Camp.* Trans. William Templer. Princeton, N.J.: Princeton University Press, 1997.

Solé i Sabaté, Josep M. *La repressió franquista a Catalunya. 1938–1953.* Barcelona: Edicions 62, 1985.

Solé i Sabaté, Josep M., and Joan Villarroya. *Cronologia de la repressió de la llengua i la cultura catalanes (1936–1975).* Barcelona: Curial, 1993.

Sombart, Werner. *Händler und Helden.* Munich: Duncker & Humblot, 1915.

Sophocles, "Antigone." Trans. Robert Whitelaw. In *Fifteen Greek Plays.* New York: Oxford University Press, 1943: 211–48.

Sorel, Georges. *Reflections on Violence.* Trans. T. E. Hulme and J. Roth. Glencoe, IL: The Free Press, 1950.

Sosa-Velasco, Alfredo. "Spain is Ill! Sick Body and Political Discourse in Twentieth-Century Spain: Santiago Ramón y Cajal, Pío Baroja, Gregorio Marañón and Antonio Vallejo Nágera." Doctoral dissertation, defended at Cornell University on 25 April 2007.

Soto Fernández, Liliana. *La autobiografía ficticia en Miguel de Unamuno, Carmen Martín Gaite y Jorge Semprún*. Madrid: Pliegos, 1996.

Southworth, Herbert R. *Guernica! Guernica! A Study of Journalism, Diplomacy, Propaganda, and History*. Berkeley: University of California Press, 1977.

Stackelberg, Karl Georg von. *Legion Condor. Deutsche Freiwillige in Spanien*. Berlin: Verlag Die Heimbücherei, 1939.

Strubell i Trueta, Toni. *El moment de dir prou*. Lleida: Pagès Editors, 2008.

Sturken, Marita. *Tangled Memories: The Vietnam War, the Aids Epidemic, and the Politics of Remembering*. Berkeley: University of California Press, 1997.

Surroca, Robert. *Joan Ballester i Canals (1913–1980)*. Barcelona: Omnium Cultural, 2007.

Tahmassian, Lena. "Carl Schmitt and the Basque Conflict: From the Design of Francoism to Spanish Democracy." *Journal of Spanish Cutural Studies* 33.1 (2012): 59–81.

Thomas, Gordon, and Max Morgan Witts, *Guernica. The Crucible of World War II*. New York: Stein and Day, 1975.

Thompson, Paul. *The Voice of the Past: Oral History*. 2nd edn. Oxford: Oxford University Press, 1988.

Torra i Pla, Quim. *Periodisme? Permetin! La vida i els articles d'Eugeni Xammar*. Barcelona: Símbol, 2008.

T.P.F., "Se dio la orden de eliminar a varios altos cargos del Gobierno y del Congreso." *Levante* (23 February 2009). <www.levante-emv.com/secciones/noticia.jsp?pRef=2009022300_19_559017__Comunitat-Valenciana-orden-eliminar-varios-altos-cargos-Gobierno-Congreso>.

"El Tribunal Supremo dicta que TV-3 no atentó contra el honor en 'Sumaríssim.'" *El País*, Catalonia edition (18 March 1999): 15.

Ugarte Tellería, Javier. *La nueva Covadonga insurgente: Orígenes sociales y culturales de la sublevación de 1936 en Navarra y el País Vasco*. Madrid: Biblioteca Nueva, 1998.

Unamuno, Miguel. 1905. "La crisis actual del patriotismo español." *Obras completas*. vol. 1. Madrid: Escelicer, 1966: 1286–98.

—. *El Cristo de Velázquez*. Madrid: Austral, 1963.

Unamuno Adarraga, Miguel, et al. "Carta al alcalde de Salamanca." <www.abc.es/hemeroteca/historico-14-12-2005/abc/Opinion/carta-al-alcalde-de-salamanca_1012980601452.html>.

United Nations Office of the High Commissioner for Human Rights. "Universal Declaration of Human Rights." <www.ohchr.org/EN/UDHR/Pages/Language.aspx?LangID=eng>.

Vallejo Nágera, Antonio. *Eugenesia de la Hispanidad y Regeneración de la Raza*. Burgos: Editorial Española, 1937.

—. *Política racial del Nuevo Estado*. San Sebastián: Editorial Española, 1938.

—. *Sinfonía Retaguardista*. Valladolid: Talleres "Cuesta." 1938.

Van Alphen, Ernst. "Symptoms of Discursivity: Experience, Memory, and Trauma." In *Acts of Memory: Cultural Recall in the Present*. Eds. Mieke Bal, Jonathan Crewe, and Leo Spitzer. Hanover and London: University Press of New England, 1999: 24–38.

Vaughan, Dai. *For Documentary*. Berkeley: University of California Press, 1999.

Vázquez Montalbán, Manuel. "Prólogo" to Mariano Sánchez Soler. *Los hijos del 20-N: Historia violenta del fascismo español.* Madrid: Ediciones Temas de Hoy, 1993: 15–20.

Vees-Gulani, Susanne. "The Experience of Destruction: W. G. Sebald, the Airwar, and Literature." *W. G. Sebald: History-Memory-Trauma.* Eds. Scott Denham and Mark McCulloh. Berlin: Walter de Gruyter, 2006: 335–49.

Verger, Frédéric. "Les Lumières et le goulag." *Revue des deux mondes.* 1 January 2011: 133–42.

Vernet Anguera, Roser. *Palabras de Opoton el viejo o El lenguaje y la recreación de la realidad.* Zapopan: El Colegio de Jalisco, 2000.

Walzer, Michael. *Thick and Thin: Moral Argument at Home and Abroad.* Notre Dame, IN: University of Notre Dame Press, 1994.

Wasianski, Ehregott Andreas Christoph. *Immanuel Kant in seinen letzten Lebensjahren: Ein Beitrag zur Kenntniss seines Charakters und häuslichen Lebens aus dem täglichen Umgange mit ihm.* Königsberg: Friedrich Nicolovius, 1804.

Weil, Patrick. *La France et ses étrangers: l'aventure d'une politique de l'immigration de 1938 à nos jours.* Paris: Gallimard, 1991.

Weinrich, Harald. *Lethe: The Art and Critique of Forgetting.* Trans. Steven Rendall. Ithaca, N.Y.: Cornell University Press, 2004.

Wilms, Wilfried. "Speak no Evil, Write no Evil: In Search of a Usable Language of Destruction." In *W. G. Sebald: History-Memory-Trauma.* Eds. Scott Denham and Mark McCulloh. Berlin: Walter de Gruyter, 2006: 183–204.

—. "Taboo and Repression in W. G. Sebald's *On the Natural History of Destruction.*" In *W. G. Sebald: A Critical Companion.* Eds. J. J. Long and Anne Whitehead. Edinburgh: Edinburgh University Press, 2004: 175–89.

Wieviorka, Michel. *La violence.* Paris: Balland, 2004.

Wittgenstein, Ludwig. *On Certainty.* Eds. G. E. M. Anscombe and G. H. von Wright. New York: Harper & Row, 1972.

—. *Tractatus-Logico-Philosophicus.* Trans. C. K. Ogden. London: Routledge and Kegan Paul, 1981.

Wolf, Eric R. *Europe and the People Without History.* Berkeley: University of California Press, 2010.

Wolton, Dominique. *Éloge du grand public. Une théorie critique de la télévision.* Paris: Flammarion, 1990.

Xammar, Eugeni. *L'ou de la serp.* Barcelona: Quaderns Crema, 1998.

Index